MEN UNDER FIRE

Austrian and Habsburg Studies

General Editor: Howard Louthan, Center for Austrian Studies, University of Minnesota

Before 1918, Austria and the Habsburg lands constituted an expansive multinational and multiethnic empire, the second largest state in Europe and a key site for cultural and intellectual developments across the continent. At the turn of the twentieth century, the region gave birth to modern psychology, philosophy, economics and music, and since then has played an important mediating role between Western and Eastern Europe, today participating as a critical member of the European Union. The volumes in this series address specific themes and questions around the history, culture, politics, social, and economic experience of Austria, the Habsburg Empire and its successor states in Central and Eastern Europe.

Recent volumes:

Volume 26
Men under Fire: Motivation, Morale and Masculinity among Czech Soldiers in the Great War, 1914–1918
Jiří Hutečka

Volume 25
Nationalism Revisited: Austrian Social Closure from Romanticism to the Digital Age
Christian Karner

Volume 24
Entangled Entertainers: Jews and Popular Culture in Fin-de-Siècle Vienna
Klaus Hödl

Volume 23
Comical Modernity: Popular Humour and the Transformation of Urban Space in Late Nineteenth-Century Vienna
Heidi Hakkarainen

Volume 22
Embers of Empire: Continuity and Rupture in the Habsburg Successor States after 1918
Edited by Paul Miller and Claire Morelon

Volume 21
The Art of Resistance: Cultural Protest against the Austrian Far Right in the Early Twenty-First Century
Allyson Fiddler

Volume 20
The Monumental Nation: Magyar Nationalism and Symbolic Politics in Fin-de-siècle Hungary
Bálint Varga

Volume 19
Tropics of Vienna: Colonial Utopias of the Habsburg Empire
Ulrich E. Bach

Volume 18
Sacrifice and Rebirth: The Legacy of the Last Habsburg War
Edited by Mark Cornwall and John Paul Newman

Volume 17
Understanding Multiculturalism: The Habsburg Central European Experience
Edited by Johannes Feichtinger and Gary B. Cohen

For a full volume listing, please see the series page on our website:
http://berghahnbooks.com/series/austrian-habsburg-studies.

Men under Fire

Motivation, Morale and Masculinity among Czech Soldiers in the Great War, 1914–1918

Jiří Hutečka

berghahn
NEW YORK • OXFORD
www.berghahnbooks.com

Published in 2020 by
Berghahn Books
www.berghahnbooks.com

English-language edition
© 2020, 2023 Jiří Hutečka
First paperback edition published in 2023

Czech-language edition
© 2016 Jiří Hutečka

Originally published in Czech in 2016 as *Muži proti ohni: motivace, morálka a mužnost českých vojáků Velké války, 1914–1918*, by Nakladatelství Lidové Noviny

All rights reserved. Except for the quotation of short passages
for the purposes of criticism and review, no part of this book
may be reproduced in any form or by any means, electronic or
mechanical, including photocopying, recording, or any information
storage and retrieval system now known or to be invented,
without written permission of the publisher.

Library of Congress Cataloging-in-Publication Data
A C.I.P. cataloging record is available from the Library of Congress
Library of Congress Cataloging in Publication Control Number:
2019040211

British Library Cataloguing in Publication Data
A catalogue record for this book is available from the British Library

ISBN 978-1-78920-541-1 hardback
ISBN 978-1-80073-930-7 paperback
ISBN 978-1-78920-542-8 ebook

https://doi.org/10.3167/9781789205411

To Vašík and Lukáš

Contents

List of Illustrations   viii
Preface to the English Edition   x

Introduction   1
1. Tournament of Manliness: Mobilization   29
2. Compromises of Manliness: Everyday Experience   62
3. Transformation of Manliness: Comradeship   115
4. Degradation of Manliness: The Military Authorities   142
5. Venues of Manliness: Home   181
6. Manliness under Fire: Combat and the Body   219
Conclusion   251

Bibliography   260
Index   279

ILLUSTRATIONS

1.1 Heeding the call. An example of the propaganda that divided the wartime social space into the masculine frontline and the feminine home front (wartime postcard, Regional Museum in Olomouc). 32
1.2 In prewar Austria-Hungary, military masculinity was an integral part of male childhood, as shown on this prewar postcard (Regional Museum in Olomouc). 35
1.3 A ritual of manliness. A ceremonial mass for the troops of k.k. Landwehr Infantry Regiment 13 in the Olomouc town square, before leaving for the front in July 1914 (Regional Museum in Olomouc). 42
1.4 A ritual of manliness. 3rd Battery, k.u.k. Field Artillery Regiment 27, marching to the train station through the streets of Hradec Králové, accompanied by its own band and a large numbers of curious, but rather passive onlookers (Museum of Eastern Bohemia, Hradec Králové). 48
2.1 A postcard sent by 'Emil' on 1 April 1915, eloquently articulating the core reality of a soldier's experience: heavy work, bad weather and more heavy work (Museum of Eastern Bohemia, Hradec Králové). 71
2.2 Defining bodily masculinity – conscripts being sorted according to their physique by a military board, Brno, March 1915 (Military History Institute, Prague). 79
2.3 Austro-Hungarian military brothel, complete with opening hours, 'nur für Österreichische Soldaten!' ('Austro-Hungarian Soldiers Only!'), location unknown (Alois Žipek, *Domov za války: Svědectví účastníků*, vol. 3, Prague, 1930, 412). 88
2.4 Masculinized femininity or feminized masculinity? Wartime propaganda showing a woman dressed in uniform, for now only as a military nurse (a 1916 calendar of the Austro-Hungarian Red Cross, Museum of Eastern Bohemia, Hradec Králové). 96
2.5 'A Battlefield Dream': official, idealized notion of womanhood on a wartime postcard (Museum of Eastern Bohemia, Hradec Králové). 99

3.1	Physical closeness in the cramped conditions of the frontline, infantry dugout of k.u.k. Infantry Regiment 75, Eastern Front, 1917 (Military History Institute, Prague).	119
3.2	Male nudity in the field, Galicia, 1915 (Museum of Eastern Bohemia, Hradec Králové).	121
4.1	The officers' access to 'resources' in wartime, military hospital in the town of Czernowitz, Bukovina, in eastern Austria-Hungary (today Chernivtsi, Ukraine), spring 1915 (Museum of Eastern Bohemia, Hradec Králové).	150
4.2	Access to resources as experienced by the rank-and-file soldiers, an unknown unit in Bukovina, spring 1915 (Museum of Eastern Bohemia, Hradec Králové).	152
4.3	A drawing by Karel Rélink of k.u.k. Infantry Regiment 28, entitled 'A Field Punishment for a Lost Can', vividly capturing the oft-abused practice of 'binding' (Karel Rélink, *Album obrazů ze světové války: Utrpení českého vojáka v poli*, Brno, 1922).	163
5.1	'In the Trenches. Gifts from Home.' A wartime postcard bringing home the message of how important mail and especially packages of useful supplies are for the soldiers' wellbeing and morale, 1915 (Museum of Eastern Bohemia, Hradec Králové).	188
5.2	'I am in good health and doing well.' A military-issue postcard given to soldiers when all other types of messages to their loved ones were banned because of operational necessity (Military History Institute, Prague).	190
5.3	'Auf Urlaub!' ('On Leave!') A propaganda image of the military hero's homecoming, promising the men to maintain or even improve their position in the gender order (Regional Museum in Olomouc).	204
6.1	'A reaper in the school for the disabled soldiers.' One of a series of postcards promising the men to keep their masculinity and status in the workforce, even if their body is permanently damaged, 1915 (Museum of Eastern Bohemia, Hradec Králové).	235
6.2	'Silent Heroism.' The positive side of a soldier's disability in wartime propaganda, postcard, 1915 (Museum of Eastern Bohemia, Hradec Králové).	236
6.3	The gruesome reality of bodily destruction in modern warfare, a military hospital in the town of Czernowitz, Bukovina, 1915 (Museum of Eastern Bohemia, Hradec Králové).	240

Preface to the English Edition

This text represents a substantial reworking and extension of the Czech original that was published by Nakladatelství Lidové noviny in Prague in 2016. While following the same ideas and arguments, important historiographical context and secondary research has been added since, with the sole purpose of presenting to a wider global audience a more rounded study of a topic that in the past has suffered all too often from oversimplification. With the hopes that the abovementioned efforts were not in vain, I would like to express my heartfelt thanks to those who made this work even remotely possible, in both versions. My early research into the vast depths of gender theory and gender history would never have been possible without the support of the Fulbright Commission, whose Research Scholarship helped me to spend several months in the cavernous depths of the Mugar Memorial Library at Boston University. Many thanks are also due to the Czech Science Foundation (GAČR), whose financial support for the project of this book was crucial. I am also forever indebted to my own Philosophical Faculty at the University of Hradec Kralove, which financed the proofreading of the translation so as to ensure that it is actually comprehensible to readers. And, finally, sincere thanks to Berghahn Books for their willingness to pick up this rather specific topic for publication.

On a personal level, I would like to express my sincere thanks to all my colleagues at the Institute of History, University of Hradec Králové, who had to bear the brunt of the problems created by their often absent Chair. In particular, I wish to thank Dana Musilová, Jan Mervart, Rudolf Kučera and Milena Lenderová for their comments on the earlier drafts, which greatly helped to improve the text. I am also very thankful to Etienne Boisserie, Helena Trnková, John Paul Newman, Rok Stergar and Gerald Steinacher, who gave me much-needed feedback on my work and supported me in my idea of preparing a translation. And, last but not least, many thanks go to Christa Hämmerle, Laurence Cole, Milan Hlavačka and the anonymous reviewers at Berghahn Books for being so helpful with their comments on the later versions of the text.

I would also like to thank Tomáš Kykal from the Military History Institute in Prague, who introduced me to a field of research that was completely new to me, and David Pazdera, who was willing to share his unpublished and decidedly undervalued work with me. Karel Podolský and Josef Šrámek, from the Regional Museum in Olomouc and the Museum of Eastern Bohemia, respectively, were of invaluable help when it came to the iconographic materials presented in this text, as well as in helping me to find ever more personal accounts of Czech soldiers. This neverending search would never have been possible without the help of a number of my students, who constantly supplied me with tips on these sources in local archives or private collections, and without the kind willingness of the current owners to let me access them. For that I would like to thank Jitka Měřínská, Martin Čihák, Václav Mach, Josef Nešněra and Jana Javůrková, as well as Jan Čundrle, Jan Janošík and Eva Horová, who made their collections accessible to me one way or another. Last but definitely not least, I must thank Ashley Davies, whose exceptional proofreading skills and infinite patience with my language have made it possible for English-speaking readers to be able to read these words in the first place.

Beyond the realm of academic concerns, my greatest thanks of all belong to my family. To my beloved wife, Mirka, who was supportive and patient beyond possible throughout all those years, and to our sons, Vašík and Lukáš, who were both born during the process of writing, rewriting and then translating this book, and have been teaching me ever since on masculinity in general and the difficulty of performing it in parallel arenas in particular. Without their ever-present smile and laughter, getting the job done would be nigh impossible.

Jiří Hutečka
Olomouc, October 2019

INTRODUCTION

Czech Soldiers in the First World War

Anglophone histories of the First World War are not usually very balanced when it comes to covering the respective participants, fronts and battlefields. While the proverbial 'Flanders Fields' of the Western Front have been subjected to repeated analytical efforts, most other areas of operations, as well as many of the participating countries, have received substantially less attention. Barring specific moments such as the very beginning of the war in the case of Austria-Hungary and the Balkans, the Gallipoli Campaign in the case of Turkey, and the Bolshevik Revolution in Russia, even key powers are left on the fringes of the great drama that mostly plays out, both in terms of the general narrative as well as deeper analysis, in France, Germany and Great Britain.[1] East-Central Europe and its experience of the war is one of the many casualties of this discourse, which may be surprising given the importance Austria-Hungary and Central Europe had for the world events in the twentieth century.[2]

The western part of the future Czechoslovakia, known in 1914 as the Bohemian Crown Lands and comprising of the historical lands of Bohemia, Moravia and a small part of Silesia, is no exception to this treatment. Neither are the roughly 1,500,000 men from these lands who went to fight in some of the war's bloodiest battles in the ranks of (initially) twenty-four k.u.k. infantry regiments,[3] some of them with a tradition reaching back to the aftermath of the Thirty Years' War, sixteen k.k. regiments of *Landwehr* infantry,[4] sixteen k.k. *Landsturm* (militia), nine *jäger* (light infantry) battalions, fifteen cavalry regiments, numerous artillery units, as well as innumerable support and staff units, and most of the ships of the *Kaiserliche und Königliche Kriegsmarine*. There are no exact statistics on how many of them were Czech by identity, as nationality as a category did not exist in the official Austrian census, which only recorded the language of everyday use (*Umgangssprache*). As a consequence, particularly the population of multilingual areas often lacked a clear-cut identity based on the national idea.[5] Also, the Austro-Hungarian military, as a consciously supranational dynastic institution, did not have any separate categories for ethnic or even linguistic groups, and its administrative entities did not always conform to the land borders. Consequently, we may only estimate that from the above quoted number – itself an estimate – about two-thirds of the troops were predominantly Czech-speaking, as this conforms to the percentage of the population that defined itself as Czech-speaking in the supposedly 'Czech' Lands.[6] This book is their story in the First World War of 1914–18.

The historiography of the Czech soldier during the First World War has so far usually suffered from a simplification often bordering on stereotyping, with the debate being framed by the lens of nationalism. According to the traditional consensus, Czech-speaking soldiers serving in the Austro-Hungarian military enlisted only because they were forced to do so, most of them supposedly thoroughly despised the war on the side of the Habsburgs, particularly one against their Serb and Russian Slavic brethren, and they spent their time in service either trying to desert or sabotaging the imperial war effort through decidedly lacklustre military performance. In general histories, they are often defined as 'passive supporters of Russia', always on the verge of 'mutinies' and 'large-scale desertions', or at least 'popular demonstrations'.[7] Two recent projects summarizing contemporary First World War scholarship, when mentioning Czechs outside of the developments leading towards an independent Czechoslovakia, similarly point to disputable loyalty, 'mass surrenders' and 'national conflict' as key topics regarding this particular minority in the ethno-linguistic patchwork of the monarchy.[8] At best, the Czech subjects of Franz Joseph I were defined as 'ambivalent patriots', and even a respected expert in Central European history such as Mark Cornwall once wrote about the 'underlying apathy or hostility towards the war effort' among Czechs.[9]

While there is certainly some grain of truth in these qualifying judgements, it must be asked why it is that Czechs, out of all the minorities of Austria-Hungary, became a prime symbol both of disloyalty and passive national resistance to state power. As Mark Cornwall recently noted, 'the evidence suggests some opportunism on the part of Czech politicians, but also some real Czech commitment to Austria which later accounts tried to conceal'.[10] It is these 'later accounts' that need to be seen as the main source of the 'disloyal Czechs' paradigm, which closely reflected the need of the postwar societies and political entities of Central Europe. On the one hand, in its own variant of the *Dolchstoßlegende*, Austrian conservative historiography found it easy to continue the trend already established by Austrian-German politicians and partially by the Army High Command during the war, blaming not only the disintegration but also the very military defeat of the old empire on its national minorities. In this particular form of the 'blame game', Czechs were always popular as 'usual suspects' and there was little need to change this view after the war was over.[11]

Even more important was the fact that this interpretation fitted very well into the national myth of the newly created Czechoslovak Republic. The country based its origins firmly in the 'foreign action' of its first president, Tomáš G. Masaryk, and other wartime exiles, as well as, in military terms, in the Czechoslovak Legion, a 90,000-strong army of expatriate Czechs (and Slovaks) and former Austrian prisoners of war (POWs), which fought successfully on the Eastern Front and saw some action in Italy and also in France, serving the exiles as a primary propagandistic tool in their push for independence.[12] After the establishment of Czechoslovakia, the dominant discourse of the war sought to legitimize the new statehood as a part of a worldwide 'fight for liberty', and the experience of the Legion, barring its radical elements, became the cornerstone of the official founding myth.[13] However, the war experience of the majority of the Czech-speaking population (the large German and Magyar minorities of Czechoslovakia notwithstanding) differed starkly from this discourse, as 90 per cent of the Czechs who fought in the war did so in the Habsburg uniform on the battlefields of the Balkans, in Galicia, northern Italy, France, in the Mediterranean Sea and even in Palestine, and more than 160,000 men from Bohemia, Moravia and Austrian Silesia lost their lives in the process.[14] Thus, an essential discontinuity between myth and reality had emerged, and the need to bridge it came to the fore. The image of Czechs as coerced malingerers, deserters and traitors, which the government in exile embraced for the purposes of political propaganda during the war, was a welcome solution that enabled the majority of the nation to reinterpret their past in nationally acceptable terms. In the early postwar years, this quickly became accepted as the mainstream – and thoroughly positive – version of the nation's participation in the monarchy's war effort, and the soldiers' past became the subject of substantial reinterpretation.[15] As a part of this process, several instances of mass surrenders of Czech-dominated units, such as the infamous 'crossing of the lines' by the k.u.k. Infantry Regiment 28, which supposedly went into Russian captivity 'with the band playing' in April 1915, became a legend that was inseparable from historical reality.[16] Supported by the ever-increasing popularity of Jaroslav Hašek's famous anti-war novel *The Good Soldier Švejk* (1921–23), which – again in a unified effort of Czech and German readership – soon became reinterpreted as a further self-evident example of Czech attitudes towards Austria and military service, the image of Czechs as anti-Austrian 'Švejks' became forever entrenched in the historical memory and spread worldwide.[17] In the Czech historical writing, little changed over the years, as the historiography of the communist era resulted only in a shift regarding the motivation of the disloyal attitude of Czechs from nationalism towards class struggle, with the resulting image remaining the same.[18] After 1989, the 'nationalistic' interpretation re-emerged and while it was, particularly in popular historiography, confronted with substantial efforts to 'rehabilitate' the image of Czechs as loyal soldiers of the monarchy and reject the 'Švejk' imagery, it remained strong in the public discourse as well as in the historical writing.[19] As a consequence, Czech historical writing on the military experience of the First World War was caught in an unproductive, analytically barren, neverending discursive loop of debate that has hardly changed in the past one hundred years and has brought little in terms of an understanding that would go beyond the few competing images.

Fortunately, there are several exceptions to the rule in Central European historiography, which at least enable us to escape the limiting constraints of this eternal argument and to see the issue in a different light. It was Ivan Šedivý who, in his now classical synthesis of the history of the Bohemian Lands in 1914–18, concluded that the traditional discourse had all too often mistaken anti-war feelings, exhaustion and economic despair for nationally motivated resistance, ignoring the all-important process of change that occurred in this area over the course of the war.[20] Martin Zückert has identified the small but vocal group of political radicals around the prewar Czech National Socialist Party as the source of the popular image of the anti-war and anti-Austrian Czech.[21] In an unpublished thesis that unfortunately still remains the most thorough analysis of the mobilization in Bohemia, David Pazdera has argued that while Czech soldiers did not go to war with much enthusiasm, they were steadfast in their determination to do their duty, hoping that the war would be over soon.[22] Rudolf Kučera, in his short essay on the issue of loyalty of Czech soldiers in the war, has identified a gradual shift from class to national loyalties, brought about by increasingly desperate material conditions and other perceived injustices of the wartime service, as instrumental in the decline in the combat-worthiness of Czech-speaking troops.[23] And finally, Richard Lein thoroughly analysed the above-mentioned 'affair' of the 28th Infantry as well as a similar case of the 75th and 35th Infantry Regiments at Zborov in 1917, concluding that more than anything else, the spectacular failures of these Czech-dominated units were the result of botched command decisions on the part of the Austro-Hungarian command structure, as well as inexperience and general exhaustion, and showed that the subsequent interpretation was a result of immediate superiors trying to find a scapegoat for their own blunders. This led to some highly politicized and public decisions of the Army High Command that, rather ironically, gave ammunition both to Austrian-German nationalists and Czech politicians in exile to claim that all Czechs were traitors after all.[24]

Goals and Methods

What most of these texts have in common, and what inspired the original idea behind this book, is that they, each in its own way, try to overcome the shortcoming that is common to most historical writing on the issue. The discourse defined by the dual framework of loyalty and national identity seems to be so powerful as to overshadow all other considerations. As a consequence, the men who went to war speaking Czech have always been studied as *Czechs* first and foremost, only rarely as *soldiers* and never as *men*. The immodest goal of this text is to invert this logic and shed a completely new light through a lens never used before, one rarely used in military history in general. The core of our analysis will rest with the elementary identity of the Czech soldier, the fact that he defined himself as a *he* – a man. Only then will the focus shift on the way in which this *primary* identity influenced the way these men experienced their *soldiering*, i.e. their attitudes and motivations towards their participation in warfare. And as it is impossible to completely overlook the topic of national identity in a discussion of Czech soldiers' morale and motivation, we will ultimately try to find a link between these two analytical frameworks and the ever-present issue of *Czech* national self-identification and loyalty.

The traditional 'neverending debate about the Czech soldier in the Great War' will therefore be ultimately approached here, only this time through methods so far ignored or underused, in the firm belief that it will help to forge a new path in understanding men in war and those in Czech history in particular. It will be argued, over the course of this book, that masculinity, particularly the way in which ordinary men turned soldiers experienced it, indeed played an important role in the way in which these men experienced the war as such, and that in turn, war had profound effect on their understanding of their masculine self. It will be claimed that while specific understanding of masculine ideals led men to war, the same war had ultimately subverted the basic concepts of modern masculinity through its upsetting everyday realities and practices. As a result, a strong connection between the notions of masculinity and military morale will be established, and, using the specifics of the Czech case, it will be shown that the inherent instability of this connection may have had serious repercussions regarding the soldiers' motivation and even political loyalty, when a crisis of wartime masculine experience opened a path to alternative loyalties and notions of self-identification, based on refuting the war along with the state that made men to take part in it.

To fulfil this rather ambitious thesis, several intertwined questions will have to be answered first. In his summary of the recent historiography of the First World War, Alan Kramer noted that much recent writing is inspired by, among other factors, the following question: 'what enabled men to mobilise for war and endure it for so long?'[25] In this regard, historiography is traditionally torn between 'coercion' and 'consent', and while it needs to be acknowledged that the overall motivational framework incorporates both in a myriad of combinations, our focus here will be primarily on 'consent'. In his study of coercion and consent in the French army, Leonard Smith has rightly criticized the tendency to see consent as a creation of external pressures, as it relieves the men of any individual will or agency, and removes the possibility for their position in the system to be negotiated.[26] However, in social analysis, the general assumption is that human beings primarily operate within the framework of pre-existing structures and meanings that define their position *before* it may be renegotiated through individual experience and agency, which may then lead to changes in the structures and meanings in question. For us, therefore, even active consent is contingent upon the underlying cultural and social framework, as even free will does not exist in a void. Our analysis will be concerned primarily with that framework, as it will focus on the very core of the question posed by Kramer – the fact that we are talking about *men* – and it will be asked whether the social experience and construction of *manhood* had any bearing on the way in which men understood their plight.

The key issue of our study will therefore be masculinity, which forms one part of the 'constitutive element of social relationships based on perceived differences between the sexes', as Joan W. Scott defined gender in her famous essay on its 'usefulness for historical analysis'. She also added that gender is 'a primary way of signifying relationships of power … a primary field within which or by means of which power is articulated'.[27] While in Czech historiography this concept has long been sidelined in favour of the more traditionally oriented women's history, only establishing itself firmly in the past decade and a half, historical writing elsewhere had a head start and, as early as the late 1980s, turned its attention not only to the limited 'new men's studies', but also to the study of masculinity (or manliness) as a previously 'hidden' social category.[28] In other words, historians turned to what it *meant*, from the point of view of both society and the individual, to be a man. The Australian sociologist R.W. Connell's theory of *hegemony* in gender relations, defining hegemonic masculinity as the pillar of patriarchal power, was soon adopted as a key analytical framework.[29] In this theory, inspired by Gramsci's model of cultural hegemony in class relations, Connell assumes a whole series of 'inherently historical' masculinities to exist in any given human society, whose 'making and remaking is a political process affecting the balance of interests in society and the direction of social change'. Of the manifold masculinities present in a given gender order, one is always seen as 'hegemonic', i.e. one that 'is not a fixed character type … rather, [one] that occupies the hegemonic position in a given pattern of gender relations, a position always contestable'. Masculinities therefore always form a hierarchy that is 'inherently historical'. Their relations are 'historically mobile', but always based on the positions of hegemony, subordination, complicity or marginalization ('deviance'). The primary purpose of this structure is the distribution of social power, with hegemonic masculinity ensuring the actors the best and most direct access to the 'patriarchal dividend', entailing symbolic power over other men and particularly over femininity, i.e. persons defined as women.[30] Even though the concept has been repeatedly criticized and consequently re-adjusted, the basic thesis arguing for the existence of historical masculinities, one of them situated in a hegemonic but ever contested, challenged and dynamically changing position has remained.[31] As such, it has inspired a new field of study that has spread successfully throughout the historical profession in the past two decades.[32]

Surprisingly, however, this inspiring process all but bypassed the field of military history, particularly in the Czech Republic, where the historiography of warfare has mostly devolved into a methodological emptiness of descriptive positivism, with little reflection of contemporary trends.[33] While it is possible to agree with Rudolf Kučera, who, in his recent summary of the current state of research on masculinities and twentieth-century world wars, argues that 'it is the phenomenon of modern total war in men and men in modern total wars ... which enables us to fulfil the potential' offered by masculinity as an analytical category, his call remains unanswered by his colleagues.[34] Ironically, the only inspiring treatment of the issue when it comes to the First World War in Bohemia and Moravia – albeit not military history – comes from the same author, who devotes one chapter of his study of wartime industrial workers to the important issue of working-class masculine identity under the pressures of the changing economy and ensuing shifts in the gender order.[35]

However, the discursive gap between the study of gender and the study of warfare is also apparent within the wider context of European historiography. Staying with the example of Central Europe in the First World War, we find plenty of studies dealing with the issue of gender. Yet, they generally tend to approach the issue from the point of view of either women or the gender order viewed through the home/front relationship, or its symbolic frontiers such as female nursing. At best, they address the temporality any re-alignment to the 'double helix' of gender relations, as in the famous essay by Margaret and Patrice Higonnet in 1987, where the authors argue that whatever radical shifts occur in wartime, subsequent social pressures will always ensure that masculinity will return to its hegemonic position.[36] The situation is not so different from the broader perspective either – the recently published collection of essays summarizing the current research on 'gender and the Great War' is rather exceptional in that it actually includes a chapter (albeit one in thirteen) on 'gender and warfare', where Susan Grayzel portrays men and their masculinity mostly as victims of modern military technologies.[37] Similarly, the vast majority of part II of volume 7 of the recent massive history of the First World War edited by Jay Winter deals with the issue of women and femininity in the war, while only one chapter by Joanna Bourke comes close to the essence of warfare when it deals with 'gender roles in the killing zones'.[38] The tendency to conflate the study of gender in wartime with the issues relational to femininity or sexuality is nothing particularly new, as it has always been prevalent even in works dealing directly with the combatants' experience.[39] As often happens in the social and cultural study of warfare, it almost seems as if gender identities fall silent when the firing starts, the combatants almost being ungendered as a result.

The rather limited connection between military history and gender history is particularly surprising if one realizes how extremely gendered the social and cultural institution of warfare has always been.[40] As anthropologies of war have long been telling us, 'war is not merely action … It is a condition of and between societies, with innumerable correlates in virtually every dimension of culture'.[41] As argued by John Lynn in his inspiring study of combat and culture, war is indeed a continuation of culture by other means.[42] It is therefore obvious that an important cultural category such as masculinity is impossible to ignore when studying warfare. Studying war experience without reflecting masculinity is problematic because in most known cultures, war is seen as being closely related to the performance of qualities defined as masculine. The idea of organized armed conflict is often 'gendered' into the notion of 'military masculinity' – a system of values that defines manliness through legalized violence against other groups.[43] Among these values, specific character traits come to the fore – personal courage, self-sacrifice for the greater good, and internalized fear of social shame in the case of failure.[44] Many of the characteristics of military masculinity may also be culturally specific, changing over time and place – while some military masculinities extol violent aggression, pride and individual skill in killing, others may value blind obedience, discipline and collective spirit the most, while for some, trickery and a cloak-and-dagger approach is preferred; the number of combinations is perhaps infinite. Institutionalized through written or unwritten rules of militaries, mercenary bands or warrior classes, these values serve as a mirror against which manliness is measured by institutions, peer-groups or whole societies, particularly in wartime.

In European culture, military masculinity has always had a complicated relationship with the hegemonic gender structures, and in the modern era it has usually been far from constituting their integral part. There are plenty of historical examples where military masculinity had been relegated to a marginalized or, at best, complicit status at the very edge of the social hierarchy, while the hegemonic image of manliness hardly included any of its traditional traits. However, because masculinity is by nature a fluid, dynamic construct, always contested and open to rapid change, events such as suddenly perceived danger to the group may cause the hegemonic masculinity to adopt some or all of the characteristics of military masculinity, therefore militarizing itself and pushing previously marginalized or even shunned values into the spotlight of social discourse, preference and adulation. Looking at the numerous cultural studies of manliness, it actually seems that for the most part, military masculine traits and behavioural patterns generally tend to exist 'in the background' of hegemonic structures, only being 'activated' from time to time, sometimes for years, sometimes for decades. We may well agree with Christopher Forth, who once argued in favour of the idea that the man-warrior image was the most enduring and persistent 'residual element', occupying a position at the very roots of European hegemonic masculinities long after warfare ceased to be the raison d'être of European elite manhood.[45] Siniša Malešević too sees traits such as physical courage, endurance, strength and skill, and honour as cultural mainstays of masculinity with strong roots in the 'warrior ethos'.[46] And, finally, John Tosh includes the concept of man as a 'protector' in his list of specific 'numerous relatively constant and resilient gender structures', one that he succinctly defines as 'the gender *longue durée*' of European culture.[47] Consequently, while early twentieth-century European society may have encompassed a number of 'hegemonic masculinities' depending on a divide of class, urban or rural origin, or cultural background, some of them radically rejecting the militarized notion of masculinity, the very individual characteristics that made up the core of this notion have always been in an ambivalent but close relationship to most of these hegemonic discourses. In a way, warfare has always been the 'backstage' of socially construed manhood.[48]

The 'discursive gap' between the study of war and the study of *men at war* is so endemic and prominent that several noted historians have actually commented on the need for more reflection on the issue, often in connection with the already four-decades-old phenomenon of 'new military history'. In 1997, John Lynn identified 'the promise of gender history' in his essay on 'the embattled future of military history', analysing the danger of it being forever sidelined by cultural and social studies. In particular, he argued that 'there is much to be said about [masculinity in war], and it will come out most clearly in discussing combat' and even went on to say that 'in this sense, gender could be really sexy'.[49] Leo Braudy, in his sweeping study of the relationship between war and masculinity, argued the same, seeing warfare and masculine identity as fluid but tightly interconnected social constructs with a common history that goes back for millennia.[50] Joanna Bourke has acknowledged the importance of masculinity in studying war both in her own work on killing in combat and in her summary of 'new military history', where she has identified 'the specifically masculine nature of war' as a particularly important issue.[51]

When it comes to the First World War, it is particularly the analysis of gendered war remembrance that had entered the historical discourse with the works of authors such as Klaus Theweleit or George L. Mosse.[52] It was Mosse who saw 'the warrior image of masculinity' as an elementary part of masculine identity 'since the French revolution and the Napoleonic Wars'.[53] In her summary of German historiography of gender and war, Christa Hämmerle also identified the study of masculinity as an integral part of the 'new debate' on military institutions and practices, and actually used the discourse surrounding the notion of 'war experience' as an example.[54] However, it is her short essay on the possible uses of Connell's concept of hegemonic masculinity that must receive the most attention here, as it introduces this theorem to the study of the Austro-Hungarian military.

Subscribing to the notion of masculinity as a dynamic process reproducing social hierarchies and power, Hämmerle pinpoints several areas where Connell's theory might be particularly useful for historical analysis and where the notion of universal military service, introduced in 1868, connected with the discourse of manliness: first, she identifies the army in the prewar era as an institution deeply interested in producing 'full men', offering an 'education in manhood' through compulsory military service; second, she argues that while men were 'complicit' to an extent with this view, their civilian economic and social status still took precedence in their self-perception of their own position in the masculine hierarchy, and 'military masculinity', which included defining 'manly' bodily forms through the army's evaluation of the physical fitness of its recruits, was mostly confined to the social space of the military; third, she states that in the social space of 'active' service, which for most men meant a three- or later two-year training period upon reaching twenty-one years of age, masculinity constituted a key identity formed through the process of symbolic feminization and subsequent 'masculinization' of the recruits who were instilled (through body-reflexive practices ranging from drill to sexualization) with the notion of 'full manhood' they were supposed to represent in opposition to everything civilian; and, fourth, she concludes that in Austria-Hungary, the complicated nature of the state and the body politic prevented the process described as 'militarizing of hegemonic masculinity' typical of countries such as France or Germany in the prewar years, as military service carried many different meanings for different groups in the monarchy. Only with the beginning of the war in 1914, finally, did the moment come when hegemonic and military masculinities became aligned in the public discourse, rallying behind the idea of 'true men' fighting for 'God, the Emperor and the Fatherland'.[55]

This is the moment when Christa Hämmerle concluded her outline and is also the moment when our application of Connell's theory falls in, hoping to analyse both the way in which the war changed the individual experience of manliness and the way in which 'the category of gender intertwined with other categories such as age, ethnicity, or religion'[56] to produce new social hierarchies specific for wartime and pertinent to the ultimate goal of all military institutions: fighting. What results is an analysis of the Czech military experience of the First World War through the lens of a history of masculinities, one that hopes to methodologically elevate the current debate on this particular issue, as well as to alleviate some of the criticism raised by Jeremy Black against the inability of gender analysis to 'offer more to the issue of military capability'.[57] In this context, the question posed above – what enabled men to mobilise for war and endure it for so long – will have to be supplemented by a set of supporting questions that also need to be answered – how did the Czech men in the uniforms of Austria-

Hungary experience their masculinity and the way it was influenced by the war? How did the war, mobilization and frontline service connect to their perception of themselves as men? What exactly did they imagine under the category of masculinity in relation to their military duties? How did they experience the interaction of various masculinities and femininities amidst the shockwaves of the wartime gender order? How did the war influence their perception of the gender order as a whole? And, last but not least, returning to the 'neverending debate about the Czech soldier', did this experience of one's own masculine identity in war influence the men's motivation to enlist and fight for the Habsburg Empire and, if so, how? Put simply, what did it mean *to be a man in war* for Czech soldiers, and how did it influence their attitudes, behaviour, feelings and morale?

Study along these lines would obviously not be possible without reflecting upon the broader issue of military morale and motivation, which has long been a subject of interest in the rather specific field of military history. It all started with Ardant du Picq, a colonel of the French infantry in the late 1860s who saw battle as a conflict of individuals, small groups, and their discipline and morale.[58] Later, in the twentieth century, the problem of individual morale and motivation became an important part of the military discourse. Shortly after the end of the Second World War, the British First World War military surgeon Lord Moran published an influential essay on courage, and J. Glenn Gray, himself a veteran of the U.S. Italian campaign of 1943 to 1945, soon added an insightful analysis of the psychology of the combat soldier.[59] In the late 1940s, a heavily researched sociological study by Samuel A. Stouffer and his team on the 'hearts and minds' of the GIs during the Second World War appeared,[60] as did the much shorter and more controversial work by S.L.A. Marshall on the same,[61] both of which influenced similar later works such as the classical study of morale in the *Wehrmacht* by Edward Shils and Morris Janowitz.[62] It took a few decades for this debate to trickle down into the field of military history, where it took a firm hold after Richard Holmes published his seminal work, offering a sweeping historical perspective on human behaviour not only in combat, but also in military service in general, with heavy emphasis on the First World War.[63]

Turning our attention to this conflict, much has been said about the groundbreaking study of battle by John Keegan, which included a brief analysis of the motivational factors that caused British troops to walk slowly towards the German trenches on the Somme on 1 July 1916.[64] In parallel with Holmes, Tony Ashworth's sociologically minded study analysed the 'live and let live' system of the Western Front, arguing – among other points – that the 'masculine code of behaviour' played a part in compelling men to 'perform in combat roles'.[65] A decade later, Leonard Smith applied the Foucaultian theory of proportionality to the power relations in the French army in order to explain how the soldiers' attitudes shifted on a scale 'between mutiny and obedience' in accordance with the pressure from above and the situation in the lines.[66] The same author also took on the subject of the soldiers' narrative of the war experience, with emphasis placed on the notion that willing consent (i.e. positive internal motivation) indeed played an important role in soldiers' motivation.[67] His claim was part of a longstanding argument and went against the belief held by mostly German historians like Wilhelm Deist or Anne Lipp, who argued – at least with regard to the German experience – that men were more or less coerced into combat by the combination of harsh discipline, propaganda and symbolic concessions made by the army to alleviate their condition, with thousands of them ending up shirking their service by the end of the war.[68] In a similar vein, Benjamin Ziemann concluded that the ability to acquire additional supplies from home, the variability of frontline exposure, fear of punishment, regular furloughs and readily available escape in the form of strong Catholic faith were key factors in the cohesion of German troops originating from rural areas of southern Germany.[69]

When Alexander Watson went on to add to this debate with his inspiring comparative study of British and German armies on the Western Front, he concluded that 'contrary to the impression given by some historiography, neither resilience nor collapse was the norm among men' of both armies, their motivation being fuelled by 'a combination of societal influences, military factors and human psychological defence mechanisms' and supported by propaganda, pre-existing beliefs and ideology, as well as primary group loyalty.[70] Watson actually comes close to admitting that masculinity and gender identity played an invisible role in motivating men as a part of the 'societal influences' underlining the overall consent with the military role, but like all the authors mentioned above, he does not dwell on the issue much more.[71] And the same is true for Benjamin Ziemann's most recent addition to the debate, which analyses 'forms of violence and the willingness to perpetrate it' on the part of the German soldiers – while he identifies 'male fundamentalism' as a form of postwar masculine discourse celebrating military action and violence, he consciously eschews any effort at studying the 'gendering of violence' in the First World War, noting its 'infancy' in the context of research on the German army.[72]

Listing important works on military morale and motivation, we have yet to mention one that is of key importance for this text. Its author is John Lynn and the work in question is his seminal study of the French revolutionary army between 1791 and 1794, where he presents us with a conveniently structured 'model of combat effectiveness'.[73] According to Lynn, this effectiveness is a product of numerous factors, both consensual and coercive, which ensure that the men ultimately reach the fighting area and engage in combat in the most effective way possible. As a part of this theory, Lynn postulates a structured model of soldiers' motivation itself, identifying three separate phases: initial (enlisting the men into the army), sustaining (keeping them in the ranks throughout training, unit movements and the long periods of waiting), and combat (making sure the men will actually fight when facing mortal danger). In our analysis of soldiers' gender identity, this motivational structure will be used as a framework that will help us to bridge two methodological worlds: that of a gender analysis of Central European societies in wartime; and that of the ongoing debates over soldiers' experience of modern warfare and the First World War in particular. It will also enable us to cover the basic experiences Czech soldiers would have had.

To follow this intent, Chapter 1 is devoted to the initial motivation of the men upon entering their wartime service, be it in 1914 or later. Attention is given here to the issue of the gender 'remapping' of the monarchy's social space and the synthesis of hegemonic and previously compliant/marginalized military masculinities, all in an effort to explain the surprising ease with which Czech men were mobilized for the Habsburg war effort. The accompanying shifts in the social hierarchy, interpreted within the context of the theory of patriarchal dividend, are what gives the chapter its title, as the process is seen as a collective *tournament of manliness*.

While the analysis of soldiers' initial motivation fits into one chapter, the sustaining motivation as defined by Lynn covers not just most of any soldier's time in service, but also most of the book, spanning four chapters in the process. As a result, Chapter 2 deals primarily with the most elementary factors of a soldier's material and physical existence, such as weather, fatigue, shelter, supply or sexuality, defining the resulting issues as endless *compromises of manliness* that slowly but gradually took away the sense of power and control from the men. Chapter 3 then takes inspiration from the study of military comradeship, which Thomas Kühne has defined as a highly gendered social concept requiring a *transformation of manliness* for the men to be able to accommodate their close homosocial coexistence and emotionality into the framework of military primary groups, therefore maintaining control over their experience of masculinity.[74] The analysis as presented in Chapter 4 focuses on the process of gradual *degradation of manliness*, caused mostly by the dysfunctional power relations Czech soldiers had with the Austro-Hungarian authorities, particularly on the symbolic level. As we will see, the individual experience of relative loss of power and status, as well as the restructuring of masculine hierarchies, all came into play here, eventually conspiring against both Czech soldiers' sustaining motivation, consent and, consequently, combat-effectiveness. Finally, Chapter 5 follows the various *venues of manliness* in which masculinity had to be performed in order to achieve or maintain hegemonic status. Taking inspiration for this framework from John Tosh, the chapter analyses both the importance of home for the men's 'emotional survival' and their gradual inability to perform their masculine roles both there and at the front, with the accompanying sense of losing power and control in both of those arenas, efforts to restore at least a semblance of normalcy notwithstanding.

The final chapter, Chapter 6, takes the reader, along with our subjects the soldiers, out of the liminal space of sustaining motivation into the symbolic space that gives meaning to the whole war experience – to battle. Here, combat motivation as defined by Lynn takes over, rooted mostly in emotions such as fear in group dynamics, but even here gendered undertones are identifiable. Combat itself is analysed from the standpoint of masculine identity, and the various fears it brings about are connected to the soldiers' perceptions of manliness. The issue of bodily deformation or outright catastrophic destruction through the actions of modern weaponry is also analysed here, as it is not just the soldier who comes *under fire*, but also his masculinity, both in the socially psychological meaning and in the way in which the body is experienced in terms of losing control of its limits and shape.

Looking at the structure of the book, a unifying theme runs through it like a red line connecting all the angles chosen to analyse Czech soldiers' war experience – namely the process of losing power and control over various aspects of existence. As we have noted above, power projected into control is the key to understanding both the gender order in general and the hegemonic masculinity concept in particular. Thomas Kühne further argues that masculine identity is not just a system of cultural patterns and discourses; it is also their reproduction in social practice as well as a subjective process, an experience that produces power. If the ability to exercise power, or the perception of thereof, is seriously breached, the whole symbolic system that forms the primary basis for this power starts to fall apart.[75] Moreover, within the social context, power means the ability to control affairs and events in one's surroundings in terms of social relations, physical conditions and the fulfilment of one's real or perceived needs. When it comes to soldiers, it may be a process similar to the one described by Rudolf Kučera in his analysis of the politics and practices of the wartime working class in Bohemia. Kučera repeatedly points out the close connection between the militarization of wartime society and the gradual loss of control and power experienced by men in all spheres of life, including economic, social and family relations. In his view, this was one of several processes that were responsible for wartime shifts in the nature of the Central European working class. In this text, we see the same process as essential in defining, through an endless series of compromises, transformations and gendered performances, the motivation of Czech soldiers to die willingly (i.e. with at least a passive consent) for the Austro-Hungarian monarchy. Alon Rachamimov once noted in a thought-provoking analysis of German-speaking officer POWs in Russia that they had experienced 'an acute sense of masculine disempowerment' because of their captivity.[76] Our argument here is that this sense may have been actually close to what many of the men, particularly in the ranks, experienced even without being captured.

Any reader versed in the historiography of the Czech soldier of the First World War may be wary of the fact that our analysis takes us only as far as combat and its direct consequences, leaving out other key experiences of many soldiers, such as capture, medical discharge or even desertion. Obviously, these themes are closely connected to the problem of masculinity, potentially representing moments of radical restructuring of values and attitudes, along with changing social frameworks that define masculine identity from the outside. Capture or desertion often presents us with breaking points in motivation that may have had a particular bearing on the actor's masculine identity, as is obvious from the very limited number of sources originating in captivity (primarily correspondence) used mainly in Chapter 5. However, after consideration, an analysis of these issues has been left out of this text for several reasons. First, it would lead to a greater level of generalization than should be allowed even in a work based mostly on personal accounts. Second, including the highly complicated issues of capture and desertion would mean asking manifold questions regarding the very *practice* of these, as well as the following issues of the POW experience, revolution and repatriation, as well as the Czechoslovak Legion. Following this path would threaten to take the text far beyond its intended scope. Also, many of these issues, including some relating to masculine identity, have already been successfully covered by Alon Rachamimov in her seminal study on POWs on the Eastern Front, and by other authors dealing with the issue of Austro-Hungarian soldiers in captivity during the First World War.[77] Any effort to push analysis beyond the limits given by the structure of Lynn's theory of military motivation would also mean that it would enter a realm beyond the universality of the common experience Czech soldiers went through. If we disregard the vast number of men in army support services, then after the first experience with fighting, even the combat soldiers' patterns of experience have the tendency to diverge – some are dead, some are wounded and invalided, some wounded and returned to their units later, some are captured, some desert and some go on to another battle. Combat situation is therefore a sort of a breaking point in the (decidedly relative) universality of men's experience of warfare. And, finally, the way in which the argument is structured here enables us to keep the analysis of the *men*'s motivation to *stay* in service logically coherent, without embarking on issues that would threaten to tear it apart.

Note on the Sources

The key sources subjected to our analysis include mostly diaries, letters and memoirs, i.e. personal accounts written by Czech-speaking (or, in several cases, obviously multilingual) soldiers during or after the First World War.[78] Of course, the reliability of 'testimonies' with regard to the experience of war has been a subject of discussion ever since the publication of Jean Norton-Cru's massive and celebrated 'critical essay and analysis of recollections of French combatants published in France from 1915 to 1928' in 1929, a comparative study of several hundred autobiographical accounts meticulously judged by the author according to their documentary value.[79] As this book is not interested so much in the objective nature of the war as in its subjective understanding by individual participants, applying a decidedly 'cultural' approach to the analysis in search of personal convictions, emotions and feelings men harboured about issues that pertain to our subject matter, it is partially 'cleared' on the minute detail of real events skipped in the search for meaning. For similar reasons, while it is obvious that the wider use of other kinds of sources (official documents, legal records, police reports or the contemporary press, for example) may help further our analysis and potentially support much of the presented argument, a conscious decision, guided by the same considerations, was made to fully focus the attention on a critical analysis of the available personal accounts – of the ways masculinity was felt and understood by those who aspired to it at the time – and leave the above-mentioned to future research. There are, of course, several exceptions to the rule, particularly a number of civilians' personal accounts, as well as a sample of contemporary propaganda material produced to support the war effort in Bohemia, Moravia and Austrian Silesia.

The available body of sources brought up several issues that had to be addressed in the process of analysis. First, there is no way to pretend that it is more than a *sample* of all the possibly available personal accounts of the war that were ever produced in Czech, selected primarily on the basis of their authors' eloquence (or conspicuous silence) vis-à-vis the topics presented here. Also, while innumerable diaries, letter collections and memoir manuscripts were lost to the vagaries of the twentieth-century history of Central Europe, it is also a fact that in the Czech Republic, there is no single institution collecting and making available personal accounts of the war that were not produced by the members of the Czechoslovak Legion. While some archives, including the Military History Archives in Prague, have subsections in their collections dedicated to these, the most valuable sources are often to be found either in local archives' personal collections or in the family estates of the authors' descendants, which makes searching for these sources a true challenge. On the other hand, over the past hundred years, numerous accounts have been published (although in numbers nowhere near those of the accounts by the members of the Czechoslovak Legion). Following the various agendas of their authors or editors, these publications came in several waves – in the 1920s, one particularly strong in the 1930s, then in a trickle until the late 1980s, with a resurgence around the turn of the twenty-first century. In the mixture of these publications, one finds texts made famous by the celebrity status of their authors, such as the diary by the Bohemian-Jewish journalist Egon Erwin Kisch (who, while technically a German-speaking cosmopolitan intellectual, served in a regiment with a Czech-speaking majority, and whose keen eye provides us with an unparalleled insight into the experience of the first few months of the war on the Serbian front), the correspondence of the impressionist poet and writer Fráňa Šrámek with his wife, or the memoirs of the radical leftist writer S.K. Neumann and the painter and mystic Josef Váchal. There are also both scholarly and popular collections of letters, postcards and fragmentary diary entries published on the basis of territoriality, i.e. by men from the same region or village, who probably never aspired to literary fame, or by local historians. A number of memoirs and diaries was edited (often heavily) and published by the authors, often at their own expense, who did not want their plight to be forgotten, or who wanted to prove a point with regard to their war record; there are also manuscripts of these that never made it to the printing presses. There are also those that were published only by a scholarly or private effort in recent decades, these editions being of particularly variable, sometimes very poor quality in terms of their faithfulness to the original source (with some particularly egregious examples being basically rewritten by the editors, turning diaries into memoirs by proxy). There are also sources dug out from the archives in an effort to overcome some inherent limits of the published or retrospective sources, and to offer some comparison in point. And, finally, there is some supporting evidence taken from the narratives of fictionalized accounts by authors both known and unknown; however, these are limited to those instances that help make a particular point, illustrating a tendency or pattern present throughout the sample, with the full knowledge that artistic licence may be present.

The issue of the time and place of origin of a source is of particular importance in the Czech historiography of the First World War, as there is often a vast difference between the texts that originated during the conflict and those that were written or rewritten, and sometimes also those published after the war. Of course, a historian needs to be constantly aware that there is no text without an agenda, and even the most authentic diary entry or letter is not just an outpouring of feelings and thoughts, but a construction of meaning addressed not only to the writer and his or her consciousness, but also to numerous potential readers (the recipient, other people with whom he or she may share the text, future generations, censors and other unintended readers, etc.), which has severe consequences for the nature of the information and forces us to dig deep in search of slips of the tongue and often unconscious references to the subject of our study. However, the closer to the events described the text is created, the less time there is to insert hindsight and further agendas. With Czech soldiers, these agendas come to the fore after 1918, as many memoirs and some later editions of diaries tend to reinterpret the war experience in a way that better fits its outcome, primarily the dissolution of the monarchy and the establishment of Czechoslovakia. While there is no hard rule that would be of much help here (indeed, there are anti-war and anti-Austrian as well as Czech nationalist accounts written by soldiers during the war), every text written in the interwar period in particular needs to be viewed especially critically, as there were many important reasons for the authors to put a different spin on their war record in the Imperial and Royal uniform. Perhaps the best example, and also by far the most problematic source used in this book, is the well-known anthology of recollections and edited fragments of diaries published in the late 1920s and early 1930s under the editorship of Alois Žipek. Its admitted purpose was to testify 'to an age … of horrible deprivation and enormous sacrifice', thus building a monument that will forever be 'a source of encouragement for all people Czech and Slovak to value their newly acquired freedom and hold it in high esteem'.[80] The First World War is interpreted here as a Czech and Slovak struggle for freedom from its very beginning, and the selection of texts follows this logic. Most of them reflect on the conflict through the lens of nationalism, often to an extent all but unknown in texts written during the war, particularly in its early phases. This distortion, while often very obvious, is one of the reasons why Žipek's collection is a chronically unreliable source in many aspects, and is used here only in those cases that are aligned with the information in other sources, or when there is no other, more reliable alternative.

The rather limited sample of sources used here – in total, thirty-five diaries in various stages of edition, five correspondence collections (three unedited but incomplete), twenty-five memoirs, two collections of fragments of diaries and correspondence, two collections of diary entries and memoirs, and five novels or novellas – immediately raises another problem: that of representativeness and the dangers of overt generalizations. Indeed, a sample of testimonies, however accurate, can never tell us what *all* soldiers did, thought or felt, and the spectre of overgeneralization will always be around the corner of the endless diversity and complexity of human experience. However, the highly analytical nature of the text has shown that even from the rather limited number of sources available, general patterns, repetitions, themes and points conspicuously left out quickly emerged and tended to repeat themselves throughout the course of the research, confirming the emerging hypotheses. Over time, the repetitive tendency of most subjects of interest became evident, and broadening the sample further only resulted in simply accumulating further evidence. As a result, further search for source material seemed pointless and unnecessary.

Besides various agendas, the very personalities of the authors also influence the kind of information we are able to extract from the sources. While gender identity is an ever-present issue that concerns all the members of a society, it is also true that men with a higher level of education tend to be more reflective of their predicament, and their texts may therefore offer potentially deeper thoughts. Educated men are also more prone to produce substantial amounts of writings, even though, as will be seen, this is far from being a rule, particularly in the case of the First World War. However, there is higher probability of them summarizing their experience in memoirs. While Bohemia and Moravia during the 1910s offered a comparably high standard of education within the European context, with Bohemia being arguably the most industrialized and modernized region of the monarchy outside of Lower Austria, the prevalence of educated men, often ranking as noncommissioned officers (NCOs) or officers, is still obvious.

Out of sixty-five diaries, memoirs and correspondence collections, where it is possible to obtain some biographical data, we see that: fourteen men had only elementary school (eight years of *Volksschule* and then went straight to work, or trained as craftsmen) education, and five were college educated (for twenty-two, their educational level is unknown), which clearly shows an overrepresentation of the better educated (64% of the known sample reaching the level of secondary education).[81]

All the accounts in this sample were written in Czech (Egon Erwin Kisch's diary being the only exception). This, of course, does not mean that their authors necessarily identified as 'Czechs' by nationality – put strictly, it only implies their language preference. Several of the men were obviously bilingual thanks to their higher-level education or environment they lived in (for example, two lived in Vienna in 1914). On the other hand, those authors who thought it necessary to identify themselves nationally already in 1914 are defining themselves as Czech in this regard as well. Here, the general overrepresentation of the better-educated has the apparent effect of influencing the very sense of national identification the men show – the group of those who, in some way, identify themselves as being Czech at the beginning of the war strongly correlates with higher education levels, urban background and sometimes even membership in Czech nationalist organizations such as the Sokol gymnastic association (two men) or the Czech National Socialist Party (three men). Closer to the notion of initial national indifference, as presented by authors such as Tara Zahra or Jeremy King, are the men with lower levels of education or from a farming background who, while mostly aware of the basics of national discourse, seem to place much less emphasis on the issue at the beginning of the war. The same is true for some of the men coming from large urban areas like Vienna or Prague, where matters were often complicated by bilingual realities or class self-identification.[82] However, even they, almost invariably, seem to find some sort of identification with the national idea by 1918 at the latest – or at least so they claim in their accounts. But the majority of the sources used here were only being edited or published after the war, when national optics was already hard to avoid even if the authors tried – and they had little inclination or motivation to do so, which complicates any deeper analysis of the issue.

Interestingly, the level of education did not translate into rank, as only nine authors served as officers (including cadets and one-year-volunteers, i.e. officer candidates), fifteen as noncommissioned officers (rank of corporal and above), while twenty-four spent the war as enlisted men (the rest are unknown). All of these men were conscripts in one form or another, and none of the officers (with one exception) can be considered a career, or regular officer. As a consequence, almost none of them were directly subject to the specific conceptualizations of masculine honour prevalent in the regular army, particularly in the extremely class-conscious Austro-Hungarian officer corps.[83] In terms of age, the age group of young men between twenty-six and thirty-five years is represented the most, with twenty-one authors, while another eighteen are from the group of seventeen to twenty-five years, with nine men older than thirty-five (the rest, again, is unknown). A majority of men in our sample were single (thirty-one), while fifteen are known to have families. Most also came from the countryside (twenty-seven), while only seventeen are known to have lived in cities with a population of over 20,000 inhabitants before the war. As for religious affiliation, it is very difficult to identify precisely; however, none of the men was deeply religious in any sense and while some tended to invoke God or other supreme being at a time of stress or elation, these are used mostly as a figure of speech.

As for the nature of the service, the vast majority of the men served in the infantry (thirty-nine), only six with the artillery and six in support units (four medical assistants and two with the staff). Probably because of this, the great majority of the men (thirty-eight) could claim to have seen and participated in combat (at least in a passive way of being bombarded repeatedly by artillery), while another six served in the frontlines, but came into danger only occasionally, though they regularly witnessed the direct consequences of combat. Only three men served in the rear, with only secondhand knowledge of combat experience.

While it is always problematic to extrapolate from individual experience, a critical analysis still makes it possible to penetrate into the minds of the actors, analyse those areas of their existence that are pressured the most by modern warfare and try to judge overall patterns from highly subjective accounts. For example, it is clear that young men without families experienced the war, as well as their masculinity, differently from older men with dependents. Similarly, men who felt marginalized in their peacetime life tended to see war as a potential social elevator more often that those who had already possessed hegemonic social status previously. It is also obvious that the experience of wartime masculinity differed for officers and for the other ranks, as these groups were differentiated by their access to the key hallmarks of masculine status: power, resources and women. Social background as well as education often played its role in the way in which men expressed themselves, and it also influenced the specific notion of masculinity to which the individual actors subscribed, which had bearings on a whole range of issues from communication with home, through attitudes towards the army authorities all the way to the perception of sexuality.

Whatever the nature of the personal accounts used in the forthcoming analysis, there is one feature that is common to all of them – they were all written by *men*. This feature is easy to overlook and that is why it is actually so often ignored in most of the historical writing on the experience of warfare. The diaries, letters and memoirs used here all reflect the thoughts of biologically male individuals, who saw themselves socially defined as *men*, a category defined through *masculinity*. For them, *manliness* was an implicit state of being. In many of the writings, it is obvious that the word a 'man' (in Czech 'člověk', which, while masculine, denotes a 'person' or, more literally, a 'human') in their text automatically denotes 'man' (a person of masculine social status), as women are always specifically identified. For the most part, a 'man' means a 'soldier' in these wartime texts (again, nonmilitary persons tend to be defined specifically). Everything and everyone not fitting into these simple categories of 'textual normality' is then often relegated to their own different space, where men-soldiers are not present, or only as exceptions. It is as if the personal accounts of the First World War experience, written by Czech soldiers of the Austro-Hungarian army, perfected – through the intensive socialization of the authors in all-male groups – the 'invisibility' of masculinity as a social category. As noted by one American sociologist, when a man 'wakes up in the morning and looks in the mirror, [he does not see a man] he sees a human being. A generic person'.[84] When soldiers write about war, they see beings around them who just *are* men as a matter of fact. And their accounts, by this very nature, tell us how it feels to be a *man* in war.

Notes

1. For an overview of recent research, see Alan Kramer, 'Recent Historiography of the First World War (Part I)', *Journal of Modern European History* 12, no. 1 (2014): 5–27; and Alan Kramer, 'Recent Historiography of the First World War (Part II)', *Journal of Modern European History* 12, no. 2 (2014): 155–74. For a perfect example of this discourse, see 'Part I: A Narrative History', in *The Cambridge History of the First World War*, ed. Jay Winter (3 vols, Cambridge, 2014), vol. 1, 15–199.
2. For an overview of recent research on Austria-Hungary, see the review essay by John Deak, 'The Great War and the Forgotten Realm: The Habsburg Monarchy and the First World War', *Journal of Modern History* 86, no. 2 (2014): 336–80.
3. The abbreviation 'k.u.k.' standing for *kaiserliche und königliche*, i.e. Imperial and Royal, denoting the regiments being part of the 'common army' of the Austro-Hungarian dual state.
4. 'K.k.' standing for kaiserlich-königlich, i.e. Imperial-Royal, putting the regiments into the organizational structure of the territorial army of the Cisleithanian (Austrian) half of the monarchy.
5. For the recent debates over 'language frontiers' and the attached forms of national identities as they formed in prewar Bohemia and Moravia, see, for example, Tara Zahra, *Kidnapped Souls. National Indifference and the Battle for Children in the Bohemian Lands, 1900–1948* (Ithaca, 2008); or Jeremy King, *Budweisers into Czechs and Germans* (Princeton, 2002). For perhaps the best summary of the topic on a broader spectrum, see Laurence Cole, 'Differentiation or Indifference? Changing Perspectives on National Identification in the Austrian Half of the Habsburg Monarchy', in *Nationhood from Below: Europe in the Long Nineteenth Century*, ed. Maarten van Ginderachter, Marnix Beyen (Basingstoke, 2012), 96–119; see also Laurence Cole and Daniel L. Unowsky, eds, *The Limits of Loyalty: Imperial Symbolism, Popular Allegiances, and State Patriotism in the Late Habsburg Monarchy* (Oxford, 2007). For further reading on the issue of nationalism and political identity in the Habsburg Empire, again with emphasis on both local and imperial identities as strong counterweights to the emerging modern mass nationalism,

see Pieter M. Judson, *The Habsburg Empire: A New History* (Cambridge, 2016); for some of the ensuing criticism, see, for example, Deak, 'The Great War and the Forgotten Realm', 362.
6. For some basic statistics, see, for example, Ivan Šedivý, *Češi, české země a Velká válka 1914–1918* (Prague, 2001), 39–40.
7. See Hew Strachan, *The First World War* (Oxford, 2001), vol. 1, 157. Similarly, Christopher Clark in his seminal study of the outbreak of the war repeatedly raises questions about 'the loyalty of Czech reservists'. See Christopher Clark, *The Sleepwalkers: How Europe Went to War in 1914* (London, 2012), 269.
8. See Benjamin Ziemann, 'Soldiers', in *Brill's Encyclopedia of the First World War*, eds Gerhard Hirschfeld, Gerd Krumeich and Irina Renz (Leiden, 2014), vol. 1, 122; and Alexander Watson, 'Mutinies and Military Morale', in *The Oxford Illustrated History of the First World War*, ed. Hew Strachan (Oxford, 2014), 194.
9. For 'ambivalent patriots', see Claire Nolte, 'Ambivalent Patriots: Czech Culture in the Great War', in *European Culture in the Great War: The Arts, Entertainment, and Propaganda, 1914–1918*, ed. Aviel Roshwald, Richard Stites (Cambridge, 1999), 162–75; for 'underlying apathy', see Mark Cornwall, 'Morale and Patriotism in the Austro-Hungarian Army', in *State, Society, and Mobilization in Europe during the First World War*, ed. John Horne (Cambridge, 1997), 176.
10. Mark Cornwall, 'Austria-Hungary and "Yugoslavia"', in *A Companion to World War I*, ed. John Horne (Oxford, 2012), 374.
11. For the tradition of suspecting Czechs of 'treason', one that emanated from the bitter politics of prewar Austria, see, for example, Mark Cornwall, *The Undermining of Austria-Hungary: The Battle for Hearts and Minds* (London, 2000), 32–33; Gunther E. Rothenberg, *The Army of Francis Joseph* (West Lafayette, 1976), 18–19, 121–30, 184–87; Richard Lein, *Pflichterfüllung oder Hochverrat? Die tschechischen Soldaten Österreich-Ungarns im Ersten Weltkrieg* (Vienna, 2011); see also Lein, 'The "Betrayal" of the k.u.k. Infantry Regiment 28: Truth or Legend?', in *Prague Papers on the History of International Relations* (Prague, 2009), 325–48.
12. For more information on the Legion, see, for example, John F.N. Bradley, *The Czechoslovak Legion in Russia, 1914–1920* (Boulder, 1991).
13. For the 'legionary myth' and the various groups competing over its meaning and purpose in the interwar period, see Ivan Šedivý, 'Legionáři a mocenské poměry v počátcích ČSR', in *Moc, vliv a autorita v procesu vzniku a utváření meziválečné ČSR (1918–1921)*, eds Jan Hájek, Dagmar Hájková, František Kolář, Vlastislav Lacina, Zdenko Maršálek and Ivan Šedivý (Prague, 2008), 16–28. See also Jan Galandauer, 'Československé legie a jejich komemorace', in *Česká společnost za velkých válek 20. století: pokus o komparaci*, eds Jan Gebhart and Ivan Šedivý (Prague, 2003), 293–312; or Jan Galandauer, 'O struktuře české historické paměti', *Historie a vojenství* 45, no. 2 (1996): 132–36. On the very real consequences of these conflicts over memory in terms of access to government welfare programmes, see Natali Stegmann, *Kriegsdeutungen – Staatsgründungen – Sozialpolitik: Der Helden- und Opferdiskurs in der Tschechoslowakei, 1918–1948* (Munich, 2010), 63–80.
14. Šedivý, *Češi, české země a Velká válka*, 65–71.
15. See Martin Zückert, 'Memory of War and National State Integration: Czech and German Veterans in Czechoslovakia after 1918', *Central Europe* 4, no. 2 (2006): 121; see also Martin Zückert, 'Der Erste Weltkrieg in der tschechischen Geschichtsschreibung

1918–1945', in *Geschichtsschreibung zu den böhmischen Länder im 20. Jahrhundert. Wissenschaftstraditionen, Institutionen, Diskurse*, eds Christiane Brenner, Erik K. Franzen, Peter Haslinger and Robert Luft (Munich, 2006), 61–75.
16. For a summary, see Lein, *Pflichterfüllung oder Hochverrat?*, 407–16; and Josef Fučík, *Osmadvacátníci: spor o českého vojáka Velké války* (Prague, 2006).
17. See Jaroslav Hašek, *Osudy dobrého vojáka Švejka za světové války* (4 vols, Prague, 1921–23). For the most recent English translation, see *The Fateful Adventures of the Good Soldier Švejk during the World War*, trans. Zdeněk Sadloň and Emmit Joyce (3 vols, London, 1997). For the interwar shifts in interpretation of the novel, see Radko Pytlík, *Osudy a cesty Josefa Švejka* (Prague, 2003).
18. See, for example, Karel Pichlík, *Čeští vojáci proti válce, 1914–1918* (Prague, 1961); or, even better, Jaroslav Křížek, *Češi a sovětští rudoarmějci v sovětském Rusku 1917–1920* (Prague, 1955).
19. For the revisionist approach, see the works of Josef Fučík: *Soča (Isonzo) 1917* (Prague, 1999); *Piava 1918* (Prague, 2001); or *Generál Podhajský* (Prague, 2009). For the latest defence of the nationalist view, see Jindřich Marek, 'Beránci, lvi a malé děti: Nekonečný spor o českého vojáka v letech 1. světové války', *Historie a vojenství* 63, no. 1 (2014): 94–113. For the same point from the similar author, see Jindřich Marek, *Pod císařskou šibenicí: čeští vojáci na křižovatkách roku 1918* (Cheb, 2005). There was actually some criticism of the nationalist discourse as early as the 1930s, particularly on the part of the veterans of Austro-Hungarian service. See, for example, Karel Wagner, *S českým plukem na ruské frontě* (Prague, 1936). For more on this topic, see Jiří Hutečka, 'Kamarádi frontovníci: maskulinita a paměť první světové války v textech československých c. a k. veteránů', *Dějiny-teorie-kritika* 9, no. 2 (2014): 231–66.
20. Šedivý, *Češi, české země a Velká válka 1914–1918*. For a more recent interpretation, see Etienne Boisserie, *Les Tchèques dans l'Autriche-Hongrie en guerre (1914–1918)* (Paris, 2017).
21. Martin Zückert, 'Antimilitarismus und soldatische Resistenz: Politischer Protest und armeefeindliches Verhalten in der tschechischen Gesellschaft bis 1918', in *Glanz – Gewalt – Gehorsam: Militär und Gesellschaft in der Habsburgermonarchie (1880 bis 1918)*, eds Laurence Cole, Christa Hämmerle and Martin Scheutz (Essen, 2011), 199–220.
22. David Pazdera, 'Češi v první světové válce (Pokus o vymezení válečného prožitku českých vojáků rakousko-uherské armády od mobilizace a nástupu k jednotce po příchod na frontu)', Master's thesis, České Budějovice: University of České Budějovice, 1997. For a more general approach to the topic of reactions to the outbreak of the war in Austria-Hungary, see Laurance Cole, 'Questions of Nationalization in the Habsburg Monarchy', in *Nations, Identities and the First World War*, ed. Nico Wouters and Laurence Van Ypersele (London, 2018), 191–221.
23. Rudolf Kučera, 'Entbehrung und Nationalismus: Die Erfahrung tschechischer Soldaten der österechisch-ungarischen Armee 1914–1918', in *Jenseits des Schützengrabens: Der Erste Weltkrieg im Osten: Erfahrung – Wahrnehmung – Kontext*, eds Bernard Bachinger and Wolfram Dornik (Innsbruck, 2013), 121–38.
24. See Lein, *Pflichterfüllung oder Hochverrat?*; see also Lein, 'The Military Conduct of the Austro-Hungarian Czechs in the First World War', *The Historian: A Journal of History* 3, no. 2 (2014): 518–49. In his case study of a similar case of k.u.k. Infantry Regiment 36, another Czech dominated unit that was ingloriously disbanded after it failed in the face of a surprise Russian attack on the San River in late May 1915, Christian Reiter

came to a similar conclusion, pointing mostly towards mishandling of the troops and general demoralization. See Christian Reiter, 'Der Untergang des IR 36: Der "Verrat" der tschechischen Soldaten im Gefecht bei Siniewa 1915', Master's thesis, Vienna: University of Vienna, 2008.
25. Kramer, 'Recent Historiography of the First World War (Part I)', 5.
26. Leonard V. Smith, *The Embattled Self: French Soldiers' Testimony of the Great War* (Ithaca, 2007), 107–8.
27. Joan W. Scott, 'Gender: A Useful Category of Historical Analysis', *American Historical Review* 91, no. 5 (1986): 1067 and 1069.
28. For a summary of the situation a decade ago, see Jana Ratajová, 'Gender history jako alternativní koncept dějin', in *Dějiny žen aneb Evropská žena od středověku do poloviny 20. století v zajetí historiografie*, eds Kateřina Čadková, Milena Lenderová and Jana Stráníková (Pardubice, 2006), 19–32; or Denisa Nečasová, 'Dějiny žen či gender history? Možnosti, limity, východiska', *Dějiny – teorie – kritika* 3, no. 1 (2008): 81–102. For a summary of the study of masculinities, see Jiří Hutečka and Radmila Švaříčková-Slabáková, 'Od genderu k maskulinitám', in *Konstrukce maskulinní identity v minulosti a současnosti: Koncepty, metody, perspektivy*, eds Radmila Švaříčková-Slabáková, Jitka Kohoutová, Radmila Pavlíčková and Jiří Hutečka (Prague, 2012), 9–20. For stylistic reasons, the terms 'masculinity' and 'manliness' are used as synonyms here, even though the author is aware of the possible repercussions for terminological purity.
29. R.W. Connell, *Masculinities* (Berkeley, 1995, 2nd edition 2005).
30. Connell, *Masculinities*, 44 and 76–77. On the topic of masculinity and patriarchy, see also Pierre Bourdieu, *La domination masculine* (Paris, 1998).
31. See, for example, Demetrakis Z. Demetriou, 'Connell's Concept of Hegemonic Masculinity: A Critique', *Theory and Society* 30, no. 2 (2001): 337–61; or Tony Jefferson, 'Subordinating Hegemonic Masculinity', *Theoretical Criminology* 6, no. 1 (2002): 63–88. For a somewhat revised version of the theory, see R.W. Connell and James D. Messerschmidt, 'Hegemonic Masculinity: Rethinking the Concept', *Gender and Society* 19, no. 6 (2005): 829–59.
32. For key works, see, for example, Michael Roper and John Tosh, eds., *Manful Assertions: Masculinities in Britain since 1800* (Oxford, 1991); John Tosh, 'What Should Historians Do with Masculinity? Reflections on Nineteenth-Century Britain', *History Workshop Journal* 38, no. 1 (1994): 179–202; Ute Frevert, *'Mann und Weib, und Weib und Mann': Geschlechter-Differenzen in der Moderne* (Munich, 1995); John Tosh, 'The Old Adam and the New Man: Emerging Themes in the History of English Masculinities, 1750–1850', in *English Masculinities, 1660–1800*, eds Tim Hitchcock and Michele Cohen (London, 1999): 217–38; Wolfgang Schmale, *Geschichte des Männlichkeit in Europa (1450–2000)* (Vienna, 2003); John Tosh, 'Hegemonic Masculinity and the History of Gender', in *Masculinities in Politics and War: Gendering Modern History*, eds Stefan Dudink, Karen Hagemann and John Tosh (Manchester, 2004): 41–58; Martin Dinges, ed., *Männer – Macht – Körper: Hegemoniale Männlichkeiten vom Mittelalter bis heute* (Frankfurt am Main, 2005); Christopher E. Forth, *Masculinity in the Modern West: Gender, Civilization and the Body* (London, 2008).
33. The best example of this issue is the scholarly journal *Historie a vojenství* (*History and Warfare*), published by the Institute for Military History in Prague, which fails to depart from the traditional, somewhat antiquarian discourse typical of the state of the field in the Czech Republic. For a rather dated, but sadly still applicable critique of the situation, see

Ivan Šedivý, 'Česká historiografie vojenství 1989–2002', *Český časopis historický* 100, no. 4 (2002): 900–1.
34. Rudolf Kučera, 'Muži ve válce, válka v mužích: Maskulinity a světové války 20. století v současné kulturní historiografii', *Soudobé dějiny* 19, no. 4 (2011): 550.
35. Rudolf Kučera, *Rationed Life: Science, Everyday Life and Working-Class Politics in the Bohemian Lands 1914–1918* (New York, 2016; first published in Czech in 2014), 94–129. The historiography of the Slovak frontline experience is somewhat more infused with gender analysis, mostly because of the work conducted by Gabriela Dudeková. See, for example, Gabriela Dudeková, 'S Bohom za kráľa a vlasť? Problém loajality a bojovej morálky radového vojaka vo Veľkej vojne', in *Vojak medzi civilmi, civil medzi vojakmi: Pocta Vojtechu Danglovi*, eds Gabriela Dudeková and Elena Mannová (Bratislava, 2017), 163–96; or Gabriela Dudeková Kováčová, 'The Silent Majority: Attitudes of Non-prominent Citizens at the Beginning of the Great War in the Territory of Today's Slovakia', *Revue des Études Slaves* 88, no. 4 (2017): 699–720.
36. Margaret E. Higonnet and Patrice L.-R. Higonnet, 'The Double Helix', in *Behind the Lines: Gender and the Two World Wars*, eds Margaret R. Higonnet, Jane Jenson, Sonya Michel and Margaret Collins Weitz (New Haven, 1987), 31–50. For the most important works on gender identity in wartime Austria-Hungary, see Christa Hämmerle, *Heimat/Front: Geschlechtergeschichte/n des Ersten Weltkriegs in Österreich-Ungarn* (Vienna, 2014); Maureen Healy, *Vienna and the Fall of the Habsburg Empire: Total War and Everyday Life in World War I*, (Cambridge, 2004); or *Gender and War in Twentieth-Century Eastern Europe*, eds Nancy M. Wingfield and Maria Bucur (Bloomington, 2006).
37. Susan R. Grayzel and Tammy M. Proctor, eds., *Gender and the Great War* (Oxford, 2017).
38. *The Cambridge History of the First World War*, vol. 3, 153–78.
39. For an example from the history of the First World War, see Frederic Rousseau, *La guerre censurée : Une histoire des combattants européens de 14–18* (Paris, 1999); for an example from a general study of war, see Richard Holmes, *Acts of War* (New York, 1985). Both works, while excellent in their own right, conflate the issue of gender into descriptions of soldiers' attitude towards women, sex, heterosexuality and connecting issues.
40. For a sociological analysis, see Siniša Malešević, *The Sociology of War and Violence* (Cambridge, 2010), 275–307; for a general overview, see Joshua Goldstein, *War and Gender: How Gender Shapes the War System and Vice Versa* (Cambridge, 2001), particularly 10–21.
41. R. Brian Ferguson, 'Explaining War', in *The Anthropology of War*, ed. Jonathan Haas (Cambridge, 1990), 26.
42. John A. Lynn, *Battle: A History of Combat and Culture* (Boulder, 2003).
43. For examples of various past and present cultures where war is socially construed around masculinity and vice versa, see Bryan Hanks, 'Constructing the Warrior: Death, Memory and the Art of Warfare', in *Archaeology and Memory*, ed. Dušan Boric (Oxford, 2010), 122–23; John Robb, 'Violence and Gender in Early Italy', in *Troubled Times. Violence and Warfare in the Past*, eds Debra L. Martin and David W. Frayer (Amsterdam, 1997), 111–44; Lawrence H. Keeley, *War before Civilization* (New York, 1996); Jean Guilaine and Jean Zammit, *The Origins of War: Violence in Prehistory* (Oxford, 2001), 158–94; R. Brian Ferguson, 'Violence and War in Prehistory', in *Troubled Times*, 321–55; R. Brian Ferguson, 'A Paradigm for the Study of War and Society', in *War and Society in Ancient and Medieval Worlds: Asia, the Mediterranean, Europe, and Mesoamerica*, eds Kurt

A. Raaflaub and Nathan Rosenstein (Cambridge, 2001), 389–437; or David D. Gilmore, *Manhood in the Making: Cultural Concepts of Masculinity* (New Haven, 1991). For a more essentialist approach, see Azar Gat, *War in Human Civilization* (Oxford, 2006), 77–86; and Maurice R. Davie, *The Evolution of War: A Study of its Role in Early Societies* (New Haven, 1929), 23–45; or Lionel Tiger, *Men in Groups* (London, 1969). For a feminist critique of the same, see, for example, Barbara Ehrenreich, *Blood Rites: Origins and History of the Passions of War* (London, 1997).

44. Robert A. Nye, 'Western Masculinities in War and Peace', *American Historical Review* 112, no. 2 (2007): 418; see also Paul R. Higate, ed., *Military Masculinities: Identity and the State* (Westport, 2003).
45. Christopher E. Forth and Bertrand Taithe, eds., *French Masculinities: History, Culture, and Politics* (London, 2007), 5–6.
46. Malešević, *The Sociology of War and Violence*, 302.
47. John Tosh, 'Hegemonic Masculinity and the History of Gender', in *Masculinities in Politics and War: Gendering Modern History*, eds Stefan Dudink, Karen Hagemann, and John Tosh (Manchester, 2004), 45–48. A conclusion that goes even beyond the theorem of 'residual elements', that 'historically societies have valued military masculinity and the personal characteristics of manliness that it comprises more highly than civic virtue and its masculinities', is argued by Nye, 'Western Masculinities in War and Peace', 418.
48. For the author's take on the issue of military masculinities in modern Europe, see Jiří Hutečka, 'Militární maskulinita jako koncept historického bádání', in *Konstrukce maskulinní identity v minulosti a současnosti*, 36–47.
49. John A. Lynn, 'The Embattled Future of Academic Military History', *Journal of Military History* 61, no. 4 (1997): 784–85; for a more recent summary of the same issue, see Robert M. Citino, 'Military Histories Old and New: A Reintroduction', *American Historical Review* 112, no. 4 (2007): 1070–90.
50. Leo Braudy, *From Chivalry to Terrorism: War and the Changing Nature of Masculinity* (New York, 2003).
51. Joanna Bourke, 'New Military History', in *Palgrave Advances in Modern Military History*, eds Matthew Hughes and William J. Philpott (London, 2006), 271; see also Joanna Bourke, *An Intimate History of Killing: Face-to-Face Killing in Twentieth Century History* (London, 1999).
52. Klaus Theweleit, *Male Fantasies* (2 vols, Cambridge, 1987–89); George L. Mosse, *Fallen Soldiers: Reshaping the Memory of the World Wars* (Oxford, 1990); George L. Mosse, *The Image of Man: The Creation of Modern Masculinity* (New York, 1996).
53. Mosse, *The Image of Man*, 115.
54. Christa Hämmerle, 'Von den Geschlechtern der Kriege und des Militärs: Forschungseinblicke und Bemerkungen zu einen neuen Debatte', in *Was ist Militärgeschichte?*, eds Thomas Kühne and Benjamin Ziemann (Paderborn, 2000), 229–30 and 252.
55. Christa Hämmerle, 'Zur Relevanz des Connell'schen Konzepts hegemonialer Männlichkeit für "Militär und Männlichkeit/en in der Habsburgermonarchie (1868–1914/18)"', in *Männer – Macht – Körper*, 103–21.
56. Ibid., 114.
57. Jeremy Black, *Rethinking Military History* (London, 2004), 51.
58. Ardant du Picq, *Battle Studies: Ancient and Modern Battle*, trans. John N. Greely and Robert C. Cotton (New York, 1920). Most of the work was originally published (posthumously) as *Études sur le Combat* in 1880.

59. Lord Moran, *The Anatomy of Courage* (London, 1945); J. Glenn Gray, *The Warriors: Reflections on Men in Battle* (New York, 1959).
60. Samuel A. Stouffer, et al., *The American Soldier* (2 vols, Princeton, 1949).
61. S.L.A. Marshall, *Men against Fire: The Problem of Battle Command* (New York, 1947).
62. Edward Shils and Morris Janowitz, 'Cohesion and Disintegration in the Wehrmacht in World War II', in *Military Conflict: Essay in the Institutional Analysis of War and Peace*, ed. Morris Janowitz (Beverly Hills, 1975), 177–220.
63. Holmes, *Acts of War*.
64. John Keegan, *The Face of Battle* (London, 1976).
65. Tony Ashworth, *Trench Warfare 1914–1918: The Live and Let Live System* (Basingstoke, 1980).
66. Leonard V. Smith, *Between Mutiny and Obedience: The Case of the French Fifth Infantry Division during World War I* (Princeton, 1994), particularly 15–17.
67. Smith, *The Embattled Self*.
68. See Wilhelm Deist, 'The Military Collapse of the German Empire: The Reality behind the Stab-in-the-Back Myth', *War in History* 3, no. 2 (1996): 186–207; Anne Lipp, *Meinungslenkung im Krieg: Kriegserfahrungen deutscher Soldaten und ihre Deutung 1914–1918* (Göttingen, 2003).
69. Benjamin Ziemann, *War Experience in Rural Germany* (Oxford, 2007).
70. Alexander Watson, *Enduring the Great War: Combat, Morale and Collapse in the German and British Armies, 1914–1918* (Cambridge, 2008), 232–33.
71. Ibid., 54.
72. Benjamin Ziemann, *Violence and the German Soldier in the Great War: Killing, Dying, Surviving* (London, 2017), 11–15, 64.
73. John A. Lynn, *The Bayonets of the Republic: Motivation and Tactics in the Army of Revolutionary France, 1791–94* (Urbana, 1984), 21–40.
74. Thomas Kühne, *The Rise and Fall of Comradeship: Hitler's Soldiers, Male Bonding and Mass Violence in the Twentieth Century* (Cambridge, 2017).
75. Thomas Kühne, 'Männergeschichte als Geschlechtergeschichte', in *Männergeschichte – Geschlechtergeschichte: Männlichkeiten im Wandel der Moderne*, ed. Thomas Kühne (Frankfurt am Main, 1996), 22–23.
76. Alon Rachamimov, 'The Disruptive Comforts of Drag: (Trans)Gender Performances among Prisoners of War in Russia, 1914–1920', *American Historical Review* 111, no. 2 (2006): 364.
77. Alon Rachamimov, *POWs and the Great War: Captivity on the Eastern Front* (London, 2002); see also Hannes Leidinger, Verena Moritz, *In russischer Gefangenschaft: Erlebnisse österreichischer Soldaten im Ersten Weltkrieg* (Vienna, 2008).
78. On the potential of so-called ego-documents, see, for example, Wilfred Schulze, 'Ego-Dokumente: Annäherung an den Menschen in der Geschichte? Vorüberlegungen für die Tagung "EGO-DOKUMENT"', in *Ego-Dokumente. Annäherung an den Menschen in der Geschichte*, ed. Wilfred Schulze (Berlin, 1996), 11–30. For their possible use in the field of military history, see the Introduction to Michael Epkenhans, Stig Förster and Karen Hagemann, eds., *Militärische Erinnerungskultur: Soldaten im Spiegel von Biographien, Memoiren und Selbstzeugnissen* (Paderborn, 2006), ix–xviii. For examples, see Helmut Berding, Klaus Heller and Winfried Speitkamp, eds., *Krieg und Erinnerung. Fallstudien zum 19. und 20. Jahrhundert* (Göttingen, 2000); Wolfram Wette, ed., *Der Krieg des kleinen Mannes: Eine Militärgeschihcte von unten* (Munich, 1992); Klaus Latzel,

'Vom Kriegserlebnis zu Kriegserfahrung: Theoretische und methodische Überlegungen zur erfahrungsgeschichtlichen Unterschung von Feldpostbriefen', *Militärgeschichtliche Mitteilungen* 56, no. 1 (1997): 1–30; Gerald Lamprecht, *Feldpost und Kriegserlebnis. Briefe als historisch-biographische Quelle* (Innsbruck, 2001); Péter Hanák, 'Die Volksmeinung während des letzten Kriegsjahres in Österreich-Ungarn', in *Die Auflösung des Habsburgerreiches: Zusammenbruch und Neuorientierung im Donauraum*, eds Richard G. Plaschka and Karl-Heinz Mack (Munich, 1970), 58–66; or Fritz Fellner, 'Der Krieg in Tagebüchen und Briefen: Überlegungengen zu einer wenig genützten Quellenart', in *Österreich und der Grosse Krieg 1914–1918: Die andere Seite der Geschichte*, eds Klaus Amann and Hubert Lengauer (Vienna, 1989), 205–13. In Czech, the only relevant effort is Vítězslav Prchal, ed., *Mezi Martem a Memorií: Prameny osobní povahy k vojenským dějinám 16. – 19. století* (Pardubice, 2011).

79. Jean Norton-Cru, *Témoins: Essai d'analyse et de critique des souvenirs de combattants édités en francais de 1915 à 1928* (Paris, 1929).
80. Alois Žipek, ed., *Domov za války: Svědectví účastníků* (5 vols, Prague, 1929–31), vol. 1, 8.
81. Compare with educational statistics for Bohemia, Moravia, and Austrian Silesia from 1920, where only 1% of the adult population (2% of men) were college educated and 10% (13% of men, 6% of women) reached the level of secondary education. See Ludmila Fialová, Pavla Horská et al., *Dějiny obyvatelstva českých zemí* (Prague, 1998), 341.
82. See Zahra, *Kidnapped Souls*; and King, *Budweisers into Czechs and Germans*. See also Tara Zahra, 'Imagined Noncommunities: National Indifference as a Category of Analysis', *Slavic Review* 69, no. 1 (2010): 93–119.
83. On the Austro-Hungarian officer corps, its wartime experience and the values and attitudes that permeated its professional core of career men in particular, see Martin Schmitz, *'Als ob die Welt aus den Fugen ginge': Kriegserfahrungen österreichisch-ungarischer Offiziere 1914–18* (Paderborn, 2016); see also István Deák, *Beyond Nationalism: A Social and Political History of the Habsburg Officer Corps, 1848–1918* (Oxford, 1990). For the consequences these values carried into the officers' experience of wartime (and postwar) gender, see, for example, Hämmerle, *Heimat/Front*, 183–201. It is of note that the one exception to the rule, Major Karel Wagner of k.u.k. Infantry Regiment 88, led the way in the abortive postwar efforts of some of the Austro-Hungarian Czech-speaking veterans to save the memory of their service, strongly emphasizing the notion of honour in the process. See Wagner, *S českým plukem na ruské frontě*, 7–9.
84. Michael S. Kimmel, *The History of Men: Essay on the History of American and British Masculinities* (New York, 2005), 5.

Chapter 1

TOURNAMENT OF MANLINESS
Mobilization

All the young people down the ages
They gladly marched off to die.

—The Clash, 'The Call Up'[1]

By the end of June 1914, the generally sleepy summer streets of the city of Brno (or Brünn, as it was known to its mostly German-speaking inhabitants) were uncharacteristically lively. Tens of thousands of Czechs not only from the Habsburg monarchy, but from all over the world, arrived to watch the massive celebration of Czech nationalism in the form of the Sokol gathering ('slet', meaning literally a flocking of birds, namely 'sokols', or falcons). That year, for the first time, the Czech gymnastic and sports movement bearing that name organized its mass meeting outside of Prague. The whole event was considered a high security risk by the Cisleithaenian authorities, who quite reasonably expected a conflict between the Sokols and the local German population. The Germans considered the entire gathering to represent a provocation against the very nature of 'their' 'German town'. Violent clashes, so common in the nationally divisive atmosphere of many regions of the monarchy at the beginning of the twentieth century, resulted in several dozen arrests on both sides, but could not disrupt the proceedings on the old military training ground of Královo Pole. The *slet* was primarily a celebration of unity between the aestheticized individual human body and the collective national body, which drove its point home through the absolute subordination of the individual to the national mass, and it proceeded well and according to plan following its opening on 27 June.[2] The thousands of spectators were more than satisfied: 'We all but forgot the close proximity of German hatred. The final march [during the male gymnastics finale] sounded like a war fanfare to us'. However, the militaristic idyll did not last long because bad news was arriving from the southern provinces of the old monarchy:

> Suddenly, there was an inexplicable commotion and bustle in the crowd. We asked everyone around what had happened, but nobody knew a thing. Then, one brother climbed on the instructor's stage and announced that the heir to the throne, Archduke Francis Ferdinand, had been murdered in Sarajevo and that the *slet* was to be suspended ... The *slet* was forgotten. There was only one thought in everyone's mind – there would be a war!³

Although this particular Moravian Sokol and his fellow travellers on the train home from Brno were quite certain of it, in the afternoon of 28 June 1914, it was actually not at all clear that there would be a war, not to mention its possible scale. Even the Austro-Hungarian government took three weeks to finally act upon its fateful decision that would lead to one. Meanwhile, the public had forgotten Sarajevo as quickly as it was reminded of its existence by the fateful shootings. As Max Brod, a close friend of Franz Kafka, remembered, 'the tragedy ... was the topic of all talks for a few days and then everybody forgot about it'. In his opinion, most people in Bohemia and Moravia condemned 'the Sarajevo murder' as 'a brutal crime', but in general paid little attention to it.⁴ 'Therefore, the Czechs were extremely surprised when that death re-emerged on that beautiful July Friday and took on the form of an ultimatum, a word almost nobody knew before that day'.⁵ Two days later, on Sunday, 26 July 1914, Brod and his wife were returning back from a field trip and a social visit to their friends' house:

> When we entered the city, the walls of Prague welcomed us with their lights, giving us strange and hostile looks. The outskirts of the Dejvice suburb. It was already dark. People were standing in front of the doors of their houses, whispering. Fear, fear! Unwittingly, we quickened our pace. What had happened? No, it's not possible. No, it's not possible. I approached a man: grudgingly, with a listless look, he passed a special edition of a Czech newspaper and said: 'War is coming'.⁶

A day before, on Saturday, 25 July, upon receiving word that the Serbs had refused to accept one of the many points of his ultimatum, Emperor Franz Joseph I ordered a partial mobilization of eight army corps, including the VIII Corps stationed in Prague and the IX Corps based in the north Bohemian town of Litoměřice. Mobilization was to start on Tuesday, 28 July. On that day, Austria-Hungary declared war on Serbia. A short time after midnight, the roar of gunfire resounded on the River Danube beneath Belgrade. The Moravian Sokol had been right after all.⁷

The war that started at the end of July 1914 and escalated into a global conflict within the following week was destined to change the lives of millions in the Bohemian Crown Lands. Few of them could imagine that it was actually going to happen and even fewer people had any idea whatsoever of what was coming next: 'For forty-five years ... there has been no war in the heart of the world', Max Brod mused about the recent events:

> War was a word that sounded almost medieval to us, echoing the ridiculousness of a knightly rattling of arms. For the present, it floated in the air like some unbelievable shiny ball or a soap bubble. War was thought to be something historically discredited, gone forever, a thing of fantasies, a thing past human generations believed in (those poor devils!) – but not us, realists armed with reason.[8]

However, one of the few conceptual notions regarding war that was common to everyone was the general understanding of its highly gendered nature. War, most of the population felt, was redrawing the social order almost overnight, and its very existence as an event suddenly made the gender order more visible than ever before.

In almost every memory and recollection of images seen around the country, picturing the crowds reading the Emperor's declaration *To My Peoples* (*An Meine Völker*) that announced mobilization, those present are clearly divided in their behaviour. Men read silently or grumble in a low voice. Women, on the other hand, are louder, more emotional and often openly critical of the situation, with tears of sadness and protest appearing now and then. František Chmela, a gunner in the k.u.k. Field Artillery Regiment 24, remembered: 'People were walking around the town, women and children crying, because they had to say goodbye to their father ... husband ... son ... in a few hours'.[9] In a similar way, Václav Poláček added a laconic note in his diary on 26 July 1914: 'All the womenfolk crying a lot'.[10] The beginning of the war seems to divide the seemingly unified peacetime world into two visibly separate spaces – that of men, soon to be associated with military uniform and frontline service, and of women, associated with 'keeping the fires burning' back home. Both of these notions were, of course, grossly inaccurate both in terms of statistics and general experience.

It was Maureen Healy who rightly claimed that the traditional image of the 'feminized home front' and 'masculinized frontline' was more than anything else a product of government propaganda and consequent contemporary discourse that made it into modern historiography. In reality, about 70% of men of military age (18–52 late in the war) were conscripted into the army between 1914 and 1918, amounting to 8,420,000 by 1917.[11] Out of this number, hundreds of thousands of men serving in the army staff and logistical services never came close to the frontlines or combat. There were hundreds of thousands of men in Bohemia and Moravia who stayed at home because of their occupation, health or age, as well as many others who were soldiers only by being designated so by their uniform. As a result, at best, only about one-third of the male population of the Crown Lands left for 'the front' during the war.[12] In the same way, there were always a substantial number of women present at

Figure 1.1 Heeding the call. An example of the propaganda that divided the wartime social space into the masculine frontline and the feminine home front (wartime postcard, Regional Museum in Olomouc).

or close to combat areas, whether voluntarily or otherwise. However, it seems that most of the participants in the events of 1914 were structuring their experience along the lines of a clearly gendered social space: 'Son, brother, even father had to go', one of them concludes his description of the events, referring to the most basic categories of masculine existence, 'leaving their loved ones behind, they hurried to join their regiment'.[13] Here, everyone who was 'a son, brother or a father' was leaving for the front and those who stayed at home were defined through not being sons, brothers or fathers, i.e. by being women. The same simplified picture of spatial gender hierarchy remained in people's minds during the war years, the reality around them notwithstanding: 'Thank you for the photograph', wrote a girl to *Fähnrich* Janošík, serving on the Eastern Front in June 1916. 'Really pretty company you have there, it is such an injustice! The gentlemen are alone, the ladies are alone'.[14] This geography of war, composed of 'gentlemen' in the army and 'ladies' at home, appeared to be an insurmountable framework that easily stood for the wartime reality, as in the minds of the people, statistics did not matter.

The famous Bohemian-Jewish journalist Egon Erwin Kisch, whose close and poignant observations of his Czech comrades (he was serving with the k.u.k. Infantry Regiment 11, composed of 45% Czech-speaking soldiers) make him a source that cannot be neglected in any analysis, saw the situation in the same vein. As he noted in his diary after he and his comrades had rummaged through the mail of the fallen after the first battle: 'Letters, in which a mother, mistress, or wife is writing how lonely she is and how she yearns for the moment of reunion'.[15] In his world and that of his comrades, it did not appear that there could be anyone else writing a letter from home other than a person belonging to those categories. It seemed to him that there were no 'men' back home. It is clear that the wartime construction of hegemonic masculinity was militarized not only in the public space, as Rudolf Kučera claims in his study of the Czech working class during the war, but in the personal views of the actors as well. Of course, it is beyond doubt that the Austro-Hungarian authorities spent much effort and resources in promoting 'the ideal male recruited soldier, who quickly acquired the position of hegemonic masculinity' throughout the Empire's population.[16] However, this norm was actually already present in the minds of the population, and people went on to define war in gendered categories almost by default from the beginning until the very end. Whatever their attitude towards war, most contemporaries agreed that it was a business of men.[17] For example, Jan Šlesingr, a Czechoslovak legionnaire on his way through Siberia, met 'a young Russian soldier, tastefully attired … I look at him closely and to my surprise I see that, it is not a soldier, it is a girl, a volunteer in a women's military unit'. To Šlesingr, the categories of 'girl' and 'soldier' evidently do not mix and if there is some overlap between them, the result is necessarily a negative deformation of one of the forms: 'Although the girl was altogether pretty and all, she repelled me because of her coarse voice. The war did not do well in raising her to girlish bashfulness'.[18] The disruption of gender geography was bound to leave its mark on the 'natural' femininity of a woman who reached its limits.

As mentioned above, this way of thinking ran parallel to the official discourse of war as presented by the Austro-Hungarian state, which went to great lengths to ensure that whatever the population thought, enthusiasm was the only emotion that made it to the public space in 1914, carrying gendered discourse of wartime social space with it. However, this discourse was nothing new; it merely became momentarily widespread with the declaration of war.[19] Military service had been presented as a sort of rite of passage ever since the introduction of general conscription in Austria-Hungary in 1868.[20] As Laurence Cole has demonstrated, a process of 'societal militarization took place in later imperial Austria during the second half of the nineteenth century, much as it occurred in other European countries'. Through veterans' associations, public rituals and dynastic self-presentation, or officially embraced cults of military heroes, war had become a constant presence in the subconscious background of the population's peacetime existence.[21] And, of course, all these venues of societal militarization designated warfare as a purely masculine enterprise, further entrenching its highly gendered nature. Also, as mentioned by Christa Hämmerle, the Habsburg 'common army' was never enthusiastic about the whole idea of building an army out of conscripts and was particularly hostile to the philosophy of 'citizens at arms'. After it had been more or less forced to adopt the principle of universal conscription following the defeat of 1866, it held tight to its notion of soldiers as obedient tools unquestionably loyal to dynastic policies and kept the citizen-soldier ideal firmly in the background. However, by the turn of the twentieth century, even the Common Army ended up adopting those elements of the concept that it found acceptable to its conservative tastes. From the point of view of gender identity, most important was the idea that military service is actually the place where the (masculine) citizen-subject is created, i.e. it constituted 'a school of the nation' with the purpose of 'making sons into men'.[22] When war came in 1914, the army naturally lost no time in invoking its appeal to the 'strength and manliness' of 'the handsome men' it had supposedly helped to forge.[23]

The discourse of manly duty had been disseminated not only through military service, but also through schools as well as in families where one generation of men passed it on to the next, and it seems that it was highly successful. A year before he went to fight on the Serbian front in 1914, the poet Jaroslav Kolman summoned images of militarized masculinity of the young generation in his poem *Baptism of a Gun*: 'The child had played in the field till now / chasing quail and rabbits, he is a man now / A man he has become, wild questions he will ask… / Sons no longer fear their fathers / In metal boxes, plates of steel / have they hidden their fathers' unmanly deeds / You'll have, you boy, plenty of toys'.[24] Young men aged around twenty, who in 1914 donned the imperial uniform in the

Figure 1.2 In prewar Austria-Hungary, military masculinity was an integral part of male childhood, as shown on this prewar postcard (Regional Museum in Olomouc).

initial stages of the war, were generally in agreement with the official propaganda and its discourse that going to war meant an undeniable 'leap into life' as if no life had been there to live before.[25] In many cases, not even several years of the experience with 'often undeniable cruelty' of war kept them from holding on to this logic in later years: 'Military service … is always the best school of life and a cornerstone of a man's character', wrote one soldier to his sister in 1918.[26] The author seems to be pursuing a traditional military argument, pushing it further towards where service and the war itself become a test of character. And he is not alone, as many seemed to make the connection between masculine adulthood and war even as children: 'I remember', wrote a private of the k.u.k. Infantry Regiment 18, 'that even as a small boy I knew that I would be going to war. I wished to see it!'[27] Similarly, a one-year volunteer of k.u.k. Infantry Regiment 75 remembered reading 'in the *Květy* [Flowers] magazine a short story about the Thirty Years' War, where a boy of about 10 years of age somehow got to the area behind his village where there was a fight going on, people shooting, murdering each other … It sounded like a great experience and I thought, I will not have any such a great experience in my life. The story was alive in my memory and to some extent, I even envied that boy for all the things he had seen'.[28] And another soldier remembered late in the war that 'my childhood wouldn't be complete without paper and tin soldiers of all armies, without guns both tin and wooden, and without wars … My biggest Christmas wishes all revolved around getting a drum or a rifle, a cuirass or a regimental colour, and many soldiers'.[29] When the war had started and fathers went to war, their little sons were often happy at first that their 'dad is a soldier, he has a gun and eats out of a tin cup',[30] clearly interpreting these objects as attributes of adult militarized masculinity.

The deeply ingrained notion that saw military service as a rite of passage from boyhood to manliness therefore seems to be not so much a product of war propaganda as a part of the prewar discourse of military masculinity.[31] This specific form of masculinity, based on positive image of military service, clearly became a dominant factor in the hegemonic image of true manliness in wartime society.[32] Of course, it is difficult to ascertain the exact measure to which the gendered interpretation of military service can be attributed to the efforts of the army authorities and to extent to which it is possible to theorize that this phenomenon resulted from the 'residual masculinity element' with roots in the *longue durée* of the Western masculine construct itself, as mentioned in the Introduction.[33] While it is not the purpose of this text to dwell on such far-reaching theories, it has to be remembered that the idea that captivated the minds of many in 1914, namely that war is the business of men and military service is their 'school', was not necessarily a product of wartime or institutional propaganda. It could be, at least to some extent, a direct consequence of a deep-seated and ever-present element of masculinity, cleverly manipulated by the state authorities of the late nineteenth century and moved into a hegemonic position in the gender order after the war had begun. What is important for us is the fact that the idea of war as a natural, indivisible part of gender identity, a thoroughly gendered event, might have played a formative underlying role in the way Czech soldiers understood and interpreted their experience of 1914.

Duty

At the time when Emperor Franz Joseph I ordered first the partial and then, one week later – after the Russian army had mobilized – full mobilization of the Austro-Hungarian military, the country's population went into a state of war fever. As demonstrated by Jan Galandauer, there was some level of enthusiasm even beyond the German populace of Bohemia and Moravia, which was generally more susceptible to spontaneous outbursts of emotion, particularly amongst the vocal urban middle classes. Especially in Prague, several occasions were recorded when even Czechs gathered to show their loyalty to the House of Habsburg in the upcoming conflict, vindicating the claim by Laurence Cole that 'prior to 1914, national identities included – for the majority of the population – acceptance of the Habsburg state, and often positive endorsement'.[34] It seems that the major difference that separated them from their German-speaking compatriots was their much more distanced attitude to the only ally Austria-Hungary had, an ally that had only recently ceased to be an arch-enemy – namely Germany, still seen to be a more or less successor to Prussia.[35] Even so, in many places in Prague during the first weeks of August 1914, one could hear not only proud collective renderings of the 'Wacht am Rhein', but also numerous versions of 'Kde domov můj?' ('Where Is My Home?' – the future national anthem of Czechoslovakia) used as an expression of Czech patriotism and support for the war effort.[36] On numerous occasions during the summer of 1914, regiments with a Czech majority even sung the same song as they were leaving for the battlefield while flying the historical colours of Bohemia – white and red.[37]

The Austro-Hungarian High Command did not foresee any positive reaction from Czechs and somewhat by default expected the people's attitude to war to be decidedly negative. As part of the partial mobilization, it called up not seven army corps as originally planned, but eight. The additional Styrian III Army Corps was supposed to compensate for expected 'difficulties in the process of mobilization in Bohemia'.[38] However, to everyone's surprise, the whole process of collecting, equipping and dispatching hundreds of thousands of men within several days went smoothly and, according to police reports, in 'a quiet mood'.[39] The k.u.k. Ministry of the Interior reported only nine cases of desertion for the whole of Bohemia in August 1914, compared with 124 in South Tyrol, 133 in the Austrian Littoral, and 600–700 in Croatia and Slavonia.[40] Karel Wagner, who in July 1914 was serving as a regular major at k.u.k. Infantry Regiment

88 in Beroun, remembered that both he and his superiors were 'surprised at the unusually quick enlistment of our reservists … and by the serious, almost astounding calm and demonstrative order all around'.[41] Even contemporaries who were later critical of Czech participation in the Austrian war effort were forced to grudgingly acknowledge that the 'Czech soldiers enlisted immediately, quietly, and in an orderly fashion to their regiments, as if they were enlisting for ordinary military manoeuvres. Their masters in Vienna also were taken aback by the manner and speed with which the whole mobilization was completed'. Tellingly, the same author added without any trace of irony: 'I had … enlisted too … It all went well'.[42]

Mobilization depots were not ready for such a wave of loyal obedience and soon faced a logistical nightmare. Many soldiers remembered being only registered and sent home with orders to come back two days later.[43] On the way to their regiments, 'people frantically climbed into the cars until the gendarmes had to stop them. They were afraid that they will not make it in those 24 hours'.[44] The desire to arrive at one's unit in time and avoid accusations of failing mobilization orders was strong even among Czechs temporarily located in distant lands. Whether they were miners in Westphalia, 'collecting their bags and rushing one after another to their stations … Just not to be late on arrival in Bohemia was what was on their minds', or intellectuals in Berlin, fearing not only that 'in any case I am going to war, but I may be punished as well' for their delay on the way to the regiment, or convalescents in Dalmatia, running 'immediately … to the harbour … so I do not have to be transported by force', many men seemed to be in a hurry to be mobilized.[45]

The question is how did the men rushing to the mobilization depots of the k.u.k. regiments understand and interpret the whole process as well as their loyalty to the monarchy? What motivated them at this stage of their war experience and why they did not protest, but, on the contrary, surprised the authorities and probably even themselves with their apparent consent? To put the question within the context of John Lynn's theory, what constituted their 'initial motivation'? The historical writing that has attempted to answer this question in the past has usually been influenced by a nationalist perspective, portraying the Czechs as unwilling subjects of the Empire. Certainly, there is a grain of truth to the claim that 'war enthusiasm of Czechs had been weak', written by one of the authors of the massive collection of war memoirs dedicated to this very interpretation.[46] It is clear from many sources that Czechs were not very keen on the general idea of war, especially one waged against Russia and on the same side as the German Empire. However, accepting this claim as an all-encompassing truth makes it hard to explain all the scenes described above. What caused Czech men to join the ranks with such apparent ease? Did their masculine identity, passing through the troubling times of a gender order in a process of being 'remapped', play any role in this?

Before actually asking the latter question, we must address other factors that undoubtedly also featured. First and perhaps foremost, as was the case throughout Europe, almost everyone was convinced that the war would end soon, before 'the plums are ripe' or 'before Christmas'. When Egon Erwin Kisch was about to leave his home in Prague to continue his trip to the 11th Regiment in Písek, his attentive mother wanted to pack him 'with a third pair of long johns and another nightgown'. He refused these, saying: 'What do you think, that I'm going to the Thirty Years' War?!'[47] A similar opinion predominated in a company of potential conscripts in Nové Pleso near Jaroměř: 'There's a long debate. Conclusion – the war will be over soon. In six months at worst. Can you imagine what all the modern war machines can do in an hour? Therefore, the war cannot be very long'.[48] Almost no one could imagine it being so:

> I was terrified when I read somewhere that the English leader named Kitchener was rumoured to say: In 1914, we (i.e. England) declared war, in 1915 we will start it, in 1916 we will wage it, and in 17 or 18 we will end it. I was mad with horror just imagining that it could last for years. We all thought we were going to be back home before St. Martin's Day! What a madness![49]

There were even more specific (and optimistic) notions about the length of the war: 'In general, people think it will be over in two weeks, one month at worst'.[50]

Second, men in the Austrian part of the Habsburg monarchy were used to joining the ranks from time to time – not only to participate in 'ordinary military manoeuvres', but also to be mobilized. Or, at the very least, they were accustomed to reading about some of the Common Army units being mobilized in the newspapers all the time. During the six years prior to the outbreak of the First World War, there were three separate (partial) mobilization efforts in different parts of the Habsburg state, specifically in 1908–9, 1912 and 1913. The first two directly affected most of the army units stationed in Bohemia and Moravia.[51] Within this context, it is clear that in the minds of many of the reservists, to be called up for a partial mobilization was a familiar experience, a completely pointless but grudgingly tolerated 'exercise'. As a one-year volunteer of the k.k. Landwehr Infantry Regiment 13 wrote in his memoir, 'the mobilization of several army corps on St. Anne's Sunday, 26 July, was deemed to be merely a support act for a diplomatic solution. In fact, Austria had staged this demonstration against Russia a short time before that … Why shouldn't they repeat this rather expensive festival again?' Although one may suspect the quoted infantryman of being unusually optimistic, and therefore an exception, as he 'did not believe in the war' even after 31 July, it can be assumed that this was a crisis like many others in the past, all of which had always dissipated. Many of the Czech soldiers rushing to their regiments during the partial mobilization of 26 July may have actually believed that they were not going to war at all.[52]

In his outline of soldiers' initial motivation to join the ranks, John Lynn identifies compliance as constituting a key factor in their consent. In his further analysis, he identifies three distinctive types of compliance that feature in a soldier's motivation: coercive, remunerative and normative.[53] Of course, the traditional meaning of remunerative compliance in terms of loot or payment probably did not play any role in causing Czech men to join the ranks in 1914 – they never mention it and it would be rather surprising if they did so, since European armies in general, including that of Austria-Hungary, had moved on from that kind of motivation for wartime service by 1914. However, as will be seen, it may be intriguing to interpret this type of positive compliance – one motivated by a prospect of symbolic reward – in broader terms and also to include social capital under its umbrella as well.

On the other hand, while few men were physically (or violently) forced to enlist in 1914, there is little doubt that recruits' compliance with orders was often based on their fear of punishment, making their compliance coercive in its nature. As we have seen, fear of failing to present oneself at the regiment on time played its role in the effort to rush to the recruiting stations. However, looking at the sources, it is only those who failed in this obligation who actually voice concerns – see the example of Egon Erwin Kisch. Not even the postwar memoirs put much emphasis on the element of outright coercion. It seems that most of the men were actually barely thinking about possible punishment or maybe barely thinking about any alternatives at all – they simply went, as they had been accustomed to going before. We may agree here with the general conclusion by Alexander Watson, who stated that 'fear of being shot by one's own side was not a major motive to fight' for most combatants in the First World War.[54] If they actually report on thinking about finding a way out in 1914 – and such reports are surprisingly rare, given the strong social motivation one had to present his anti-Austrian attitudes in postwar writings – the most radical steps the men were willing to take were rather limited: 'For a soldier categorized as an A, meaning capable of military service, there was no way out but to subordinate one's individual self to the situation and be content with passive resistance', recalled one infantryman of k.u.k. Infantry Regiment 57, adding with an air of proud defiance: 'And so I enlisted, but not until a fortnight after the mobilization decree, when a gendarme called upon me for the third time and threatened me with an escort'.[55]

However, it seems that normative compliance was much more important. Normative compliance, as defined by John Lynn, depends mostly on the internalized values, self-discipline and self-control of the individual who is willing (not forced) to subordinate himself to any behavioural norm he deems to be reflecting dominant social opinions. These are exactly those norms the k.u.k. military tried to ingrain into the soldiers' minds during its 'school of manhood', i.e. during the years of compulsory military service. It seems to have been particularly effective as there were not many men who doubted the notion that their new status in wartime was essentially a given. Karel Vaněk, who would go on to become Jaroslav Hašek's successor in describing the good soldier Švejk's adventures in the First World War, commented on the situation in August 1914: 'Everyone is resigned to their fate, as it is a given fact that cannot be changed'.[56] In fact, resignation to their fate seems to be one of the primary emotions that soldiers recalled about their enlistment in 1914 and can be found in many primary sources with men describing their attitude as that of 'a resigned little calf'[57] or as that of 'a slave'.[58]

As described in Vaněk's diary, many soldiers understood their resignation to fate to be tightly connected to powerful, if unvoiced social pressure: 'I have to go! The word of law and the threat of punishment saying it has to be so … make the turn of events easier and less painful … But I have to go, because everybody's going'.[59] Looking at the primary sources, it is clear that it was mostly this kind of pressure that made it impossible for the soldiers, at least from their own viewpoint, to even think of alternatives to enlistment – for them, there were none. Moreover, according to their understanding of their social status, this was their destiny. Anyone who thought about going against the grain not only risked a confrontation with the 'word of law' and subsequent punishment – coercion works here as the ultimate argument, covered over with other, more effective layers of motivation – but also faced the even more profound risk of actually stepping outside the general definition of wartime masculinity as well as outside the circle of their acquaintances, friends and male relatives, who were generally thinking 'it has to be so' and 'were going'. It is no coincidence that, especially in the sources describing the mobilization in the countryside, we can find many images of groups of neighbours and friends leaving their villages for the nearest train station together. Whatever the individual's attitude towards the war – and it could be decidedly negative as well as somewhat positive – the fact that everyone participated in this 'manly business' led most of the men to the conclusion that there was no way out other than to accept their fate: 'Even though I did not like the whole idea of war at all, what could one do against it? Nothing'.[60] Motivation based on a network of friendships is clearly to be seen in the words of an infantryman serving in k.u.k. Infantry Regiment 8: 'I was not keen to join the party, but then I saw that we're all in this together … There was a lot of crying in the village, but we were not the first nor the last ones, and people got used to it'.[61]

The whole concept of military obedience lying at the very centre of military masculinity was also reinforced by contemporary social norms. In accordance with the strictly patriarchal order that governed most social interactions, especially outside urban areas, the population of the Bohemian Crown Lands at the beginning of twentieth century was generally used to following all sorts of rules. In fact, the Austro-Hungarian state ideology of the Emperor-Father was basically an extension of the same universal order of things. It is therefore no wonder that

Figure 1.3 A ritual of manliness. A ceremonial mass for the troops of k.k. Landwehr Infantry Regiment 13 in the Olomouc town square, before leaving for the front in July 1914 (Regional Museum in Olomouc).

men, accustomed to being subjected to social pressures in their everyday lives, were perfectly willing to be mobilized for war, thus entering the vicious circle of collective pressure described in Vaněk's diary. In the words of an artillerist enlisting to k.k. Landwehr Infantry Regiment 13, 'they were mostly sons of peasants, people with little education and simple needs, used to obeying and working hard … They took it as a fact'.[62] An almost perfect expression of this attitude, based on simple, passive obedience to the powers that be, is present in a letter written by a young man who had just left his small village in northeastern Bohemia to serve in the ranks of the *jäger* battalion of k.u.k. Infantry Regiment 98: 'I must learn a lot, do things well, and everyone must obey'.[63]

Of course, not every recruit was so passive about his situation, but it seems that most men who were not willing to 'obey' in the summer of 1914 limited their acts of disapproval to what amounted to rather pointless rhetorical exercises. For example, the majority of primary sources, especially those written after the war and based on the authors' (re)interpretation of their own past, mention the instance of the military oath which many of them, attempting to appear as if they had at least tried to put up some kind of resistance, claim to have sabotaged metaphorically by remaining silent.[64] Referring bitterly to another manner of 'rhetorical resistance', one contemporary vividly recalled 'the camp talk of all the people's leaders: "In case of war, not a man, not a penny!"',[65] while the aforementioned Karel Vaněk describes in his diary what could happen to those who struggled to come to terms with their manly destiny of soldiering: 'Tůma, who so often indulged in radical talk about the Czech nation and its hatred towards the government in Vienna, proposed that we should sing "Hej Slované" [a pan-Slavist hymn] on our departure from the barracks; better to be shot now than go against our Russian brothers … I wonder what's he up to'. A day later: 'Departure from the barracks was quiet; Tůma didn't start any revolution; he walked in front of me, a bit drunk, singing "No-one loves me anymore"'.[66] Having received little support from resigned or perhaps simply scared comrades, the self-proclaimed rebel ends in a state of resignation himself – social pressure at work could hardly be made more blatant.[67]

Based on the conclusions above, it may seem that Karel Wagner, former major of k.u.k. Infantry Regiment 88 and a postwar general in the Czechoslovak army, was right when he claimed in his memoir that Czech soldiers fought for the Emperor and the monarchy 'only because that duty and obedience to their laws made them to', referring – through not so veiled allusion to Simonides' famous epigram – to the ancient code of the citizen-warrior.[68] What Wagner tried to prove in his memoir was that Czech soldiers were primarily citizen-warriors, self-conscious patriotic soldiers in the style of Leonidas' Spartans, legionaries of the Roman republic or *citoyens* of the French First Republic. However, the conservative, traditionalist Austro-Hungarian military was not keen on invoking the spectre of a citizen-soldier at all, because it smacked too much of liberal nationalism that threatened to tear the old monarchy apart during the nineteenth century. The authorities very much preferred to base the official discourse of military masculinity on the much less internalized and more self-conscious virtue of obedience and sense of duty to the Emperor and the state. 'Austria was a state, not a nation', wrote the historian Maureen Healy. 'State and nation allow (or demand) different levels of commitment from individuals; one may be loyal to a state, but one does not "belong to" a state in the same way that one belongs to a nation'. Healy uses this argument to support her claim about the highly problematic nature of wartime 'mobilization of Austrian women'. However, the same may well be claimed about the mobilization of Austrian men, Czechs included.[69]

Ultimately, Czech soldiers ended up being almost exactly the passive servants of the state that the official discourse of military masculinity wanted them to be – in their version of the wartime world, it was the destiny of men to go to war, and they were men, so they went. The modern discourse of military masculinity, based on a conscious fulfilment of civic duty by a citizen (i.e. member of a political community, the nation), such as that which Karel Wagner was trying to portray, was mostly foreign to them. The passive, resigned loyalty to the state, as defined by Maureen Healy, which the conservative Austro-Hungarian authorities tried (successfully it seems) to instil in their subjects, became the norm of their behaviour. There were some who were even aware of this: 'I'm going to fight, destroy the enemy, but I don't feel any hatred', noted Karel Vaněk on the way to the front in his diary in February 1915. 'But that huge, complicated machine called "the state" is at work and I'm just a small, unimportant cog driven by the sprockets of the others. I cannot stop'.[70] The same feeling was expressed by another diarist, this time immediately during the summer of 1914. The reason why 'people go to their deaths against their will', she concluded, lies in the 'enormous power of the state idea'.[71] Others were perfectly aware of the difference between loyalty to the state and the sense of belonging to a nation – and found true heroism, and correspondingly also real masculinity, only in the latter: 'On Sunday, the 91st Regiment boarded a train … How difficult it is to leave a family and children and go to war. What for? If only we were going to defend our Czech land, we would be going with a heroic spirit'.[72] It was not by chance that many postwar critics of the Czech behaviour during the mobilization used the emasculating word 'cowards' to describe it.[73] Looking back from the independent state that emerged in 1918, an entity that emphasized an absolutely different concept of military masculinity as embodied by the Czechoslovak Legion (more or less a volunteer force), the passive sense of duty made little sense. But in 1914, men felt the normative pressure for their obedience to be too strong to be avoided. Furthermore, the social pressure created by the fact that majority of the population followed this logic was too powerful to withstand, even for those who had some misgivings about this definition of their wartime manliness.

Prize

Hegemonic masculinity, in mid to late 1914 invariably connected to military service through its militarized form, brings to its beneficiaries the 'patriarchal dividend' of power, control and social status above women and other men.[74] And it is precisely within this context that the self-interest to fulfil one's perceived social role during mobilization comes to the fore. Authors with families and established careers, i.e. men who could lose a lot in the war and who left dependents at home, are invariably the most critical of the whole situation. 'The hardest was the goodbye for those who were leaving their families', remembered a one-year volunteer of k.u.k. Infantry Regiment 53.[75] The man, husband or son was not a breadwinner only under the present gender discourse, but in the lived life experience of many working- and middle-class families as well. Concerns for the family's wellbeing or for the family business or farm, especially if we realize that the mobilization came just before the harvest season, represent an eternal theme running through many of the sources.[76]

On the other hand, young men around their twentieth year of age often seemed to be rather careless in their attitude, occasional melancholy notwithstanding. 'Young soldiers, quite jovial, had no idea what was in store for them', remembered a one-year volunteer serving in k.u.k Infantry Regiment 75,[77] while another soldier noted that 'only the youth were not that pessimistic about their prospects'.[78] One of the young men saw the contrast clearly: 'So we enlisted. We, rookies, saw only an unknown adventure in war and therefore were not afraid that much; old dads were scowling, as their family was weighing down their spirits like a heavy stone. And then there were the others, thieves, gypsies and other riff-raff, people with nothing to lose'.[79]

Besides the subtle notion of the traditional hierarchy of masculinities, in which the 'rookies' are only now about to aspire to full manhood while the 'dads' are those who have already attained it, and 'the others' are the marginalized groups on the very edge of social manhood, it is important to note here the 'nothing to lose' argument. This notion can be widened to also include the 'rookies', i.e. the young men who can see the war as a chance to attain at least some of the privileges usually attributed to hegemonic masculinity, while avoiding going through time-consuming and uncertain endeavours on the traditional 'path of manliness' – getting a respectable job and economic independence, finding a female sexual partner and starting (and feeding) a family. The wartime redrawing of the gender order presented young men with a shortcut to full masculine status, and this shortcut led through the rite of passage of wartime military service. Within this context, young men could reasonably expect to be able to escape the peacetime rules created, among other purposes, to 'pacify' young men and keep them in check under a strict hierarchy of masculinities.[80] Moreover, if we define masculinity not only as social expression of power over women, but also as relational power structure dividing categories of men, what we have here is an ideal example of a process that can be referred to as 'a tournament of manliness'. In this particular tournament, individual categories of men compete for symbolic capital and the real power that is closely related to it. By winning in this tournament, young men were able to escape the rules of the peacetime hegemonic masculinity and use its redefined wartime construction to attain such a status along with its benefits.

The fact that most of these young men never actually reached the very top of the masculine hierarchy, i.e. never became officers with all their privileges and real benefits of power, did not seem to matter to them initially. From their point of view, the chance to rise in the hierarchy of masculinities was a reward of sorts that they received for their compliance with the official discourse. On the other hand, men whose existence, masculine identity and status had been firmly rooted in peacetime society could, on the battlefield, lose most or all of it in the blink of an eye, and were deeply aware of that fact. Augustin Mudrák, writing in his diary, was 'as calm as ever' in 1909 when he was drafted into the army, because 'at least I can get out of becoming an animal castrator, which I hate', mentioning a career his father had selected for him. He lived through the years of the three-year compulsory service, was discharged and became the only breadwinner in the family after his father died. In 1914, he was about to start a family of his own when the mobilization came. This time, his feelings were radically different from those of five years ago: 'Devastated, I say goodbye to everyone. Especially to my wife Anička'.[81]

The hypothesis that this tournament of manliness was a part of the lived experience for many a young man in July 1914, and therefore a part of their initial motivation, can be supported not only by a general dissonance between the attitudes of young single men and those of fathers of families. Some of these men experienced 'victory' in the tournament even in their civilian life before they actually enlisted, as their social status changed in the direction of hegemonic masculinity thanks to war. Suddenly, many young men just below military age had to step in for those who had already been conscripted and sent to the front, as was the case for František Šmída, who was 'ever so conscious of his manly importance' while helping with the summer harvest of 1914.[82] To most, however, this feeling only came when they donned the uniform.

An especially effective way for a young man to move up the masculine hierarchy was to become an officer. A possible result is described in the war novel written by Karel Poláček and published under the title *Hrdinové táhnou do boje* (*The Heroes Go to War*). One of the characters named Král, a small-town teacher who became a *Fähnrich* (warrant officer), acquired 'an air of stiff arrogance' along with his epaulettes. He used to stand in the town square and imagined 'commanding everyone in that provincial town. The president of the district council, the mayor, the whole town council, the high school headmaster, the doctor [i.e. everyone who stood above him in the hierarchy of masculinities of a small town], all of them standing to attention in ranks'.[83] The feeling of belonging to the officer corps is also reflected upon by František Šmída, who attained the metaphorical peak of the wartime social hierarchy by entering a cadet school: 'I will come back an officer, a lord, respected and admired by people back home'.[84] To receive such an award, one did not even need to be very positive about the war. The well-known leftist radical and poet Stanislav Kostka Neumann described a friend, a pacifist and 'fanatical anti-militarist' whom he met in 1917 at a depot: 'My friend is young, and he certainly suffered a lot when leaving his home and his life behind, thinking desperately and in vain of how to escape the inescapable; he came to me all handsome, in a *Fähnrich*'s uniform, tanned, masculine … reconciled to the inescapable, and happy'.[85] However, becoming 'masculine' could be a reward attainable not only by those near the top of the hierarchy, but also by those at the bottom, since even a marginalized person could become 'a man' by donning a uniform (which makes all men look equal, at least on first glance). A good example here is the village idiot František, the main character from Vladislav Vančura's novel *Pole orná a válečná* (*Fields of Harvest, Fields of War*): 'František was … happy … he looked like the other guys. He had become a soldier'.[86] For him, as for many of the men going to war in 1914, this social integration could be worth the risk of joining up.

In gender theory, 'patriarchal dividend' means primarily social capital that is easily translated into power, especially power over women and access to them in terms of a possible sexual relationship.[87] Consequently, it may be easily argued that this specific form of capital represented one of the key perceived rewards soldiers received for their compliance. This is especially true for those men whose access to women had been limited because of their age, class or character. It is difficult to provide a definitive answer with regard to the precise importance of this 'masculine dividend' within the framework of Czech soldiers' motivation, but primary sources tell us that the soldiers themselves put a considerable amount of faith in it.[88] There are some verses in the prewar poetry of Jaroslav Kolman that directly refer to the expected appeal of the military attributes of masculinity to women: 'He smelled of dirt, stalls, and iron / and of gunpowder… / He came, as misfortunes come / like a wild animal about to jump / he whispered kindly / then looked in my eyes / He came, nodded, and I had to go with him'.[89] Similar ideas can also be identified in several descriptions of events during the mobilization of 1914. It is Poláček's 'heroes going to war' who throw 'manly handsome looks' at women, believing in their own masculine prowess.[90] 'Pilsen! … The city is one big camp of civilians turned soldiers. Uniformed privates, but especially officers, are the centre of attention. And they know it very well', wrote one of his contemporaries.[91] As another diarist noted, 'wives and mistresses were hugging their loved ones. They loved them more than ever before. These men became the heroes of the day, and had the mobilization been cancelled, they might even have been disappointed'.[92] In the same way, Egon Erwin Kisch noted that even among the otherwise depressed reservists who were forced to leave their families, there were some instances of awareness of their social promotion. When his battalion was taking its oath, 'ladies were blowing kisses towards us and every one of the poor reservists who only yesterday had been saying tearful goodbyes to their wives and children, was thinking these were meant for him and for him only, and responded in kind'.[93] Jan Šmatlán is even more direct in his description of the way he experienced the departure of his battalion and is not able to hide his delight at being the centre of attention of the crowds: 'All over the town, people were looking at us'.[94] As we have seen, in the gendered geography of the wartime world, 'people' out of uniform usually meant 'women'. Not surprisingly, the whole transport of the field regiments from their home bases in Bohemia and Moravia, via Vienna and Hungary, to the Serbian frontier takes on a very special quality in many a soldier's description, elevated to the status of a masculine *via triumphalis*. Soldiers, often depressed inside, are being celebrated and admired at every station by the local belles, and many of them happily take notice of the fact.

At least some of the newly inaugurated soon-to-be warriors were lucky enough – from their point of view – to attain the most coveted reward that could come with reaching the top of the hierarchy of masculinities, namely a sexual relationship with a woman. In his diary, František Skála mentions the case of a

Figure 1.4 A ritual of manliness. 3rd Battery, k.u.k. Field Artillery Regiment 27, marching to the train station through the streets of Hradec Králové, accompanied by its own band and a large numbers of curious, but rather passive onlookers (Museum of Eastern Bohemia, Hradec Králové).

young corporal: 'Back home he was in a respectable relationship. He was looking forward to get a leave, imagining what it would be like. And it was great indeed, but the days passed too fast. There were only three left and so he became obsessed with the idea that he would not return. In particular, he agonized about what would happen to Mařka, his girl. Should he leave her to someone else without making her all his, completely, at least once?' The girl refused him at first, but the corporal's social role of a man leaving for the front seems to have helped:

> I had felt, she said, that you were demanding something too great, something I could not understand. I don't share your fears ... but ... God forbid ... I would not forgive myself for the rest of my life if I did not fulfil your last wish. It's not a sin if I give you what is truly and rightfully yours ... I want to be all yours tonight, even if there are consequences for me.[95]

The idea, fixed in many a soldier's mind, that accepting military masculinity increases man's popularity with the opposite sex, possibly increasing his sexual attractiveness as well, worked as a 'reward' of a kind not only during the mobilization, but also during the war years. Many soldiers held to the notion that enlistment turned them into a kind of manly warrior and presented themselves as such in their writings. František Šmída, when he became a cadet, felt himself to be 'a complete man, full of life and longing for adventure … a warrior with the right and license' to conquer women.[96] When Josef Ulrych's unit was transferred for rest and refit to the town of Pottendorf near Vienna in March 1917, he and his comrades went to the local dance hall where local male and female workers were also present. Immediately, they became the hit of the evening, undoubtedly with the girls as well: 'There were several Czech boys and girls, who mostly worked in local ammunitions factories … When we made it clear to them that we were coming from the war, they flooded us with beer … and we danced a lot'.[97] A similar development, but from the perspective of the 'other side' (i.e. the men who were, thanks to their wartime work assignment, left out of the tournament of manliness altogether), is described by Rudolf Kučera: 'Any kind of work performed at the home front was drastically devalued … Hard-working workers faced the dilemma of how to remain a man according to the dominant public discourse that automatically identified full-fledged manhood with a soldier', one that made hegemonic masculinity and military service nearly synonymous.[98]

Reward in the form of the ability to quickly acquire or defend one's hegemonic masculine status was not necessarily the only 'absolution' of the mobilization process. There were of course many others and it is beyond of scope of this text to include them all. To mention only those prominent in the sources used here, there was, first, the very homosocial nature of the mobilization. A specific and exclusive group of men, the army was indeed keen to present itself as a school and a bastion of its own idea of hegemonic masculinity superior to all other masculinities.[99] The opportunity to be 'among men', often old friends from the years spent on the three years' service before the war, made the process of adaptation to the fact that men had to leave their civilian life behind all the more palatable. Things like alcohol, singing and vulgar humour, so typical of masculine socialization, were all present, as was the social pressure to suppress overtly unmanly displays of sadness, especially tears.[100] 'Hat to the side, flower behind it, cigars, cigarettes, a bottle of schnapps in a pocket or in the hand', that was the image one recruit remembered after he and his friends had been successfully conscripted.[101] 'An unlimited number of old friends. How they had changed since we saw each other last time!'[102] Meeting friends after a long time was always a thing to celebrate, whatever the circumstances: 'Our first steps back in town led us to the café … where we used to go to read Czech newspapers while on active service. We ended up staying there all the way till dawn'.[103] 'We have a nice little pub here at the Locomotive, where the whole bunch meets. J. Tyl plays the piano. If this is war, then it's no bad thing'.[104] 'Drinks were ordered by the dozen' in every pub of all garrison towns, 'the tragic destiny being drowned in beer'.[105] Homosocial company could ultimately even succeed in erasing the despair of leaving loved ones: 'With the wife, mother, children, it was the worst!

But on the train with the guys, it felt much lighter'.[106] 'How moving it was to watch the reservists say goodbyes to their families ... On the train, everyone suppressed their grief and it looked like a holiday in garrisons'.[107] Rowdy partying in such manly company was able to put most of the memories of home to rest: 'The soldiers finally got rid of the unnecessary hypersensitiveness and some raucous fun found its way into their hearts again'.[108]

There was also the sense of adventure.[109] Many of the soldiers' diaries have an almost Baedeker quality to them, featuring many paragraphs expressing awe at the beauty or peculiarities of foreign lands. In addition, it is necessary to realize the limited horizon that people of the early twentieth century had – war was often the first time they had had the chance to leave the region they grew up in. Jan Šmatlán, for example, describes with outright fascination first Jaroměř (a small town), then 'the beautiful big city of Hradec Králové' (in fact, a local metropolis at best) about 50 kilometres from his home village. 'Who could have said that I'd get to Hradec in my life'.[110] For many, the idea of being taken out of their ordinary lives to see the world could be rewarding by itself: 'But we're playing heroes ... Inside it boils and bubbles, but on the outside, everyone is happy, because we are going to see the wide world'.[111] It was especially the younger men who were more positive about 'seeing far-away lands', willing to view all the travelling as a part of their rite of passage that would enable them to acquire a hegemonic masculine identity: 'We were roving and fearless boys, full of manly dreams ... and so, we welcomed the war that promised us a journey to all the far-away lands for free, with great enthusiasm'.[112] Even in the memoirs of the ultimate anti-soldier, the painter and mystic Josef Váchal, we can find a note of 'feeling that it may be worth seeing a trench and an assault once in my life', experienced during a café discussion filled with 'enthusiasm and well-hidden fears of being conscripted'.[113] Of course, the desire for adventure together with one's homosocial group played only a secondary role in motivating Czech men to enlist, as it was usually cultivated only once the men had arrived at their units and could (re)identify with these groups and dreams. However, it is possible to argue that it played its role in their ultimate consent, especially if it was to be only a short reprieve from a somewhat boring peacetime life.

However, during August 1914, instead of the expected series of quick victories, the Austro-Hungarian army took part in several immensely bloody engagements that mostly thwarted all advances both against Serbia (the Battle of Cer in mid August, followed by the bloodbath of the Drina in early September) and Russia (where the victories at Krasnik and Komarów were followed by defeats at Gnila Lipa and Rawa, causing a panicked retreat of the eastern army all the way to Krakow). By the end of August, it was clear that the war would not be over soon. The first transports of wounded started arriving back in the Bohemian Crown Lands and the population, not prepared for suffering on such a horrific scale, veered in its mood towards growing disillusionment and pessimism:

As long as we could believe that the war would be over soon, people were always talking about ongoing peace talks etc., but all these rumours proved to be false. It seemed as if people didn't want to believe in something that they weren't willing to admit to themselves ... But now, after a month, which is the time usually reserved for regular military manoeuvres, there was no triple blast of trumpet to call it all off, and all the hopes of a quick return gave way to desperation.[114]

The first *Marchbattalione*, replacement battalions leaving the Bohemian Crown Lands to bring new men to the depleted field formations in mid September, left their depots in much more sober mood, both from the perspective of the soldiers and their loved ones. The same was true for the k.u.k. authorities, who were becoming nervous with the disappointing start to the campaign and guided by the powerful nationalist discourse present even in the generally supranational High Command, they started to look for scapegoats. They found them in the seemingly unsatisfactory war enthusiasm of the Empire's minorities. Czechs, along with Serbs, Ruthenes or Jews, were the traditional 'usual suspects' here. In the army, punishments started to be dealt out based on soldiers belonging to a specific language group; in the hinterland, a wave of more or less arbitrary arrests and convictions of real or imagined 'national radicals' ensued.[115]

There is considerable degree of irony in the fact that the Austro-Hungarian authorities quickly adopted the same image of 'the rebellious Czechs' that became a cornerstone of the postwar Czechoslovak interpretation of the First World War, one so successful that it made its way into most of the general accounts of the war. The fact is that during the summer and early autumn of 1914, the same authorities were tolerating or even supporting the same displays of Czech patriotism that they started to outlaw and even punish later on. As mentioned previously, in the first weeks of the war, many regiments were leaving Bohemia with ribbons and flags in the heraldic colours of Bohemia (white and red) instead of those of the Empire (gold and black) while singing many typically Czech patriotic songs. Reinterpreting incidents such as the departure of the III Replacement Battalion of k.u.k. Infantry Regiment 28 from Prague on 23 September 1914, when the local populace who had gathered to bid farewell to the unit momentarily clashed with the police, postwar and later on even Marxist historiography attempted to portray some of the events during the 'autumn of disillusionment' as revolutionary acts of the defiant Czechs. In fact, it seems that the reality was much more prosaic and owed much to the general drop in morale, as well as to some other factors.[116] For example, older men were now finally leaving for the front after undergoing the six-week retraining, and this also included the *Landsturm* battalions, i.e. men of thirty-two years of age or more, who had little to gain from the 'tournament of manliness', but had plenty to lose both in terms of their status and their existence. As a result, their feelings may be well summarized in the words of a Budweis *Landsturm* NCO: 'The terrible moment I dreaded so much has arrived ... There was a lot of crying at home. The wife was crying, the little son was crying ... And I, remembering that I have to leave them, leave my solid life and go off to see unforeseen hardships, was crying as well'.[117] In some specific cases, such as the aforementioned 28th Infantry Regiment, it is also possible to see an important role played by the class origin of the men in question, as working-class soldiers were more likely to manifest their discontent collectively in the same way as they were accustomed to in terms of negotiating their social and economic status in peacetime.[118]

The fact is that the Austro-Hungarian authorities, suffering from a longtime nationalist paranoia, were only too happy to jump to the same conclusion, as this fit well into their search for a scapegoat responsible for less than not-so-successful beginning of the war. By the end of the year, most of the replacement battalions started to leave their garrison towns at night and any public displays of affection for the troops were banned. In late 1914 and early 1915, the whole process of estrangement between the army and some of its soldiers peaked, with several Czech regiments having their reserve battalions ('cadres', meaning garrison depots) moved to Hungary in an exchange with their Hungarian counterparts.[119] As for the images of the increasingly difficult moments of units leaving garrison towns, at least one thing did not change – under the new 'social geography' of wartime society, the crowds accompanying soldiers to the train stations with increasing anger were still, in the soldiers' accounts, conspicuously gendered, composed exclusively of women and children; it still seemed as if all men were in uniform and those who were not were not men.[120]

August and September 1914 were, for most of the soldiers of the First World War, only a small taste of things to come. A war of movement was quickly replaced by a war of increasingly sophisticated trench lines, and the neverending marches in the scorching heat and dust of Galicia or the deadly game of hide-and-seek in the corn fields of Serbia gave way to autumn sleet, frost and a subsequent flurry of snow that no one was prepared for – the armies in particular. The Galician front, pushed all the way to the Carpathian mountain range by the Russian counteroffensive, turned into an icy grave for thousands of ill-equipped and ill-supplied soldiers of the Austro-Hungarian army. 'When it began, they said it would be over soon, before Christmas. But it went on and on, and the end was nowhere in sight'.[121]

The Czech-speaking recruits of the Austro-Hungarian military in 1914 went to war more or less willingly, confounding generations of future historians and perhaps even themselves by acting against not only against their natural 'self-interest' as defined by John Lynn, but also against their 'national feelings', as repeatedly claimed ever since the First World War. Whatever these feelings were, they played a lesser role in the summer of 1914 than has traditionally been argued. Multiple factors were obviously more important at that time, such as the mobilization of that year being the third such event in the past five years; the popular perception that if war ever started, it would be quickly over; or simple 'coercive compliance' – fear of being punished for not fulfilling one's duty. But it is the very notion that it is the duty of a subject, a citizen, a man, to serve in war that points to the well-hidden structures based on gender identity and the contemporary ideas of masculinity, proving that these indeed influenced the way in which Czechs thought about their situation in 1914.

The moment war erupted in East-Central Europe, the population of Bohemia and Moravia began to redefine its social space in a thoroughly 'gendered' way. While in no way corresponding to reality, the image of men leaving for the front and the home being populated by women, children and the elderly permeated most of the popular thought, creating a symbolic masculine space of war and a feminine space of peace. The very existence of such thought reflected the propaganda efforts of the Austro-Hungarian authorities, but its roots ran deeper than that, to the prewar discourse of military service oriented around the values of loyalty and honour in obedience,[122] and even beyond, to the *longue durée* of 'residual elements' of masculine identity. As a result, the question of one's masculinity stood at the centre of every recruit's understanding of the mobilization and created a normative structure, a set of societal attitudes that presented men going to war as a natural phenomenon. Accordingly, the behaviour of most men at the beginning of the war amounted to an absolute acceptance of the discourse of military masculinity, as mobilization was its institutionalized manifestation. In the simple words of an author who was otherwise highly critical of the Austrian war effort, 'they force-fed us the Austrian spirit, especially that dumb Austrian militarism … Our necks were so used to this yoke that we had stopped trying to get rid of it. That is why the mobilization went so well … We were cowards'.[123] Moreover, the very sense of duty, used in retrospect by many recruits to explain their behaviour, sprang partially from a pervasive spirit of obedience to patriarchal authority that was ever-present in early twentieth-century society where 'everyone had to obey'. In combination, these considerations then caused a powerful social pressure that forced even those who more or less opposed the idea of going to war to enlist with little resistance. All they could see around was 'everyone' (meaning men of course) 'going' – and they went too, because any resistance seemed futile and, in 1914 at least, socially unmanning.

While staying out of the space of war, i.e. out of service and out of uniform, endangered many man's masculinity, joining that space by contrast represented a once-in-a-lifetime opportunity to attain full masculine status almost overnight. If we include social capital in John Lynn's definition of 'remunerative' compliance, we can identify its influence precisely here, in creating a situation that presented recruits with a massive motivation to ignore whatever doubts and fears they had. The militarized hegemonic masculinity in wartime society created powerful new points of access to this coveted social status for those who could not hope to possess it in peacetime society due to their age or economic position. Young men especially often understood mobilization as a chance to become 'full men' through military service, with full access to the patriarchal dividend – status, resources and women. Even those who already occupied the hegemonic position were caught by this logic as, willingly or not, the only way they could *keep* this status was to prove it under altered conditions – in war. To keep winning in the 'tournament of manliness', basically a social dialogue concerning the ever-changing notion of hegemonic masculinity, one had to stay on top of whatever game was being played, and in war, being a man meant becoming a soldier, even if somewhat involuntarily. All this social pressure deeply rooted in gender identities meant that anyone who was considering standing aside had to think twice, as such defiance would mean not only punishment by the force of law, but also social discrimination, echoing Lynn's definition of coercive compliance. The Czech-speaking soldiers of Austria-Hungary were well aware of it in 1914 and even later. Consequently, soldiers' consent, if we return to the term from the ongoing historiographical debate, may well have been, in the end, induced by societal coercion.

The whole process was made easier by some specific characteristics of the mobilization experience, appealing to 'manly dreams' of adventure and seeing the world, which again attracted especially the young and restless. The fact that mobilization was a process of re-creating a homosocial community also helped – one that should have been, ideally, translated into a primary group cohesion in order to bolster combat effectiveness, as Lynn states. Such an environment, however depressing, offered the participants – especially in the first weeks of service – many psychological outlets in the form of collective behaviour typical of all-male groups. As a result, the k.u.k. authorities were able to put the abrupt change in the hierarchy of wartime masculinities, 'the tournament of manliness', to good use in their effort to overcome the sometimes substantial ideological conflicts that many Czech men had with the idea of going to war against Russia or Serbia, or of going to war at all.

Notes

An earlier, much abbreviated version of this chapter has been published as Jiří Hutečka, '"Looking Like the Other Guys": The 1914 Mobilization as a Masculine Experience in Czech Soldiers' Writings', *Revue des études slaves* 88, special issue '1914, l'Autriche-Hongrie entre en guerre: récits de soldats et civils', no. 4 (2017): 667–82. Its fleshed-out form appears here courtesy of the editors.

1. The Clash, 'The Call Up' (CBS-Epic, 1980).
2. For more on the Sokol and the body, see Filip Bláha, *Frauenkörper im Fokus: Wahrnehmung zwischen Strasse und Turnplatz in Prag und Dresden vor dem Ersten Weltkrieg* (Frankfurt am Main, 2013). On the Sokol movement in general, see Claire E. Nolte, *The Sokol in the Czech Lands to 1914: Training for the Nation* (Basingstoke, 2002).

3. Quotations from František Šmída, *Vzpomínky z vojny 1914–1919*, ed. Miroslav Kobza (Olomouc, 2014), 9.
4. Max Brod, *Život plný bojů* (Prague, 1994), 75–76.
5. Ibid., 76.
6. Ibid., 78.
7. Out of the vast number of works on the beginning of the First World War, the best reference today is probably Clark, *The Sleepwalkers*. See also Hew Strachan, *The First World War: To Arms* (Oxford, 2001), 64–102; or Holger H. Herwig, ed., *The Outbreak of the World War I* (Boston, 1997). On the July Crisis as it happened in the Bohemian Crown Lands, see Šedivý, *Češi, české země a Velká válka 1914–1918*, 21–31.
8. Brod, *Život plný bojů*, 73–74.
9. František Chmela, *Vzpomínky z 1. světové války* (Týn nad Vltavou, 2014), 7.
10. Jaroslav Poláček, ed., *Zápisky Václava Poláčka ze světové války a ze života v Hojkově* (Jihlava, 2011), 37. Tellingly, many recruits expressed surprise, even disgust, with women who not only did not cry (as would apparently be fitting for any woman at the beginning of war), but aggressively proclaimed their pro-war stance by demanding 'death to the Serbs'. In the eyes of many authors, these women, almost invariably identified as 'German' in the postwar memoirs, seem to have breached the constraints of the role ascribed to them at the moment: 'What the fairer sex was doing [in a German-speaking town of Iglau/Jihlava] was disgusting. Waving the black and yellow flags, screaming and shouting "You guys kill a thousand Serbs each and the war will be over quickly!"' Josef Chalupecký, 'Na hranicích Černé Hory', in *Domov za války*, vol. 1, 107.
11. See Maureen Healy, *Vienna and the Fall of the Habsburg Empire: Total War and Everyday Life in World War I* (Cambridge, 2004), 258–64. Healy's criticism is directed to such claims as the one made by Elizabeth Domansky, who wrote: 'Men did leave in sufficient numbers to make the home front seem to be women's territory … the female noncombat zone of producing and reproducing the means of destruction'. Elizabeth Domansky, 'Militarization and Reproduction in World War I Germany', in *Society, Culture and the State in Germany, 1870–1930*, ed. Geoff Eley (Ann Arbor, 1996), 459.
12. See also Wilhelm Winkler, *Die Totenverluste der öst.-ung. Monarchie nach Nationalitäten: Die Altersgliederung der Toten. Ausblicke in die Zukunft* (Vienna, 1919); or Zdeněk Boháč, 'Wilhelm Winkler, Die Totenverluste der öst.- ung. Monarchie nach Nationalitäten: Die Altersgliederung der Toten. Ausblicke in die Zukunft. Wien 1919', in *Československý statistický věstník* I (Prague, 1920), 67.
13. František Černý, *Moje záznamy ze světové války* (Prague, 2014), 27. Scenes of troops leaving for the front were an ideal moment to almost ritually reconstruct gender roles in society. In most accounts, it is the quiet, resigned soldiers marching in straight ranks to the train stations, while 'women fall to their knees, praying to the Lord to stop the horrible war … Perhaps never in their lives had they prayed more fervently … It was all in vain'. Josef Kápar, *Cestou kamenitou* (Prague, 1922), 21.
14. 'Božka' to Jan Janošík, June 14, 1916, Státní okresní archiv (SOkA – State District Archive) Olomouc, Fond Janošík Jan, pplk. v. v.
15. Entry for 21 August 1914, Egon Erwin Kisch, *Vojákem pražského sboru* (Prague, 1965), 55 (first published in Berlin as *Soldat im Prager Korps*, 1922).
16. Kučera, *Rationed Life*, 103. As noted by Siniša Malešević, 'in times of war social organizations have different priorities … [and] it becomes paramount to redefine "civilian" as weak, passive, dependent and in need of protection while "military" acquires the

attributes of strength, leadership, determination and assertiveness ... This change is grounded in already familiar and institutionalized dichotomies' of gender order, and it 'often resonates well with the larger population' because of it'. See Malešević, *The Sociology of War*, 307.

17. In the thoughts of some of the soldiers, this idea reached almost philosophical heights in retrospect: 'If the world's destiny was being decided by women-mothers, there would be no wars ... But it is men who make history'. Ferdinand Lirš, *S Osmadvacátníky za světové války* (Prague, 1936), 8.
18. See Jan Šlesingr, *Legionáři* (Olomouc, 2005), 61.
19. Using various leverages with the press as well as official channels of regional and authorities, the government was rather succesful in fostering this image, even though various segments of the population were less than enthusiastic abot the war's prospects. See Mark Cornwall, 'The Spirit of 1914 in Austria-Hungary', *Prispevki za novejšo zgodovino* 55, no. 2 (2015): 7–21.
20. It is necessary to realize that the Habsburg state never had the financial and logistical means (and, partially, even the political will) to recruit more than a fraction of each year's class of young men into its 'school of manhood' of the three-year service. As a result, while population rose by 40% between 1870 and 1912, the annual intake of recruits only rose by 12%. See Günther Kronenbitter, *'Krieg im Frieden' Die Führung der k.u.k. Armee und die Grossmachtpolitik Österreich-Ungarn, 1916–1914* (Munich, 2003), 145–232.
21. Laurence Cole, *Military Culture and Popular Patriotism in Late Imperial Austria* (Oxford, 2013), 308–9. On the other hand, A.J.P. Taylor has famously argued that 'the "military monarchy" of the Habsburgs was the least militarized state in Europe', and Christa Hämmerle concluded that while recruits were innoculated with the militarized discourse of masculinity during their years on active service, hegemonic masculinity of peacetime society proved more or less resistant to the level of militarization we know from other European countries of the same era. See A.J.P. Taylor, *The Habsburg Monarchy, 1809–1918* (London, 1948), 247; Hämmerle, 'Zur Relevanz des Connell'schen Konzepts hegemonialer Männlichkeit für "Militär und Männlichkeit/en in der Habsburgermonarchie (1868–1914/18)"', 107–10. See also Rothenberg, *The Army of Francis Joseph*, x, for a further endorsement of this argument. For a comparison with other European countries in the nineteenth century, see Christian Jansen, ed., *Der Bürger als Soldat: Die Militarisierung europäischer Gesellschaften im langen 19. Jahrhundert: ein internationaler Vergleich* (Essen, 2004).
22. See Christa Hämmerle, 'Back to the Monarchy's Glorified Past? Military Discourses on Male Citizenship and Universal Conscription in the Austrian Empire, 1868–1914', in *Representing Masculinity: Male Citizenship in Modern Western Culture*, eds Stefan Dudink, Karen Hagemann and Anna Clark (New York, 2007), 160. For more on the notion of the citizen-soldier in modern European society and politics, and its connections with masculine identities, see the following collections and articles: Katherine Aaslestad, Karen Hagemann and Judith Miller, eds., *Gender, War and the Nation in the Period of Revolutionary and Napoleonic Wars: European Perspectives* (Philadelphia, 2007); Ida Blom, Karen Hagemann and Catherine Hall, eds., *Gendered Nations: Nationalisms and Gender Order in the Long Nineteenth Century* (Oxford, 2000); Stefan Dudink, Karen Hagemann and John Tosh, eds., *Masculinities in Politics and War: Gendering Modern History* (Manchester, 2004); Ute Frevert, 'Das Militär als Schule der Männlichkeiten',

in *Männlichkeiten und Moderne: Geschlecht in den Wissenskulturen um 1900*, eds Ulrike Brunotte and Rainer Herrn (Bielefeld, 2008), 57–76. For a brief summary, see Robert A. Nye's concluding remarks in Christopher E. Forth and Bertrand Taithe, eds., *French Masculinities: History, Culture, and Politics* (London, 2007), 232–41.

23. Quoted from a government propaganda pamphlet: Rudolf Peerz, *Vlast volá! Slovo k obyvatelstvu Rakouska-Uherska* (Vienna, 1916), 6 and 55.
24. Jaroslav Kolman, 'Křest děla', in Jaroslav Kolman, *Cassiovy listy* (Prague, 1921; first published in the magazine *Přítomnost* in 1913).
25. Diary entry of Alois Dolejší, an eighteen-year-old private of Infantry Regiment 28, 11 May, 1917. Alois Dolejší, *Válečné vzpomínky z první světové války vojína Dolejše z Nového Strašecí*, ed. Dagmar Neprašová (Brno, 2014), 75.
26. Josef Janošík to his sister, Anna Janošíková, 16 July 1918, Josef Janošík Papers, private collection of his great-grandson, Jan Janošík.
27. Josef Ulrych, 'Moje zápisky, 1893–1922' (unpublished manuscript, 1922, Archivní sbírka Vlastivědného muzea v Dobrušce, digital archives, CD no. 115), 45.
28. Vladislav Květoň, *Vzpomínky z první světové války* (Prague, 1995), 3.
29. Jaroslav Havlíček to Marie Krauseová, 1 June 1918, quoted in Hana Taudyová, 'Válečná milostná korespondence Jaroslava Havlíčka', *Historie a vojenství* 52, no. 1 (2003): 102.
30. In his diary, Karel Vaněk described the views held by his four-year-old nephew in this way. See diary entry, 4 January 1915, in Karel Vaněk, *Charašó pán, da? Zápisky všelijakého vojáka, 1914–1919* (Prague 2013, first edn Prague 1920), 26.
31. For a comparison, see the inspiring analysis of the connection between children's education and the dissemination of the militarized concept of masculinity in prewar Canada in Mark Moss, *Manliness and Militarism: Educating Young Boys in Ontario for War* (Oxford, 2001).
32. Hämmerle, 'Zur Relevanz des Connell'schen Konzepts hegemonialer Männlichkeit für "Militär und Männlichkeit/en in der Habsburgermonarchie (1868–1914/18)"', 103–21, especially 118–19.
33. See Christopher E. Forth, 'Introduction', in *French Masculinities*, 5–6; see also Tosh, 'The Old Adam and the New Man', 219, 238; or John Tosh, 'Hegemonic Masculinity and the History of Gender', in *Masculinities in Politics and War: Gendering Modern History*, 45–47.
34. Cole, 'Differentiation or Indifference?', in *Nationhood from Below*, 112.
35. Marie Koldinská and Ivan Šedivý, *Válka a armáda v českých dějinách. Sociohistorické črty* (Prague, 2008), 333–39; see also Jan Galandauer, 'Wacht am Rhein a Kde domov můj: Válečné nadšení v Čechách v létě 1914', *Historie a vojenství* 45, no. 5 (1996): 28–29.
36. Galandauer, 'Wacht am Rhein a Kde domov můj: Válečné nadšení v Čechách v létě 1914', 32–34.
37. See, for example, L. Padevět, 'Pražský domobranecký pluk č. 8 na bojišti', in *Domov za války*, vol. 1, 141–42; František Bouška, 'Zápisky ze světové války 1914–1920 a z čsl. revolučního vojska na Rusi' (unpublished manuscript), 5–6; František Skála, *Válečný deník, 1914–1918* (Kyšperk, 1937), 12; or František Tonar, ed., *Válečný deník: Český voják bojující v Rakousko-uherské armádě na východní frontě za 1. světové války* (Brno, 2008), 36, diary entry from 15 August 1914.
38. See Šedivý, *Češi, české země a Velká válka*, 37. According to Martin Zückert, the image of 'the unreliable and disloyal Czech' was mostly based on the very vocal activities of several (rather small) groups of anti-militarist nationalist radicals headed by the Czech National

Socialist Party. It was this party that was responsible for the First Anti-militarist Congress in Prague in 1907, and for the anti-war demonstrations against the annexation of Bosnia and Herzegovina a year later. See Martin Zückert, 'Antimilitarismus und soldatische Resistenz', in *Glanz – Gewalt – Gehorsam*, 199–220. However, there were indeed several 'military strikes' of Czech-speaking units during the early stages of the 1912 mobilization against Serbia, apparently motivated by pan-Slavic national discourse. See Richard G. Plaschka, 'Serbien und die Balkankriege als Motivationselemente in der österreichisch-ungarischen Armee', in *Nationalismus – Staatsgewalt – Widerstand. Aspekte nationaler und sozialer Entwicklung in Ostmittel- und Südeuropa*, ed. Horst Haselsteiner et al. (Vienna, 1985), 232–45; or Richard G. Plaschka, '"... a střílet nebudem!" Ein Modellfall zur Frage der Auswirkung der Balkankriege auf Österreich-Ungarn', in *Nationalismus – Staatsgewalt – Widerstand*, 246–52.

39. Quoted in Pazdera, 'Češi v první světové válce', 34.
40. Manfried Rauchensteiner, *The First World War and the End of the Habsburg Monarchy* (Vienna, 2014), 165.
41. Wagner, *S českým plukem na ruské frontě*, 15.
42. See L. Padevět, 'Pražský domobranecký pluk č. 8 na bojišti', in *Domov za války*, vol. 1, 136. For a similar example, see Jaroslav Vítek, *V cizích službách: deník ze světové války* (Česká Skalice, 1937), 20: 'They enlisted immediately and the mobilization went smoothly, so smoothly, that even the army was not expecting this'.
43. See, for example, Bouška, 'Zápisky ze světové války', 1b. The situation was the same at every garrison. For example, Václav Poláček did not reach the *presentierung* in Jindřichův Hradec until three days after his arrival because the regimental office was flooded by men coming to enlist. See Poláček, *Zápisky Václava Poláčka ze světové války*, 37, diary entry from 31 July 1914.
44. Chmela, *Vzpomínky z 1. světové války*, 7.
45. Josef Krejza, 'Vzpomínky z válečné doby', in *Domov za války*, vol. 5, 195; Kisch, *Vojákem pražského sboru*, 8, diary entry from 31 July 1914; recollection of Karel Pokorný, 'Vzpomínky z první světové války', ed. Ladislava Šuláková, *Malovaný kraj. Národopisný a vlastivědný časopis Slovácka* 6, no. 1 (2002): 8.
46. Josef Šula, 'Vzpomínky z Krakova r. 1914', in *Domov za války*, vol. 1, 223.
47. Diary entry from 31 July 1914, in Kisch, *Vojákem pražského sboru*, 8.
48. Ulrych, 'Moje zápisky', 22
49. A. Černý, 'První měsíc války', in *Domov za války*, vol. 1, 166.
50. Šmída, *Vzpomínky z vojny*, 10.
51. It was the behaviour of some of the Bohemian regiments during the mobilization of 1912 that led Austro-Hungarian authorities to doubt Czech soldiers' loyalty, as some units openly refused to be sent to war against their 'Serbian brothers'. See Rothenberg, *The Army of Francis Joseph*, 148 and 170.
52. Bedřich Opletal, *Anabáze hanáckého medika, 1914–1920* (Prague, 1998), 5.
53. Lynn, *Bayonets of the Republic*, 24–25.
54. Alexander Watson, 'Mutinies and Military Morale', in *The Oxford Illustrated History of the First World War*, vol. 2, 178–79. There are of course exceptions to this observation; one to be found in our sources came from Jaroslav Vítek's description of a night attack in the Kras Mountains in September 1917, where he specifically mentions being 'motivated by the revolver' in the hands of the lieutenant to follow orders. See Vítek, *V cizích službách*, 158.

55. Vítek, *V cizích službách*, 23.
56. Diary entry from 6 August 1914; Vaněk, *Charašó pán, da?*, 10.
57. Černý, *Moje záznamy ze světové války*, 31.
58. Kápar, *Cestou kamenitou*, 13. The author sees the passivity as amounting to 'cowardice', seemingly understanding it as an antithesis to manly behaviour. The feeling of being a slave is sometimes present even in contemporary diaries; see Skála, *Válečný deník*, 9. However, it is especially popular *topoi* in retrospective, as many authors are using their memoirs to vindicate and explain their actions in 1914 in a way that would make them look to be Czech patriots. This leads to a popular vocabulary based on the idea of 'slavery' in many of the memoirs; see, for example, A. Černý, 'První měsíc války', in *Domov za války*, vol. 1, 162; or Josef Šefl, *Paměti domobrance 28. pluku z války světové 1914–1918* (Budweis, 1922), 10.
59. Diary entry from 16 February 1915, in Vaněk, *Charašó pán, da?*, 36.
60. Josef Jarkovský, 'Kronika ze světové války od roku 1/2 1915 do 4/9 1919' (unpublished manuscript, Archivní sbírka Vlastivědného muzea v Dobrušce, sig. XIV/300), 2.
61. Oldřich Jurman, ed., *Legionářská odyssea: Deník Františka Prudila* (Prague, 1990), 9.
62. Jan F. Tříska, ed., *Zapomenutá fronta: vojákův deník a úvahy jeho syna* (Prague, 2001), 23. Published in English as *The Great War's Forgotten Front* (New York, 1998).
63. Jan Šmatlán to his parents, 19 December 1914, in *Zapomenuté hlasy: korespondence, deníkové záznamy a kresby z první světové války*, eds Milada Krulichová and Milan Jankovič (Hradec Králové, 1986), 18. For a rather similar conclusion regarding the ultimate unenthusiastic passivity of the Czech soldiers' Slovak counterparts, see Dudeková Kováčová, 'The Silent Majority', 718–20.
64. The topic of taking or not taking military oath is almost obsessively mentioned by many of the most anti-Austrian authors of Žipek's collection *Domov za války*, but is also apparent in some of the sources written during the war itself – see, for example, the diary of František Bouška, who was not present during the ritual of oath-taking and spends several paragraphs of making a point of it – Bouška, *Zápisky ze světové války*, 2b. This only confirms the psychological importance of this symbolic act of military obedience in the early twentieth century, as mentioned by Richard Holmes. See Holmes, *Acts of War*, 45–47.
65. František Konipásek, 'Železnice za války', in *Domov za války*, vol. 1, 65.
66. Diary entries of 15 and 16February 1915, in Vaněk, *Charašó pán, da?*, 33–34.
67. As Karel Pichlik bitterly concluded in his study, written with the purpose of proving that Czech soldiers actively opposed the war (actually referred to in its title), in 1914, Czechs were enlisting 'in a resigned mood and with much indifference'. See Pichlík, *Čeští vojáci proti válce*, 26. The Austrian historian Richard Lein later concurred with this point of view, adding in one of his texts that the 'Czech troops marched willingly to fight for the Emperor and their country'. Lein, 'The "Betrayal" of the k.u.k. Infantry Regiment 28', 326. Perhaps the most extensive analysis of the topic, the unpublished thesis of David Pazdera, concluded in 1997 that 'most Czechs fulfilled their duty … without any dissent or enthusiasm, hoping it would all be over soon'. See Pazdera, 'Češi v první světové válce', 42.
68. Wagner, *S českým plukem na ruské frontě*, 7–8.
69. Healy, *Vienna and the Fall of the Habsburg Empire*, 165.
70. Diary entry from 15 February 1915, in Vaněk, *Charašó pán, da?*, 36.
71. Diary of Anna Lauermannová-Mikschová, entry from the summer of 1914, quoted in Milena Lenderová, *A ptáš se knížko má. Ženské deníky 19. století* (Prague, 2008), 135, footnote 87. Within the same context, Marie Gebauerová noted in her diary on the day

her boyfriend went to war: 'He is going, angry in his soul that he has to'. Quoted in ibid., 134, footnote 84.
72. Chmela, *Vzpomínky z 1. světové války*, 7.
73. See, for example, Jan Morávek, *Špatný voják* (Prague, 1929), 63; or numerous instances in the *Domov za války* collection.
74. See Connell, *Masculinities*, 76–77.
75. Šmída, *Vzpomínky z vojny*, 12.
76. See František Kylar, 'Vzpomínky z vojny: Válečné paměti 1917–1918', in *Rodové paměti v Kunčicích*, eds Alois Kněžek and Emil Vondrouš (Ústí nad Orlicí, 2006), 34; Josef Slezák, *Paměti Josefa Slezáka k I. světové válce* (Archival Collection, Regional Museum in Dobruška, unprocessed manuscript), vol. 1, 3.
77. Květoň, *Vzpomínky z první světové války*, 3.
78. Opletal, *Anabáze hanáckého medika*, 6.
79. Jindřich Hušák, 'Dvacetiletý ve válce', in *Domov za války*, vol. 3, 203.
80. On young men and their position in masculine hierarchies, see John Tosh, 'What Should Historians Do with Masculinity? Reflections on Nineteenth-Century Britain', *History Workshop Journal* 38, no. 1 (1994): 184–87.
81. Augustin Mudrák, *Bojoval jsem za císaře pána*, ed. Jiří Červenka (Brno, 2011), 14.
82. Šmída, *Vzpomínky z vojny*, 13.
83. Karel Poláček, *Hrdinové táhnou do boje* (Prague, 1994), 26.
84. Šmída, *Vzpomínky z vojny*, 25.
85. Stanislav Kostka Neumann, 'Válčení civilistovo', in *Spisy Stanislava K. Neumanna* (Prague, 1976), 9.
86. Vladislav Vančura, *Pole orná a válečná* (Prague, 1966), 108.
87. See Connell, *Masculinities*, 76–77.
88. Alexander Watson has identified the same phenomenon of social pressure created because of, and even by women, also as a part of British soldiers' motivation. See Watson, *Enduring the Great War*, 53–54.
89. Kolman, 'Vojačka' [A Soldier-Girl] (1913), in *Cassiovy listy*, ed. Jaroslav Kolman (Prague, 1921).
90. Poláček, *Hrdinové táhnou do boje*, 22.
91. František Kellner, 'Vzpomínky', in *Domov za války*, vol. 1, 162.
92. Vítek, *V cizích službách*, 20.
93. Diary entry from 1 August 1914, in Kisch, *Vojákem pražského sboru*, 12.
94. Jan Šmatlán to his parents, 20 January 1915, in *Zapomenuté hlasy*, 24.
95. Skála, *Válečný deník*, 235–36.
96. Šmída, *Vzpomínky z vojny*, 60.
97. Ulrych, 'Moje zápisky', 65.
98. Kučera, *Rationed Life*, 103–5.
99. Hämmerle, 'Zur Relevanz des Connell'schen Konzepts hegemonialer Männlichkeit für "Militär und Männlichkeit/en in der Habsburgermonarchie (1868–1914/18)"', 114–16.
100. 'The attraction of sharing the exclusively male company is usually strongest among the young, single men who are yet not able to enjoy the full benefits of masculinity'; Tosh, 'What Should Historians Do with Masculinity?', 487. See also Ute Frevert, *Nation in Barracks: Modern Germany, Military Conscription, and Civil Society* (Oxford, 2004), 173–76; or Schmale, *Geschichte der Männlichkeit in Europa*, 151.

101. Jurman, ed., *Legionářská odyssea*, 9.
102. Diary entry from 31 July 1914, in Kisch, *Vojákem pražského sboru*, 9.
103. Václav Weinstein, 'U válečného loďstva', in *Domov za války*, vol. 3, 81.
104. Diary entry from 24 May 1916, Dolejší, *Válečné vzpomínky z první světové války vojína Dolejše*, 11.
105. František Mikulášek, 'Slovácko na počátku války', in *Domov za války*, vol. 1, 123; and Vaněk, *Charašó pán, da?*, 10, entry for 6 August 1914. Vaněk noted the escape to social drinking as early as 27 July: 'The pubs are full and people are having debates everywhere... Many a headache there...' Entry for July 27, 1914, ibid., 10.
106. Vaněk, *Charašó pán, da?*, 10, entry for July 27, 1914.
107. Vítek, *V cizích službách*, 20.
108. Hušák, 'Dvacetiletý ve válce', in *Domov za války*, vol. 3, 205.
109. For a thesis on how the expectation and longing for adventurous experience influenced the prewar generation in Great Britain and the United States, see Michael C. Adams, *The Great Adventure: Male Desire and the Coming of World War I* (Bloomington, 1990).
110. Šmatlán to his parents, 15 or 16 January 1915, in *Zapomenuté hlasy*, 22.
111. Dolejší, *Válečné vzpomínky z první světové války vojína Dolejše*, 7, entry from 11 May 1916.
112. Šmída, *Vzpomínky z vojny*, 15.
113. Josef Váchal, *Malíř na frontě: Soča a Italie 1917–18* (Prague, 1996), 12.
114. Diary entry from 3 September 1914, in Kisch, *Vojákem pražského sboru*, 74.
115. By the end of 1914, 950 people were arrested in Bohemia for political offences. See Rauchensteiner, *The First World War and the End of the Habsburg Monarchy*, 267–68.
116. For early criticism of the whole 'revolutionary action thesis', see Milada Paulová, *Dějiny Maffie*, vol. 1 (Prague, 1937), 202–4. For a thorough analysis of the event, see Pazdera, 'Češi v první světové válce', 101–10.
117. Černý, *Moje záznamy ze světové války*, 28.
118. In the early 1990s, the historian Petr Havel came to the conclusion that 'regiments recruited in the countryside and among the peasant population appeared to be more disciplined than those originating from cities and industrial agglomerations', seeing the roots of this phenomenon in the different normative circumstances of individual class experience. See Petr Havel, 'K otázce bojové morálky českých vojáků v počáteční fázi první světové války', in *Od Sarajeva k velké válce/Ab Sarajewo zum Grossen Krieg* (Prague, 1995), 47–55.
119. The army general staff first came up with the idea, motivated by security reasons, in 1913. It only came to fruition in late 1914, after the initial lack of success in the war brought the Army High Command back to its deeply held stereotypes of 'suspect nationalities' in the ranks. See Rothenberg, *The Army of Francis Joseph*, 171.
120. For typical examples of these scenes, see Kisch, *Vojákem pražského sboru*, 13; Kápar, *Cestou kamenitou*, 19–21 and 25; Slezák, *Paměti Josefa Slezáka k I. světové válce*, 10 and 16; Chmela, *Vzpomínky z 1. světové války*, 9; and many others.
121. Jurman, ed., *Legionářská odyssea*, 10.
122. See Cole, *Military Culture and Popular Patriotism in Late Imperial Austria*, 309–10.
123. Morávek, *Špatný voják*, 63.

Chapter 2

COMPROMISES OF MANLINESS
Everyday Experience

Lost souls praying only for warmth, bread, and sex.

—Josef Váchal

Josef Slezák, a 24-year-old farmer and the only son of a widowed mother from České Meziříčí in Eastern Bohemia, received the first news of mobilization while preparing the family farm for the harvest: 'Everybody was devastated by the news … My mother hugged me, crying'. Later, on Tuesday, 27 July 1914, he finally left his home for the garrison town of Hradec Králové, to join the 3rd Company of k.u.k. Infantry Regiment 18: 'It's hard to describe how I felt during those first few days. Just the thought! Harvest coming, just bought a young horse, and suddenly, I'm leaving all that to my old, sick mother'.[1] After seeing combat on the Galician front in September, he was wounded during the first siege of Przemysl and was sent home to recover: 'The thought that I'd have to go back there in two weeks was always on my mind. But we were hoping the war would be over soon. Oh Lord, please let it end soon! Dear Lord, hear us out!'[2] His prayers went unanswered and he was finally sent back to his unit in April 1915, more or less reconciled to his fate. After joining the regiment in the field, he served as an infantryman and later a section commander both in Galicia and, since March 1916, in the Tyrolean Alps. While clearly homesick, he left only sparse comments on his service during those days. However, by mid 1916, he was becoming increasingly disaffected. In June 1916, he was wounded in the leg in a skirmish with an Italian patrol (after the war he reinterprets the wound as self-inflicted, perhaps to make it sound more 'patriotic'). After spending a few months in several hospitals, he was finally sent to recover at a convalescence centre back in Eastern Bohemia and later to a training unit, where he assumed training duties.

Most of the time, he was content with his rather comfortable situation, dividing his time between lazy service with the unit and long 'agricultural leaves' at the family farm during the spring and summer of 1917. He was happy as long as he was not sent back to the front: 'I hope this is my last diary entry', he wrote on 25 June 1917. 'I have no desire to go back there again'.[3] When the moment finally came in late August 1917, it was not to the front but to the fields of Eastern Galicia, where his mixed unit of previously wounded veterans and fresh *Landsturm* conscripts was ordered to help with the harvest. Clearly dismayed by this task and the ever-present danger of real frontline duty ('What's in store next?')[4], Slezák checked out sick, feigning at least some of his ailments, only to live in constant fear of being sent back: 'Thank God, just not anywhere near the front', he wrote in late October, when he finally managed to be sent to a field hospital. Even though he was finally sent back to the hinterland later in the month, he was deeply depressed, 'praying to God that I won't have to go back, hoping he'll hear me out'.[5] This time, his prayers were apparently answered and he spent the winter of 1917 back in Eastern Bohemia, doing whatever he could to stay there (i.e. malingering and bribing both officers and officials with foodstuffs from his farm), partly recovering, partly on 'agricultural leave'. When he was finally ordered back to his unit in February 1918, it drove him 'to the edge of despair' and thoughts of suicide.[6] He returned to the Piave front anyway and served the Empire as a depressed, uninspired, but still physically present soldier until he was granted further leave in early November 1918. When he came down from his position high on an Alpine glacier, he was swept along with the mass of the disintegrating army and became a prisoner of war soon afterwards.

The wartime story of Josef Slezák, based on his five-volume diary-memoir (a retrospective diary he was completing during and immediately after the war from his notes), is a typical both in terms of the story itself and in the way it is presented. While the early draft of the manuscript brings us a textured narrative with the main protagonist's 'character development' from compliance to one's manly duty, fuelled by hopes of a quick war in 1914, through gradual disappointment, self-denial and disillusionment, all the way to his ultimate psychological as well as physical exhaustion bordering on an outright anti-war (but not anti-Austrian) attitude, the additions written after the war (ranging from 1931 to 1964) increasingly try to reinterpret many of the events (especially the protagonist's combat record and the wounds he sustained in service) in such a way that would portray him as anti-war and possibly anti-Austrian from the very beginning. While it is difficult to ascertain the real truth here, this tendency is rather typical of Czech narratives of the First World War in general. Memoirs more often than not take on an anti-Austrian and anti-war tone, adopting the ever-more popular image of Josef Švejk in the process. Their goal is to create a general impression that Czech soldiers, with a few loathsome exceptions, objected to the war from the very beginning and sabotaged the imperial war effort through various forms of resistance throughout, even though they remained in service until the very end. On the other hand, the accounts written during the war, especially those that escaped later editions, put forward a different picture, more or less similar to that of Slezák's original narrative. While in the former case there is a clear effort to connect one's own life experience with the official Czechoslovak memory of the war,[7] the latter is a much more faithful image of motivational dynamics in wartime.

Josef Slezák's quest through the horrors of war seems to provide an excellent example of the quiet, grudgingly compliant wartime existence, one that the historian Richard Lein neatly defined as lying between 'acceptance and refusal'. Studying 'soldiers' attitude towards war', Lein came to the same conclusion that can be assumed from many a soldier's personal writings – that the morale of the Austro-Hungarian army dropped sharply after the illusion of a short war dissolved during the first winter of the war, which also revealed the army's ill-preparedness. The crisis escalated when casualties topped one million in November 1914 and became even worse during the disastrous Carpathian campaign in early 1915.[8] However, after the Austro-Hungarian army succeeded, with substantial help from Imperial Germany, in stabilizing the Eastern Front after the Gorlice-Tarnów Offensive in May 1915, Czech soldiers' morale seems to have reached a sort of equilibrium, which then lasted almost two years. Only the events of 1917, with the number of inconclusive battles on the Isonzo River reaching ten, and after the bloody Kerensky Offensive in July 1917, seem to have once again pushed the soldiers' morale into a downward spiral. The collapse of the Russian war effort along with the Bolshevik Revolution and the worsening economic situation in the hinterland only seem to have exacerbated this trend. 'The war still going on, without end, sucks all the remaining joy of being alive out of us', wrote Bohumil Sperling in his diary in October 1917, reflecting upon his situation on the eve of the Caporetto offensive. 'If only it all went to hell'.[9]

War was increasingly seen as an affair without end, regardless of the number of offensives, victories or casualties. When POWs started to be repatriated from Russia in early 1918, some of them brought home ideas of revolution, while most were strongly disinclined towards any further combat service. The collapsing economy not only made the soldiers hungry, it also brought the threat of famine to their families at home, while the Central Powers' advances on the Italian front showcased that the enemies, whatever their military abilities, were now much better supplied than the Austro-Hungarian army. Then, when disaster struck in the form of the hellish experience during the final unsuccessful offensive of the Habsburg army on the Piave in June 1918, soldiers' morale hit rock bottom. As a staff officer wrote of the general situation in the 10th Army in September 1918, 'enthusiasm for the war is completely missing. Most of the men are apathetic, but they will fulfil their duty … The longing for peace is widespread … Morale is indeed being damaged by material hardships, but especially by the conditions in the hinterland'.[10] In combination with the reports of German armies retreating on the Western Front, Czech soldiers were increasingly susceptible to reacting positively to the propaganda of the politicians in exile promoting the idea of Czechoslovakia.[11] However, most of them, like Josef Slezák, merely ended up waiting it out. The end finally came on 24 October 24 1918, when the already disintegrating army fell apart in the face of the final Italian offensive. When retreat turned to flight, it was no longer the once glorious imperial army, as each national group made a retreat of its own. It was only now, in early November 1918, that the longtime crisis of morale in the Austro-Hungarian army finally rose to the surface with all its destructive force.

In our sources, there are actually many examples of those who, like Josef Slezák, 'fulfilled their duty' to the very end, apparently unable to break with the motivational structures that kept them in service. As a member of k.k. Landwehr Infantry Regiment 4 remembered after the war: 'I had been reading the papers every day and knew for sure that the Italians would start an offensive against us, and I knew that our guys would lose badly because there were too few of them'. Even so, men stayed, waiting for official permission to leave as they always had. Many, including the *Landwehr* infantryman, were loyal enough to return from their furloughs even as late as October 1918: 'I didn't want to go back ... But they could have been really tough on me, you know, and so I decided to return to the field of war'.[12] Fears of punishment, an excellent example of coercion, were still strong enough in 1918 to motivate men to keep fighting. This is something to keep in mind throughout the following chapter, which analyses the motivational structures that *sustained* most of the Czech men in the army until the very end of the war. We will see that the experience of masculinity, which played an important role in getting men into the army, was gradually compromised by the nature of the war itself and by the emergent social changes. As a result, men were left increasingly doubting the meaning of the war and, at the end, even the legitimacy of the state that made it. Over time, it was the ultimate argument of law, force and power that grew more important than ever in shaping soldiers' compliance, to remain almost the sole motivational factor at the very end.[13]

The theory of military motivation advanced by John Lynn places everything that a soldier experiences between enlistment and entering combat under the structural umbrella of 'sustaining motivation'.[14] According to Lynn, the primary group and willingness to follow the authorities' orders play a key role here, in addition to a wide range of smaller factors that make up a soldier's morale – starting with faith in the cause and ending with soldiers' relationship with their home. While Czech-speaking soldiers in the Austro-Hungarian army did not see much sense in the war, their normative compliance nonetheless caused them to heed the call to serve. Subsequently it was the sustaining motivation that kept them going for up to four years.

The primary group cohesion and its dynamics is something that Czech soldiers often understood and described under the notion of *comradeship* – a notion that is, as we will see, one with heavily gendered overtones, as is the relationship with the authority figures and with the hinterland. These are all factors that will be covered in the following chapters. However, before starting on this, it is necessary to pause for a while over those topics that receive only minor treatment in Lynn's theory of sustaining motivation, but that represent a backdrop to the complex picture of the Czech soldiers' experience not only of the war itself, but also of their masculinity caught in its midst.

Bread

Josef Váchal, the painter, illustrator, sculptor, poet and mystic all at once, 'became stuck in the Austrian military machine forever' in 1916, becoming an acute observer of the war itself, but also of his comrades, whom he later described as 'lost souls, praying only for warmth, bread, and sex'.[15] Writing about his service with an artillery regiment on the Isonzo front, he noted the change in the subject of his fellow soldiers' debates when the logistical crisis erupted in full: 'The one and only thing we were constantly talking about was *food* ... We did not care about anything else but food and hunger; it must be said that my comrades were truly the blessed meek, blinded by the sin of their birth, being driven to the slaughterhouse'.[16] Reflecting upon the situation, he would probably agree with George Orwell's colourful observation of the effects hunger and poverty have on one's perception of reality: 'Only food could rouse you. You discover that a man who has gone even a week on bread and margarine is not a man any longer, only a belly with a few accessory organs'.[17] Believing that such a state of mind is only a consequence of true human nature stripped of the protective layers of civilization, Váchal further claimed that war had revealed the fact that man is 'nothing but a cluster of nerves and digestive organs'.[18] As a result, when the situation became critical, the only thing most people *really* cared about was food, and everything else was secondary as long as this primary need was satisfied. Only then, in his view, did 'warmth and sex' come to the fore.[19]

Other soldiers concurred, including Egon Erwin Kisch, lying in a skirmish line somewhere in Serbia during a summer night in 1914:

> Half asleep, I got something like an erotic thought running through my mind. It was a first such excitement I'd had here, and as it was really out of place, it dissipated quickly. I think it's the same with the others, as there are no crude jokes to be heard these days. It seems that the great desire for peace ... is firmly planted in the insatiable craving for a good piece of pork and a pint of Písek or Smíchov lager.[20]

It seems that in many a soldier's mind, even home had shrunk to an image of good food and drink, and that this idea was able to push sexual desires into the background, even in a mind so erotically charged as Kisch's.

Regarding the Czech soldiers' personal writings, it indeed seems that the main worries of most of the men revolved around a few simple dichotomies: hunger/food, cold/warm, wet/dry, rest/fatigue, healthy/sick, safety/danger.[21] 'Good chow', safety and a warm place to stay are perennial topics in most of the sources used here, and some of the men scarcely talk about anything else, perhaps beside their other favourite topic – mail.[22] 'Peace and quiet, rest, something to eat, time to sleep, and nothing biting me', noted Jan Tříska, a happy artilleryman, in his diary on leave, summarizing everything that counted in a soldier's life.[23] In the same vein, the infantryman František Černý happily relished the fact that that the army's retreat during the Brusilov Offensive of June 1916 became much less tiresome after 'we had something to eat again and did not have to run for our lives for a while'.[24] Josef Slezák has described the same elementary need of having a full stomach and a feeling of safety in a rather unremarkable poem, written while in a hospital: 'Here it's all tolerable / most of it to those able / chow is good, wine enough / no-one's sleeping in the rough'.[25] The all-important role played by simple basic needs in a soldier's life is perhaps best summarized in the words of another, somewhat more capable poet:

> Oh war, we should not remember you smiling, perhaps we should not find anything worthy of a smile while thinking of you. You were a bitch. You were a cunt. But sometimes you looked at us with sparkling, sky blue eyes, and life was never more promising than at those moments ... Sometimes the wind brought a smell from the woods that we had never smelled before; and while on a bad day we could die in those woods, they never hugged us more gently or with more tenderness. Sometimes we were wet to the bone for three days in a row, but on the fourth day we got dry and felt so happy, as if it only took a dry coat for us to see the light of the ultimate, perfect happiness.[26]

According to this summary, penned by Fráňa Šrámek, a writer, poet and combat medic who served on the Serbian, Italian and Romanian fronts, soldiers' physical needs were satisfied in such a haphazard and unpredictable manner, never enough in general, that even the most fleeting moments of peace, comfort and abundance had to be enjoyed to the maximum while they lasted. The situation on the battlefield was changing with every moment and all that was available now could be taken away a few seconds later. What is even more important for us here, though, is that fulfilment of these needs was mostly beyond the soldiers' control.

The key importance of 'bread' in the range of a soldier's elementary needs is obvious from many sources. 'It was so happy I could hardly breathe', Egon Erwin Kisch noted in his diary when he finally received some quality food while on the Serbian front in the autumn of 1914. 'It's always the same, soup and beef, it's killing me. Now, when I was given a plum cake, tears came to my eyes'.[27] Kisch's note shows us clearly that references to food in personal sources are highly relative – at the beginning of the war, men were quick to complain about monotonous meals consisting of earthy vegetable soups and hard beef, while a few years later, or even at the same time, but in a different unit with less military luck or less logistically competent leadership, these would be considered heavenly gifts. The same went for tobacco, of course, as its importance in many a soldier's eyes surpassed even that of a full stomach: 'My comrade next to me fully agreed with me. Rather miss the evening chow than lose one's tobacco ration', Josef Váchal recalled.[28] The fact that rank-and-file men were 'happiest when given cigarettes' during ration distribution was also noted by another artilleryman, Karel Jaroš, who served with the Austro-Hungarian detachment in Palestine.[29] The infantry was naturally no different, as a soldier from a Galician regiment observed: 'Out there, at the front, one just had to have enough smokes to make it through, one didn't even have to eat that much. Especially heavy smokers were like that'.[30]

The known side-effect of nicotine, i.e. that it lowers the appetite, would become useful to those who served through 1917 and 1918, when the Austro-Hungarian state slowly became incapable of supplying its field armies properly. The periods familiar to every soldier, when there is nothing to eat except what is stolen, were becoming distressingly longer. The successful offensive at Caporetto in late October 1917 had only a limited effect in that it enabled the participating formations to plunder and pillage their way through the newly acquired Italian territory before the riches of the previously untouched countryside north of the Piave quickly ran out.[31] Then, in 1918, most of the accounts invariably shift their attention towards the one and only problem – where to get some food. Sometimes it seems that whole units of the Austro-Hungarian army were doing nothing else.[32] The desperation of this situation is clear even from the privileged point of view of an officer: 'War shortages are starting to manifest themselves in our food supply', František Šmída recalled of his experience with the Croatian k.u.k. Infantry Regiment 79 in the Dolomites in July 1918:

> Bread rations were miserable, mostly corn, and too little anyway. Meat was scarce as well, especially with regiments such as ours which refused horse meat ... We made spinach out of nettles ... We also had little success in searching for the once ubiquitous wine. The wine we got in our rations was getting worse by the day, almost undrinkable. The officers' food supply was still acceptable, and we did not starve or anything, but the days of feasts were definitely over.[33]

In other units, 'soldiers were horribly weakened from starvation',[34] 'stealing food constantly',[35] and often fought with their comrades over the miserable rations the army was still able to get to them: 'The mess they made when the kettles were put on and rations distributed ... is beyond description. People were all over the cauldrons, fighting each other like dragons ... Come the time to distribute the rations to the men in the tunnel, even the wops in Monfalcone must have heard the ruckus the guys were making'.[36] Even before the final offensive on the

Piave, the official, rarely met daily ration was 250 grams of bread and 170 grams of horsemeat per man; on the first day of the attack, 15 June 1918, even this meagre quantity was lowered further still in some units, sometimes being almost halved.[37] By the end of the summer, the supply situation had become critical and some of the soldiers made the clear connection between material wellbeing and their sustaining motivation: 'About noon I went to get my rations, but ugh, what a piece of shit. Dried vegetables soup with worms floating around, looking like noodles, dried sea fish, all smelling like fish oil to me ... If the officers had to eat the same as we do, the war would have been over ages ago'.[38]

As noted by Mark Cornwall, 'the underlying food crisis ... which had its roots in the Entente blockade, deepened substantially ... 1918 notoriously became the year when the army was "living from hand to mouth" while the authorities frantically improvised with short-term solutions'. While identifying the crisis as one of the factors in the army's decline (alongside internal ideological divisions rooted in nationalism and related enemy propaganda), he pointedly identifies it as 'always the most basic threat to morale', making ideological discontent much worse and dangerous to the army's cohesion in the process.[39] In a telling example, the infamous military mutinies that occurred during 1918 (as in the Bay of Kotor (Cattaro) in February, or in Rumburk in May 1918, to name those with substantial participation of Czech-speaking servicemen) were to a large extent initially motivated by miserable supply conditions, only to grow into anti-war rebellions momentously inspired by the events in Russia.[40] The failure of the army to supply the troops properly was increasingly damaging their motivation at its core, undermining the legitimacy of the army and the monarchy at the most fundamental level: 'Hunger and general war-weariness were wearing down even the most loyal Austrians. Soldiers were going on leave and not coming back. The gendarmes were powerless'.[41] Desertion rates skyrocketed in 1918 as – fears of punishment notwithstanding – men started to succumb in large numbers to war-weariness and the depressing emptiness of their stomachs.[42]

The clear connection between the supply situation and motivation is obvious not only from soldiers' complaints, but also in the moments when 'the war looked at them with sky blue eyes' of abundant foodstuffs, safety and comfort. Josef Slezák describes 'a merry indeed march' of his battalion in May 1918, with 'good chow', beautiful sunny weather, bathing breaks and 'patriotic songs' being sung, as if it were a holiday trek through Italian countryside, not a redeployment from one part of the Piave front to another.[43] In addition, it is hardly surprising to see that the men whose supplies were relatively plentiful thanks to their position in the army hierarchy were usually more optimistic and loyal to the war effort. For example, the rear-echelon troops experienced a distinctively different war from that lived through every day by the soldiers in the frontlines: 'My life is just wonderful right now', noted regimental surgeon's assistant Alois Dolejší in his diary in February 1918. 'I'd be happy to live like this till the end of the war, even if it takes three years'. However, his diary is a rather typical example of the relative nature of human existence, because he soon started to complain about 'always the same vegetables and polenta'. Also, as evidence of the fact that in war nothing is certain, he then suddenly lost his privileged position in July 1918, being transferred to the malarious hell of the Albanian front, soon longing to taste 'vegetables and polenta' once again.[44]

The underlying importance of food for soldiers' morale and motivation is particularly obvious in the moments when it influenced their very willingness to fight. Egon Erwin Kisch's diary provides us with two examples, first mentioning 'the biggest cowards ... leaving cover under fire when there's a chance to get food', only for he himself to become one of them when his company abruptly changed its attitude to frontline service when they were told that 'chow had been brought up front ... Starved to death, we were immediately eager to go over to the firing line'.[45] The fact that this was not an isolated case of the stomach triumphing over fear is further proven by an example from Josef Váchal's memoir where he describes two soldiers in his supply train (therefore quite far towards the rear) who volunteered for trench-digging duty in the second line (under fire of Italian artillery), saying: 'At least we'll get something to eat there'.[46]

Warmth

While it is possible to speculate on the extent to which the offensive actions of the Austro-Hungarian army during 1918 were motivated by the soldiers' eagerness to occupy the much better-supplied enemy trenches, there is little evidence in the soldiers' writings that the same could be in any way applied to Váchal's metaphorical 'warmth'. Feelings of comfort and safety are almost always (with the exception of the most horrific positions in the worst places imaginable) associated with one's own trench or dugout, especially if dry and well-built, but surprisingly often even with one that felt somewhat improvised or outright symbolic. It seems that safety especially was more about *feeling safe* that really *being safe*: 'I think that had a shell hit the roof, the gingerbread walls full of woodworm wouldn't do. But sometimes it's just the feeling of cover that is enough for one to feel safe'.[47] Besides stray shells, there were many other negative external factors influencing a soldier's physical wellbeing or the way in which he experienced it. Vagaries of weather, ranging from the heatwaves of Galicia through the deadly frosts in the Carpathians to avalanches in the Alps, were often responsible for suffering that was dangerous not only to the men's physical health, but also to their morale and mental stability: 'Uncovered trenches, knee-deep in water, lashed by freezing rain mixed with hailstones and snow. One of the comrades who could not suffer any longer had shot himself'.[48] Fatigue bordering on exhaustion is a staple image of several sources, as the largest part of a soldier's service was taken

Figure 2.1 A postcard sent by 'Emil' on 1 April 1915, eloquently articulating the core reality of a soldier's experience: heavy work, bad weather and more heavy work (Museum of Eastern Bohemia, Hradec Králové).

up not by combat, but either by hard physical labour or – particularly in 1914 and 1915 – long, exhausting marches: 'Sixteen hours a day on foot. Day after day', recalled one *Landwehr* infantryman.[49] Individual sense of masculinity may have well played a role in fighting fatigue, as for example with František Černý, who, during the retreat after the Brusilov Offensive in July 1916, repeatedly told himself to 'man up' and go on, instead of waiting to be captured.[50]

Adding to the exhaustion was a constant lack of sleep that is noted even more often – even when the operational situation had stabilized and the armies had settled in entrenched positions, the digging, repairs and supply operations were almost exclusively nocturnal affairs, with incessant artillery and machine-gun exchanges becoming a constant feature of the frontline, sporadically erupting into lengthy whirlwinds of actual barrages of fire. When too many of these factors occurred around the same group of men for too long, the 'vegetative state' described by Richard Holmes threatened to take over their existence after a while (sixty to ninety days of sustained combat on average), with men giving up on caring about anything, including whether they were alive or dead.[51] Czech soldiers were susceptible to this breakdown as much as anyone else – one of them wrote the following in a letter to his family in 1917: 'Often I have no idea what day of the week it is. It could be Tuesday, or Saturday, I don't care anyway. I just don't care about anything'.[52] Three years earlier, another soldier described the same feeling: 'I kind of don't care about anything these days. I'm not scared of death. I even expect it, unconcerned and calm'.[53] The 'unconcerned' attitude was, according to another man, 'a product of complete physical and spiritual fatigue, of one's whole body being exhausted'.[54]

Besides exhaustion, insufficient hygiene could also be destructive to the soldiers' morale, especially when it brought a large array of parasites in tow, causing extreme discomfort. There is hardly a Czech soldier's diary or a memoir that fails to mention this topic – most of the men, even the officers, tend to be rather obsessed by it, whether are they describing their frontline experience or their service at the rear: 'It is getting colder and colder. Moreover, there are the insects. Our skin is on fire, raw from all the scratching and chafing'.[55] The issue seems to be a rather universal one in any soldier's experience. As noted by Stéphane Audoin-Rouzeau in his study of French trench newspapers, rain, mud, weather, 'brutality and barbarity of existence', lack of hygiene, rats, lice, as well as the current state of food supplies, idleness and boredom, are 'always the object of close attention'.[56]

Each of the above-mentioned factors influenced the soldiers in its own specific way, but what they had in common was their cumulative character. And as the British military surgeon and Western Front veteran Charles McMoran Wilson (later Lord Moran) said about the nature of human courage: 'Courage is will-power, whereof no man has an unlimited stock; and when in war it is used up, he is finished. A man's courage is his capital and he is always spending' in war.[57] What Moran is talking about here is courage in war, not necessarily in combat itself, i.e. sustaining motivation. However, combat is at the core of the war experience, almost synonymous with death or wounds, and the very *idea* that one could actually end up in such a situation therefore also weighed heavily enough on the structure of sustaining motivation. As Egon Erwin Kisch noted in his diary, 'we're going into battle against the Serbs tomorrow. It's a depressing idea … When one is already in the water, it doesn't feel that cold, and it's the same with being under fire. It's the feeling *before* one gets there that makes men quiver with fear'.[58] It actually seems that the very *idea* of combat was worse than the experience of it, as while at the rear, away from the sensory overload of being under fire or firing back, men had enough time to think about what lay ahead: 'It was the thinking that hurt more than the physical suffering when in the trenches, marching, attacking or retreating … The worst psychological torments always came in reserve'.[59] One of the problems was the very nature of modern warfare as it developed in the early twentieth century – more or less static lines, quick-firing long-range artillery and later, on the Italian front, even bomber aircraft, all these factors brought a previously unknown sensation of almost constant danger to the soldier's experience, along with the poor capacity that a common soldier had to confront these dangers. The only way to leave them behind was to leave the combat zone, which, however, now covered hundreds of square miles.⁶⁰ As a result, although engagement in actual combat was rare enough, men *felt* they were in combat most of the time, with all the consequences mentioned above.

Even though the Austro-Hungarian command, after the first few months of hard-earned experience, was well aware of the limits of endurance of its troops and accordingly tried to rotate troops in the frontline as much as possible, operational reasons or even the terrain itself (typically mountains such as the Carpathians or the Alps, often in connection with inclement weather) often conspired against this, prolonging frontline duty from a week or two into months. Lack of manpower had to be factored in as well, forcing units to stay put simply because there was no one to replace them, or to skip rest periods and simply march from one sector of the line to another. These situations, often reflected upon in the sources, frequently brought resentment not just because many men came close to complete exhaustion and a vegetative state in the process, but also because any movement lost them the hard-earned small comforts of their own trenches, in exchange for increased danger in unknown territory. These troubles rose to the surface especially during the crisis the army experienced in the winter of 1914 to 1915 in Galicia (combat fatigue was probably one of the key factors in causing the infamous surrender of k.u.k. Infantry Regiment 28 in April 1915)⁶¹ and again during 1917, only to deteriorate substantially further during 1918. Whatever the army command tried to do, its inability to relieve the frontline troops for any sensible amount of time undoubtedly contributed to the general malaise and disillusionment spreading through the ranks in the final months of the war.⁶²

As the static conditions of trench warfare gradually came to dominate the war experience, replacing the centuries-long military reality of long marches, foraging and winter quarters with a year-long siege on a massive scale, many Czech soldiers commented on this process in their writings. Interestingly, they tended to project this experience onto a geographical template, often drawing a sharp distinction between the way in which war was conducted in Russia and in Italy. Of course, there were manifold differences between fighting in the Isonzo valley, in the Dolomites or the Alps, and on the wide plains of Galicia, the steep slopes of Carpathian forests or in the swamps of Russian Poland. Moreover, the mountainous, sometimes even alpine conditions in the mountains were often completely foreign both to the training and general experience of the men – most of them came from starkly different regions in terms of geography, with the result that avalanches, frostbite and other specifics of this type of warfare made conditions all the more insufferable. Also, with traditional mass attacks by infantry nigh impossible in such terrain, technological development came to the fore on the Italian front, introducing all kinds of new and more 'effective' methods of combat – poison gas, heavy mortars and mountain artillery – along with new tactics.⁶³

As a result, the men often felt the war in Italy to be a completely different (and new) affair: 'In general, physical labour and exhaustion was not as bad in Italy as it was in Russia, where marches of ten miles or more were fairly common. On the other hand, combat in Italy was positional, generally more intense and horrifying. Sapping and mining enemy positions was the norm, and blowing them to pieces pretty common'.[64] The resulting difference was usually not appreciated, and it seems it was not just the landscape itself (when not in combat, soldiers tended to enjoy Italy more than they did Galicia or the Carpathians, as it felt somewhat closer to home), but the very intensity of combat and the industrial, material nature of attritional warfare that was hated the most.[65] As Augustin Mudrák, a medical patrol commander with k.u.k. Infantry Regiment 3 put it:

> New circles of hell opened to us, perhaps even worse than what we saw in Russia. A bad omen seemed to hang around ... The artillery barrage lasted the whole night, spitting flame like the huge mouth of a volcano. It lit up the night sky as if it were a bright day ... All rush and hurry everywhere ... Hundreds and hundreds of guns standing in rows on the plateaus ... Hundreds of aeroplanes are flying over our positions every day.[66]

An infantryman from k.u.k. Infantry Regiment 18 agreed: 'Soldiers who came from the battlefields of Serbia and Russia said that the artillery fire here was beyond anything they had ever seen'.[67] 'A terrifying barrage had started', a member of k.u.k. Infantry Regiment 91 recalled:

> The mountains were shaking, earth and stone was thrown into the air. I was a veteran of three years, and I hadn't seen anything like it before. Three days later, the infantry went over the top ... The [Tyrolean] *Edelweis* division was obliterated. Then the Moravians, the 18th Division, went in, guys who were in Russia from the beginning... We told them it was going to get much worse than it ever was in Russia soon.[68]

The rocky terrain of the Isonzo front before the breakthrough at Caporetto in October 1917 made things even worse. Combined with the ever-increasing scale of artillery operations, it tended to generate a deadly mix of secondary projectiles made of thousands of razor-sharp pieces of rock, as dangerous as shell fragments and shrapnel themselves. 'When a shell explodes among the rocks, it is horrible. Rocks big and small are thrown out with extreme velocity, flying for hundreds of meters. Most of the wounds are caused by them, all of them heavy'.[69]

The prevailing perception that the war in Italy was generally worse than anywhere else led many soldiers to express a desire to avoid the 'dreaded Italy' for as long as possible[70] or to 'get out of the damned Alps' as quickly as possible, respectively.[71] Sometimes it almost seems that soldiers willingly accepted both the contemporary and the postwar Austrian official interpretation of the war in the southwest, based on the legend of manly 'mountain warriors' (*Gebirgskrieger*) fighting a heroic battle against a traditional, treacherous enemy.[72] If this were so, it may be said that the propaganda had the unintended effect of exacerbating fear and worries instead of cultivating pride in one's efforts in difficult conditions. On the other hand, when the main frontline finally descended into the Venetian plain, things only got worse, as the stage opened for the Second Battle of the Piave in June 1918. Here, mass death by aerial bombing and perfected artillery barrages reached such horrific levels that it prompted a participating French veteran to note that this kind of war was 'worse than Verdun'.[73] It is little wonder that, as far as personal accounts are concerned, the Piave marked the moment when the morale of the soldiers broke down for good, turning the rest of the war into a mere waiting game.

Souls

Whatever the perceived specifics of fighting in different areas of Europe were, it is obvious that longtime service had psychologically disruptive effects on the men. In his psychohistorical study of the war experience between 1914 and 1918, Eric Leed claims that the soldiers of the First World War experienced an incomplete, unfinished, twisted form of psychological ritual, resulting in them being stuck in a transitional, 'liminal' phase. It seems that Czech soldiers would agree. The war had torn them from their past, but they felt they had no future; they were not dead, but they often felt less than alive; the purpose of existence was not to live, but merely to not die. In the words of a Czech veteran turned writer, they had become 'living mummies'.[74] They existed outside of time and space, life or death. The feeling of alienation, arising from the incomprehensible monotonous nature of modern warfare, is ever-present in the sources. Egon Erwin Kisch captured it best when he noted in his diary:

> A quarter of a year ago it was different. Hundreds of relationships, tasks, duties, affairs, meetings, plans, intentions and motives were connecting me to the present as well as to the future. I would not have believed it if I'd been told that the feeling of the fullness of life could be taken from me in one moment. Now it's just different. Ties to friends and the world are loosened, connections to the present, the future notwithstanding, broken.[75]

Even though soldiers stayed in contact with their loved ones and even though they usually had some idea where they were (often vague at best, as it was the officers who held the monopoly on spatial orientation), their world lost its inner compass, the link between the past and the future. The past had lost its connection to the present, and the future was deprived of meaning, because there was none. Consequently, time also lost its meaning. Looking at some of the diaries, there are a number of chronological lapses, providing clear evidence that the author has difficulty remembering dates – events are relevant only in relation to themselves, locked forever in the enclosed universe of war. Placing them within the context of an external time frame of human civilization (the calendar) seemed superficial at best.[76] Losing a sense of time is one of the basic experiences of the wartime military life of ordinary soldiers: 'Sundays, holidays, never mind, all the same here'.[77] 'We have completely lost track of time, cannot tell what day of the week it is'.[78] 'In the chaos of war, we only knew when day changed into night. No other time frame was important to us'.[79] In war, time had meaning only in the monotonous cycle of light and darkness. As a result, losing any tangible timeframe of living, of the beginning and the end, only added to the physical stress and fatigue, effectively pushing men onto a slippery slope towards a vegetative state.[80]

The thesis concerning the liminal character of war experience is useful for us as it points to one important characteristic that directly endangered soldiers' masculinity. In many cultures, Central European culture at the peak of modernity being no exception, there are a series of elements that define the masculine individual's relationship to the universe. Among other factors, man is often defined as active, action-seeking, aggressive, influencing and controlling the world around him, i.e. possessing certain level of *power* over himself in relation to the context of his social, economic and physical being. As noted above, military masculinity as defined by the Austro-Hungarian army propaganda (which enveloped the concept of hegemonic masculinity as soon as the war started) was built upon character traits that suppressed these characteristics in favour of obedience and discipline. Men were supposed to fulfil their duty and go to war. However, the image of the determined, purposeful, action-oriented and enterprising hero still made it into the official representations of wartime masculinity, translated into hero cults of fighter aces or submarine captains.[81] It was all the same, as the idea that masculinity is inherently an *active process* was deeply ingrained in the social psyche, forming one of the above-mentioned 'residual elements' that traditionally define manliness.[82] It was when this ideal was confronted with the realities of modern war (which was supposed to be a masculine event) that problems arose.

As Eric Leed states, 'the early expectations became a dream, a fantasy … Trench warfare is a paradigm of compromise, of the repression of aggressive energies'.[83] The soldiers' sustaining motivation was therefore constantly undermined by the fact of them living in a world where there was no place for public performance of traditional masculine virtues. As noted by Alois Dolejší: 'We all think we rule the world while in fact, we are just little worms'.[84] The situation simply did not allow the majority of the participants to 'act manly' – they were constantly being moved around, with no idea where and why; they had little knowledge of their surroundings beyond what they could see over the trench's parapet; they rarely saw an enemy who was not dead or captured, but were constantly being fired upon; and they had little to no control over what they would be doing the next minute or even second, where they were to sleep, what they were to eat, what they would look like or whether they would even live.[85] In other words, they were no longer subjects – they had become objects, the world's passive victims. 'I follow someone else's will the whole day long. I have to obey, willingly or not, day in, day out, as if I were a mere boy ... I feel terrible ... I'm always dominated ... I only have to do things'.[86]

As a result, the war became an endless compromise of manliness, an eternal contradiction between the ideal and the reality, where men – like Jaroslav Havlíček above – felt being disempowered and infantilized by lack of control or even individual will.[87] The official propaganda did not in fact help much here, as its heroes were mirror images of the traditional masculine concepts mentioned above. Looking at the 'letters from the front' published in the press throughout the Habsburg monarchy, we can see this notion at work. Although directed primarily at the 'feminine' hinterland, these cultural images nevertheless served as subconscious points of reference for how soldiers valued themselves or were valued against by others. These letters, published as a part of the government propaganda effort and with much editing, were filled with 'the most courageous platoons', 'manly reservists', 'massive efforts' and 'brave dragoons' proving their 'virtue' by 'behaving in a lion-hearted, resolute, brave ... courageous manner, particularly when assaulting the enemy', 'gallant heroes beyond reproach, simply put: the best soldiers one could wish for'.[88] When reading these definitions of themselves, soldiers were often huddling in dugouts or makeshift huts, freezing or in stifling heat, wet or thirsty, hungry, always waiting. They were waiting even while in the firing line – waiting for orders to come, for something to happen, for a shell to be fired and bury them indiscriminately in the ground: 'Waking up, one is horrified by the thought that there's nothing else to do the whole day but to stay awake and stare forward, to starve and do nothing'.[89] 'That horrible feeling when we just wait helplessly, huddled in a trench, for a shell to come and smash us to pieces'.[90] The resulting contradiction led, not surprisingly, to resigned fatalism, a somewhat conscious variant of the vegetative state, a willing acceptance of the unmanning reality based on the realization that one has no power or control over his own fate, as a true man should.

There are several examples of men who, trapped in the liminal state, concluded that the only purpose of war was death: 'Well, it was out there, waiting for all of us ... After all, it was war and that was why we were there'.[91] Some abandoned their fate to the 'fortunes of war': 'We no longer hide from bullets, as we no longer care. Many would say: "The one that is made for you will find you anyway"'.[92] Others put their faith in the hands of God: 'I'm in His hands now. If the Lord protects me, nothing will happen to me. The Virgin Mary is by my side, protecting me, and I sincerely hope that she will not let me die'.[93] In the process, soldiers were redefining their masculinity internally, introducing the obedience principle that defined masculinity in their social and institutional space deep into their identity, one that was defined by a loss of control over their existence. 'I'm going into the trenches for the first time today, and I don't know if I'm coming back' was a typical situation calling for stoical virtues coming to the fore, as can be seen in a rather similar case of a soldier waiting for the military machine to send him to the front: 'I'm waiting calmly though. Let's see what happens. There is nothing else I can do anyway, only, as they say, *maul halten und weiter dienen* ... And if it comes to that, well, there's no help, I can't do anything about it, just hope I make it through alive. It's best not to think about it'.[94]

The spectre of losing control, which threatened to compromise one's manliness, also relates directly to the above-mentioned 'bread' and 'warmth' obsession manifested by many soldiers. For example, modern armies invariably usurp for themselves the decision on when, where and how soldiers are to sleep. Also, especially in the latter phases of the war, men had very little control over when, what and how they ate. While the military was indeed a thoroughly disciplinarian force in this area, as evidenced by countless complaints about harsh punishments for eating one's 'iron reserve' can of meat, the deteriorating logistical conditions made rationing increasingly dysfunctional and therefore noticeable to the men, with negative consequences for their feelings of self-worth.[95] Food, in the words of Rachel Duffett, was also not just a way to replenish the body with calories – it has carried much 'emotional significance' and 'social importance', because it has always been confronted with the ideal notions of idealized domesticity and masculine status, respectively. In particular, priority access to available food was a 'masculine prerogative' throughout all social classes, with fathers and grown sons having the first pick at the family table. However, this important symbolic function of food consumption 'could not be replicated in the exclusively masculine environment of the army' and every distribution of meals – their quality notwithstanding – served as a painful reminder a lost social position.[96]

Bodies

With the supply crisis peaking and the army unable to provide soldiers with much-needed rest in 1918, the gap between the *active* discourse of hegemonic masculinity and the *passive* reality of soldiers' lives widened alarmingly. In a similar vein, the worsening food supply accentuated the difference between the ideal and the real masculine body. The body, along with (hetero)sexuality, is a key to understanding modern masculinity. It is not just an operational 'tool' of manliness – it is integral to it as a constitutive part. As stated by R.W. Connell, 'the physical sense of maleness and femaleness is central to the cultural interpretation of gender'.[97] Aesthetics is integral to this sense, shaping the body into a culturally defined ideal. Moreover, as Christopher Forth adds, 'bravery, strength, endurance and sexual potency figure prominently in most lists of ideal

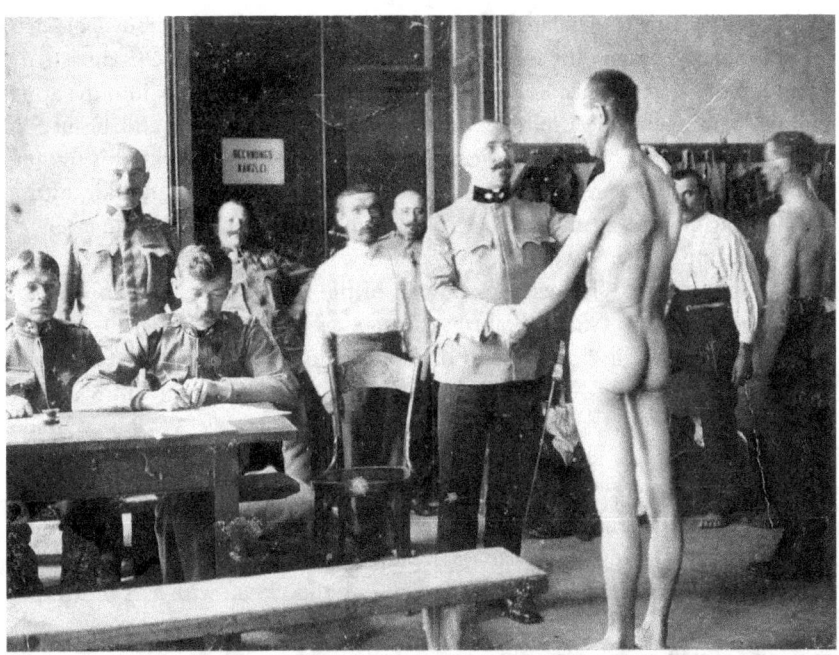

Figure 2.2 Defining bodily masculinity – conscripts being sorted according to their physique by a military board, Brno, March 1915 (Military History Institute, Prague).

male bodily attributes, as do grace, beauty and harmony of form'.[98] According to Sabine Kienitz, this form is not 'simply a symbolic metaphor nor a passive surface of discursively attributed interpretations and reinterpretations, but rather both an active part itself in social processes of negotiation and their product'.[99] Therefore, the body and masculinity are an indivisible continuum, not in a biological sense but in a symbolic one, as they are two social categories that mutually influence and shape one another.

In accordance with these conclusions is the fact that a specific form of male body was integral to wartime hegemonic masculinity. It was actually rooted in the institution of military service itself, officially defined and formally evaluated in every individual understood to be a man – a body accepted as *tauglich*, i.e. fit for service in category A (combat service), was the equivalent of the officially approved bodily expression of masculinity in its perfect form.[100] Moreover, the official propaganda always worked with the images of 'sturdy' and 'handsome men', whose bodies seemed to reflect their loyalty, courage and aggression.[101] In soldiers' accounts, this logic may have been mocked at times, but it was still acknowledged as a natural state of affairs regarding the body-masculinity dialogue – it is the 'good men' who possess truly masculine bodies, while cowards and thugs are always presented as disfigured in the sources. We have also seen the importance of coordinated movement of men's bodies (or bodies of men) for the Sokol culture. Indeed, many members of the movement carried the notion of the close connection between masculinity and the body into the army. František Šmída, who admired 'the unified show of strength and beauty' of male gymnasts in July 1914, had a rather similar experience during his training as a one-year volunteer, seeing his comrades as 'young bodies in full kit, hitting the floor again and again'. He even viewed himself through the same lens of manly age and shape: 'Twenty years of age, I was a lad as handsome as they get, ready to get it all'.[102] The widespread cult of the male body is also apparent in the imagery used by Gustav Habrman, leader of the Czech Social-Democratic Party, when describing the process of mobilization: 'Boys and men so strong! A joy to behold! Thin, beautifully strapping … Boys and men full of spunk, strength and energy'.[103] Josef Šrámek, a POW in France, also saw his comrades as a mirror image of the official discourse of men at arms, calling them 'our boys, tall and strong'.[104] Ferdinand Lirš, who ended the war as a lieutenant, used similar language when describing the prewar barracks in his memoir: the 'young, supple boys, marching in a brisk, jaunty step' were in direct opposition to his description of a comrade in training, 'small in build, weak, with ears protruding far away from his skull', whom he called a victim of 'cruel mother nature'. In his opinion, 'a man so robbed of his stature and strength … [was] bereft of manliness' and 'should and could never have become a soldier'. On the other hand, when describing another soldier, 'comrade Knobloch', he saw the opposite: 'A handsome man of strong build, a pleasant face to look at'.[105] To him, the body blends into masculinity to create one perfect form, as was the case in the diary of Alois Dolejší, who in 1917 admired a platoon of stormtroopers, employing the phrase 'guys as huge as pine trees'.[106]

However, the notion of perfect body form was a curse more often than not. Of course, bodies tended not to conform to it from the very beginning, projecting their deficiencies onto the masculine identity of the men in question (particularly those labelled as *untauglich* on enlistment). Many other bodies were deemed fit, only to be changed radically (and brutally) through combat (see Chapter 6), while many more were subjected to the pressures of hard labour, starvation and disease. As Josef Ulrych complained bitterly in his diary in 1918, 'no one in the whole company is affected by starvation worse than I am … My body is so decimated that there's only skin and bones left of me, nothing else'.[107] The feeling must have been widespread at the time, as István Deák mentions that the average body weight of Austro-Hungarian soldiers dropped to under 55 kilograms in mid 1918.[108] Also, as Kaja Silverman wrote in her analysis of the psychosomatic dynamic of masculinity, 'when the male subject is brought into a traumatic encounter with lack, as in the situation of war, he often experiences it as impairment of his anatomical masculinity'. Material deficiency, producing deficiency in one's physical form, then produces a psychic 'disintegration of bound and armored ego, predicated upon the illusion of coherence and control'.[109] Malnutrition and exhaustion stimulate feelings of anatomical and, consequently, psychological 'unmanning', a situation in which 'the tortured body' is anything but close to the officially endorsed ideal of the masculine body.[110] Alois Kaiser expressed these feelings in a fictionalized account of his wartime service, writing about his ravaged body at the end of the war:

> It is embarrassing how weak I am. My body became a miniature of itself. My legs are but sticks and my arms are terribly bony. I feel so ashamed when they uncover me. Last time, it was the Croatian doctor who uncovered me and, with the help of a nurse and that tall Italian girl, they propped me up so I could sit up. I was so ashamed. Not because I was naked, but because I was so skinny.[111]

In a similar vein, Jan Morávek presented his body, deformed through dysentery, as 'a miserable collection of pain and suffering lying on soiled straws', in direct contrast with 'myself, that hero, lover, proud and virile boy who wanted to conquer the world!'[112]

For the men who realized the contrast between the perfect form and the physical reality of their own bodies under the strain of war, the added insult to injury was often that it carried no social capital of the 'red badge of courage' usually attached to war wounds: 'It's all because of the war. If you have a bad leg as a civilian, everybody will just look down on you', Karel Vaněk noted in his diary. 'But now it has changed. I could actually walk well enough, but I keep my limp on purpose, because I know people notice … Everybody's eyes fill with tears, their mouths whispering: "Poor bastard, so young and suffering so much."'[113] But being only sick and skinny from starvation hardly qualified one for the same reactions, and the men were well aware of the fact.

Soldiers experienced a process of gradual unmanning not only through the way in which their bodies changed shape under the pressure of war. Many of them also mentioned an increasing level of dehumanization through the way in which they perceived their situation and position in the war machine. And since human is synonymous with *man* in their outlook, there was another front on which their masculinity became compromised. The conclusion expressed by the disillusioned Karel Vaněk in his diary that the 'huge, complicated machine called "the state" is at work and I'm just a small, unimportant cog driven by the sprockets of the others' was already mentioned in Chapter 1. Vaněk did not leave his machine-like imagery there, also seeing himself and his comrades as dehumanized machines on other occasions: 'A weary walk, indifferent eyes bereft of life, staring at the back of the head of the guy in front … They walk like machines. He'll walk for a day, a week, a month, all the way to the edge of the world'.[114] Many soldiers actually agreed with Karel Vaněk's feelings, viewing themselves as passive victims of a gigantic impersonal and industrialized entity, 'War' as a machine-like 'beast yearning for blood', 'a war monster leaving only destruction behind', a monster 'spitting flames' from 'its gun-like mouths ... crushing everything in its path', 'the machine of war' pushing little men 'into helplessness'.[115] František Skála, an infantryman with k.u.k. Infantry Regiment 98, summarized these feelings in his statement that 'the perverse human spirit turned progress against itself'. 'Man, the ruler of the world, is degraded, spit on and trampled into the dust by his own fury. The horror – the horror – the horror!'[116] Under the pressure of industrialized warfare, man ceased to be a man as well as a human being, becoming an automaton in his own eyes. 'Violence, a machine, a mechanism', mused Jaroslav Křenek in his memoir.[117] This metaphor effectively reflected all the above-mentioned angles of the impact that war had on men, from a vegetative state through liminal existence, all the way to fatalist tendencies, connecting them in one massive push against the masculine identity of the soldiers. War deprived men of ways to satisfy their needs, tearing apart any notion of their temporal existence, as well as their capacity to enact their will – the machine metaphor, in its negative sense, seemed more than fitting. As noted by Rudolf Kučera, the working-class men of Bohemia had actually experienced a similar symbolic shift from masculine pride in one's hard work towards its compromised, mechanized interpretation, which became widespread during the war years. And whether viewed positively or negatively, the 'mechanization' of human experience was a staple of many learned debates on social issues in the early twentieth century.[118]

A soldier's manliness was endangered not only through the feeling of unmanly helplessness that he perceived through every minute of his experience and that only worsened over time, pushing his stoic sustaining motivation to its limits and beyond. War also washed away the many layers of culture and civilization that form the basis of modern masculinity. Some men saw their comrades' obsession with the food supply as evidence of layers of civilization being shed, and even the culture of eating left a lot to be desired as, according to food historians, the ever-present discomfort, indecency, disorder and violence of many meals only highlighted the 'lack of civilization' of their situation, threatening their 'social person' in the process.[119] Also, as we saw, the notions of self-denial and self-discipline formed the core of the official discourse of wartime hegemonic masculinity. However, according to Christopher Forth, these traits were integral to the way in which modern European masculinity had been structured during eighteenth and nineteenth centuries, shaping itself as an image of the 'civilizing process' described by Norbert Elias.[120] As Forth claims, the modern concept of hegemonic masculinity gradually pushed everything deemed 'barbaric' and 'animal' to the margins of the prevailing gender discourse, using a symbolic contrast with other cultures or previous eras in order to demonstrate its supremacy based on public decency, respectability, self-restraint, self-control and social discipline.[121] And it was precisely the compromising descent into savagery, associated with the loss of everything civilized including self-control and succumbing to unbound aggressive violence, that seems to be one of the particular fears harboured by Czech men during the war.

War as a barbarizing, dehumanizing, unmanning force is a staple of many sources, especially when dealing with difficult situations such as combat, starvation or extreme exhaustion.[122] The authors' vocabulary is almost always the same, betraying the sense of losing control not only over one's body, but over one's humanity in general: 'We are losing human dignity. Both brain and heart are silenced, man's cultural habits thrown away. Culture is left behind, we are becoming human primitives'. In František Skála's opinion, one could only become a part of the 'world of war' by losing whatever it was that made him a *modern* human, with 'culture' meaning the 'bourgeois rationalist model idealizing competitive individualism, reason, and self-control or self-denial', i.e. traits that the 'war primitive' distinctively lacks or is soon about to lose.[123] Lying on a hospital bed at the end of the war, Alois Kaiser let his fictional self to muse about the same: 'It seems I have ceased to be a civilized man'.[124] Rudolf Wagner, *Fähnrich* (officer candidate) with k.u.k. Dragoon Regiment 10, saw 'unbelievable barbarity' in a sacked church somewhere in Russian Poland,[125] while Josef Váchal observed what the 'raging beast in man' did to northern Italy after Caporetto.[126] It is often hunger that turns men into 'animals ... with a half-crazed stare in their eyes',[127] starving men become 'wolf-like', and ration distribution is all too often described as 'feeding wild creatures in a menagerie'.[128] 'It was a war, and people, especially soldiers, lost many of their natural inhibitions. A hungry soldier does not ask questions', a *Landsturm* infantryman wrote in his diary with resignation. For him, hungry men no longer have the morals that previously defined them as civilized and as men.[129] Subsequently, combat itself only further reduces men to the level of 'game animals', 'wild animals' or 'beasts of prey'[130] who have already 'lost all sense of humanity' and now are 'losing their mind and reason' under a day-long artillery barrage.[131] It is particularly the repeated mentions of one losing control over his own *mind*, losing the power to exercise reason, a prime characteristic of masculinity since the Age of Enlightenment at the latest, which provides further evidence for our thesis that for most men, the loss of control they experienced because of the war was a disturbing compromise of their manliness.[132]

It may be assumed that the above-described fears of many soldiers facing the cumulative pressures of war represent one, usually unconscious but still important factor in Czech soldiers' sustaining motivation and its dynamics during the First World War. As the war dragged on and escalated in its intensity, its military and economic demands encroaching upon more and more areas of existence, men were increasingly forced to compromise their masculine identity. While the official discourse presented hegemonic masculinity through the images of military heroes and heroics, in reality, in trying to keep to that role, men lost control not only over themselves and their existence, but also over the very things that made them men – civilization and culture. As a result, they felt they were losing their manhood along with their humanity, becoming mere animals, machines or just passive victims. As Augustin Mudrák noted when he realized he had been at the front for almost a year in July 1916: 'One long, endless year. How much pain, suffering, hunger, cold and danger ... This lot is good for a convict, a criminal, not for a man thrown out of his home, away from his family. It's a miserable, bitter life, filled with hatred for all those who are responsible ... I've been thinking a lot about my miserable situation, one which befell me at my manliest age'.[133] The 'manliest age' of the man here is in obvious opposition to the marginalized categories of 'convict' or 'criminal' that are deemed unmanly by the social discourse. What is also clear is that the author's motivation is close to zero, and it is probably the negative compliance – i.e. coercion – that keeps him in combat for the moment, as it seems he has completely lost any faith in the idea that military service may bring him any useful social capital. For him, any perceived dividends of hegemonic masculinity ultimately seemed unable to overcome the cumulative effect of physical and psychological exhaustion, and of the perceived threat to the way he experienced masculinity on an intimate, individual level. Modern warfare and its realities, it seems, pitted two components of wartime hegemonic masculinity against one another – its militarized part, inherited from the peacetime military masculinity through mobilization and official propaganda, and the part that traditionally made men into men. As a result, and in order to reconcile these two conflicting layers of masculinity, a soldier's wartime manliness was gradually turned into an endless compromise.

Sex

Turning back to Josef Váchal's definition of the average soldier's basic needs and worries, it is clear that both 'bread' and 'warmth' played important roles in soldiers' sustaining motivation. Additionally, both categories were gendered in their effects on men's bodies and perceptions of themselves as human beings. 'Sex', which he identified as the third component in the 'holy trinity' of soldierly wartime existence, seems destined to be a thoroughly gendered category from the beginning. In fact, there are several historical studies on the 'tight relationship between love and war'.[134] However, love is not the category Josef Váchal had in mind when contemplating his comrades' behaviour. While emotions and emotional attachments play a key part in soldiers' morale and motivation (see Chapters 3 and 5), Váchal is adamant that his observation referred only to pure sexuality, particularly the seemingly insatiable desire of many soldiers to find carnal fulfilment, which overtook them as soon as they donned their uniforms and caused them to spend all the money they brought with them in 'the temples of Venus'.[135] He is in agreement with a majority of other sources here –

heightened sexual drive along with lessened social control in wartime are a staple in many of them, often as part of a general criticism of war as a vehicle of moral turpitude and decadence. As Vladislav Vančura wrote in his novel *Pole orná i válečná* (*Fields of Harvest, Fields of War*), 'stealing became widespread and people fornicated more eagerly than ever. Intimate moments spilled out of stables and barns, unchecked and uncontained'.[136] While Egon Erwin Kisch's recollection of food trumping the sex drive was clear in that when the situation was bad enough, 'bread' and 'warmth' took precedence, his diary as well as other sources also clearly tell us that the sex drive came a close third if the situation improved even slightly: 'I wondered how erotic and sexual desires could prosper in that putrid smell, in a place lacking any condition whatsoever for such a thirst'.[137]

However, war is a social event just like any other, which is therefore able to inspire many shifts in the social and cultural understanding of reality, including behavioural patterns. Our goal here is to analyse the way in which Czech soldiers experienced (or, more precisely, interpreted in writing) their own sexuality during the war, focusing on how the war influenced and changed this experience in relation to their masculine identity. As many authors argue, sexuality, along with the biologically defined sex, male or female, construed – through modern medical science – as a simple dichotomy of man or woman, represents one of the key pillars of modern masculinity.[138] In recent research, some reservations were raised concerning the way in which this underlying conclusion is applied to our understanding of sexual identities during the First World War, warning against projecting a truly 'modern' understanding of sexual identity onto masses of men who were in all probability unaware of the fact that their identity should be defined by their sexual behaviour: 'The crucial point is that the current belief that sexual behaviour and inclinations determine one's identity as heterosexual or homosexual has come about as a result of historical forces that took place after the First World War'. More than absolute identities to adhere to, for example, heterosexuality and homosexuality were rather personal preferences of fulfilling one's needs, moral choices based on one's sense of respectability, which was as much class-bound as it was gendered.[139] As George Chauncey demonstrated a long time ago in his case study of U.S. sailors, between 1914 and 1918, most men still tended to define themselves based on 'what they did, rather than who they were'. However, he also concludes that with most men (mostly young and lower class, with only elementary education), the social construct of masculinity was still bound to heterosexual behaviour as a preferred option.[140] Czech soldiers also seem to fit this trope, as they rarely mention homosexual behaviour at all in their writings, and when they do so, this is usually within a context of trying to prove the moral turpitude and perversity of the upper classes (i.e. officers).[141]

Of course, this silence on the issue of homosexual behaviour may simply be a reflection of acute legal awareness, since under both the civil and military law of Austria-Hungary, 'sodomy against nature, i.e. with persons of the same sex' was illegal and punishable with the sentence of 'hard jail from one to five years'.[142] Both diaries and correspondence would therefore implicate the author or his comrades, and while the army seemed to harbour a rather tolerant attitude to such behaviour as long as it involved 'consenting adults' of the same class, it may well have served as a strong factor for reports of any 'acts of sodomy' to be left out of written accounts.[143] However, this would not explain the similar silence on the matter in soldiers' memoirs. With the few exceptions noted above, memoirs also treat sexual intercourse between men in the army in this way, an observation also made by István Deák in his now-classic study of the Austro-Hungarian officer corps: 'One looks in vain for evidence [of homosexual behaviour], the only available source of information being court reports … [even though] it must have been widespread as one could expect in an all-male society where women were either absent, unapproachable, or possibly infected'.[144] Moreover, assuming that Czech soldiers were no different from the above-mentioned U.S. seamen or from their German counterparts, who, according to Jason Crouthamel, while they 'otherwise defined themselves as heterosexual … in the remote, otherworldly environment of the war experimented with homosexual relations', we must come to the conclusion that homosexuality was also a sort of a taboo in retrospect.[145] It may well be argued that in the memoirs, mostly written in the 1930s, the modern discourse of identity firmly rooted in sexual behaviour was finally taking hold; however, it seems that most Czech soldiers indeed understood homosexual behaviour to represent an exception to the norm defined not necessarily by biology, but certainly by their sense of morality attached to a general notion of proper masculinity. Homosexual behaviour was something that placed this morality, and one's ability to hold on to it throughout the war years, in doubt, rendering it just another danger that threatened to compromise a soldier's 'proper' manliness. As such, it was rarely mentioned, with perception of sexuality focused almost invariably on its 'straight', potentially more masculine form.[146]

While homosexual behaviour was relegated into the 'big nothing' by most soldiers' writings, another 'alternative' form of sexual practice received a more extensive treatment in the sources, being probably both more widespread and also less problematic for the authors, namely masturbation. The extent to which the practice was commonplace is a question that is again very difficult to answer, as by the early twentieth century, it was both thoroughly medicalized and demonized at the same time – one historian actually called it 'an obsession of the Western civilization' of this era.[147] However, it seems that men were more willing to mention it simply because they ultimately found it a more morally acceptable (and respectable) alternative to either homosexual relations or to the option of sexual abstinence, which was both unbearable and foreign to most of them, especially as erotic literature circulated among them even in the trenches.[148] 'Oh, how the desire for women has tortured us while in Italy', complained František Šmída in his diary in the oblique fashion typically used when tackling the issue. 'As for me, I make do with memories *more often than not*'. The question, of course, is as to what happened in those *less often* situations, as he was in an all-male environment all the time.[149] The only author who comments openly on the topic is the acute observer of military life in the Austro-Hungarian army, Egon Erwin Kisch. On 2 January 1915, he noted in his diary: 'There's a guard in front of the brothel, and a prophylactic post. Back in the camp, everyone who's still satisfying himself sexually in the way that's the only option in the trenches is subjected to ridicule and laughter. Why do that now when there are whores around'.[150] It seems that masturbation was widely regarded as a stop-gap measure necessary for survival at the front where there were no women available. However, when the 'proper' outlet of masculine sexuality was at hand, most men thought it absurd to keep the habit, be it out of preference, lack of money or fear of venereal disease. What is also worth noting here is the fact that in a wartime military environment deprived of intimacy and personal space, sexuality is more or less a public matter – any sexual practice was clearly difficult to perform without at least the closest comrades knowing, which is telling regarding the limited reporting on both masturbation and homosexual relations.

As is clear from Kisch's note on a military guard being set up at the entrance to a brothel while his unit was back at the rear for refitting and replacement of losses, soldiers' sexuality was, just like essentially every other aspect of their physical existence, subject to the disciplining efforts of Austro-Hungarian military authorities. To paraphrase the title of Rudolf Kučera's book on the issue of increased social control in the hinterland during wartime, what soldiers experienced almost from the beginning of the war can be generally referred to as 'rationed sex'. The Austro-Hungarian military command soon realized that it was more or less impossible to keep 'men in the best years of life' away from sexual activities, but faced the conundrum of how to keep the attendant venereal diseases under control at the same time. Whatever measures it took were therefore motivated not by concerns over morals, but rather by a desperate effort to keep men in fighting condition. Consequently, officially sanctioned prostitution was seen as a necessary evil important for soldiers' morale (or sustaining motivation). What resulted, besides a continuous and mildly successful prophylactic-educational campaign warning soldiers against venereal disease, was a tight regulation of prostitution anywhere near military bases and in the rear areas (*Etappenbereich*) of the front. These measures, which greatly expanded upon the prewar regulation of prostitution (peacetime regulation also primarily revolving around the hygiene and health of registered prostitutes, i.e. women's bodies), focused primarily on the bodies of the 'official' prostitutes and only secondarily on men's access to them.[151]

While 'clandestine', unsanctioned prostitution was never wiped out, and in fact flourished during the war years, hand in hand with the economic and social collapse, the army spent a great deal of effort keeping the bulk of the trade under

Figure 2.3 Austro-Hungarian military brothel, complete with opening hours, 'nur für Österreichische Soldaten!' ('Austro-Hungarian Soldiers Only!'), location unknown (Alois Žipek, *Domov za války: Svědectví účastníků*, vol. 3, Prague, 1930, 412).

strict control in official army brothels, which were divided according to rank (separate for officers and men) and staffed by women whose health was under the control of military medical personnel.[152] Army-operated brothels became widespread both in the hinterland as well as in the occupied territories, at the army's immediate rear. 'The army would not, or could not feed our stomachs', noted one soldier. 'But they at least paid a lot of attention to our sexual needs, introducing the "noble" institution of "field puffs" … At the rear, these brothels were everywhere'.[153] Egon Erwin Kisch described one such brothel in his diary: 'A typical military brothel. The price is one *koruna* per room, no more – by order of the army command! Hundreds of soldiers wait eagerly in front of the rooms, in the hallways, and all the way down the street'.[154] There were obligatory prophylactic checks before and after using the services of the brothel, as well as a strictly limited time for each 'customer'. Like everything else in a soldier's life, even the minutiae of his sex life were increasingly mechanized, disciplined and taken away from him.

It is worth noting that the primary target of the army authorities' regulatory efforts were women, as it was them who was generally blamed for the massive spike in venereal disease cases not only in the army, but also in society as a whole. While women were perceived as inherently immoral, male sexuality was to be regulated strictly by limiting access to women (the source of immoral behaviour) and by education (mostly about the immorality of women seeking illicit sex). Ultimately, soldiers' sex drive was seen as an undesirable but excusable consequence of war, a specific part of wartime hegemonic masculinity.[155] Blaming morally corrupt women for soldiers' promiscuous behaviour also became an attractive option for many soldiers in their attempt to understand the perceived shifts in the gender order. However, the home front interpretation of male sexuality released from the confines of respectable citizens' homes often tended towards two opposite extremes – denial, i.e. faith in the soldiers' sexual abstinence, and fear of the barbarizing effect war had on men even in this area of life, unleashing 'wild' 'animal instincts' in them, deforming them for life in the same way the violence of combat was alleged to.[156] It is precisely these three specific discursive elements that form a perfect framework for our analysis of soldiers' perception of sexuality in their personal writings – dehumanization and moral corruption of *women*, increasingly savage and dehumanized *other* men, and the sexually abstinent, respectable *self*.

In contrast to homosexual practices, heterosexual relations are described more freely in the sources, which can be interpreted as a reflection of their 'mainstream' status in the contemporary discourse of both sexuality and masculinity. However, looking more closely at the way in which the topic is treated by the soldiers, it is more than obvious that there was a line most of the men refused to cross – usually their own self. In most of the narratives on sexual behaviour, the author is a mere observer, not a direct participant. For example, Josef Šrámek describes in his diary from French captivity 'our lads, well-built, brawny ... have established many relationships, intimate even, with local girls as well as with soldiers' wives', while he keeps himself to writing love letters in his comrades' names, as he is the only one who speaks French. Nevertheless, he still admits that he was as much smitten as anyone by the local girls: 'We all drool over the sight of the plump hot daughters of France's south, strange ideas getting into our heads. Little wonder, as none of us had been intimate with a woman for 23 months, missing all the pleasures of love dearly'.[157] In a similar way, Josef Ulrych complains in his diary of 'May Day, the time of love ... Eleven months since we last saw a Czech girl'.[158] However, when it comes to the services of local prostitutes, it is always his friends, not himself, who enjoy them. Even František Šmída, who is generally more open in his diary, only hints at the possibility that he had actually visited brothels and courted local beauties. However, when dealing with the adventures of 'the other men', he is much more explicit and usually adds a slight hint of moral outrage:

> The men's sexual drive, their desire for the female body, was out of control. The things I saw there [in an official army brothel] I could find no excuse for ... There was one woman and a whole platoon of horny men. My neighbour, a one-year volunteer as I was, could not understand my disgust. After she had been through those seventy men, I saw her lying under the stairs, exhausted, half-passed out. She was horribly wretched and worthless in her misery.[159]

It is worth noting two things here – it is the woman, not the men, who is 'wretched and worthless', and it is the author who is the only one who kept his morals, the men sliding into what Paul Göhre has described as a purely instinctive and impersonal heterosexual relationship, turned into a purely mechanical exercise fulfilling a basic physical need.[160]

One of the most explicit descriptions of wartime sexuality is presented in the diary of Jaroslav Vítek, in his lengthy description of a journey from his leave back to the front in early 1918:

> A few moments before train finally took off, Corporal Foltýn brought in a girl, an eighteen-year-old looker from Moravia, saying she was coming with us ... I tried to talk her out of the idea, describing all the horrors and dangers in vivid detail, as she was just a girl after all, and so she simply couldn't come with us ... But she took on one man's coat, put his cap on her head and huddled in a corner saying that she'd just go into another car if we threw her out, and that she was going anyway ... We're moving now, it's all dark in the car ... The boys are taking care of the girl. There's a sergeant on one side, a staff sergeant on the other, others sit across from her. Their hands often meet on her body. It's the lance-corporal who lights a match from time to time, causing the 26 pairs of eyes of those not engaged with the girl to shoot lustful, jealous stares at the scene to see how far the things have got. It was the lance-corporal who finally went first, with the others following right after him ... During the night, the soldiers

are having fun with the girl, hardly ever sleeping … She's tired as hell, I can see it, but she's got no scruples or regrets, she's even enjoying herself, and at least she's not hungry. I'm so disgusted by it all, trying to reason with her, but she wouldn't move and the men would stop her anyway. The staff-sergeant, who was the car commander, used her few times himself, and I couldn't go against the majority opinion anyway. It took five days and nights before they'd finally had enough of her … and dumped her off at some station.[161]

There are similar stories, albeit usually less explicit, in several of the sources, but it is this one that draws together some key motifs.

First, sexuality in wartime was indeed a public matter, shared with many in an ad hoc community of those present at the time – in this case, the community of a train car going to the front. Of course, we may assume that sexuality was more or less a public matter for anyone who was not of one the urban middle class, as life in crowded workers' quarters or peasant huts often bore little difference to the everyday wartime experience of thousands, such as when eighteen men shared a room with a flock of sheep and a 'young, pretty Polish girl' somewhere in Galicia, one of them 'plundering the girl's body' on a 'creaking bed' at night.[162] With the exception of the officers, war usually did not provide the men with much more intimate space than what the army brothels had to offer – and with the long queues in front of them, men were forced to exchange the luxury of intimacy for the benefit of time, having only few minutes to 'enjoy' themselves. There were apparently several witnesses to a large number of sexual acts, which, however, does not explain why men refrained from describing these acts 'first-hand'. It seems that the key motive here is the effort to place oneself in an unequivocally moral, respectable and self-restrained position in relation to the story, and therefore in terms of masculinity itself, at least in the way the author imagined was expected of him.

Second, the author repeatedly stresses how disgusted he is, distancing himself from the situation, even claiming that he tried to stop it. While Vítek's diary was only published in a rewritten, narrative form almost two decades after the war, we may assume the author was always trying to *present* himself as a moral beacon in a sea of debauchery, as this is a thread that continues through the entire text (and not only his at that). Thus, even if he had actually taken part in the events, he would probably have treated it in a way not dissimilar to a lance-corporal in another soldier's diary, who spent a night in a brothel, only to beseech the author afterwards 'to be quiet about it, so no-one at home knows'.[163] The author's direct participation in any sexual acts is clearly a borderline not to be crossed, at least in the way soldiers preferred to report on their experience. Even when František Šmída actually decides to 'conquer' an 'available woman' in the name of 'masculine aggression and passion' while stationed in Slavonia, moral inhibitions 'somewhere deep in my mind' come to the surface in the last moment, halting him in his endeavour.[164] What the author does here, therefore, is to present himself as someone who, while naturally attracted by women (like Ulrych or Šrámek above, i.e. proclaiming his heterosexuality, obviously perceived as natural and manly), takes the moral high ground in suppressing the 'primitive urge', exercising the right amount of self-control and restraint needed to prove his bourgeois masculinity. In this way, both his sexuality and his masculinity are in fact bolstered in the eyes of the audience (and possibly himself). Since the audience many authors had in mind, even when writing diaries, was the home front, such a manner of construing the image of a soldier's sexuality effectively worked towards further reinforcing his public image. It mixed the ideal notion (the author's self) with the feared consequence of war (the savage, adulterous, sex-obsessed 'others'), along with the basic trope of the official discourse – the inherent corruption of women: 'Women feel no shame …', Václav Doležal, a private in k.k. Landsturm Infantry Regiment 22, wrote in his diary dedicated to his children. 'They do bad things, particularly at night, my comrades say. It didn't work on me, though, because my thoughts have been and are with you, my beloved children, and with my little wife. Mostly it's just tailors and shoemakers here, and too many whores'.[165]

Women

It is clear that many authors tend to adopt the official discourse regarding women as inherently corrupt, weak and sexualized. As this discourse represents only a more pronounced and officially embraced reflection of the modern gender order, where femininity is systemically placed in a subordinate position to masculinity and more or less defined as its opposite, the way in which soldiers perceived and interpreted the feminine may tell us a lot about the way in which they understood and experienced their masculinity and its position in the wartime gender order. Indeed, it was Robert Nye who correctly pointed to the fact that 'one thing about which I think we can be fairly confident is that women and the "woman question" cannot be left out of any story about men'.[166]

In the light of the quotes above, it may easily be assumed that the image of women in Czech soldiers' writing is indeed precisely congruent with the traditional (and, at the time, official) discourse of femininity, picturing women as passive, weak, subordinate objects. Indeed, in many texts, soldiers attach only one important trait to women – sexuality: 'Their world was simpler, more carefree, seemingly happier', wrote František Šmída of the local women in a village where his battalion was quartered, while tellingly reducing them to 'female bodies' in the same way he did regarding the prostitutes in a brothel in Osijek, Habsburg Croatia: 'Flesh, older and less fresh … for the men … much prettier and younger goods … for the officers'.[167] In the same way, Egon Erwin Kisch described the women he saw after his unit finally stopped retreating from Serbia in late 1914 as 'masterful pieces of art', while Karel Jaroš, a one-year volunteer with an artillery detachment in Palestine, mentions women only within the context of men being 'interested in them'.[168]

However, women are not just passive, sexualized objects in Czech soldiers' writings. Many authors actually feel pity for them, seeing them as victims of their own unmanageable – feminine – sexuality, unleashed by war and loosened social control (of husbands and fathers). The image presented of a 'young Polish girl' from a Galician village provides a clear example: 'Dorka, what a poor girl, fighting in vain against the nature of her healthy, lush, vigorous body, stood no chance – she regretted deeply her weakness, often sighing in an eager lover's ear: "Oh, Mary, Virgin of Czestochowa, my man's at the front, what am I doing here, wretched soul!"'[169] The 'respectable women' who regularly sell themselves to soldiers for a piece of bread (even in the hinterland),[170] jump into bed with any passerby in an officer's uniform,[171] 'are keen on starting an intimate relationship' with the lance-corporals quartered in their house[172] or seek to 'receive their duties of manhood' are often described as ordinary examples of womanhood, 'nice women in general, only looking to get as much as possible out of life. Who would blame them?'[173] Moral corruption therefore does not necessarily mean negative judgement – for many of the authors, it is again the very nature of the feminine that makes women sexualized objects.

Of course, objectifying women serves a distinct purpose in soldiers' writings, especially in those where the author actually touches upon his own sexual endeavours. Here, women as objects are used as a proof of one's virility and therefore masculinity. For example, Ferdinand Lirš 'conquers' an unnamed beauty, only to brag to his readers about 'the days ... filled with tender love and nights of wild pleasure' he came to experience when he succeeded. While he tends to present her as a 'beloved' person and his relationship to her does not seem to lack emotional attachment, its whole purpose in the narrative comes to the fore when the time of parting arrives. While he is sad about leaving, he is also immensely proud to finally make the relationship public to the whole town, regarding it as a 'trophy' and a proof of his manliness: 'The local Poles were stunned, especially the pharmacist [who had always doubted the author's chances]'.[174] A woman is a one-dimensional plaything, a passive object on offer to be admired, conquered or turned down on a whim, thus proving the ultimate superiority of the man and his masculinity. Even when it seems that the woman in question is an exception, as in the case of a 'saint', the 'young, pretty, 19-year-old Mrs. M'. who 'steadily refuses to share a bed with me, reminding me every day that she's married and has a husband, which saddens me immensely', the contemporary discourse of feminine weakness ultimately occupies the narrative: 'As I've been told, after I left for the front, she was raped by a lance-corporal, fell in love with him, and he used her so much and so often that she was thinner than a finger'.[175] However, the author is able to put a positive spin on the story at the end – he is barely able to hide his pride and sense of moral superiority over the lance-corporal, who had obviously failed in proving to be a true, respectable, self-controlled man.

There is one important element of Czech soldiers' writings we have not tackled so far, one that will play an important part in our analysis in the future – all the stories cited above deal with women 'in foreign lands', from Hungary through Russian and Polish parts of Galicia, its Austrian frontier, all the way down to Slavonia and the Western Balkans. While there is little evidence that would show the men differentiating morality of women based on whether these are Czech or not, seeing them first and foremost as women and only so often mentioning other characteristics, it seems that Czech soldiers' optics mirrored the gendered wartime geography. For them, these women were part of the masculine world of war – at the rear of the combat zones, close to the front, away from home. In general, a woman's purpose in this world was, according to many men, to 'serve the country on her back'.[176] In this world, women are objects of male desire, either morally corrupting (when men fail) or uplifting (when men uphold their respectable masculinity). And more than anything else, in order to fulfil this purpose, women must be seen as *passive*, and their femininity must constitute the opposite of the men's masculinity (active, dominant, aggressive). On one level, it is possible to interpret the result as a disturbance of the prevalent moral order, endangered by women enthralled by their own nature (as claimed by the official discourse); however, on another level, most of the authors are able not only to use the narrative to further the case for the existing gender order, one where femininity is subordinate to masculinity, but also to present themselves as true men who rose above the moral challenge, proving themselves through sexual prudence.

Yet, there is also a rather different and from the soldiers' point of view much more disturbing picture of femininity. While the usual emotions reserved for women in the sources are sympathy and compassion, in some cases we encounter a mix of bewilderment, disapproval and disgust. What is important for us is that these cases present women as sexually aggressive, i.e. in a role that should belong to men. It is no wonder that soldiers' reactions to women perceived as such are decidedly negative – for them, they represent a serious dislocation of the gender order, since they acquire masculine characteristics in the worst imaginable way – through active sexuality. 'These animal, primitive women were hungrier for men than they were for bread', František Šmída noted about the women who crossed the line for him. 'A fresh batch of men made them lose the last ounce of respectability they may have had left'.[177] Another author expressed similar thoughts in his recollection: 'Once we were passing a barn on our way back from an exercise to Velká. Three women were threshing wheat there. Seeing us, they immediately invited us over to have some fun with them'. The soldiers, allegedly united in their disgust for such behaviour in women of certain age, refused: 'We told them we had no time. They were old, 35 to 45 at best'.[178] František Skála was similarly wooed by 'a passionate Magyar girl' while stationed in Kaposvár – and he, as well as his friend, resisted the temptation, adding that it was improper for a woman to 'hunt for men'.[179] Even Josef Šrámek, so infatuated with French girls, sometimes regarded their skills of seduction as going beyond acceptable limits, calling them 'flirts',[180] while Alois Dolejší seemed genuinely scared by the behaviour of the local girls in Haidenschaft (Ajdovščina in today's Slovenia) during a celebration of St Mary's Day: 'Women shoot us gleaming glances like cats, performing their orgies much to our horror'.[181] And finally, in his time as a POW in Russia, Vladislav Květoň had difficulty understanding the behaviour of the local girls and ladies who 'enjoyed showing us' their naked bodies while bathing in a stream, two of them even approaching him at a station in Rowno while he was urinating behind a shack:

> Two girls of perhaps twenty-years of age appeared from nowhere, frantically whispering and constantly prodding one another. They came all the way to me and one of them pulled fifty kopeks out of her purse and pushed it into my hand, saying something all the time while blushing ... It took me a while to understand that they wanted to see my thing. It embarrassed me and I hastily climbed back into the car.[182]

Of course, the reality behind these stories and the perception of it by the authors are two separate categories, and it seems that the soldiers may have had a tendency to see sexual overtones even in behaviour not necessarily connected to sexuality. For example, the same Vladislav Květoň was shocked when 'women from a village in Kerensk started to miss men a bit. Their husbands being at the front, they came for us and demanded to take us home'.[183] It may very well be speculated that the women in question were not so much enamoured by the idea of having a man in bed as much as they missed the workforce on their farms. Similarly, many other soldiers' stories apparently tell us more about sexuality constantly occupying their minds and the way they saw the world than about the women themselves. However, even if it was only a perception, it is clear they were deeply resentful of such behaviour, and it needs to be asked why. We may assume that, from their point of view, these women crossed a line in transforming themselves from objects into subjects, therefore upsetting the gender order at its core. Sexually active and aggressive women entered a territory where they had no place, threatening the soldiers' masculinity by acquiring one of its key traits whilst being female. By exhibiting masculine sexual qualities, these females in fact discredited and devalued the entire concept of manliness for the men.

The fact that soldiers were reluctant to allow women to enter what they perceived as the sphere of masculine identity and existence is most apparent in the way in which they treat female nurses in their writings, both those in field hospitals and those serving in the hinterland. Except for more or less random encounters with local women, it is the nurses who are the 'feminine type' reflected upon the most by frontline soldiers, often serving as a projection of their masculine fears and worries. In the spring of 1917, however, another

Figure 2.4 Masculinized femininity or feminized masculinity? Wartime propaganda showing a woman dressed in uniform, for now only as a military nurse (a 1916 calendar of the Austro-Hungarian Red Cross, Museum of Eastern Bohemia, Hradec Králové).

category of 'frontline woman' appeared – the *weibliche Hilfskräfte für die Armee im Felde*, the Women's Auxiliary Labour Force in the Field, numbering about 50,000 women by the end of the war.[184] These women not only carried out duties firmly rooted as much in the contemporary discourse of femininity as those of the nurses (for the latter caring for the wounded and the sick; for the former as cooks, washerwomen, seamstresses, etc.), but also got dangerously close to jobs traditionally perceived as masculine (clerks, drivers, switchboard operators, etc.). And whatever their job, they often performed it in areas perceived by the home front audience as 'the front line', even though they were actually far at the rear. As mentioned in Chapter 1, 'the frontline', 'the military' and 'the army' were all symbolic spaces associated, from the very beginning of the war, with masculinity. The fact that these women often seemed to share the many discomforts of military life with their male colleagues was disconcerting to many, as these discomforts were supposed to be the 'badges' of wartime hegemonic masculinity.

As Bianca Schönberger wrote in her study of female nurses in the German army, 'the fact that women were employed "in the field" – a sphere with a genuinely masculine connotation – played an important role in the social and cultural formation of gender images in wartime society'.[185] Under the official discourse, nurses and auxiliary corps-women were, of course, painted as prime examples of 'womanly service to the country'.[186] However, at the same time, there is an underlying effort to make sure that the frontline was still fully understood to be a masculine space populated by 'real men': 'There was a civilian nurse in Nisk who wanted to go and help the men in the front line at all costs. She was crying when I refused the idea', wrote an anonymous officer in one of the propaganda 'letters of our soldiers' published in the press, the text pointing to both the patriotism of the nurse and at the fact that the true frontline is no place for a woman.[187] What is also important regarding the public discourse is the fact that it strenuously endeavoured to picture nurses as asexual 'angels in white', describing their relationship with the wounded men as 'sisterly' or 'motherly' in an effort to quell any doubts about their true femininity and chastity in the face of the brutality of war.[188]

However, it was the sexuality of the nurses or, generally, of all the women present in the 'space of war', and sexual discipline as a basis of their moral qualities, which was in doubt anyway.[189] It was not just the moral guardians at home who may have felt threatened by the notion of women being too close to the horrors and mayhem of war – upon looking at the Czech soldiers' writings, it seems that they more or less internalized these fears into their own vision of the wartime gender dynamics. Of course, we encounter a number of sources that stay true to the official discourse, which is hardly surprising since when painfully wounded, exhausted and scared men are confronted first-hand with the comforting touch of a nurse, they easily accept her as the perfect 'angel in white', a human touch of femininity in the masculine world of war: 'A young Jewish nurse enters', František Jaroš recalls of his stay in a field hospital on the Eastern Front in 1917. 'She stops by every bed and talks to the wounded. Finally coming to me, she sits beside me, tells me stories, smiles, strokes my head and left arm – and I feel wonderful'.[190] But the idealized imagery, rooted in undoubtedly sincere feelings of relief and tranquillity, is all too often subverted by morally problematic undercurrents ensuing from the sexualized notion of 'frontline' femininity: 'A female doctor comes to us twice a day, dressed in a white coat. Her face is like that of a madonna when she passes our beds, seemingly distant and cold-hearted, but in fact both attentive and sensitive'. Up to this point, František Skála adheres faithfully to the idealizing trope, but the text continues: 'There are rumours that she's under a medical clerk's spell. These rumours may have originated in the fact that he gets whatever he wants from her'. Even the 'madonna' imagery did not stop men from regarding a woman as an inherently morally corrupt, sexualized object: 'Men who have barely recovered from their wounds and diseases are salivating with lust, their eyes pinned on Anna the pretty nurse'.[191]

It seems that while the men tended to accept the angelic and asexual image of the nurse to an extent, internalizing it especially in those moments when they appreciated the tender physical touch the most (when in pain and suffering), their general view of women in hospital service was still under the influence of the notion that war and the military are inherently masculine symbolic spaces, and any woman present in such an environment had been driven there by her sexual desire for men's bodies. As a result, her morally proper femininity is placed in serious doubt. These doubts are often expressed innocuously, such as when a soldier is somewhat struck by the fact that nurses do not even blush at the sight of naked men waiting for their clothes at a delousing station, something he would expect from decent girls,[192] or when soldiers contemplate nurses who, they are convinced, 'offer their services' to the officers in the hospital's dark corners.[193] In the diary of Josef Slezák, there are plenty of nurses, 'loose types by the look of them, thinking only about having fun with the men instead of taking care of us properly'.[194] And, finally, it is Josef Skála who, in his diary, claims that all nurses are invariably prostitutes:

> Most of the nurses in the hospital have given themselves fully to whoring around. They and their lovers have no shame whatsoever … Out at the back, behind the rehabilitation hut, there is a large and empty hospital ward with several surgical tables and gurneys lying around … Soldiers used them to shag nurses, often in broad daylight. They had no qualms about copulating even when someone on our side came to the fence. If that happened, they just stuck out their tongues at you and went on with their business.[195]

As expected, the image of the other 'intruders' into the masculine space of war – the members of the auxiliary women's force – was no better: 'There are

Figure 2.5 'A Battlefield Dream': official, idealized notion of womanhood on a wartime postcard (Museum of Eastern Bohemia, Hradec Králové).

only girls employed in staff offices these days, writing reports and such. They are surrounded by officers who flirt and fool around with them', wrote Alois Dolejší in his diary while staying in hospital in Ljubljana in 1917.[196] All these women were particularly dangerous to the gender order – first, they existed in environments where a woman had no place, except perhaps as a sexualized object, a prostitute; and, second, they refused to fit into that category by shedding the notion of passivity. Perhaps the best and most complex summary of the soldiers' puzzlement and disgust at this gender chaos is to be found in the forgotten war novel *Voják statečný* (*A Brave Soldier*) by Alois Kaiser:

> But the thing that hurt Julek the most was the arrival of the 'hilfskräfte'. The very word 'hilfskräfte' elicited contempt and hatred in him. The 'hilfskräfte' were the women's auxiliary forces ... The staffs are full of them now ... Upon arrival, beautiful faces of luscious, immaculately dressed women stare at the miserable and hungry soldier. This is where the true social life is happening, with all its fads, affairs, smiles and flirting. There is no War here ... He thinks of the moments of carnal love hidden behind the blinds of the officers' quarters, mad and hungry at the provocative womanhood that has come to make his wretched life insufferable... one that knows no tears, no despair, no strokes of misfortune, one that only laughs out loud...[197]

In war, women should cry, not enjoy the 'dividend' that should be reserved for the warriors. The 'provocative womanhood' not only endangers 'true', passive and suffering femininity, it also worsens the soldier's condition by the very fact of its existence – it is he who should be masculine, provocative, sexually aggressive, it is he who deserves rest and the chance to flirt and smile. Instead, he is miserable, exhausted, hungry and unmanned – whereas the system to an extent allowed these women to be in a position of dominance and sometimes even power over men like him. Similarly, as he felt all his power and control being taken away from him, nurses were making daily decisions concerning his very body.

Soldiers, fighting in a war that was supposed to confer or confirm their full manliness, slowly realized that they were gradually losing control over their eating habits as well as living standards; they had no influence over their own life and their own death. They had become passive victims, spiritless animals or machines without will. They had lost all social power. At the same time, it appeared that women were becoming more powerful with every day. For the ordinary rank-and-file men, women were almost out of control, taking over many traditional aspects of masculinity – uniforms, aggressive sexuality, as well as patriotic service in war, even in the army, one that was supposed to be a 'school of manhood'. The worst part is that the soldiers regarded these women not just with anger, but also with lust. In the same way that they compromised on their manliness in the trenches, they also did so in their relations with women – they yearn for them, they seek their comfort when wounded, but they are afraid of them at the same time. They are afraid of the fact that the sexualized objects are becoming subjects of their own – and they, according to the logic of gender dichotomy, are becoming passive objects themselves.

Because this whole process took place in the relatively stable system (at least from a temporal point of view, since our focus here is on just four years) that is the gender order, its consequences vis-à-vis sustaining motivation were probably only subordinate, covered by many layers of more immediate factors such as those we have already discussed (the supply crisis and exhaustion producing war-weariness on the background of a sense of compromised masculinity) or will discuss below (such as the overall economic collapse and failure of the authorities, threatening some of the key elements of masculine identity). If, from the point of view of its contemporaries, war was a gendered event and the 'tournament of manliness' was one of the elements in soldiers' initial motivation, then it must be conceded that the wartime reality, combined with shifts in the reciprocal positioning of femininity and masculinity within the dynamics of the gender order, delivered severe blows to this notion throughout the duration of the war. The constantly questioned discourse of war as a masculine enterprise was arguably played out on the very background of Czech soldiers' motivation, being perhaps the most subconscious part of it, but there is no doubt that it helped to transform the war, from the point of view of the men thrown into its midst, into one great compromise of manliness.

Based on the previous paragraphs, it may seem that our interpretation of Czech soldiers' masculinity is close to that presented by Klaus Theweleit in his classic psychoanalytical study of members of the *freikorps*, the paramilitary force formed during the postwar chaos in many areas of Germany. In one of his conclusions, Theweleit stated that 'bourgeois masculinity' is one of the keys to unlocking the ideology behind the 'white terror' in the early years of the Weimar Republic. In his understanding, it is a masculinity freed of all inhibitions in the name of the struggle against the 'red tide' of communism, a 'male fantasy' glorifying purely homosocial institutions of fighting units, one that sees femininity as something 'foreign', pigeonholing it into three specific categories: 'whore', 'mother' and 'madonna'.[198] However, this impression is wrong. The reality that most men, including Czech soldiers, experienced during the First World War differed significantly from the fantasy world that Theweleit's specific and rather small group of men created for themselves shortly afterwards.[199]

Starting with their attitude to women, it was much less schematic and a lot simpler. In general, they tended to see the women they met while in service primarily as sexual objects. As long as these women did not behave like independent subjects, posing a threat to men's masculine dominance and feeling of power, soldiers often felt compassion for them, with a clear tendency to blame the war (along with their feminine nature) for their sorry moral state. Ironically, this was the same logic that many men used in their general musings over their own situation, worrying about what war was doing to their own humanity, dignity and masculinity.[200] There are almost no sources exhibiting an outright dislike for femininity itself, or to particular characteristics that are seen as feminine. On the other hand, there are also precious few authors who attempt to idealize the military and its homosocial institutions. While going to war may have been a sort of involuntary, albeit adventurous escape from a boring civilian life for some, the realities of army life and modern warfare quickly caused them to change their opinion.

The same is true for what Theweleit describes as deliberate distancing from everything civilian – as will be seen in Chapter 5, soldiers lived as much with their own concerns as with those of their loved ones at home, seeing the women there as a source of much-needed intimacy and positive emotions. There is no need to go far for an example, since there is one presented in Alois Kaiser's war novel. While its main character certainly hates the *hilfskräfte*, he also dreams 'of the immeasurable, unrelenting tenderness of an unknown woman, who will come, in whom he puts his faith as he did in God, in whom he places many great hopes … and watches his comrades with envy when they receive letters from their wives and lovers'.[201] It almost appears as if many soldiers saw two opposite worlds – the one they inhabited at that moment, and the idealized image of a respectable home where, as Stanislav Kostka Neumann wrote in his memoir, 'the most natural woman's function is realized, as a keeper of the warming flames in the midst of that one firm place without which one is only an eternal nomad through the world'. For Neumann and many others like him, a woman was primarily 'the good flame of my own life' in 'that little lighthouse of living' – his home.[202] It is hardly surprising that it is women (and children) who are more often than not on the minds and lips of men dying in battle or in a hospital, at least according to their surviving comrades, as it is women who usually receive the symbolic 'last kiss' of those who 'go into the trenches'.[203]

The masculine 'world of war' may well be interpreted as a symbolic space serving as a living embodiment of everything that home is not, including morals: 'Life in the city is a little freer than we are used to back home', František Skála wrote of the garrison town of Kaposvár. 'On the main promenade, ladies in the ground floor windows are looking out at us with their bosoms half-naked'.[204] While the world of war was, in the soldiers' minds, connected with promiscuity, anonymity and masculinity, home (hopefully) offered much-needed emotional support, as well as continuous reassurance that they were still those decent, respectable men they used to be. While the role expected of women in the 'world of war' was limited to mechanized, impersonal sexual pleasure, the women at home were a key element of emotional survival. 'You guys at home feel like strangers to me now', one of the men complained in a letter to his male friend. 'You actually make me to turn to women to get some of those good memories one needs so much. Bye'.[205] However, as these women were hundreds of miles away, and leave was a rare commodity for most of the men, soldiers almost constantly felt the acute shortages of those 'most natural functions' of femininity, i.e. nurture, care, emotional understanding and intimacy. As a result, it was much too difficult to cope with the massive stress of wartime existence, and as a means of emotional survival, a certain 'remapping' of wartime military masculinity became an attractive option.

Notes

1. Slezák, *Paměti Josefa Slezáka k I. světové válce*, vol. 1, 2–5.
2. Ibid., 79.
3. Ibid., vol. 3, 76.
4. Ibid., vol. 4, 11.
5. Ibid., 33 and 36.
6. Ibid., vol. 5, 8.
7. On the topic of the 'official war memory' in interwar Czechoslovakia, see Ivan Šedivý, 'Legionáři a československá armáda 1918–1938', in *České země a Československo v Evropě XIX. a XX. století. Sborník prací k 65. narozeninám prof. Dr. Roberta Kvačka*, eds Jindřich Dejmek and Josef Hanzal (Prague, 1997), 209–30; see also Jan Galandauer, *2. 7. 1917. Bitva u Zborova: Česká legenda* (Prague, 2002); Nancy Wingfield, 'The Battle of Zborov and the Politics of Commemoration in Czechoslovakia', *East European Politics & Societies* 4, no. 2 (2003), 654–81; and Natali Stegmann, 'Soldaten und Bürger. Selbstbilder tschechoslowakischer Legionäre in der Ersten Republik', *Militärgeschichtliche Zeitschrift* 1, no. 1 (2002): 25–48.
8. See Lein, *Pflichterfüllung oder Hochverrat*, 53–72; see also Cornwall, 'Morale and Patriotism in the Austro-Hungarian Army, 174–75. The level of exhaustion reached its nadir in March and April, while combat effectiveness plummeted with more and more ill-trained, ill-commanded and inexperienced replacements being conscripted into their ranks to make up for the losses. As Lein proves, the infamous affair of k.u.k. Infantry Regiment 28 from Prague was a direct consequence of deploying an exhausted unit back to the front in April 1915 – during the ensuing battle, its three battalions were surrounded by a Russian assault, isolated and soon surrendered to the enemy almost completely. When a few months later a similar fate affected another regiment with a Czech-speaking majority, the k.u.k. Infantry 36, and both units were swiftly and very publicly disbanded by the Austrian command, trying to cover up its own lapses and appease the Austrian-German nationalists, a legend was born of the heroic patriots (from the Czechoslovak point of view) or treacherous Czechs (according to Austrian Germans) 'going over to the enemy'. See Lein, *Pflichterfüllung oder Hochverrat*, 73–199; and Reiter, 'Der Untergang des IR 36', 26–68.
9. Bohumil Sperling, *Český důstojník na frontách monarchie: válečný deník*, ed. Leonard Hobst (Brno, 2003), 114, diary entry from 13 October 1917.
10. Quoted in Corwnall, 'Morale and Patriotism in the Austro-Hungarian Army, 1914–1918', 189.
11. See Cornwall, *The Undermining of Austria-Hungary*, 142–173 and 202–68.
12. Jarkovský, 'Kronika ze světové války', 89.
13. Fears of punishment could go well beyond one's individuality, encompassing the soldier's family as well: 'What would Božena do, if his desertion would became known to the army command in Vienna?' mused an artilleryman on the Piave front. Tříska, ed., *Zapomenutá fronta*, 84. His fears were not unsubstantiated, as the army often stopped paying any pensions and benefit payments to the families of those soldiers who were suspect of desertion or voluntary surrender. In 1918, this could well mean the difference between starving and survival. See Lein, 'The Military Conduct of the Austro-Hungarian Czechs in the First World War', 530.

14. Lynn, *Bayonets of the Republic*, 35.
15. Váchal, *Malíř na frontě*, 13–14.
16. Ibid., 90.
17. George Orwell, *Down and Out in Paris and London* (London, 1933), 19–20.
18. Váchal, *Malíř na frontě*, 254.
19. On the issues of food supply in the Austro-Hungarian army and the importance it had for soldiers' morale, see the case study of Slovenian troops by Rok Stergar, 'Hrana na bojiščih 1. svetovej vojne: izkušnje slovenskih vojakov', *Prispevki za novejšo zgodovino* 55, no. 2 (2015): 22–53. For a British comparison, see Rachel Duffett, *The Stomach for Fighting: Food and the Soldiers of the Great War* (Manchester, 2012).
20. Kisch, *Vojákem pražského sboru*, 59, diary entry from 26 August 1914.
21. Sabine Haring confirms this conclusion in her sociohistorical study of the 'emotional world' of Austro-Hungarian soldiers during the first few months of the war on the Eastern Front: 'As is clear from both [of our] sources, combat soldiers' mood was heavily dependent upon their material situation at any given moment, especially upon the supply situation regarding food and water, on weather conditions, and on the quality of roads'. Sabine A. Haring, 'K.u.k. Soldaten an der Ostfront im Sommer und Herbst 1914: Eine emotionssoziologische Analyse', in *Jenseits des Schützengrabens*, 84.
22. Dolejší, *Válečné vzpomínky z první světové války vojína Dolejše*, 62, diary entry from 10 January 1917. For other examples, see Květoň, *Vzpomínky z první světové války*, 14–20; Černý, *Moje záznamy ze světové války*, 91 ff; Jarkovský, 'Kronika ze světové války', passim; Poláček, *Zápisky Václava Poláčka ze světové války*, 43; or Slezák, *Paměti Josefa Slezáka k I. světové válce*, vol. 2, 13–16. Food, its quality and quantity are also one of the favourite topics in soldier's correspondence. See, for example, the collections of letters Jan Šmatlán or Ludvík Maršík. *Zapomenuté hlasy*, 7–31 and 65–88.
23. Tříska, ed., *Zapomenutá fronta*, 110.
24. Černý, *Moje záznamy ze světové války*, 117.
25. Slezák, *Paměti Josefa Slezáka k I. světové válce*, vol. 3, 113.
26. Fráňa Šrámek, 'Popová', in Fráňa Šrámek, *Žasnoucí voják: povídky z vojny* (Prague, 1924), 258.
27. Kisch, *Vojákem pražského sboru*, 116, diary entry from 27 September 1914.
28. Váchal, *Malíř na frontě*, 166.
29. Karel Jaroš, *Z turecké armády do britského zajetí*, edited by Petr Havel (Prague, 1995), 32.
30. Jurman, ed., *Legionářská odyssea*, 11; see also Tříska, ed., *Zapomenutá fronta*, 55.
31. 'On the 26th day of October, the hungry Austrian armies, half-crazed after two years of horrific fighting in the Alpine wastelands, entered the plains of Italy on a rampage worthy of the wildest animals. The wine that was to be found in every house and every cellar made the situation even worse, as the hungry men got quickly drunk and knew no limits'. See František Jaroš, 'Pochod benátskou rovinou až k Piavě', in *Domov za války*, vol. 4, 470. For the sheer scale of pillage, plunder and rape that Austro-Hungarian and German troops brought upon the Venetian Plain, see Mark Thompson, *The White War: Life and Death on the Italian Front, 1915–1919* (London, 2008), 348–51.
32. For comparison, see Stergar, 'Hrana na bojiščih 1. svetovej vojne: izkušnje slovenskih vojakov', 43–45.
33. Šmída, *Vzpomínky z vojny*, 133.
34. Tříska, ed., *Zapomenutá fronta*, 84, 89

35. Slezák, *Paměti Josefa Slezáka k I. světové válce*, vol. 5, 16.
36. Bohuslav Hála, 'Vzpomínka na 11. sočskou bitvu', Vojenský historický archiv – Vojenský ústřední archiv (Central Military Archives – Military Historical Archives Prague), Sbírka osob II, Pozůstalost Bohuslava Hály, Vzpomínky: *Vzpomínka na 11. sočskou bitvu* (typescript), 58.
37. Deák, *Beyond Nationalism*, 202.
38. Dolejší, *Válečné vzpomínky z první světové války vojína Dolejše*, 285, diary entry from 28 September 1918.
39. Cornwall, 'Morale and Patriotism in the Austro-Hungarian Army', 182. Similarly, Gunther Rothenberg agrees that while 'nationalist propaganda' has played its role in mass desertions during the Kerensky offensive (which included the Battle of Zborov and the infamous 'affair' of the Czech-dominated k.u.k. Infantry Regiment 75), 'they were also due to the growing war-weariness appearing in all armies and to the totally inadequate rations'. See Rothenberg, *The Army of Francis Joseph*, 205 and 211. On the topic of the 75th Infantry and its failure at Zborov, see Lein, *Pflichterfüllung oder Hochverrat?*, 203–344.
40. This is especially true in the case of Rumburk in Northern Bohemia, where it was the repatriated POWs from Russia who mutinied against the supply conditions due to a combination of suspicion-fuelled maltreatment on their return as well as against the prospect of being sent to the front again. See Marek, *Pod císařskou šibenicí*, 15–96. On the ill-treatment of former POWs by the Austro-Hungarian authorities, motivated by suspicions regarding their loyalty and political beliefs, see Rachamimov, *POWs and the Great War*, 191–95. On the Kotor mutiny, see Richard Plaschka, *Cattaro-Prag: Revolte und Revolution, Kriegsmarine und Heer österreich-Ungarns im Feuer der Aufstandsbewegung vom 1. Februar und 28. Oktober 1918* (Graz, 1963); or more recently Richard Plaschka, *Matrosen, Offiziere, Rebellen: Krisenkonfrontationen zur See 1900–1918* (Vienna, 1984), vol. 2, 155–278.
41. Šmída, *Vzpomínky z vojny*, 138.
42. On desertion rates in the Austro-Hungarian army late in the war, see Rauchensteiner, *The First World War and the End of the Habsburg Monarchy*, 981–82; see also Richard Plaschka, Horst Haselsteiner and Arnold Suppan, *Innere Front: Militärassistenz, Widerstand und Umsturz in der Donaumonarchie 1918* (Vienna, 1974), vol. 1, 278–90 and 374–400. On the limited importance of political motivations for desertion before 1918, see Oswald Überegger, 'Politik, Nation und Desertion: Zur Relevanz politisch-nationaler und ideologischer Verweigerungsmotive für die Desertion österreichisch-ungarischer Soldaten im Ersten Weltkrieg', *Wiener Zeitschrift zur Geschichte der Neuzeit* 8, no. 2 (2008): 109–19. For the most radical form of 'military resistance' springing from the mixture of escapism, defence of the community and rural political radicalism – the 'green cadres' – see, for example, Jakub Beneš, 'The Green Cadres and the Collapse of Austria-Hungary in 1918', *Past & Present* 236, no. 1 (2017): 207–41. See also Jakub Beneš, '"Zelené kádry" jako radikální alternativa pro venkov na západním Slovensku a ve středovýchodní Evropě 1917–1920', *Forum Historiae* 9, no. 2 (2015): 20–34. For a wider overview of the issue in the context of the Austro-Hungarian military law and traditions, see Christa Hämmerle, 'Desertion vor Gericht: Zur Quellenproblematik von Militärgeschichtsakten am Beispiel der k.(u.)k. Armee 1868–1914/18', *Wiener Zeitschrift zur Geschichte der Neuzeit* 8, no. 2 (2008): 33–52.
43. Slezák, *Paměti Josefa Slezáka k I. světové válce*, vol. 5, 42–43.

44. Dolejší, *Válečné vzpomínky z první světové války vojína Dolejše*, 162 and 216, entries for 23 February and 6 July 1918.
45. Kisch, *Vojákem pražského sboru*, 109 and 42, entries for 19 September and 16 August 1914.
46. Váchal, *Malíř na frontě*, 45.
47. Šmída, *Vzpomínky z vojny*, 82.
48. Recollections of Josef Rezek, infantryman in k.u.k. Infantry Regiment 18, in *Když naši dědové bojovali a umírali v 1. světové válce*, ed. Miloš Konečný (Vlkov, 2014), 39. There are many similar cases described in the sources quoted here; see, for example, Slezák, *Paměti Josefa Slezáka k I. světové válce*, vol. III, 13. See also the diary of Karel Vaněk, entry from 1 April 1915: 'It is quite unpleasant to be wet from the waist down and sleep, or rather just lie, on the ground. I'm shivering like a little dog from the cold'. Vaněk, *Charašó pán, da?*, 44.
49. Hušák, 'Dvacetiletý ve válce', in *Domov za války*, vol. 3, 206.
50. Černý, *Moje záznamy ze světové války*, 114–16.
51. Holmes, *Acts of War*, 214.
52. Václav Jílek to his wife, 28 June 1917, in *Zapomenuté hlasy*, 107.
53. Josef Klejna, *Voják – zajatec – legionář*, ed. Michaela Mrázová (Velké Přílepy, 2014), 53. Egon Erwin Kisch describes a similar state of consciousness in his diary: 'Here and there, an apathetic soldier passes us. If only there was a spark of life in him, a little spark of hope … he would hurry up. But he just does not care'. Kisch, *Vojákem pražského sboru*, 194, entry from 9 December 1914. For other vivid descriptions of the 'vegetative state', see also Skála, *Válečný deník*, 89; or Tříska, ed., *Zapomenutá fronta*, 52.
54. Vítek, *V cizích službách*, 152.
55. Mudrák, *Bojoval jsem za císaře pána*, 36.
56. Stéphane Audoin-Rouzeau, *Men at War, 1914–1918: National Sentiment and Trench Journalism in France during the First World War* (Oxford, 1992), 36–42.
57. Lord Moran, *The Anatomy of Courage*, 13.
58. Kisch, *Vojákem pražského sboru*, 80, diary entry from 7 September 1914.
59. Morávek, *Špatný voják*, 153.
60. While numerical strength of militaries grew at an ever-increasing rate during the modern era, technological and logistical changes in the late nineteenth and early twentieth centuries enabled them cover battlefields spanning increasingly massive areas. By the end of the Second World War, the ratio of men to space was one soldier to every 27,500 square metres. In the American Civil War eighty years before, it was one man to every 257 metres. See Bourke, *Intimate History of Killing*, 6.
61. Lein, *Pflichterfüllung oder Hochverrat*, 120–47.
62. As noted by István Deák, only about 500,000 troops out of 3 million were involved in combat duty by October 1918, which made it nigh-impossible to relieve larger units for any sensible amount of time. See Deák, *Beyond Nationalism*, 202.
63. For specific summaries of Austro-Hungarian operations on the Southwest and Eastern Fronts, respectively, see Günther Kronenbitter, 'Die k. u. k. Armee an der Südwestfront', in *Krieg in den Alpen: Österreich-Ungarn und Italien im Ersten Weltkrieg (1914–1918)*, eds Nicola Labanca and Oswald Überegger (Vienna, 2015), 105–27; Christa Hämmerle, 'Opferhelden? Zur Geschichte der k.u.k. Soldaten an der Südwestfront', in *Krieg in den Alpen*, 155–80; and Richard Lein, 'A Train Ride to Disaster: The Austro-Hungarian Eastern Front in 1914', in *1914: Austria-Hungary, the Origins, and the First Year of*

World War I, eds Günter Bischof, Ferdinand Karlhofer, and Samuel R. Williamson (Innsbruck, 2014), 95–126.
64. František Loubal, 'V kraji Doberda, Rovereta a Tridentu', in *Domov za války*, vol. 4, 185.
65. On the Austro-Hungarian soldiers' perception of the 'landscapes of war', see Jason C. Engle, '"This Monstrous Front Will Devour Us All": The Austro-Hungarian Soldier Experience, 1914–1915', in *1914: Austria-Hungary, the Origins, and the First Year of World War I*, 153–158.
66. Mudrák, *Bojoval jsem za císaře pána*, 73–74 and 77.
67. Ulrych, 'Moje zápisky', 44. 'In Russia we were lucky', agreed a telephone operator serving with k.u.k. Infantry Regiment 98. 'But here we are losing men every day … The Italians start to rage as early as seven o'clock. It is not just one hell being torn open; it is a hundred infernos. We cannot tell individual guns firing, it all blends into one deafening noise'. Skála, *Válečný deník*, 182–83.
68. Chmela, *Vzpomínky z 1. světové války*, 23, diary entry from 30 November 1917.
69. Mudrák, *Bojoval jsem za císaře pána*, 80.
70. Ulrych, 'Moje zápisky', 85. 'The front in Italy was feared. Everyone wanted to make it to Russia instead', recalled a one-year volunteer of k.k. Landwehr Infantry Regiment 7 from Pilsen. František Leitl, 'Má účast v Brusilovově ofenzivě', in *Domov za války*, vol. 3, 348. František Šmída, a junior officer in k.u.k. Infantry Regiment 79, observed the same. See Šmída, *Vzpomínky z vojny*, 60.
71. Slezák, *Paměti Josefa Slezáka k I. světové válce*, vol. 3, 61.
72. See Christa Hämmerle, '"Es ist immer der Mann, der den Kampf entscheidet, und nicht die Waffe": Die Männlichkeit des k.u.k. Gebirgskriegers in der soldatischen Erinnerungskultur', in *Der Erste Weltkrieg im Alpenraum/La Grande Guerra nell'arco alpino: Erfahrung, Deutung, Erinnerung/Esperienze e memoriam*, eds Hermann J.W. Kuprian and Oswald Überreger (Innsbruck, 2006), 35–60; see also Fernando Esposito, 'Über keinem Gipfel ist Ruh. Helden- und Kriegertum als Topoi medialisierter Kriegserfahrungen deutscher und italienischer Flieger', in *Der Erste Weltkrieg im Alpenraum*, 73–90. See also Vincenc Rajšp, ed., *Isonzofront 1915–1917: Die Kultur des Erinnerns* (Vienna, 2010).
73. Paul Pireaud to Marie Pireaud, 16 June 1918, quoted in Martha Hanna, 'A Republic of Letters: The Epistolary Tradition in France during World War I', *American Historical Review* 108, no. 5 (2003): 1356.
74. Alois L. Kaiser, *Voják statečný: Fragment posledního náporu třistaleté armády* (Prague, 1930), 139.
75. Kisch, *Vojákem pražského sboru*, 129, diary entry from 4 October 1914.
76. See, for example, Bouška, 'Zápisky ze světové války'; or Skála, *Válečný deník*.
77. Jan Šmatlán to his parents from Galicia, 1 June 1915, in *Zapomenuté hlasy*, 30.
78. Skála, *Válečný deník*, 106.
79. Jan Sýkora, 'Tarnavka – Obrázek ze světové války', Central Military Archives – Military Archives in Prague, Sbírka historických prací, kart. 7 (manuscript), 8.
80. For a summary of a similar state of mind experienced by the British soldiers, see Dennis Winter, *Death's Men: Soldiers of the Great War* (London, 1978), 80–106; see also Michael Roper, *The Secret Battle: Emotional Survival in the Great War* (Manchester, 2009), 261.
81. For some general examples, see René Schilling, *Kriegshelden: Deutungsmuster heroischer Männlichkeite in Deutschland, 1813–1945* (Paderborn, 2002), 252–86; Burkhard Fuhs,

'Fliegende Helden: Die Kultur der Gewalt am Beispiel von Kampfpiloten und ihren Maschinen', in *Gewalt in der Kultur*, eds Rolf W. Brednich and Walter Hartinger (Passau, 1994), 705–20.

82. Bourdieu, *Le domination masculine*, 11–33; Gilmore, *Manhood in the Making*, 9–28 and 220–30; Connell, *Masculinities*, 185–203; or R.W. Connell, 'The Big Picture: Masculinities in Recent World History', *Theory and Society* 5, no. 2 (1993): 597–623. For the specific case of European culture of the late nineteenth century, see the analysis of masculine honour in relation to the duelling culture of the European bourgeoisie in France and Germany: Robert A. Nye, *Masculinity and Male Codes of Honor in Modern France* (Oxford, 1993); Ute Frevert, *Men of Honour: A Social and Cultural History of the Duel* (Cambridge, 1995).
83. Eric J. Leed, *No Man's Land: Combat and Identity in World War I* (New York, 1979), 114.
84. Dolejší, *Válečné vzpomínky z první světové války vojína Dolejše*, 18, diary entry from 8 July 1916; see also Skála, *Válečný deník*, 243: 'In these horrible moments, man feels so infinitely small'.
85. For details on everyday realities of trench warfare, see John Ellis, *Eye Deep in Hell: Trench Warfare in World War I* (Baltimore, 1976); or Winter, *Death's Men*.
86. Quoted in Taudyová, 'Válečná milostná korespondence Jaroslava Havlíčka', 98.
87. For a similar conclusion on the 'disempowering nature' of the specific conditions typical for First World War warfare (including the massive use of artillery, the constricted nature of the trenches, the 'empty battlefield' and 'missing enemy', creating a general feeling of 'isolation', 'inability' and 'incapacity' in the participants), see Watson, *Enduring the Great War*, 28–34.
88. The so-called 'letters from our soldiers' were a regular staple of most daily newspapers and their purpose was, among other things, to disseminate a militarized version of hegemonic masculinity in the public discourse. The quoted references are from a collection of such letters, also published during the war, undoubtedly with the same propaganda intentions. See *Listy našich vojáků. Co nám píší z bojiště* (Prague, 1915) – references are from several letters available in volumes 1–4.
89. Dolejší, *Válečné vzpomínky z první světové války vojína Dolejše*, 29, diary entry from 13 September 1916.
90. Bouška, 'Zápisky ze světové války', 30.
91. Jurman, ed., *Legionářská odyssea*, 14.
92. František Škoda to Marie Škodová, 20 October 1914, in *Zapomenuté hlasy*, 92. For the 'fortunes of war', see Josef Janošík to his brother Jan, 21 December 1914, Josef Janošík papers, private collection of Jan Janošík.
93. Jan Šmatlán to his parents, 20 January 1915, in *Zapomenuté hlasy*, 24.
94. 'Bohuš' in a letter to Róza Kropáčková, 1 June 1918, in *Zapomenuté hlasy*, 111; and Karel Šulc to Marie Šulcová, 20 March 1918, in *Zapomenuté hlasy*, 111.
95. Rachel Duffett, in her study of food in the British army during the First World War, noted similarly that 'it was not only the poor quality of the food that distressed the men but the lack of control they had over their diet'. See Duffett, *The Stomach for Fighting*, 2. It is also interesting to see how quickly these inherent traits of military institutions spread into the hinterland subject to sudden militarization under war economy measures, and how similar the consequences were for those who experienced them. For the example of Bohemia, see Kučera, *Rationed Life*, 12–56.

96. Duffett, *The Stomach for Fighting*, 3–10 and 47.
97. Connell, *Masculinities*, 52; see also Connell and Messerschmidt, 'Hegemonic Masculinity', 837–38.
98. Forth, *Masculinity in the Modern West*, 8. For more on masculinity and the body, see Martin Dinges, '"Hegemoniale Männlichkeit" – ein Konzept auf dem Prüfstand', in *Männer – Macht – Körper*, 7–33; Andrea Cornwall and Nancy Lindisfarne, 'Dislocating Masculinity: Gender, Power, and Anthropology', in *Dislocating Masculinity: Comparative Ethnographies*, eds Andrea Cornwall and Nancy Lindisfarne (London, 1994), 34–37; or Kathleen Canning, 'The Body as Method? Reflections on the Place of the Body in the Gender History', *Gender & History* 3, no. 2 (1999): 499–513.
99. Sabine Kienitz, 'Body Damage: War Disability and Constructions of Masculinity in Weimar Germany', in *Home/Front: The Military, War and Gender in Twentieth Century Germany*, eds Karen Hagemann and Stefanie Schüler-Springorum (Oxford, 2002), 186.
100. Hämmerle, 'Zur Relevanz des Connell'schen Konzepts hegemonialer Männlichkeit für "Militär und Männlichkeit/en in der Habsburgermonarchie (1868–1914/18)"', 110–12.
101. Peerz, *Vlast volá! Slovo k obyvatelstvu Rakouska-Uherska*, 42. For the general tendency of early twentieth-century armies to project expectations of combat effectiveness onto specific male body types, see Bourke, *Intimate History of Killing*, 109.
102. Šmída, *Vzpomínky z vojny*, 9, 21 and 64.
103. Gustav Habrman, *Mé vzpomínky z války: Črty a obrázky o událostech a zápasech za svobodu a samostatnost* (Prague, 1928), 27.
104. Josef Šrámek, *Paměti z první světové války Josefa Šrámka z Ústí nad Labem, 1914–1918* (Brno, 2007), 73, diary entry from 9 July 1916.
105. Lirš, *S Osmadvacátníky za světové války*, 7 and 28.
106. Dolejší, *Válečné vzpomínky z první světové války vojína Dolejše*, 121, diary entry from 5 November 1917.
107. Ulrych, 'Moje zápisky', 106.
108. Deák, *Beyond Nationalism*, 202.
109. Kaja Silverman, *Male Subjectivity at the Margins* (London, 1992), 62.
110. Mudrák, *Bojoval jsem za císaře pána*, 68.
111. Alois L. Kaiser, *Od Piavy ke Komárnu* (Prague, 1931), 10.
112. Morávek, *Špatný voják*, 127.
113. Vaněk, *Charašó pán, da?*, 18, diary entry from 12 September 1914.
114. Ibid., 36 and 40, diary entries from 19 and 22 February 1915.
115. Jan Šindelář, *Proti vlastní vůli: z deníku bojovníka první linie, 1914–1918* (Prague, 1932), 236; Vítek, *V cizích službách*, 177; Tonda Mádl, 'U 102. pěšího pluku', in *Domov za války*, vol. 4, 399; Mudrák, *Bojoval jsem za císaře pána*, 40; Stanislav Kostka Neumann, *Bragožda a jiné válečné vzpomínky* (Prague, 1928), 61.
116. Skála, *Válečný deník*, 251. For further discussion of the topic, see Rolf Spilker and Bernd Ulrich, eds, *Der Tod als Maschinist. Der industrialisierte Krieg 1914–1918* (Bramsche, 1998).
117. Křenek, *Vzpomínky na vojnu v Albanii*, 164.
118. Kučera, *Rationed Life*, 59 ff; Forth, *Masculinity in the Modern West*, 169–200.
119. Duffett, *The Stomach for Fighting*, 10–18.
120. Norbert Elias, *On the Process of Civilization* (Dublin, 2012).

121. Forth, *Masculinity in the Modern West*, 21–24. It is necessary to mention that this facet of the modern ideal of masculinity was, in Forth's opinion, in an almost permanent grip of the 'modern paradox', i.e. fears that *too much civilization* results in men being *feminized*, forcing them to search repeatedly for new paths of 'manly' escape out of a perceived 'crisis' (from sporting cults and athleticism, through the liberating use of machines (airmen), all the way to the cults of 'frontiersmen', imperial 'gentlemen', rowdy duellists or other rough-and-ready alternatives to over-civilized manliness). Ibid., 21–66. For a historical summary of 'domesticated' bourgeois masculinity, see also Connell, 'The Big Picture', 607–10; or Dinges, 'Hegemoniale Männlichkeit', 14–33.
122. Stéphane Audoin-Rouzeau talks about 'the dignity that was the first victim of the trench life', the articles in the French soldiers' trench newspapers being 'full of these outcast men's feeling of humiliation ... [and] daily degradation'. Audoin-Rouzeau, *Men at War*, 46.
123. Skála, *Válečný deník*, 13. For the definition of 'culture', see Charlotte Hooper, 'Masculinist Practices and Gender Politics: The Operation of Multiple Masculinities in International Relations', in *The 'Man' Question in International Relations*, eds Maryška Zalewski and Jane Pappart (Boulder, 1998), 33. See also Connell, *Masculinities*, 187–91; George L. Mosse, *Nationalism and Sexuality: Respectability and Abnormal Sexuality in Modern Europe* (New York, 1985), 2–23; John Tosh, 'Domesticity and Manliness in the Victorian Middle Class: The Family of Edward White Benson', in *Manful Assertions*, 44–72; or Dinges, '"Hegemoniale Männlichkeit" – ein Koncept auf dem Prüfstand', 18–25. On the gendering of the concept of culture and civilization, see also Gail Bederman, *Manliness and Civilization: A Cultural History of Gender and Race in the United States, 1880–1917* (Chicago, 1995), 9–42. For a discussion of value systems as a part of 'culture' within the context of Central Europe, see Jaroslav Krejčí, *The Paths of Civilization: Understanding the Currents of History* (Basingstoke, 2004), 7–12.
124. Kaiser, *Od Piavy ke Komárnu*, 11.
125. Diary of Rudolf Wagner, entry from 26 October 1915, in *Zapomenuté hlasy*, 24.
126. Váchal, *Malíř na frontě*, 155.
127. V.P. Hájický, 'Křížová cesta Čsl. vojska – z mých zápisků ze Srbska', Central Military Archives – Military Historical Archives in Prague, Sbírka historických prací, kart. 7 (manuscript), 2.
128. Jan Laška, *Pochod hladu Albanií (Z Niše do Valony)* (Prague, 1920), 78 and 132.
129. Černý, *Moje záznamy ze světové války*, 119.
130. Mudrák, *Bojoval jsem za císaře pána*, 35 and 40.
131. Černý, *Moje záznamy ze světové války*, 76 and 82.
132. See Rousseau's *Emile* for a prime example: Jean-Jacques Rousseau, *Émile, ou De l'éducation* (Paris, 1762). For a general discussion, see Genevieve Lloyd, *Man of Reason: 'Male' and 'Female' in Western Philosophy* (Minneapolis, 1984); or Dena Goodman, *The Republic of Letters: A Cultural History of the French Enlightenment* (New York, 1994).
133. Mudrák, *Bojoval jsem za císaře pána*, 42.
134. Holmes, *Acts of War*, 93. See also Jason Crouthamel, *An Intimate History of the Front: Masculinity, Sexuality, and German Soldiers in the First World War* (New York, 2014), 10–14 and 41–42; R.W. Connell, 'Masculinity, Violence, and War', in *Men's Lives*, eds Michael S. Kimmel and Michael A. Messner, 3rd edn (Boston, 1995), 125–30; Reid Mitchell, 'The GI in Europe and American Military Tradition', in *Time to Kill: The Soldier's Experience of War in the West, 1939–1945*, eds Paul Addison and Angus Calder (London, 1997), 313–14; and Kathy J. Phillips, *Manipulating Masculinity: War and*

Gender in Modern British and American Literature (London, 2006). From an anthropological point of view, the connection between sexuality and war is a result of the traditional motivation of warriors based on gaining access to 'reproductive resources'. See, for example, Ferguson, 'Explaining War', 46; or R. Brian Ferguson, 'Introduction: Studying War', in *Warfare, Culture, Environment*, ed R. Brian Ferguson (Orlando, 1984), 37–38.

135. Váchal, *Malíř na frontě*, 14.
136. Vančura, *Pole orná a válečná*, 102.
137. Váchal, *Malíř na frontě*, 235.
138. See Dinges, 'Hegemoniale Männlichkeit', 7–33; Connell, *Masculinities*, 52–56 and 103–6. On the connection between modern medicine, sexuality and modern gender structures, see Thomas Laquer, *Making Sex: Body and Gender from the Greeks to Freud* (Cambridge, 1990), 193–243.
139. See Ann Carden-Coyne and Laura Doan, 'Gender and Sexuality', in *Gender and the Great War*, eds Susan R. Grayzel and Tammy M. Proctor (Oxford, 2017), 95–96.
140. George Chauncey, Jr., 'Christian Brotherhood or Sexual Perversion? Homosexual Identities and the Construction of Sexual Boundaries in the World War One Era', *Journal of Social History* 19, no. 2, (1985): 190–94.
141. For the only explicit comments on the matter in this vein, see Rudolf Vlasák, *Vojáci císařovi* (2 vols, Prague, 1932), vol. 2, 23–30; see also a memoir written in 1952 by an unknown soldier, who remembered refusing repeated advances made by his commanding officer, 'an unhappy man with perverse tastes'. On an interesting note, the author's argument for his ultimate refusal was that 'he was not a teenage boy'. Unknown, 'My Memoir', manuscript, author's collection.
142. Quotations from the imperial Criminal Code 117/1852, §129 and §130, as quoted in Jan Seidl, *Od žaláře k oltáři: Eampcipace homosexuality v českých zemích od roku 1867 do současnosti* (Brno, 2012), 22–23.
143. István Deák reports on the army's tolerance towards homosexual behaviour between officers (as opposed to that involving minors or subordinates, where there were doubts about consent), in his study of the prewar officer corps. See Deák, *Beyond Nationalism*, 145.
144. Ibid., 143.
145. Crouthamel, *An Intimate History of the Front*, 59. For a somewhat crude comparison, less than a hundred people a year were sentenced under Section 129 of the Criminal Code in Bohemia and Moravia before the war, mostly with punishments ranging from one to three months in jail. See Seidl, *Od žaláře k oltáři*, 34–36.
146. On respectability, sexuality and modern masculinity, see Mosse, *Nationalism and Sexuality*.
147. Jean Stengers and Anne van Neck, *Masturbation: The History of a Great Terror* (Basingstoke, 2001), 101.
148. See, for example, the diary of Josef Janošík, a first-lieutenant with k.u.k. Infantry Regiment 3 who, in January 1915, was fighting boredom with the help of light erotic novels such as *V opojení slávy a rozkoše* (Prague, 1915); see diary entry from 4 January 1915, Josef Janošík papers, private collection of Jan Janošík.
149. Šmída, *Vzpomínky z vojny*, 114. In a similar way, František Skála complains with disgust in his diary of 'young lads' who, upon witnessing very public sex acts between nurses and patients in an empty hall of the Kaposvár military hospital, 'were seduced to things

... they would have never done at home', pointing towards possible auto-erotic or even homosexual activities. Skála, *Válečný deník*, 283.
150. Kisch, *Vojákem pražského sboru*, 221, diary entry from 2 January 1915.
151. Nancy M. Wingfield, *The World of Prostitution in Late Imperial Austria* (Oxford, 2017), particularly 213–20; see also Nancy M. Wingfield, 'The Enemy within: Regulating Prostitution and Controlling Venereal Disease in Cisleithanian Austria during the Great War', *Central European History* 46, no. 3 (2013): 568–98; Jovana Knežević, 'Prostitutes as a Threat to National Honor in Habsburg-Occupied Serbia during the Great War', *Journal of the History of Sexuality* 20, no. 2 (2011): 312–35; or, for wartime administrative practices, Tamara Scheer, *Zwischen Front und Heimat: Österreich-Ungarns Militärverwaltungen im Ersten Weltkrieg* (Frankfurt, 2009). For a general overview, see Roger Davidson and Lesley A. Hall, eds, *Sex, Sin and Suffering: Venereal Disease and European Society since 1870* (London, 2001).
152. For a comparison, see Michelle K. Rhoades, 'Renegotiating French Masculinity: Medicine and Venereal Disease during the Great War', *French Historical Studies* 29, no. 2 (2006): 293–327; Angela Woollacott, '"Khaki Fever" and its Control. Gender, Class, Age and Sexual Morality on the British Home Front in the First World War', *Journal of Contemporary History* 29, no. 2 (1994): 325–47; or Genadii Bordiugov, 'The First World War and Social Deviance in Russia', in *Facing Armageddon: The First World War Experienced*, eds Hugh Cecil and Peter Liddle (London, 1996), 539–53.
153. František Zajíček, 'Z Ruska se vracejí zajatci', in *Domov za války*, vol. 5, 80.
154. Kisch, *Vojákem pražského sboru*, 25, diary entry from 10 August 1914.
155. Oswald Überegger, 'Krieg als sexuelle Zäsur? Sexualmoral und Geschlechterstereotypen im kriegsgesellschaftlichen Diskurs über die Geschlechtskrankheiten. Kulturgeschichtliche Annäherungen', in *Der Erste Weltkrieg im Alpenraum*, 351–366; see also Crouthamel, *An Intimate History of the Front*, 43–63.
156. The same fear has played an important role in the way in which postwar Austrian society viewed its returning soldiers – as brutalized, sexualized and bereft of any civilized modes of behaviour. See Maureen Healy, 'Civilizing the Soldier in Postwar Austria', in *Gender and War in Twentieth-Century Eastern Europe*, eds Nancy M. Wingfield and Maria Bucur (Bloomington, 2006), 47–69.
157. Šrámek, *Paměti z první světové války Josefa Šrámka z Ústí nad Labem, 1914–1918*, 73 and 80–81, diary entries from 9 and 18 July 1916, respectively.
158. Ulrych, 'Moje zápisky', 50.
159. Šmída, *Vzpomínky z vojny*, 98 and 61, cited from 40–41.
160. Paul Göhre, 'Der Krieg und die Geschlechter', *Der Flieger* 1/2 (1917), cited in Crouthamel, *An Intimate History of the Front*, 105–6.
161. Vítek, *V cizích službách*, 214–15.
162. Viktor Flaišer, 'Novica', in *Domov za války*, vol. 3, 383.
163. Skála, *Válečný deník*, 270. It is worth noting here, regarding this particular story, that the author was also in the brothel, but reportedly spent the evening sitting at a table commenting on the proceedings with words such as 'this filth is so repugnant'.
164. Šmída, *Vzpomínky z vojny*, 61.
165. Diary of Václav Doležal, entry from 19 August 1918, private collection of Martin Čihák.
166. Robert A. Nye, 'Kinship, Male Bonds, and Masculinity in Comparative Perspective', *American Historical Review* 105, no. 5 (2000): 1666.
167. Šmída, *Vzpomínky z vojny*, 74 and 97.

168. Kisch, *Vojákem pražského sboru*, 202, diary entry from 14 December 1914; Jaroš, *Z turecké armády do britského zajetí*, 158.
169. Flaišer, 'Novica', in *Domov za války*, vol. 3, 384.
170. Vladimír Soušek, *Z Olomouce na perské hranice: Vzpomínky ze světové války* (Brno, 1930), 8; Šmída, *Vzpomínky z vojny*, 41.
171. Šmída, *Vzpomínky z vojny*, 64–65.
172. Skála, *Válečný deník*, 80.
173. Ibid., 265
174. Lirš, *S Osmadvacátníky za světové války*, 174–81.
175. Vítek, *V cizích službách*, 84.
176. Karel Rélink, *28. pluk 'Pražské děti': Osmadvacátníci, veselí kluci, ve válečné vichřici* (Prague, 1932), 286.
177. Šmída, *Vzpomínky z vojny*, 63.
178. František Křížek, 'Z válečných zkušeností chudého vojáka', in *Domov za války*, vol. 3, 199–200.
179. Skála, *Válečný deník*, 276.
180. Šrámek, *Paměti z první světové války*, 90.
181. Dolejší, *Válečné vzpomínky z první světové války vojína Dolejše*, 107. A perfect example of gender role reversal is also presented in the final chapter of Alois Dolejší's memoir, describing a maid ('a sea nymph') only willing to allow him and his friends to stay in her house if one of them 'took the sacrifice' and 'accommodated her lust'. See ibid., 306–9, diary entry from 31 October 1918.
182. Květoň, *Vzpomínky z první světové války*, 35.
183. Ibid., 34.
184. See Alexandra Hois, 'Weibliche Hilfskräfte in der österreichisch-ungarischen Armee im Ersten Weltkrieg', Master's thesis. Vienna: University of Vienna, 2012.
185. Bianca Schönberger, 'Motherly Heroines and Adventurous Girls: Red Cross Nurses and Women Army Auxiliaries in the First World War', in *Home/Front*, 87.
186. Hämmerle, *Heimat/Front*, 33–38.
187. *Listy našich vojáků*, 25. It is worth noting that just a century earlier, women were able to enter the 'masculine space' of the battlefield more freely. It was only after the modern gender order, based almost exclusively on a medical interpretation of the biological body reinterpreted as a bourgeois body politic, took firm hold during the nineteenth century that women were explicitly banned from the frontlines. In 1815, they could still receive awards for bravery on the field of battle from the King of Prussia. See Karen Hagemann, '"Heroic Virgins" and "Bellicose Amazons": Armed Women, the Gender Order and the German Public during and after the Anti-Napoleonic Wars', *European Historical Quarterly* 37, no. 4 (2007): 507–27.
188. Hämmerle, *Heimat/Front*, 28–29; Schönberger, 'Motherly Heroines and Adventurous Girls', 92–93; see also Regina Schulte, 'The Sick Warrior's Sister: Nursing during the First World War', in *Gender Relations in German History: Power, Agency and Experience from the Sixteenth to the Twentieth Century*, eds Lynn Abrams and Elizabeth Harvey (London, 1996), 121–41.
189. Hämmerle, *Heimat/Front*, 34; see also Schönberger, *Motherly Heroines and Adventurous Girls*, 93.
190. František Jaroš, 'Z fronty do zázemí', in *Domov za války*, vol. 4, 170. For a general analysis of soldiers' reaction to nurses, see Holmes, *Acts of War*, 98–102.

191. Skála, *Válečný deník*, 265.
192. Křížek, 'Z válečných zkušeností chudého vojáka', in *Domov za války*, vol. 3, 198.
193. Jaroslav Křenek, *Vzpomínky na vojnu v Albanii* (Jihlava, 1924), 48.
194. Slezák maintains this view throughout the war, viewing nurses in the same way both in Krakow in 1914 and in Graz in 1917. Slezák, *Paměti Josefa Slezáka k I. světové válce*, vol. 1, 74, and vol. 4, 35.
195. Skála, *Válečný deník*, 282–83.
196. Dolejší, *Válečné vzpomínky z první světové války vojína Dolejše*, 145, diary entry from 16 November 1917.
197. Kaiser, *Voják statečný*, 169–70.
198. Theweleit, *Male Fantasies*, vol. 1, 27 and 64–134.
199. For a criticism of Theweleit's conclusions in this regard, see Joanna Bourke, *Dismembering the Male: Men's Bodies, Britain, and the Great War* (London, 1996), 22–25; or Crouthamel, *An Intimate History of the Front*, 95. Michael Roper's study of soldiers' emotional survival during the Great War may also be considered a complete rebuttal. See Roper, *The Secret Battle*.
200. A typical example of this rather middle-class logic is František Šmída, writing about 'the call of instincts, of people, of women, who have nothing left in their lives except for that simple pleasure that has to make up for all its joys'. Šmída, *Vzpomínky z vojny*, 64.
201. Kaiser, *Voják statečný*, 170.
202. Neumann, 'Válčení civilistovo', 138.
203. 'Bohuš' to Róza Kropáčková, 1 June 1918, in *Zapomenuté hlasy*, 111.
204. Skála, *Válečný deník*, 275–76.
205. František Langer to Václav Vilém Štech, Literary Archive – Memorial of National Literature, fond František Langer, inv. č. 12952. I owe many thanks to Jana Javůrková for bringing this reference to my attention.

Chapter 3

TRANSFORMATION OF MANLINESS
Comradeship

> Comradeship is just another word for love.
> —Editorial of *Kamarádství*, Czechoslovak veterans' magazine[1]

The memoir of Jaroslav Křenek, who served as a cadet with k.u.k. Infantry Regiment 42 in Albania, contains an interesting part, one that does not fit well with the rest of the grim and often graphic narrative of the gradual disintegration and collapse of the Austro-Hungarian forces on the Macedonian front during the summer of 1918. In this particular part of his text, which feels like it came from a different work altogether, he introduces a recollection an unknown soldier shared with him in a field hospital somewhere in southern Albania. The man was shot in the chest 'up there, in the mountains above the Osum', fell down a ravine and knocked himself unconscious. He woke up later in a pastoral idyll of a shepherd's shelter, tended to caringly by 'a lad of a bright eye, a beautiful, oval face framed by hair blacker than night'. The boy looked after him for a week and while 'the furies of war ravaged Europe, I was enjoying the blissful feeling of powers returning to my senses in the midst of an indescribably simple and amazing idyll … We communicated only through smiles … and became attached to each other in a strange way of love, one that only the people kicked down and out by life know. We might call it a fairytale if it weren't true'. One morning, the boy hinted that he wanted to tell the soldier a secret – but it never happened, because he was ambushed by two 'Hungarian soldiers' while swimming in the river. The narrator came to the youth's defence, killing both with his rifle; however, one of them stabbed the boy with a bayonet first:

> I rush to the wounded lad as fast as I can, and what a surprise! The most beautiful girl I have ever seen is lying in the grass in front of me, crimson blood streaming down her

tanned virgin bosom, eyes shut, fainting, long hair loose on her shoulders. I cleaned her wound, she woke up, her arms around my neck, tears in her eyes, she pressed her lips against mine, whispering softly: I am dying! Her body was growing cold and collapsing. In anger I threw the hideous corpses of those brutes into the torrent of the Osum, and put my only love on a soft bed of moss. Then I dug her a grave and sprinkled it with fragrant flowers. When I was finished, I sunk to my knees by the grave and cried like a helpless child.[2]

In Křenek's memoir, the purpose of the recollection, supposedly told by a soldier who was lost in the mountains soon afterwards, is primarily to pinpoint the criminal absurdity of war. However, at the same time, it is a celebration of the human ability to experience emotionally and aesthetically, even erotically charged moments in its midst, of an intensity rarely seen in ordinary peacetime life. As the same soldier challenged Křenek during their dialogue: 'Do you recall a moment in your past when you felt life more deeply, more intensely, than you do right now?'[3] Besides that, the main storyline here revolves around an intimate, emotionally powerful and ultimately eroticized relationship between the narrator and 'the beautiful lad' who turns out to be 'the most beautiful girl' at the story's tragic climax. Looking closer, we see that the youth's characteristics as stated in the text place him more or less outside the traditional categories of masculinity, as he is defined through the language usually reserved for idealized, even mythological feminine qualities: 'beautiful face', 'hair blacker than night', tenderness, care, kindness, as well as an idealized female 'virgin body'. Moreover, the narrator defines his relationship to this *vision* of femininity in an (originally) male body as 'a strange way of love', being saved from seemingly homoerotic repercussions only by the boy's ability to 'change' his perceived sex at the last moment.

It is rather symptomatic that the story above ends with an elaboration of 'the dying kiss', which Santanu Das identified as a trope common in both First World War literature and in personal accounts, betraying shifts towards intimacy within the boundaries of gender-specific behaviour between men in the trenches.[4] As Thomas Kühne wrote in his influential study of military comradeship in German culture, 'the concept emerged to address small or primary group relations', but at the end, it 'was all about ambiguity', 'was not just a German peculiarity' and 'any attempts to precisely determine its proliferation are doomed to fail'. While 'the virtue of comradeship was invoked to fuel combat cohesion and fighting power – the aggressive side of soldiering ... at the same time, it served as a synonym for male friendship, even male love, of homoeroticism and tenderness'.[5] And it is precisely this latter trait of comradeship that will be the focus of this chapter, as it has indeed played an important role in the way Czech soldiers tackled the ways in which wartime stress and unforeseen modes of male sociability threatened to subvert their masculine identity. Following this path of interpreting the concept, it was Kühne again who argued that comradeship was formed as 'the opposite of outward aggression as much as of the violence that governed the community of soldiers inwardly. Comradeship was explicitly encoded as feminine; it was "personal warmth and the language of mutual consent and warm-heartedness", in short: the "warmth which lies within the woman'".[6] However, femininity projected through comradeship is not femininity per se. It is merely an *idea*, a vision of femininity, a stereotype based on men's concept of the nonmasculine, unmanly – the concept that, in the modern gender dichotomy, serves as the opposite number of masculinity. It is therefore a collection of qualities that modern masculinity generally tries to avoid, is afraid of, ignores or tries to push to the margins of its image of itself. However, under the umbrella of comradeship, it is possible for men to incorporate more traditionally feminine traits into their identity as they experience it, 'smoothing over the symbolic contradictions, social differences and emotional tensions which existed in a world of war dominated by men'.[7] Dehumanizing brutality, the mechanization of soul and body, loss of control and power, enforced existential as well as sexual passivity only occasionally interrupted by explosions of aggressive violence or animal sexuality – all these experiences created tensions between the *ideal* of manliness and the *reality* as the men perceived it.

On an emotional level, the resulting conflict led to a suppressed longing for femininity in its idealized form, which bordered dangerously on homoerotic or even homosexual feelings projected onto the other actors, i.e. the fellow members of the group.[8] Accepting the notion of comradeship made these feelings possible in a way that rendered them harmless in terms of men's perception of their own masculinity, turning them into a stabilizing force that gave the otherwise alienated all-male social group a much more humane and emotionally bearable form.[9] Meanwhile, the masculinity of the actors remained unchallenged, along with their position in the social hierarchy. As such, the transformation of military masculinity through the incorporation of the concept of comradeship became an integrating factor, accommodating the stressful wartime reality into the existing framework, thus keeping the sense of continuity and normality as strong as possible.[10] Comradeship was therefore a key symbolic space where masculinity was unconsciously transformed in an effort to save it – as a psychological as well as a social identity – from whatever men *perceived* and feared to be feminine traits in themselves.

Feminine Within, Feminine Without

As mentioned above, the official discourse of wartime masculinity turned to terms like bravery, strength, endurance, dependability, controlled aggression, courage, discipline and stoical self-control in the face of mortal danger whenever it discussed individual soldiers' qualities or even the ideal 'community of men' in war. As Egon Erwin Kisch ironically commented on the letters his comrades were writing home from the Serbian front three weeks into the war, there were 'bloody skirmishes, dangers overcome, heroic deeds performed'.[11] They had obviously subscribed to the official discourse of manly behaviour in war and it is of little importance to us how exactly true their stories were, as in our analysis it is their perception and/or way of presenting themselves that counts. Kisch himself, incidentally, subscribes to the brave soldier paradigm when he extols the efforts of a certain Vintner, an infantryman in his platoon, who saved the only remaining boat the platoon had left during a retreat by swimming twice across the Drina River, under fire and with a bullet wound in his hand. Reflecting the gendered dimension of the act, he literally refers to it as 'manly', thus matching the expected standards.[12] In the same vein, it is the 'manliness' of František Černý and his comrades that keeps them 'dragging our feet along' during the arduous marches of the Brusilov Offensive of 1916.[13] In Josef Klejna's diary entry from October 1914, men find space for a gesture of true manly brotherhood even in the midst of a tense combat situation, when a captain of k.u.k. Infantry Regiment 88 addresses his men moments before charging the Serbian positions, with the following words: '"Boys, we're going against the enemy's positions at Banovo Polje. Keep steady, be brave. Many of us won't make it, I guess, so let's shake hands." We shook hands with him, and with our friends and comrades, then the order came and we charged forward'.[14] Even Josef Slezák, in his more or less doctored diary, depicts himself as a stoical patrol commander who repeatedly calms down his inexperienced 'rookie chicken' in Italy in 1916.[15] It is he again who, against the general gist of his diary, reflects upon the competitiveness of masculine bravery a little earlier when he describes how 'Lieutenant Štark, Corporal Holý, Corporal Barvínek and myself were the first ones to jump into the Russian trenches … with a thunderous hoorah' and only regrets not receiving the Silver Medal for bravery he was promised because the lieutenant was killed in combat a few minutes later and there was no one left who could legally recommend him for the award.[16]

These 'images of manliness' point to the all-encompassing influence that the official discourse of military masculinity and sociability held over soldiers' existence. However, it was ultimately all up to them to internalize this discourse. John Tosh, in his analysis of masculinity as a historical concept, places a great deal of emphasis on the dichotomy between the objective (social) and subjective (individual) constructs of masculinity, claiming that the psychological development of early childhood, 'negotiating a path through dual identifications', results in 'men having feminine bits of themselves (just as women have masculine bits). Peer-group pressure among men in the public arena requires them to disown their feminine side, in the process setting very rigid boundaries for the self. And the unacknowledged feminine within is disposed of by being projected onto other categories of men, often with socially repressive results, as in the case of homosexuals'.[17] In other words, *social* discourse is not necessarily in sync with the *individual* experience of the actors. And even if these two

Figure 3.1 Physical closeness in the cramped conditions on the frontline, infantry dugout of k.u.k. Infantry Regiment 75, Eastern Front, 1917 (Military History Institute, Prague).

categories are more or less in accord at one moment, any external pressure may well cause the social construct of masculinity to become unattainable, physically impossible or emotionally unbearable – with one of the possible results being that men rediscover the 'unacknowledged feminine' within themselves in an effort to accommodate new realities of existence. It was the radical leftist poet and wartime corpsman S.K. Neumann who interpreted his military service as a call of 'sensual greed and lust, those merry, eager, manly enemies of that whining, dawdling, effeminate spirit'.[18] He goes on to create an almost Freudian dichotomy between the 'manly' death drive of war and the 'effeminate' life instinct, more or less associated with peace.[19] However, the reality of industrial war brought, even in his observation, an inhuman, mechanized horror of 'bloody combat' rather than supplying any manly inputs or 'heroic challenges'. Feelings of eternal boredom, hunger, exhaustion and passivity were only occasionally interrupted by explosions of brutal, impersonal and mostly unheroic violence. Manly ideals were turned into physically as well as psychologically unmanning gestures, and while men suffered emotionally from being away from their homes for years, they had to adapt to close, almost intimate coexistence with other men. The resulting situations often did not fit comfortably into any possible definition of a 'heroic challenge' or 'manly sensuality'. Escaping towards one's own 'effeminate spirit' was a possible way out; however, it posed a threat to the whole concept of masculine identity.

The very physical closeness to other men was something many soldiers were not accustomed to from their civilian existence, particularly not on an everyday basis, as was common in wartime. Bohuš Adamíra wrote in his diary that in a new hut built by his pioneer company to shelter troops from the vagaries of the Alpine weather in November 1916, 'we have a measured space of 35 cm for each man'. Although he agrees that this was an extreme solution to a crisis and 'most men could not sleep', there were many instances when similar spatial conditions, leading to unwelcome intimate coexistence, were a common occurrence in frontline conditions.[20] Of course, there were few other options, so most men had to accept the situation and make the best of the comforts of even a rudimentary shelter. And if the chosen dwelling, be it a hut, tent, dugout or an open trench, lacked warmth, physical closeness and intimacy became a necessity. As Egon Erwin Kisch noted in his diary on 6 September 1914: 'The night is cold. My neighbour and I are cuddling together to keep at least a bit warm'. The same situation, when he was 'pressing bodies together as much as possible' with two other men he did not even know, occurs again in his diary three months later.[21] Similarly, Jan Šmatlán wrote to his parents in November 1914 that he 'used to lie down under a blanket with an acquaintance of mine from Přelouč',[22] while Augustin Mudrák and his comrades 'huddled together, breathing on one another to keep a bit warm', in the Carpathian forests in February 1917.[23] This inherently corporeal practice of homosocial coexistence was, in general, considered to be an archetypal manifestation of comradeship: 'The only thing that warms us here is our buddy's body next to us'.[24] However, the homoerotic undertones of such behaviour did not remain hidden from the men, although they only rarely elaborate upon it. In Josef Slezák's diary, however, we find language that points more directly to such an interpretation: 'I shared a blanket with *Zugsführer* Doskočil. Although we pressed ourselves against one another like lovers, we were still cold'.[25] He clearly saw soldiers 'cuddling' to shelter themselves from the cold as possessing a homoerotic dimension, which was in turn neutralized by incorporation into the complex notion of masculine comradeship. Concurrently, intimacy bordering on homoerotic contact serves here as a way to 'soften' the thoroughly masculine war experience. Rough soldierly manliness, of a type that is supposed to distinguish it in social discourse, is transformed here into a milder, more easily tolerable form that makes war more bearable in terms of bodily experience, strengthening the bond between the participants in the process.

A similar effect may be noticed in the sources, when their authors discuss another area where men's bodies came into close proximity with each other or, respectively, were displayed publicly – communal hygiene. With the units in the field, its rare occurrence made it a special moment in every soldier's life, often interpreted as a reassurance of one's own humanity – as Josef Váchal recalled,

Figure 3.2 Male nudity in the field, Galicia, 1915 (Museum of Eastern Bohemia, Hradec Králové).

a soldier 'became a new man' after taking a bath after several weeks.[26] As Josef Kápar, a POW on the way to the island of Asinara, noted in his diary on 24 December 1916, 'the very possibility that we will be returned to a state of cleanliness' made all the men 'happy as children at Christmas'.[27] However, the presence of naked male bodies during the communal experience of bathing in rivers and lakes was not only charged with homoerotic undertones, but also seemed to liberate the men from the emotional baggage of militarized wartime masculinity, evoking behaviour that made the stoic warrior image considerably softer or even feminine. In Jaromír John's collection of *Letters from War*, there is a description of his platoon taking a swim in a Tyrolean stream in August 1915: 'Within a minute, we were calming ourselves in its crystal clear water, soldiers splashing about and at each other, pushing and tripping each other, those who hesitated were caught and thrown in, or at least sprayed. There was a lot of shouting, swearing, whooping and laughter … We took a swim and frolicked in a way only soldiers can do'.[28] 'Whooping', 'laughing' and 'frolicking' naked is rather typical imagery used by many authors to denote – usually in an eroticized way – women taking a bath in public.[29] In John's prose, however, it is without doubt a type of behaviour that relieves men from stress while bordering on the limits of what is acceptable within the context of masculine identity.

There is one other specific form of behaviour that appears regularly in the sources, which in the literature is usually interpreted as either an unconventional disruption of the gender order or, more often, as a confirmation thereof via the normalizing effects of a tolerated stress release – cross-dressing. Alon Rachamimov, in her study of female impersonation in POW camp life on the Eastern Front, claims that while 'drag is by definition ambivalent' with regard to the prevalent gender order, it carried an 'ability to counter … lethargy, improve bad moods, and channel sexual anxiety without it leading to … "moral transgressions"'.[30] While the elaborate drag performances of officers' POW camps differed in many ways from impromptu eruptions of cross-dressing among combat troops, the latter were only rarely a product of wartime shortages (although, apparently, this may have happened from time to time, especially in an army so desperate for supplies such as the Austro-Hungarian army).[31] Such behaviour, which temporarily feminized one's self and even made men behave in ways deemed feminine for a while, was clearly pushing the boundaries of the gender order and the hierarchies attached to it (including those in the military), which made it an excellent means of releasing accumulated stress and breaking down rules, only for them to be rebuilt after the momentous carnival was over. For example, when František Skála's comrades found 'suitcases full of lingerie' in the cellar of a Tyrolean school in May 1916, 'the whole detachment was soon dressed in nightgowns … Someone brought a piano, Svatoš was playing it and all the others were dancing around like forest fairies … I cannot stop laughing at the image of my comrades going wild'.[32] The presence of 'wild comrades' is the key here, as it makes the whole affair tolerable. Everyone present is aware of the temporary suspension of gender boundaries that makes cross-dressing and even transgender behaviour possible without any social reprimand. When Alois Dolejší's unit passed through the ruins of Gorizia in November 1917, some of the men discovered a collection of women's dresses as well as men's suits in one of the destroyed palaces. 'Everyone grabbed some nice clothes, men's or women's. Some guys actually dressed completely as women … they made a lot of comedy out of it'.[33] Only a few miles into Italy, a similar scene unfolded in another unit: 'We dressed in whatever we could find. Ladies' silk blouses, ladies' pumps … When we looked at ourselves in the mirror, we almost died laughing. We looked like ballerinas'.[34] Soldiers not only *look* like women, they almost *feel* like them for a moment. It may be argued that it was particularly in these moments of improvisation that cross-dressing enabled men, through the fantasy of a shared 'comedy', to escape from the emotionally exhausting world of war (and discursive masculinity) through what can be called a feminine myth, an idea of femininity otherwise feared and buried deep within oneself. In a liberating gesture, men put on dresses and, secure under the guise of a humorous act, they restabilize not only the gender order itself, but also their own individual masculinity by testing its rigid boundaries. Even though these performances were usually short-lived and are often connected to alcohol consumption, they may well be interpreted as spontaneous carnivals, stabilizing the social order through what Mikhail Bakhtin called the 'authorized transgression' of the bizarre.[35]

However, soldiers felt their masculine identity being called into question and subsequently transformed not only by visibly pushing the limits of masculinity in an effort to escape both the physical and psychological stress of wartime existence. There were actually many everyday chores designated as traditionally feminine, which men carried out as part and parcel of their service in the field. In his work on the wartime working class in Bohemia, Rudolf Kučera mentions the way in which the male workers' sense of masculinity was threatened by the fact that they were 'stripped of their freedom to decide what, and when, to eat', as it was their wives who became 'the respected bearers of public, as well as private, authority' with regard to 'the time and manner of family meals'.[36] As we have already mentioned, men at the front had the same experience with the Austro-Hungarian war machine taking away their authority over how and when (and if) they would eat, failing badly in the process, especially during the second half of the war. As a result, most accounts of frontline service either during the first weeks of the war (when the army logistics was still unprepared and placed in a difficult position by the armies being constantly on the move) or later in Italy and the Balkans in 1917 and 1918, paint a bleak picture of men spending large portions of their days trying to find and steal food for themselves and their comrades. Soups made out of virtually anything, cooking goulashes or slaughtering and preparing animals ranging from pigs to dogs – all these required the men's cooking skills, forcing them into a new, traditionally feminized position of the one who actually *prepares* the meal. And it was not just the army cooks who were expected to do so by their position; in contrast to the experience of peacetime service, war forced most of the men into these new realms. 'Everyone was a good cook ... or at least they thought so', Jan Laška noted in his diary while in a POW camp on the island of Asinara. 'He was beaming at how good he was at it and how glad his wife would be when he came home, that he could easily stand in for her in the kitchen if needed'. The man in question, upon discovering his cooking skills, obviously concluded that one day he would be able to replace a woman.[37]

However, soldiers' 'housekeeping' efforts were not limited to cooking. Circumstances turned many men into 'housewives' in many other areas, forcing them, for example, to wash their own clothes, as laundry was seldom available while deployed at the front: 'When there's time, we do our washing as much as we did while stationed in the barracks; all available fences are put to use', Ludvík Maršík reported on the way in which washing was practised at his *Landsturm* unit in Galicia in 1915.[38] Washing of clothes was usually preceded by another often communal activity – flea-searching. An account that would not elaborate in some way on methods and techniques deemed to keep the parasites off, or to help one to get rid of them, is hard to come by indeed. 'We looked forward to our flea-searching in the same way kids look forward to Christmas', wrote a soldier to his wife from the Russian front.[39] There were also moments when the 'heroic warrior of the monarchy' turned into a seamstress: 'We sew on our buttons, do the repairs with awkward stitching, we repair our boots, resoling them with new hobnails. If only our mothers could see us!'[40] Regarding the practicalities of wartime existence, a soldier's identity was more or less forced to adapt to the fact that in war, men do most of the woman's work. War was not just redrawing the gender order and its hierarchies – it was also, the official public discourse notwithstanding, transforming the norms of what is manly and what is not. It tested the boundaries of masculinity not only by blurring the outlines of the masculine and feminine body image, but it did so in the area of the constantly negotiated, albeit traditionally gender-specific types of behaviour that wartime reality forced on the men in the same way as it let women to intrude into areas of masculine exclusivity (see Chapter 2).

Emotions

It is not just daily chores that are thoroughly gendered in modern social discourse. The same is true for emotions and especially their public display, which became a sort of a taboo of European masculinity at the beginning of the twentieth century.[41] It is easy to recognize the way in which men understood emotional display in their descriptions of the moments they were conscripted, leaving for the front, or when their leave was up later during the war. Crying, as the most visible display of sadness in public, is thoroughly gendered in their accounts. In their eyes, it seems to be the sole prerogative of women, and while there are many men who cry in these accounts, they always try to do so in private or in the least conspicuous, most hidden manner possible, and when they are mentioned in the third person, it seems that the male authors themselves seem to be somewhat embarrassed and turn their textual eyes away. As a typically gendered account stated: 'The men – soldiers – were frowning, many had a tear in the eye, and the women cried all the way'.[42] Manly tears are allowed as long as they are not made public: 'Women are crying, looking anxiously at their husbands, who are also secretly shedding tears on their military coats'.[43] The dominant discourse of soldierly manliness defined, among other factors, through one's ability to suppress emotions and their display in public is further evidenced in the diary of Josef Klejna who, during the tragic crossing of the Drina River in September 1914, commented that 'tears ... do not befit a soldier, they say'.[44] Jaroslav Křenek noted a similar attitude when describing a Christmas celebration in Tirana: 'The infantryman Mojžíš turned to me. He was a sentimental *grenzjäger*, going too deep into the imagery of a true Christmas Eve. He tried to pull us down with his big wet eyes, gawking at us all sad and dull. But we were soldiers enough to avoid all the emotional softness'.[45] Jan Šindelář experienced the same emotional turmoil during that time, only several hundred miles away, in Italy: 'We wipe away our little tears in secret, because we're soldiers, so all the other comrades who do the same cannot see them'.[46] Facing the emotional stress of wartime service, many men were simply not able to stay true to the discourse they tried so hard to emulate. As captured by Josef Slezák in his description of the moments before an assault on Serbian positions in September 1914: '*Oberleutnant* Procházka told us to get ready, that we would get to work soon, laughing it all off, saying the devil would not take him'. The *Oberleutnant* here represents the ideal performance of military masculinity in the field of battle – bravery, even bravado, and disregard for fear and danger. But Slezák's account goes on: 'But I felt different. Many of us prayed, our eyes welled up, cherishing memories of our loved ones. Me in particular'.[47] As the author confesses here, he and his comrades, facing possible mutilation or death, are overcome by fear and consequent emotions – and they do not hold these back, as they are not able to.

In war, men experienced innumerable situations like these, creating a need to cope with them in such a way that would not, as far as possible, reveal 'unmanly' and 'unsoldierly' emotions – in other words, a framework was desperately needed that would enable the men to survive the war emotionally while remaining 'men'. As a result, what we see in many of the sources is that crying ceases to be understood as something inherently feminine, being increasingly tolerated as long as it was a part of military 'brotherhood'. Thus, for example, in František Skála's diary, there is a certain distancing effort in his description of a young soldier, shot through his shoulder, 'crying and pleading for help', finding excuses in the man's youth and therefore 'incomplete' manliness. However, a few days later, the same author notes upon saying goodbye to a friend: 'He'll be alone here after I leave. He's weeping constantly, feeling no shame. I'm crying too – we were like brothers to each other! We hugged, kissed, and parted, never to see each other again'.[48] František Šmída describes an emotionally difficult situation following an accident during weapons training, which resulted in a popular company commander being killed by a hand grenade: 'Our lieutenant, seeing it all, wept like a child ... I tried to hold back for a while, but couldn't and started crying as well. Many of our men also showed their tears. They knew that their good commander, one they all loved, was dying'.[49] Public display of emotions is turned into a shared 'manly' experience, connecting the men in an emotionally stressful moment with a powerful bond that, in all probability, strengthened their group cohesion and therefore supported their overall motivation to go on. Tears shed together made emotional survival easier, while assuring the men that they were still men indeed, since they were not alone. As Josef Slezák noted on the verge of the Gorlice Offensive in May 1915:

> it is a sad picture, men right before battle. Every one staring into the ground, their thoughts back at home with their loved ones. Every one of them shedding tears, sighing, many pressing to their lips a picture of a girlfriend, wife, kids or parents, or at least a cross or a holy picture that was given to them upon leaving home. No-one talks. Comrade is asking comrade for help, if needed, or sharing addresses of loved ones.[50]

Here, Josef Slezák is addressing another important shift in the 'emotional map' of wartime masculinity – soldiers are openly expressing love, which in the gendered spacing of wartime reality belongs to the home front, populated by the discursive image of women and children. As is generally noticeable in collections of correspondence, especially those few where both sides' letters were preserved, expressing emotions is generally reserved for women, who are expected to do so. While men express emotions too, they do so in a more restrained, seemingly less intense way, and are even chastised for transgressing this rule in communication.[51] Of course, there is no direct link between the intensity of emotions and the quality of the relationship, as the former is thoroughly culturally conditioned, with men being rather limited in their options, especially in the written form, which was traditionally deemed more feminine in itself.[52] The same cultural baggage was even stronger with regard to keeping a diary, where emotions are displayed even more obliquely and often with clear knowledge of a certain future readership. For example, Josef Klejna keeps invoking 'my beloved children' in his journal, dedicating it entirely to them with the full knowledge that it may be the only way for them to learn what their sole remaining parent experienced before he died.[53] However, emotional outpourings similar to his are rather rare in soldiers' writings or tend to revolve around general musings on how loved ones at home are faring during the man's absence. Only now and then, some of the diaries betray men's feelings of being overcome by the unending stress of war and lack of emotional support, as for example in a melancholic outburst from Jan Janošík, whose rather sketchy diary further collapses into a chaotic mixture of fragments of love songs and poems, starting with a depressed note on May Day: '1 May, 1917 – the time of love. Three years on the fields of war'.[54]

Consequently, it is particularly these moments of heightened emotionality that stand out in the soldiers' diaries. Josef Slezák, who tended to remember home in general rather than his girlfriend in particular (one he constantly suspected of cheating on him), noted on the first day of the Gorlice Offensive in May 1915: 'It was so close, I thought I would never hear those loving sounds coming out of your lips'. In a moment of extreme duress, his loving feelings for 'Mařenka' were strong enough even to make it onto paper the first – or the last – possible moment it was practically possible.[55] The final moments before going 'over the top' were especially potent, as the men were left waiting for orders, alone with their thoughts and feelings for minutes. While they were not conditioned to do so, the very nature of their situation was so emotionally intense that they were often overcome with feelings of love, which were difficult to fully express in the given environment – those upon whom they bestowed these feelings most commonly, and without fear of being seen weak or unmanly, were far away from them, and while the military post was doing its best, it was too slow by its nature. Because of this, soldiers were left with their memories and artefacts such as photographs, letters or other symbolic objects that helped to play the role of emotional support by proxy.

The use of substitute objects for investing emotions is obvious in the many cases where men encountered animals during their service. 'We have deep sympathy for that dog', Egon Erwin Kisch noted in his diary in August 1914. 'We are constantly tripping over both Austrian and Serbian dead, and we see people horribly wounded all around, but many of us feel truly distraught over one animal's fate. We cleaned its wounds and dressed them properly. Also, when we pass horses in their last moments, one hears several shouts of anger and disgust, betraying sympathy'.[56] There is a scene in František Bouška's diary when a group of recruits quartered in a brewery in Choceň, Eastern Bohemia, during the July mobilization in 1914 invested considerable effort in saving a young sparrow: 'Poor thing – entangled in the wire, it may die – it may lose its life – we can't just let it be!'[57] While it may be true that later in the war, animals tend to be viewed mostly as a walking meal, there are many moments in the sources where we encounter similar emotional investment in their suffering and fate, further proving the argument that many soldiers felt the need to project their feelings onto *something* simply to escape the violent reality around. In the words of Josef Váchal, 'empathy with the weak has never disappeared, even at the front. Turned into a beast himself, man's love for the poor beast survived the purgatory of the trenches ... Men shed blood in throngs just to save the life of a creature one level beneath them'.[58]

The increasingly tolerant attitude towards men showing emotions in front of their comrades naturally changed the very relationship they had to one another. Emotional needs manifested in these emotional displays were increasingly directed toward the soldiers' more or less immediate vicinity, be it in writing or in person. As the poet and one-year volunteer of k.u.k. Infantry Regiment 8, Jan Kotrba, wrote to his friend and future literary critic Bedřich Václavek in May 1916: 'Béďa, I love you, and those in love are quick to discern the thoughts and feelings of one another ... You are the only one who ever understood me, because us being soulmates made it actually possible'.[59] Being a true poet, Kotrba was much more open in expressing his feelings than most of his comrades in arms, but he only reflected upon the general shift in emotional boundaries to the relationship between men that the war brought about. František Šmída, about to leave 'his Bosnians' during the final retreat of the Habsburg army in early November 1918, expressed a deep sadness, forever remembering 'the human bond of men bound by gratitude and love', categories he had previously understood as expressing his relationship toward women.[60] Similarly, Jan Tříska expressed a feeling in his diary that 'the lieutenant likes me and I really like him'.[61] When Bohumil Sperling was transferred to the Tyrolean front in June 1917, he experienced more than mixed feelings upon leaving his old battery: 'Looking back, it was not all that bad, however one would like to forget some things ... There were some good memories of that horrible war! We said goodbye to the battery crew, my eyes are all watery upon leaving. They were good guys'.[62] The emotional bond with 'the good guys' is placed in direct opposition to 'the horrible war' here, being presented as something that made the war experience bearable. The price for this was obvious – transforming one's sense of masculinity by incorporating emotionality and its display such as tears: 'How difficult it is to leave one's colleagues … guys I went through 17 months of war with, good or bad', František Pluháček, an infantryman from Jindřichův Hradec, despaired in his diary. 'No words can express that. Yes, we did cry'.[63] Furthermore, as we have seen in František Skála's account above, traditionally feminine gestures of parting, such as a kiss, also found their way into the broadened notion of wartime masculinity: 'Meeting [a friend] was really moving … We shake hands, kiss, and he's got to go'.[64]

The need to cope with 'the horrible war' opened up a path for men to discover the side of their psyche traditionally identified with femininity, incorporating previously 'unmanly' emotions into their everyday behavioural patterns.[65] Of course, it is clear that crying, hugging, kisses or expressing affection or love for other men did not become the norm of coexistence in male groups in the military. Hegemonic masculinity, promoting emotional self-control and stoicism in the midst of horrors through official channels was still powerful. Also, as Joanna Bourke noted in her study of gender identity and the body during the war, the very environment of wartime militaries was too splintered and 'male bonding limited and contingent on a huge range of factors' such as individual character, age, race (Czech soldiers often held deep anti-Semitic prejudices), class, rank, education or – in the Habsburg military especially – national identity and its understanding by the particular actor.[66] As another friend of Bedřich Václavek wrote to him in October 1916: 'You write about how difficult it is to make friends these days. You're right. And even if we get to know someone pretty well, it still lacks the beauty of a true friendship. And so we are the hermits of this world'.[67] Most of the men were too focused on their survival, and the world around them was populated mostly by faceless uniforms, characterized only by their direct relationship towards oneself and to the war itself (either succumbing to it or not, physically or psychologically). In the words of Bedřich Václavek himself: 'I only know one duty in war: my own profit'.[68] Josef Slezák was a perfect example of this, pretending to suffer from dysentery in a hospital in Krakow in the autumn of 1914 so that he would not have to return to the regiment with his friends who had just recovered from their wounds (as he also had) – he persisted, even though they had cursed him, threatened him and called him a coward. Although he seemed to have had a positive relationship with them beforehand, he was obviously not attached enough to them to risk being killed just to stay in their company.[69]

The behavioural patterns mentioned therefore remained exceptional reactions to exceptional, often momentously stressful circumstances, stopgap measures enabling emotional survival under extreme duress when cynical stoicism would not suffice and hegemonic masculinity was too limiting an existential framework. However, it seems that this sort of emergency reaction occurred with such frequency that many soldiers mention it in their writings with little surprise. As was the case with cross-dressing or everyday 'feminine' chores, the boundaries of masculine behaviour underwent a shift that made experimenting with emotions a specific, tolerated thread of military masculinity in wartime. Nevertheless, all these transformations of masculine identity ultimately represented a considerable threat to the officially promoted discourse of 'heroic' manliness. They barely corresponded with the widely promoted trope of the masculine warrior, often coming dangerously close to what John Tosh has defined as 'the unacknowledged feminine within', which was, under the standard gender discourse in peacetime, 'disposed of by being projected onto other categories of men' such as the stereotyped, feminized homosexual.[70]

In order to contain this threat to their perception of their own masculinity, Czech soldiers seem to have developed a concept that made them able to reconcile the hegemonic discourse of masculinity with those elements in their wartime behaviour that they feared to be encroaching on feminine, homoerotic or even homosexual, such as when they realized that they 'find that bit of human warmth in each other's company', 'enjoyed the pleasures of being together for the evening' and addressed each other as 'sweetie' in their correspondence.[71] The resulting symbolic construct turned tears and other discursively feminized gestures such as hugs and kisses, when manifested among *war comrades*, into *manly* tears and gestures, as they were shared strictly with those *comrades*. The transformed structure of individual perception of masculinity enabled soldiers to experiment with its limitations, with intimacy and the body, as well as with displayed emotions, while preserving their sense of themselves as men safely within a transformed definition of manliness. Seen through the lens of the hegemonic discourse of wartime masculinity, soldiers were permitted to behave in feminine ways from time to time, or denote their behaviour in such terms, whilst remaining men – but they had to be comrades. Kühne's initial argument, which sees the origins of the idea of comradeship in wartime gender upheaval, is therefore plausible in our case – of course, the postwar context and therefore the consequences remained radically different.[72]

In the context of the previous paragraphs, we may now return to the recollection of Jaroslav Křenek from the beginning of the chapter and interpret it as a mythical image used to express the author's (either the narrator or the author of the memoir itself) experience of 'wartime comradeship'. It is obvious that the story triggers several questions about gender categories and identities, which are bent and transgressed as the narrative progresses. Onto the image of the young boy, a comrade, a number of ideal feminine characteristics are projected during the narration, the narrator's relationship with him is unashamedly defined as love, and the story climaxes in the discovery of ultimate feminine beauty in a body that had hitherto been understood to be masculine, in a moment of tragic intrusion of wartime brutality, symbolically encapsulated in the characters of 'two Hungarian soldiers'. The story is an indictment of a brutalized wartime masculinity, as well as a celebration of the bonds of comradeship and its power to redeem all the horrors of war. The key to its interpretation is to be found in the dichotomy between 'the furies of war' and the feminine 'beauty of comradeship', which does not cross over into homoerotic territory only because the boy turns out to be a girl sufficiently in time to spare the narrator's masculinity from any doubts.

However, the same feminizing or even homoerotic tendencies are also apparent in other reflections on comradeship, again sparing their authors from any doubts under the protective umbrella of transformed masculinity, which made the close and often intimate coexistence of male bodies acceptable: 'My neighbour, a boyish youth, kind and pretty, still a virgin in mind and body, took off his shirt and lay topless on the bench, inadvertently showing off his adorable clean body to the world', wrote S.K. Neumann in his memoir. 'I can't remember what else was in that poem of mine besides adoration for that fresh body, whose breasts resembled a pair of sealed love letters'.[73] Neumann is testing the limits of his own masculinity while exploring the possibilities of eroticizing the male body in a similar way to Křenek's narrator, reassured by the notion of comradeship. However, he too is subconsciously afraid he may transgress too far in the eyes of his readers, so he hastily adds: 'Nothing is more foreign to me than homosexuality. My verses are rooted in aesthetics pure and simple'.[74] Homosexual behaviour still seemed to be a step too far, which may well support the old argument presented by Magnus Hirschfeld in the 1930s that while war did not necessarily make homosexual behaviour a regular part of soldierly masculinity, it created a variety of forms of 'intimate comradeship', ranging from consciously erotic, through unconscious eroticization, to unerotic bonding, which were generally deemed acceptable.[75]

Comradeship therefore presented men with a way to incorporate the dangerous, potentially feminizing aspects of their wartime experience into their own masculinity as they experienced it. Using one of S.K. Neumann's metaphors, it enabled them to reconcile their 'feminine soul' (psyche) with their 'masculine' senses (body). The soldier's manliness may have been transformed in the process, but it was stabilized, and his gender identity felt safe again. Converting the argument from an individual to a group level, the result is similar – the masculine identity of the homosocial group is strengthened as its internal dynamics are spared the destabilizing tensions that result from the destabilized individual masculine identities of its members. The friction caused by the potentially disruptive consequences of 'male bonding' being interpreted as homosexual was erased by transforming the general discourse, possibly increasing (or at least not decreasing) the group's cohesion in the process. As Hirschfeld pointed out, even the militaries during the First World War understood the consequences and promoted the concept of comradeship in the ranks, even if it meant verging upon the dangers of homoerotic sociability.[76] Viewed from the point of view of the soldiers' motivation, the highly gendered discourse of wartime comradeship indeed played the role of a glue that held together the key element in any army's morale – the so-called 'primary group'.

Groups

In the general theory of military motivation, the question of primary group dynamics and its influence on the unit's cohesion in the campaign and in combat has been present at least since Ardant du Picq published his works in the 1860s. His well-known conclusion was that the battlefield, swept by the increasing firepower of modern weaponry, would render traditional linear or other mass formations physically impossible, with the result that the moral qualities of individual soldiers and the cohesion of small groups of men became the key to military performance, as these men would have to move around the battlefield individually and without direct supervision. As he argued, 'unity alone produces fighters'.[77] The importance of the 'unity' of the primary group (i.e. a group small enough for its members to know each other well and to be in close everyday contact) in maintaining soldiers' morale and motivation later became one of the key analytical tools in studying the combat effectiveness of Western armies, particularly during and after the Second World War. The massive sociological study of the U.S. army conducted between 1941 and 1945 by Samuel Stouffer and his team concluded that this unity (not patriotism or any political ideology) was the primary source of motivation that carried U.S. soldiers through the campaigns in Europe and in the Pacific, while Edward Shils and Morris Janowitz used it to explain the astounding ability of the *Wehrmacht* units to maintain their battle-worthiness even in a severely depleted state.[78] Thanks to these authors, who went to great lengths trying to get rid the whole concept of the ideological baggage identified by Kühne while keeping its logic alive, the issue became a category of analysis in contemporary military psychology and sociology,[79] as well as in the 'new military history'. John Lynn, who could well be presented as a prime example of the latter, has actually argued that the primary group dynamics are indeed a key factor influencing the 'sustaining motivation' of troops during prolonged conflict in the modern era,[80] while Alexander Watson concluded that in the case of British and German soldiers in the First World War, 'comradeship and "primary groups" were in fact crucial to soldiers' ability and willingness to fight on … generally increasing combat motivation'.[81]

Since a primary group is usually defined as a group no larger than thirty men, within the organizational structure of the Austro-Hungarian army, it is the platoon (*Zug*) that best fits this definition. The regiment then served as the basic *institutional* framework of soldiers' identification not just throughout the war, but for all their military lives, as regimental culture was particularly strong in the Imperial and Royal Army. According to Stouffer and his team, the primary function of a primary group is to 'set and enforce group standards of behaviour, and to support and sustain the individual in stresses he would otherwise not be able to withstand'.[82] It is little wonder that it resembles the socially disciplinary role of the family, as it is the concept of family that is often referred to by military primary groups when addressing their internal dynamics. Thomas Kühne even argues that 'the construction of a community of comradeship as a "family" … was the central basis for the symbolic order of war'.[83] Juraj Benko agrees, arguing that an individual's socialization in the army often took the form of a 'fictional kinship': 'The absence of traditional kinship relations in a homosocial group, along with heightened individual as well as collective danger, which leads to a heightened need for mutual support, creates conditions where military brotherhoods thrive well'.[84] However, these brotherhoods are often only a small part of a larger hierarchy, frequently compared to a wider family.[85] We will focus on the hierarchical aspects of this 'family' in Chapter 4; however, the very homosocial nature of such a family or brotherhood is important for our argument here, as its dynamics fuel a cohesion that in turn supports the members' sustaining motivation, even if it is against their immediate interest.

The fact that wartime comradeship tended to identify itself with family life is interesting, as it points to a sort of gendered structure within the symbolic 'family roles'. František Skála's diary presents a truly 'family picture' moment during Christmas Eve 1915 in Galicia. 'A signalman, a sapper, and a runner' (i.e. representatives of all the groups of rank-and-file servicemen at the battalion headquarters) were invited to report to their battalion commander, Major Müller. Skála was sent as one of the signalmen:

> A tiny Christmas tree was on the table, alight with four tiny candles. Two golden threads served as a decoration … Under the tree were chocolate bars, a few bottles of wine and various trifles. The adjutant Uher passed some of the gifts to us. We were all silent, our thoughts far away from our trench. A long stream of Christmas Eves appeared in our minds, taking us all the way back to our childhood … We felt poor – homeless, with an uncertain future. We were depressed. And even so, there was this heartwarming feeling of humanity, that we loved each other, and shared the fate of those violently thrown in here … Army regulations were put to one side under the tree, and we spoke only Czech, as we would at home with our moms. Later, we expressed our thanks and went to pass the gifts on to our comrades.[86]

The 'heartwarming feeling of humanity' and 'love for each other' like 'at home with our moms' took place in the battalion commander's dugout, and it is he who came up with the idea and defined the proceedings – for example, the language used, even though he was a 'German' (everyone else present was presumably Czech-speaking). In keeping with the family comparison, he obviously played the role of a patriarch, while his adjutant took on a motherly role and the happy soldiers receiving gifts, recalling their childhood days, were the children. The primary group defined through the family framework seemed to fulfil the participants' emotional needs very well at that moment, helping the otherwise 'depressed' men to improve their morale. It is also important to note that the family metaphor further helps to transform the framework of wartime masculinity, so it would encompass the 'heartwarming', 'loving' feelings of men towards other men. The 'military family' as described by František Skála therefore represents further support for the notion of comradeship, as it creates a viable hierarchy that enables men to cross the potentially divisive limits of class, rank or national identity inside the primary group. Consequently, it made the primary group an all-important factor in Czech soldiers' sustaining motivation, as – in those instances when it worked well – it enabled them to identify with the military organization about which they had been generally ideologically indifferent from the start.

The importance of the primary group in this regard is apparent in many of our sources. It is clear, for example, that the authors saw it as a source of all-important emotional support, well in line with the principle of wartime comradeship: 'You're right, dad, I'm in a really good mood. It's because we're always together with the guys', wrote a pioneer from Galicia at the beginning of the war.[87] Under normal circumstances, the need for emotional support was suppressed in masculine identity, but war made it so powerful and necessary for survival that men went out in search for it in their surroundings, finding it among their comrades and with the simple knowledge that they were not alone and would be taken care of if needed: 'Everyone's aware that he may need someone's help soon; and everyone knows the others would help as best as they can; that's comradeship … in spite of the different nationalities … different goals and ideas … inside the mess that is Austria'.[88] However idealized this passage from Jan Šindelář's memoir may be – and it obviously is, reflecting Kühne's analysis of the postwar enshrinement of wartime comradeship in certain circles of veterans – it may be cautiously deduced that the soldiers experienced comradeship at least as a *need* in a situation where it was too terrible to be alone. As Jaroslav Vítek wrote about the moment when a heavy shell exploded in close proximity: 'My head is spinning, body shivering … I'm alone. Being alone in such moments is particularly bad. Anxiety overcame me, I stood up and ran just to find some of my mates scattered in all directions'.[89] Similarly, when František Čapek found himself wounded in a hospital in Krakow in April 1915, there was only one thought on his mind: 'Taken away from my friends, I am alone, so alone'.[90] One rather typical feature of emotional support was the mutual assurance between comrades that their loved ones would be informed of whatever happened to them in the ensuing combat, as men were disinclined to place their faith in the army's ability to do so.

The notion of comradeship buttressed by familial imagery often helped to blur the class division in the ranks, working in both directions: 'On the one hand, I was really happy to leave the hellish maze of grey rocks', wrote František Šmída, a junior officer. 'On the other, though, I was sad to leave them. We were bound by the invisible bond of shared fortunes and danger'.[91] The same effect is, in some cases at least, apparent with regard to the issue of national identity, which was obviously becoming more important as the war went on: 'Two days have passed since I said goodbye to my friends, with whom I shared eighteen months of my existence', wrote an engineer to his father from Galicia after his unit was disbanded and the men transferred to various other outfits. 'Louda ... Steiner ... Křenek ... Strasser ... Now, there's only Czechs around, but it's just not that good'.[92]

Our sources also support the claim that the primary group is instrumental in sustaining combat-effectiveness. For example, when Jan Šlesingr tried to leave his trench under heavy fire in the hope that he would be killed, 'Bittner, an old reservist, pulled me down again and again. He worries about me. Even though he's much older than me, he feels safer with me'.[93] Even if it was not true of the author himself, the 'old reservist Bittner' felt much better as a member of a small group of two than as a lone individual on the fire-swept battlefield, enjoying the emotional support so much that he invested considerable effort in keeping the group intact. Josef Jarkovský, an infantryman in k.u.k. Infantry Regiment 18, wrote: 'I kept walking, even though my legs hurt and I probably shouldn't have ... The doc had ordered only light duty for me, but I loved the guys so much and they loved me', which led him to ignore his pain, leave the reserve and go back to his unit in the trenches around Tolmin in 1915.[94] Here, primary group cohesion kept one Czech soldier in the ranks for Austria-Hungary. He was not alone – on 1 October 1914, Egon Erwin Kisch met 'corporal Šperl', wounded for the third time and with a fresh bandage on his head. He looked 'terrible', 'a bloody bandage covering half of his face, blood dripping from it ... "So now you're staying in the hospital, right?", I asked, but he protested: "No way, I'm just going back to the dressing station to fix this ... I'll be back by noon."'[95]

Changes in the composition of the primary group were the most obvious dangers to its cohesion, and the insensitive replacement practices of the Austro-Hungarian army were often to blame. Not only were replacement battalions (*Marschbattalione*) organized more or less ad hoc, with only limited consideration for pre-existing training units and almost none for the situation of men returning from hospitals; the same battalions were, upon their arrival at the front, usually broken up into subunits, often platoons or even sections, and used to replenish numbers in the existing field units. In the words of Alois Dolejší, men often felt 'like slaves in the market' during the process, and the chance to keep any group identity or even *esprit de corps* was lost.[96] While there may have been an advantage to this method, in that it enabled the army to mix fresh and inexperienced units with surviving veterans,[97] the ultimate consequence was that many soldiers repeatedly lost those few friends and comrades they had managed to make, and their morale plunged. Convalescents were even worse off, as they tended to end up in the army replacement depots, where they were collected and sent as replacements to any unit currently in need – usually not the one they had known before.[98] The army, through what seemed to be administrative laziness more than anything else, was therefore signalling to the men that they were indeed 'cogs in the war machine' and not full men. And to make matters even worse, even this practice received its own share of the army command's paranoia – as noted by Jason Engle, efforts were repeatedly made to 'dilute' the groups suspect of disloyalty with other nationalities, sending Czech replacements to non-Czech-speaking units and vice versa. The men's morale had suffered along with their ability to properly communicate with their comrades.[99]

Besides misguided efforts of the army authorities, combat casualties were always threatening to tear the group apart over time, with the personnel rotating more quickly than the bonds in the group could establish themselves. In some cases, particularly heavy casualties could destroy the fabric of comradeship in a matter of minutes, the losses being both real and emotional: 'I have seen many torn bodies mangled horribly', wrote Jan Sýkora of k.k. Landwehr Infantry Regiment 30 in his diary. 'But the feeling every soldier knows, when he cradles a mortally wounded comrade's head on his knees … is much, much more painful than a sight of any lifeless corpse'.[100] In November 1914, Egon Erwin Kisch succumbed to depression not only because the war was obviously destined to go on into the next year, but also because the list of people he considered his friends was thinning by the day: 'The amount of casualties which has resulted from the battles of the past three days … I see many good friends on the list … I loved … many of them. And now they're dead'.[101] With men being violently ejected from the fabric of comradeship, the primary group tended to loosen or even fall apart, with the individual self-interest of its members again coming to the forefront. The logic of comradeship could also turn completely against any notion of combat effectiveness. František Čapek was captured during the Brusilov Offensive in July 1916 immediately after the preliminary barrage, when, in the ensuing chaos, he 'saw a corporal on the left throw away his rifle. So I did the same'.[102] The unspoken bond of wartime comradeship, although apparently anonymous, caused him to suddenly lose any motivation to sustain his effort. The moment the values and interests of the primary group diverge from that of the army as a whole, the group itself may become a medium of discontent or even disobedience. In other words, primary group always has an agency, and this agency may well get into conflict with the war effort if the members of the group find their interests to be at odds with those of the wider group of the army.[103] For example, during the retreat after the same Russian offensive, František Černý remembered 'many comrades purposefully leaving their units at night to surrender to the Russians, just to get something to eat'. He himself was contemplating doing the same, one of his arguments in favour being that 'the best friends I had here have gone anyway'.[104] We may well argue that during the last twelve months of the war in particular, when the Austro-Hungarian army experienced a deep crisis in terms of logistics and manpower, such moments, including the image of men despondent over the lack of food, were an all-too-common occurrence, with primary groups and their interests becoming increasingly at odds with the interests of the authorities, i.e. with the monarchy's war effort.[105]

Josef Váchal concluded in his memoir that Czech soldiers, 'according to their temperament, coped with their uncertain future more or less by themselves, looking inwards rather than outwards for strength', which made them, in his opinion, different from Germans, who 'were generally more communal types, and when addressing each other in an informal manner they sounded somewhat more sincere'.[106] While his theory might have provided an interesting starting point for comparative research, within the context of our argument, it is only possible to comment that Czech soldiers were indeed members, either passive or active, of military primary groups, and it is beyond doubt that the dynamics of these groups – when functioning properly – had helped them to sustain their motivation over the course of the war. As for the nature of the dynamics themselves, their roots can be followed to the symbolic structuring of male bonding in such groups, redefined under the notion of wartime comradeship. Its primary purpose was to defend the men's masculinity from further destabilization caused by inherent tensions both in individual gender identity, and in the specific homosocial environment of military units in wartime. These tensions were often rooted in the conflict between the hegemonic discourse of masculinity and the reality (physical and emotional) that the individual soldiers experienced in the war, which produced fears of further unmanning through one's social feminization. To resolve this conflict, masculinity was transformed under the guise of comradeship, which in turn played an important role in sustaining the men's motivation and morale.

Notes

1. V.s. Vráb, *Kamarát – kamarátom*, Kamarádství: List válečných, převratových a současných dějů 3, no. 3 (1934): 42.
2. Křenek, *Vzpomínky na vojnu v Albanii*, 175–178.
3. Ibid., 174.
4. Santanu Das, *Touch and Intimacy in First World War Literature* (Cambridge, 2005).
5. Kühne, *The Rise and Fall of Comradeship*, 30.
6. Thomas Kühne, 'Comradeship: Gender Confusion and Gender Order in the German Military, 1918–1945', in *Home/Front*, 233.
7. Ibid., 236.

8. As argued by Eve Sedgwick, 'desire among men' is unacceptable and punishable in all-male, 'homosocial societies'. Eve K. Sedgwick, *Between Men: English Literature and Male Homosocial Desire* (New York, 1985).
9. See also Roper, *The Secret Battle*, 10; Bourke, *Dismembering the Male*, 22–25; or Crouthamel, *An Intimate History of the Front*, 3–8. All these texts, including Kühne, take issue with Klaus Theweleit's original thesis on the wartime 'brutalization' of men, leading them to shun and loathe everything feminine. See Theweleit, *Male Fantasies*.
10. Kühne, 'Comradeship', 245–49. See also Robert L. Nelson, 'German Comrades – Slavic Whores', in *Home/Front*, 72–73 and 81.
11. Kisch, *Vojákem pražského sboru*, 25, diary entry from 10 August 1914.
12. Ibid., 60, diary entry from 26 August 1914.
13. Černý, *Moje záznamy ze světové války*, 105 and 114.
14. Klejna, *Voják – zajatec – legionář*, 49, diary entry from 30 October, 1914.
15. Slezák, *Paměti Josefa Slezáka k I. světové válce*, vol. 3, 65–67.
16. Ibid., vol. 2, 43–45. A similar competitiveness in the homosocial groups has been stressed above when discussing the concept of virility and soldiers' attitude towards women. On the inherent competitive nature of homosocial institutions, see Tosh, 'What Should Historians Do with Masculinity?', 186–87.
17. Tosh, 'What Should Historians Do with Masculinity?', 195; see also Tosh, 'The Old Adam and the New Man', 217–38; Tosh, 'Middle-Class Masculinities in the Era of the Women's Suffrage Movement, 1860–1914', in *English Masculinities, 1660–1800*, 103–27, 103–27; and John Tosh, *A Man's Place: Masculinity and the Middle-class Home in Victorian England*, 2nd edn (London, 2007), 102–43.
18. Neumann, 'Válčení civilistovo', 19.
19. On Sigmund Freud's theory of modern war as a consequence of an unsuppressed 'death drive' (Thanatos), which, along with the 'life instinct' (Eros), constitutes a key axis of the human psyche, see Sigmund Freud, 'Proč válka?', in *Sebrané spisy Sigmunda Freuda*, vol. 16: *Spisy z let 1932–1939* (Prague, 1998), 15–26; Sigmund Freud, 'Aktuální poznámky o válce a smrti', in *Sebrané spisy Sigmunda Freuda*, vol. 10: *Spisy z let 1913–1917* (Prague, 2002), 277–302; and Sigmund Freud, 'Mimo princip slasti', in *Sebrané spisy Sigmunda Freuda*, vol. 13: *Mimo princip slasti a jiné práce z let 1920–1924* (Prague, 1999), 7–58. See also Daniel Pick, *War Machine: The Rationalization of Slaughter in the Modern Age* (New Haven, 1993), 211–57; or Stefanos Geroulanos and Todd Meyers, *The Human Body in the Age of Catastrophe: Brittleness, Integration, Science and the Great War* (Chicago, 2018), 207–43.
20. Diary of Bohuš Adamíra, entry from 21 November 1916, in *Když naši dědové bojovali a umírali*, 72.
21. Kisch, *Vojákem pražského sboru*, 79 and 182, diary entries from 6 September and 20 November 1914.
22. Jan Šmatlán to his parents, 8 November 1914, in *Zapomenuté hlasy*, 11.
23. Mudrák, *Bojoval jsem za císaře pána*, 64.
24. Šindelář, *Proti vlastní vůli*, 177.
25. Slezák, *Paměti Josefa Slezáka k I. světové válce*, vol. 3, 53.
26. Váchal, *Malíř na frontě*, 93.
27. Kápar, *Cestou kamenitou*, 101.
28. Jaromír John, *Listy z vojny, jež psal svému synovi* (Prague, 1917), 35.
29. Květoň, *Vzpomínky z první světové války*, 35.

30. See Rachamimov, 'The Disruptive Comforts of Drag: (Trans)Gender Performances among Prisoners of War in Russia, 1914–1920', 368–72. See also Crouthamel, *An Intimate History of the Front*, 111. For a classic general study, see Marjorie Gerber, *Vested Interests: Cross-dressing and Cultural Anxiety* (New York 1992); for a comparative perspective on other militaries throughout history, see Holmes, *Acts of War*, 252–54.
31. Karel Rélink recalled a sergeant who put on 'a woman's shirt with a deep cleavage' to keep warm. Rélink, *28. pluk 'Pražské děti'*, 253.
32. Skála, *Válečný deník*, 171.
33. Dolejší, *Válečné vzpomínky z první světové války vojína Dolejše*, 129, diary entry from 7 November 1917.
34. Mádl, 'U 102. pěšího pluku', in *Domov za války*, vol. 4, 404.
35. Mikhail Bakhtin, *Rabelais and His World* (Bloomington, 1985).
36. Kučera, *Rationed Life*, 98–99.
37. Jan Laška, *Asinara* (Prague, 1928), 52.
38. Ludvík Maršík to his sister Anna, 23 September 1914, in *Zapomenuté hlasy*, 67.
39. Otakar Veselý to Gustina Veselá, 19 March 1915, in *Zapomenuté hlasy*, 95.
40. Laška, *Pochod hladu Albanií*, 29.
41. For a summary on the culture of emotions in European history, see, for example, Ute Frevert, *Emotions in History: Lost and Found* (New York, 2011), particularly 87–147 on their gendered nature.
42. Černý, 'První měsíc války', in *Domov za války*, vol. 1, 162.
43. Šindelář, *Proti vlastní vůli*, 77.
44. Klejna, *Voják – zajatec – legionář*, 43, diary entry from 13 September 1914.
45. Křenek, *Vzpomínky na vojnu v Albanii*, 38.
46. Šindelář, *Proti vlastní vůli*, 197.
47. Slezák, *Paměti Josefa Slezáka k I. světové válce*, vol. 1, 42.
48. Skála, *Válečný deník*, 22–23.
49. Šmída, *Vzpomínky z vojny*, 70.
50. Slezák, *Paměti Josefa Slezáka k I. světové válce*, vol. 2, 38–39.
51. For an excellent example, see the communication between Jan Čundrle, a junior officer in Russian captivity from late 1914, his wife and his in-laws. While Čundrle becomes increasingly emotionally upset as the war drags on, repeatedly complaining and asking for more emotional support from his wife, his in-laws and even his wife become increasingly irritated by his attitude, referring to it as 'whining' and evidently regarding it as unmanly. See Josef Čundrle papers, currently in the private possession of his descendants in the Čundrle family; the author is in possession of a digital copy, and all the future references are to this digitized version of the collection (hereinafter cited only by the name of the correspondents and the date).
52. On letter-writing as a traditionally 'feminine' form of communication see, for example, Rebecca Earle, 'Letters, Writers and the Historian', in *Epistolary Selves: Letters and Letter-Writers, 1600–1945*, ed. Rebecca Earle (Aldershot, 1999), 6–7; for more background, see Carolyn Steedman, 'A Woman Writing a Letter', in *Epistolary Selves*, 111–33.
53. Klejna, *Voják – zajatec – legionář*.
54. Josef Janošík diary, quote from 1 May 1917, Josef Janošík papers, private collection of Jan Janošík.
55. Slezák, *Paměti Josefa Slezáka k I. světové válce*, vol. 2, 48.

56. Kisch, *Vojákem pražského sboru*, 31, diary entry from 13 August 1914.
57. Bouška, 'Zápisky ze světové války', 4.
58. Váchal, *Malíř na frontě*, 137. The author is particularly susceptible to sympathizing with horses and their suffering, as he grew close to the animals during his service with the artillery and later the supply train. However, he should not be taken as a typical example, as one of his substitute objects of affection was an angora cat he left behind at home and to which he occasionally sent postcards. See ibid., 196.
59. Quoted in Hana Kábová, 'Bolestná cesta od věřícího mládí k přijetí zkonkrétněného světa (Bedřich Václavek a první světová válka, 1914–1918)', in *Armáda, společnost a první světová válka: Sborník příspěvků z vědecké konference konané v Jihočeském muzeu v Českých Budějovicích dne 8. listopadu 2002* (České Budějovice, 2003), 40, footnote 50.
60. Šmída, *Vzpomínky z vojny*, 145.
61. Tříska, ed., *Zapomenutá fronta*, 109. In this particular case, the quotation is apparently a direct transcription of the author's diary, not the editor's retelling of it, as is unfortunately the case with most of this particular edition; however, it is only vaguely dated to the time of the Battle of the Piave River in 1918.
62. Sperling, *Český důstojník na frontách monarchie*, 100, diary entry from 13 June 1917.
63. Tonar, ed., *Válečný deník*, 45, diary entry from 14 December 1915.
64. Karel Tůma, 'Na srbském bojišti', in *Domov za války*, vol. 1, 198.
65. See also Santanu Das, 'Kiss Me, Hardy: Intimacy, Gender, and Gesture in First World War Trench Literature', *Modernism/Modernity* 9, no. 1 (2002): 51–74.
66. Bourke, *Dismembering the Male*, 27 and 144–46.
67. Karel Janíček to Bedřich Václavek, 1 October 1916, quoted in Kábová, *Bolestná cesta od věřícího mládí k přijetí zkonkrétněného světa*, 44.
68. Quoted in ibid., 26.
69. Slezák, *Paměti Josefa Slezáka k I. světové válce*, vol. 1, 88.
70. Tosh, 'What Should Historians Do with Masculinity?', 195.
71. Křenek, *Vzpomínky na vojnu v Albanii*, 39; Slezák, *Paměti Josefa Slezáka k I. světové válce*, vol. 3, 41; Jan Richter to Jan Janošík, 16 August 1919, State District Archive in Olomouc, Fond Janošík Jan pplk. v. v.
72. Kühne claims that comradeship as a symbolic construct, while born out of the emotional crisis of the First World War, enjoyed the its greatest popularity in German postwar society, especially after the Nazi Party tried to build a 'state of comrades' based upon that myth. Then, Kühne argues, in the next generation of German soldiers, this time in the uniforms of the Third Reich, the idea of 'comradeship' became the key constitutional element of military masculinity. See Kühne, *The Rise and Fall of Comradeship*, 107–214. While the historical context, namely the outcome of the war itself, never allowed for such a development to happen in postwar Czechoslovakia, comradeship as a 'prized display of manly love', or 'a comradely affection and sympathy', is repeatedly invoked and praised in the Czech k.u.k. veterans' association bi-weekly magazine during the 1930s. Not surprisingly, the paper itself was titled *Kamarádství*, i.e. *Comradeship*, and its spirit is best captured by the introductory quote for this chapter. It may therefore be concluded that the tendency to 'mythologize' one's own past in a way that ensures its stability in terms of gender identity was not peculiar to German veterans. For quotations, see 'Dopis Jos. Merunky', *Kamarádství* 2, no. 6 (1933): 25; and Ladislav Hájek, 'Kamarádství', *Kamarádství* 1 no. 2 (1932): 25. For another example of the same, see Oskar Straka, 'V poli i zátiší', in *Pětasedmdesátníci vzpomínají. Z paměti účastníků světové*

války (Jindřichův Hradec, 1936), 139: 'It is impossible to forget the comradeship and true friendship that only shines through in the worst times full of danger. It was natural that comrades helped each other then, be it only by a warming look'. For more on Czech veterans' identity in the postwar period, see Hutečka, *Kamarádi frontovníci*.

73. Neumann, 'Válčení civilistovo', 101. Neumann writes that the poem he mentions was later lost; however, his use of homoerotic imagery remained. For example, in another of his memoirs, *Elbasan*, he writes of 'a one-year volunteer ... an adorable virgin boy ... all young and pretty'. Ibid., 120.
74. Ibid., 101.
75. Magnus Hirschfeld, *Sittengeschichte des Weltkrieges* (2 vols, Leipzig, 1930), vol. 1, 275–88.
76. Ibid., 288.
77. See du Picq, *Battle Studies*, 75.
78. Stouffer et al., *The American Soldier*, vol. 2, 334–58; Shils and Janowitz, 'Cohesion and Disintegration in the Wehrmacht in World War II', 177–220; see also Roger W. Little, 'Buddy Relations and Combat Performance', in *The New Military. Changing Patterns of Organization*, ed. Morris Janowitz (New York, 1964), 195–223.
79. See, for example, Anthony King, 'The Word of Command: Communication and Cohesion in the Military', *Armed Forces & Society* 32, no. 4 (2006): 493–512; Guy L. Siebold, 'The Essence of Military Group Cohesion', *Armed Forces & Society* 33, no. 2 (2007): 286–95; Anthony King, 'The Existence of Group Cohesion in the Armed Forces: A Response to Guy Siebold', *Armed Forces & Society* 33, no. 4 (2007): 638–45; and Guy L. Siebold, 'Key Questions and Challenges to the Standard Model of Military Group Cohesion', *Armed Forces & Society* 37, no. 3 (2011): 448–68.
80. Lynn, *Bayonets of the Republic*, 30–35.
81. Watson, *Enduring the Great War*, 66–67. Watson rightfully criticizes an older study of Peter Knoch, who in 1989 argued the opposite. See Peter Knoch, 'Kriegsalltag', in *Die Rekonstruktion des Kriegsalltags als Aufgabe der historischen Forschung und der Fridenserziehung*, ed. Peter Knoch (Stuttgart, 1989), 222–51.
82. Stouffer et al., *The American Soldier*, vol. 2: *Combat and its Aftermath*, 130–31.
83. Kühne, 'Comradeship', in *Home/Front*, 245. See also Roper, *The Secret Battle*, 10 and 131.
84. Juraj Benko, 'Vojnová sociálizácia mužov v armáde, v zajatí a v legiích (1914–1921)', *Forum Historiae* 3, no. 1 (2009): 1.
85. See, for example, William Arkin and Lynne R. Dobrofsky, 'Military Socialization and Masculinity', *Journal of Social Issues* 34, no. 1 (1978): 151–68.
86. Skála, *Válečný deník*, 125–26.
87. Ludvík Maršík to his father, 16 September 1914, in *Zapomenuté hlasy*, 67.
88. Šindelář, *Proti vlastní vůli*, 158.
89. Vítek, *V cizích službách*, 148.
90. Diary of František Čapek, State District Archive in Havlíčkův Brod, Sbírka soudobé dokumentace okresu Havlíčkův Brod, sign. D7A (manuscript), 2.
91. Šmída, *Vzpomínky z vojny*, 138.
92. Ludvík Maršík to his father, 27 July 1917, in *Zapomenuté hlasy*, 85.
93. Šlesingr, *Legionáři*, 17.
94. Jarkovský, 'Kronika ze světové války', 25.
95. Kisch, *Vojákem pražského sboru*, 121, diary entry from 1 October 1914.

96. Dolejší, *Válečné vzpomínky z první světové války vojína Dolejše*, 10, diary entry from 19 May 1916.
97. Jurman, ed., *Legionářská odyssea*, 10; see also Ulrych, 'Moje zápisky', 66.
98. Slezák, *Paměti Josefa Slezáka k I. světové válce*, vol. 4, 26.
99. Engle, '"This Monstrous Front Will Devour Us All"', 148–52.
100. Sýkora, 'Tarnavka – Obrázek ze světové války', 11–12.
101. Kisch, *Vojákem pražského sboru*, 162, diary entry from 9 November, 1914.
102. Diary of František Čapek (manuscript),13.
103. See Kühne, *The Rise and Fall of Comradeship*, 5.
104. Černý, *Moje záznamy ze světové války*, 114 and 116.
105. For the same argument, with particular regard to the disintegration of morale in units dominated by ethnic minorities, see Alexander Watson, 'Mutinies and Military Morale', in *Oxford Illustrated History of the First World War*, ed. Hew Strachan (Oxford, 2016), 195. While ethnic identity may well have been one of the factors forming the primary group and its interests, it seems that it only came to the fore after many other factors had made further service barely bearable (see Chapters 2 and 4 of this book in particular).
106. Váchal, *Malíř na frontě*, 39.

Chapter 4

DEGRADATION OF MANLINESS
The Military Authorities

Any stupid brute should tremble in the face of an officer's uniform.
—Karel Poláček, *Podzemní město*

In his war novel *Podzemní město* (*The Underground City*), the famous Czech writer, journalist and First World War veteran Karel Poláček presents his readers with a fascinating collection of almost real-life characters, ranging from ordinary privates to commanding officers. Poláček's talent for observation enables us to use his characters as a stepping stone, leading us to another key factor that influenced the men's sustaining motivation: the military authorities and the soldiers' relationship with them. The Austro-Hungarian army projected its power over the men primarily through junior and lower-grade senior officers (*Kadett*, *Fähnrich* (i.e. officer candidates), *Leutnant*, *Oberleutnant*, *Hauptmann*, *Major*, sometimes *Oberstleutnant*) or through ranking noncommissioned officers (*Feldwebel* or *Stabsfeldwebel*). Poláček's novel, which takes place in an anonymous sector of the Eastern Front over the course of a number of weeks sometime in 1916, more than effectively shows the multifaceted nature of that power, while revealing some of the factors that the men saw as crucial when submitting themselves to authority.

There are a number of arrogant, self-centred officers who care only about their looks, their comfort and their perceived social superiority. In fact, in Poláček's eyes, these are in a slight majority as far as his characters are concerned:

> Utschigg, commander of the 17th Company, studied the moustache supporting his pointy nose with delight in the mirror, flirtatiously raising and lowering his eyebrows again and again … The little infantryman braced himself for a torrent of shouted insults, even expected a slap or two, but the *Oberleutnant* seemed a bit absent-minded

this time. He just called him a crossbred of a dog and a pig and promised that he would let him be hanged. But he sounded indifferent saying that – the officer was leaving for the battalion HQ, for a night full of drinking and singing.[1]

However, there are others who seem to fulfil the hard-sought image of paternal authority figure a little better, ruling their military 'family' in a tough and fair spirit:

> They liked their commander. They liked his black moustache and slender legs in polished high boots. *Major* Klofanda knew very well that they liked him, and he twisted his hips and jumped over tree stumps with a charming lightness … *Major* Klofanda laughed and said: '*Schön, meine Kinder. Wirklich tadellos.* Good soldiers. Singing I like a lot'. 'Major Klofanda is a great guy, ain't he?' 'Great guy, yeah. A tough gentleman, he doesn't give a shit who's who. He's a damn tough commander, but he always looks after his soldiers'.[2]

Another theme that resonates throughout the novel is a dissonance in the understanding of disciplinary measures between the men in command ('*Oberleutnant* Král measured the officers in that group with disdain. Some gentlemen, he thought, had no sense of honour, joking and jesting in front of the rank and file. Can we keep them disciplined this way at all? Any stupid brute should tremble in the face of an officer's uniform.')[3] and the other ranks: 'The men hated *Oberleutnant* Král for making them run up and down the trenches and scolding them in a nasty way… *Oberleutnant* Král was a reserve officer. He was not supposed to be boorish and cruel. The sense of one's dignity and civil rights was an early victim in this war, but *Oberleutnant* Král worked hard to awaken it so much it burned white hot'.[4] In addition, there is a moment in the novel when the subordinate position of a soldier comes into a conflict with his social identity, degraded as it is and humiliated beyond acceptable limits by the impersonal power of the army:

> Private Trachta stared into the distance, and his confectionery appeared before his eyes … I am an affluent man, a master confectioner. I sat on the Board of Supervisors of the town savings bank. I was also a member of the Readers' Club. There is a diploma on the wall of my shop. I was a respected man, and now I am barely surviving … *Oberleutnant* Král came closer, whipping his cane on his thigh. *Feldwebel* pushed his inquests further; Private Trachta knew that he was asking about the missing ration. He remained quiet, mumbling to himself: 'I am a master confectioner. I could have been elected to the town council…' *Feldwebel* Wagenknecht slapped him again. Private Trachta licked away the blood streaming from his nose.[5]

The image of authority in Poláček's novel is thoroughly ambivalent and it also does not lack gendered connotations. There is boorishness, arrogance, and an obsession with privilege along with a parody of the masculine body image, even if this body image plays an important part in the representation of the 'good authority' that, above all else, dispenses tough fatherly justice to its 'children'. The notion of military discipline is given the same ambivalent treatment. While it seems that the men generally understand that it is necessary for the army to properly fulfil its purpose (i.e. combat), they also feel that the way in which it is applied by the military somewhat misses the point of effectiveness and unit morale, as it robs them of their humanity, rights and elementary control over themselves as beings. The way in which it physically humiliates them only reminds them how distant the world of war is from the world they used to inhabit, and the entire dissonance is shrouded in an ever-present theme of an absurd, impersonal and arbitrary power based on a hierarchy that negates all peacetime rules, including the gender order and the peacetime hierarchy of masculinities. A hierarchy where the cruel and ambitious *Oberleutnant* Král and 'the soul hollowed by regulations', *Feldwebel* Wagenknecht, are 'everything', where uncontrollable psychopaths and future deserters to be hanged, such as Private Habětín, become celebrated war heroes and therefore 'something', and where respected members of the community such as the confectioner-turned-soldier Trachta are literally 'nothing'.

Of course, the subordination principle is the key to the way in which military institutions have worked for centuries, one that has proved most effective in fulfilling their task of executing organized violence. The 'empty battlefield' of modern conflict, as once defined by S.L.A. Marshall, makes it a particular imperative for the army organization to relay information and orders in such a way that they would be acted upon in the quickest and most predictable way possible, with little to no hesitation.[6] And it is particularly this kind of battlefield, where firepower made massed formations impossible, and command and control were decentralized into small scattered units, where high-quality officer corps and NCOs, respected by the men enough to induce obedience to their command, are indispensable. Morris Janowitz and Edward Shils concluded in their study of the *Wehrmacht*'s performance in the Second World War that ultimately the soldiers' motivation 'depended upon the personality of the officer', and other authors focusing on other militaries in other eras – including the First World War – generally agree, so there is little reason to think that the Habsburg army would be an exception.[7]

To whom and *how* one is subordinated are therefore key questions for anyone in a military hierarchy. What is even more important for our analysis here is the result, which is a hierarchy of power, power of men over other men, i.e. a surprisingly open institutionalization of the power struggle that underscores any gender hierarchy, in this case a hierarchy of masculinities.[8] Like every hierarchy, and particularly one based on the notion of masculinity, this one was inherently unstable and, as a result, the position of individual actors remained open to contention, attack or renegotiation. As a consequence, the gender-based nature of the military hierarchy has created a permanent conflict. This conflict between the military authorities and their subordinates may well be interpreted as an institutionalized, militarized, large-scale version of the permanent tension between the many forms of masculinity – between the officers' masculinity and rank-and-file masculinity, between hegemonic and complicit masculinity, between mainstream and marginalized forms.[9] This conflict, taking place well inside the 'masculine'/'front' part of the wartime social space, is also open to other interpretations, particularly those which see it as a symbolic struggle to control men both as a group and as individual actors, projected upon the radically reconstructed gender order produced by war. In the following chapter, we will analyse the way in which this struggle was mirrored in the motivation and morale of Czech soldiers.

Talking about authorities in the military as viewed by rank-and-file soldiers in the Habsburg army means talking about company and battalion officers, with infantry companies of 200–250 men commanded by a captain (*Hauptmann*), and infantry battalions of about 1,000 men commanded by a major. When Austria-Hungary entered the war in 1914, the peacetime establishment of its military (the Common Army, *Landwehr*, *Honvédség* and the *k.u.k. Kriegsmarine*) numbered 415,000 men and officers. With wartime mobilization, this number quickly reached 3,260,000 by September of that year.[10] Along with the army, its officer corps also grew, but at the height of mobilization, it still numbered only 60,000 men, and the ratio of one officer to fifty-four other ranks hardly satisfied the needs of a modern army. The subsequent heavy losses in the first months of the war, which decimated the prewar cadre of regular officers (22,310 officers, i.e. one-third, were killed, wounded or taken prisoner in 1914), could hardly have improved the situation. Put simply, the hard-pressed army, exhausted by bloody battles it mostly lost, suffering from a supply crisis and miserable weather in a prolonged war few had expected, was short of experienced command, as many of its best junior officers became casualties of war.[11]

Of course, the army responded, compensating for the losses by pushing thousands of reserve officers through training and into command positions. While the same was more or less also true for the other ranks, and the Habsburg army changed forever, in the words of its official history, into 'a *Landsturm* and militia army' made of civilians in uniform, its command structure suffered from particularly grave problems, especially before the new commanders learned the basics of their trade (at the expense of results and the lives of their men).[12] In this light, the deep crisis of morale at the end of the Carpathian battles in the spring of 1915 is therefore much easier to understand, as many a command position in field companies was taken by men previously unfit for commission in terms of age, health or education.[13] In the words of k.u.k. infantryman Josef Slezák, written in April 1915, 'we have experienced a shortage of officers. Many mistakes were made as a result'.[14] However, the desperate measures carried the army through another four years of war, and by October, 1918, 188,000 Austro-Hungarian officers commanded an army numbering a total of 3,824,000 (one officer to twenty other ranks).[15] Furthermore, contrary to the popular image, they suffered disproportionate losses in the process – 13.5% of regular officers were killed in action, compared to 9.8% of NCOs and enlisted men. All in all, almost 100,000 officers became casualties during the war.[16] Nevertheless, even the statistically apparent willingness to 'lead from the front' did not spare the officers some harsh judgement from their men.

One of the oft-repeated complaints referred to the very nature of the military hierarchy or, more particularly, to its immovably fixed form. In spite of the heavy losses in the commissioned ranks, the Austro-Hungarian high command refused to waver and insisted on a strict class separation in the army. While other armies either enabled (albeit in exceptional cases) men from the lower ranks to enter the officer class or – under the combined pressure of manpower shortages and the necessity to sustain the morale of the troops – at least tried to find a way that would keep the class-bound structure intact while enabling a degree of promotion through merit, in the Common Army it was outright impossible for battle-hardened, experienced NCOs, often with informal command experience in the field, to be ever granted a commission and to become officers without the proper qualification, usually formally reflected in education. This never changed during the war.[17] From the point of view of the Austro-Hungarian military authorities, the army was forever bound to be composed of two distinct groups of men: the officers and the other ranks. As a result, while these groups seemed to represent only two different variations of wartime hegemonic masculinity, upon closer examination they represented the fixed nature of an institutionalized hierarchy of men. The key to this hierarchy was power and control, both bordering on absolute – one group had it all, while the other lacked even the most elementary forms of it. This basic dynamic reflected – in a highly institutionalized and formalized form – the way in which gender hierarchies worked, and consequently influenced the way in which the individual participants experienced their own masculinity. This experience then logically became one of the key factors influencing their general attitude to the system, i.e. their sustaining motivation.

Those who served in the higher echelons of the military hierarchy felt their masculinity being fulfilled more than the mass of those who spent the war in the compliant, sometimes even marginalized role of ordinary soldiers. While they were still part of the wartime hegemonic gender (i.e. military masculinity), their world, mostly limited to the homosocial military environment, relegated them to a position that in the end felt like a diminishing of their status as men. The biggest problem was well represented by the case of Poláček's character, Private Trachta – many a man's status in this new wartime hierarchy of manliness did not correspond well with their peacetime social standing. As shown in Chapter 1, whereas war enabled particularly young or marginalized men to access hegemonic masculinity with its attached patriarchal dividend almost overnight, many soldiers, particularly older professional men with families and successful careers, experienced the exact opposite.

Of course, the diminishing of one's humanity, let alone social status, may well have been an inherent trait of war itself, as commented upon by Jan Laška, a POW in Serbian captivity observing the wretched state of the Serbian army retreating across the mountains to Albania in late 1915: 'Intelligent people they once were, men of respect and good stature, fathers of families ... Now, they are reduced to the status of animals'.[18] In addition to the miseries of war, the military uniform itself carried with it an inner purpose of erasing any outward symbols of social status. For many men, donning it may well have cast doubt on any expectations they may have had regarding any improvement of their status as men. For example, the radical leftist poet Stanislav Kostka Neumann initially saw the whole process in a positive light:

> There is one thing that makes it all easier ... No longer are men classified on the basis of their dress, as this will be removed soon ... No one asks whether you are a cabbie or an engineer, whether your coat is made of canvas or of woollen cloth, we sit or stand here right next to each other, all equal ... At first, war seems to be the most democratic thing in the world, which makes it a lot easier to get used to whatever it brings about'.[19]

However, for many, this actually meant giving up not only their status, but also many of the social and personal habits they had internalized as an intimate part of their own individuality: 'Day after day, soldierly habits became part of our beings. The differences in the use of handkerchiefs and foot wraps gradually disappeared, and a louse or two came along', recalled another artist-turned-soldier, Josef Váchal. 'In the first few days, all those feelings of nostalgia and spiritual degradation by militarism were nothing compared to the horrible impression of filth, numbness and animal stupidity of my co-conscripts, who – alas! – were my fellow countrymen after all. Realizing this, I concluded that I would never become a democrat'.[20]

Looking closer at the 'democracy of the army', even its admirers such as Stanislav Kostka Neumann soon realized that this was merely an impression: 'The social justice and equality are only superficial ... Many of those who in peacetime were nobodies ... became "big men" with all the benefits of being "big"'.[21] Translated into analytical vocabulary, some men achieved hegemonic status, giving them a position at the top of the hierarchy that maximized their 'patriarchal dividend'. Reciprocally, soldiers who were used to hegemonic masculine status with all its dividends in peacetime now often found themselves at the very lowest levels of the *military* masculine hierarchy, as this hierarchy cared little about their previous life or its symbolic attributes: '*Oberleutnant* Licht did not like the little doctor', remembered Ferdinand Lirš. 'Right at the beginning of our glorious military careers, Koerner reported using his pompous "doctor" title during roll call ... "What doctor?!", the *Oberleutnant* shouted angrily. "You are a one-year volunteer Koerner, do you understand? We are soldiers here, we do not care about civilian rank. We are no damn club, remember!"'[22] František Šmída has described this process as a 'complete degradation of one's personality', one that 'man has to conform to'.[23] The 'diminishing' of one's personality is actually one of the primary purposes of basic military training, aiming at erasing the soldier's civilian identity and replacing it with an internalized attachment to a greater good, i.e. the unit and its goals.[24] As Thomas Kühne added, 'a significant part of certain rituals of initiation and degradation was (and is) that recruits had (and have) to carry out feminine-connoted acts'.[25] Cleaning and modifying uniforms, sewing, cooking, general cleaning of quarters and other culturally feminized tasks were perceived as passive, unmanly enterprises bereft of anything that would point to one's manly bearing and status in peacetime. Consequently, the soldiers' very masculinity came under threat.

The Officers and the Brutes

The problem of diminished manliness that many men experienced upon enlisting had other dimensions beyond simple submission to a new social hierarchy. It also carried the painful realization of *who* stood at the upper levels of that hierarchy; to use Neumann's words, who had become the 'big man' and been given power over men, which was the primary 'benefit' of his new status. It is not surprising that the sharpest criticism of the new order, where 'better people' are commanded by 'lowlife', comes from the ranks of former *Landsturm* servicemen or at least from those men who enlisted in their late twenties, thirties or even early forties. Age is one of the key categories of masculine identity, co-defining a man's position in the gender hierarchy. In the military hierarchy, however, it is largely ignored, as it often gives twenty-year-old cadets the power of command and control over 'fathers of families': 'Respected men, businessmen or master craftsmen in their civilian life were thus at the mercy of a malicious youth, whose sloppy character ... has manifested itself in the most callous, ruthless, even cruel manner', recalled S.K. Neumann, himself thirty-nine years old at the time of enlistment.[26] Experiences from cadet schools for one-year-volunteers (i.e. future reserve officers) are another rich source of similar complaints, as it placed a group of young men from the educated class (passing the *Abitur*, i.e. secondary school final exam, was a basic requirement), aspiring to hegemonic masculinity, beneath those who actually held that position currently and were given command over them in training: 'The ever-present, unrestrained Austrian military boorishness exercised by the officers pulled from the cobbler's stools, cattle shops, bricklayer's shovels, and made into instructors in the school for one-year-volunteers'.[27] 'Bricklayers, shop assistants, junior salesmen etc. Many were good men, but some of them were still far from "civilized"'.[28] 'The instructors, in general, were rough, coarse, and unintelligent men'.[29] For many, the 'tournament of manliness' did not help them to attain better social standing or to maintain their hegemonic position in the hierarchy of masculinities as the public discourse had promised them. In fact, it did the opposite – they lost their status to men who because of their class, education, age or intelligence were not supposed to have a rightful claim to such a social position. Ultimately, many felt as if they had ended up on the losing side of the tournament – and the higher their original position, the worse their fall.[30]

Within the framework of the hierarchy outlined above, the power relations attached to the positions of individual actors translated into a dynamic game of everyday practice of social negotiation, aptly described by Neumann as 'everyday abuse of power'.[31] As a prime example of its inherently gendered dimension, we can point to the way in which soldiers' or even junior officers' masculinity was diminished through a particularly sensitive area of masculine power – their women. Agreeing that one of the main purposes of socially construed masculinity is to maintain it in a dominant position vis-à-vis femininity through the ritualized possession of a woman, the breaking of this social (and sexual) control represents the most perfect form of diminishing a man's manliness. In a number of sources used in this study, a situation is described in which a superior officer forces a subordinate's wife to provide him with sexual favours in exchange for saving her husband from a frontline assignment. These apparently rare cases required the wife's presence at the base, of course, which perhaps limited the extent of such practices, but the sources repeatedly mention them in the case of depots in Hungary in 1915 (after reserve battalions of Bohemian regiments moved here in January, and some women came to visit their husbands, staying in town for a while) and also once in Bohemia proper. For example, Egon Erwin Kisch noted in his diary that a wife of an *Oberleutnant* 'visits *Herr Oberstleutnant* every day at six', earning her husband, after eight days of visits, proof that he is unfit for service in the field and the Military Merit Medal on top of that. The patriarchal dividend, translated here into sexual favours, was clearly understood by Kisch to be a projection of power over men through 'their' women: 'She is the daughter of an industrialist from Prague, a blonde, still in her late teens, and she lets the old and creaky *Oberstleutnant* abuse her just to get a small piece of metal for her husband to wear'.

Kisch also noted that 'this is a common occurrence here now', following with several other examples – an infantryman's wife 'giving herself' to a regimental medical officer, 'earning' her husband a 'travel order back to Bohemia' that 'only came into effect after three days, so the good doctor had time to enjoy the lady's company'; a staff-sergeant's wife providing the same favours to a lieutenant; or 'Mrs. H., a wife of one the reservists and a very nice lady, the mother of three children', again 'visiting' the regimental medical officer: 'I ran into her ... she

Figure 4.1 The officers' access to 'resources' in wartime, military hospital in the town of Czernowitz, Bukovina, in eastern Austria-Hungary (today Chernivtsi, Ukraine), spring 1915 (Museum of Eastern Bohemia, Hradec Králové).

was all upset and confused, and begged me to keep silent'.[32] And, as Kisch had observed, the very public nature of these affairs was seen as the most humiliating aspect: 'It was all happening quite publicly, as there were a number of people quartered in each house, and the batmen and adjutants see and tell everything'.[33] A year later at a regimental depot in Szeged, S.K. Neumann's wife, on a visit to her husband who was about to be finally sent to the front, received an offer for a similar kind of 'exchange': '*Oberleutnant* N ... actually distinguished himself one last time, when he offered my wife the chance to "pull me out" of the *Marschkompanie* in exchange for a thing ... a good little man'.[34] The fact that this kind of projection of one's status and power over those lower in the military hierarchy was not limited to Hungarian garrisons is evidenced by a note in another diary, that of František Skála, who mentions a 'lord supreme, *Hauptmann* Bibus', a commander of a replacement company of k.u.k. Infantry Regiment 98 in Jaroměř, Bohemia, who 'was only merciful to those men on whose behalf pretty ladies pleaded enough'.[35]

The question is how widespread this behaviour was, as the sources consulted here are few and far between even within a limited sample of personal writings. Also, it is obvious that the practice of spouses visiting their husbands at regimental depots was limited both by their relative wealth in terms of money and the time available for such an undertaking (i.e. the 'industrialist's daughter'), as well as by the limited 'windows of opportunity' of the war's ebb and flow (troop movements, rest and refit periods, recuperation in hospitals). It is therefore highly possible that the examples above constitute exceptional situations and were recorded as such. However, it is often such extreme forms of power relations in society that uncover deeper general trends, in this case the dynamics of power between individual positions within the structures of military masculinity.

Similar, undeniably much more common dynamics were exercised in the purely material sphere of accessing the ever-limited resources of 'warmth, bread, and sex'. The different levels of access to rations and other supplies enjoyed by officers in comparison with other ranks are an almost constant source of criticism and disapproval in soldiers' writings.[36] The division is particularly painful whenever the supply system breaks down and rations run low, which happened to most of the men during the final year of the war. Frontline troops in particular were forced to live through most of 1918 on miserable rations, such as the widely unpopular *Trockengemüsensuppe*, a vegetable soup based on beet and grass, accompanied by corn bread, while most officers still enjoyed a reasonably accommodating lifestyle. An artillery lieutenant serving with a battery of heavy howitzers on the Piave noted in his diary as late as 15 September 1918 that: 'In the evening we went to a concert and then invited some ladies to the officers' mess, where we stayed till early morning having lots of fun. Bacon, cheeses, pepperoncini, wine, chocolate and a peach punch were served'.[37] Truly, the menu was a bit limited in comparison to the one infantry *Fähnrich* Jan Janošík praised in December 1915: 'Sunday brunch – bouillon with egg, sour pike with potato, melted butter and white bread, salsa, a goose with canned fruit, beer, a chocolate cake, wine, black coffee'.[38] On the other hand, the enlisted men's rations were infinitely better in Galicia in 1915 than on the Piave in 1918, and the fact that officers' rations stagnated at worst while those of other ranks plunged below an existential minimum led to an ever-increasing spiral of condemnation in many soldiers' writings. However, their *leitmotif* hardly changed. At Christmas 1915, the *Landsturm* infantryman František Černý wrote in his diary: 'The officers were stuffing their bellies and their pockets, while men were dying of hunger … That's how it's always been in the Austrian army'.[39] Two and half years later, a regimental surgeon's assistant Alois Dolejší – located well behind the frontline at a well-supplied headquarters – voiced a similar sentiment: 'No wonder soldiers eat only vegetables and polenta day after day, when everything ends up in the *Offiziersmesse*. No wonder we have to tie our poor stomachs up with a belt and look forward to better times'.[40] As a result, every moment when meals were distributed reminded men not only of the status they had lost vis-à-vis their peacetime selves, but – even more importantly – vis-à-vis other men in the masculine hierarchy of the military.[41]

Of course, resentment towards officers' privilege based on their separate class status was not specific to the Austro-Hungarian military – during the First World War, most armies were subject to similar criticisms from their servicemen, mostly in connection to food and shelter.[42] In addition, it is hardly surprising that, given the aforementioned constant obsession of the men with 'sex', rank-and-file soldiers strongly disapproved of the officers' privileged access to women, whom

Figure 4.2 Access to resources as experienced by the rank-and-file soldiers, an unknown unit in Bukovina, spring 1915 (Museum of Eastern Bohemia, Hradec Králové).

they saw in this context as just another disproportionately distributed resource. As *Leutnant* František Šmída noted with a certain relish, the 'officers, as gentlemen', had the 'luxury of being much more picky' regarding prostitutes,[43] while many soldiers complain in their writings constantly about 'dressed-up ladies' surrounding the officers wherever they go, 'undoubtedly having a jolly good time with those of our officers quartered there'.[44] Moreover, it is no surprise that soldiers' criticism of this situation often blends in with their negative judgement of the women in question, as they reminded them of their diminished status in the masculine hierarchy in a particularly painful way. No wonder that officers, whose very public exhibition of the inequality of wartime masculinities in this area caused such pain, were subject to the most disparaging epithets: 'Arrogant vermin they are! Whores and booze, that's the only thing they care about, not war or the men!'[45]

As Alexander Watson noted in his study of German and British military morale, an officer's privilege is closely interspersed with the theme of 'paternalism', thus lending a particular poignancy to the gender theory of 'patriarchal dividend', with the dividend here being the obvious privilege of access – to power and resources.[46] As mentioned in the previous chapter, 'the construction of the community of comradeship as a "family" – with the head of the troops as "Dad" and the sergeant as the "mother" of the company, or with another distribution of roles – was a central basis for the symbolic order of war'.[47] In fact, this was the traditional basis of interpreting the military service by the conservative army command for centuries. As stated by Christa Hämmerle, the military discourse of obedience was firmly rooted in 'the nature of the bond between the soldiers and the "fatherland", especially the emperor ... that was configured as an authoritarian father-son relationship', with the patriarchal power understood as residing above daily politics.[48] As such, the army was always seen as a tool for defending the patriarchal hierarchy of the empire, a logic that once led Field Marshall Radetzky to complain about 'mere boys' ascending to power during the revolutionary year of 1848, disrupting the patriarchal social order.[49] In the eyes of the military authorities during the nineteenth and early twentieth centuries, not only the army but the entire society of the empire was an embodiment of patriarchy from to top to bottom, with 'fathers' in uniforms and in the civil administration ruling it with a strong but fair hand.[50]

Looking at the soldiers' writings, it is difficult to ascertain the level of success this discourse had in defining their thought. Czech soldiers usually all but ignore the patriarchal ideology of the army in their diaries, and the only moment the emperor receives an honourable mention is either the moment of his birthday (usually connected with extra rations of 'bread' or 'warmth') or that of his death. When Charles I succeeded Franz Joseph I to the throne after the latter's death in November 1916, the event was generally noticed by the men only within the context of the official mourning they were subjected to. In memoirs where the authors often try hard to heap criticism upon the late monarchy from the safety of hindsight, this general silence is often replaced by a lambasting of the empire and its symbols, with Franz Joseph I in particular receiving the brunt of the harsh words in a way that somewhat confirms the patriarchal discourse, sometimes in an almost Freudian manner of a son renouncing his father (with the Czech nation playing the role of mother).[51]

It seems that the 'community of comradeship' was a much closer 'family' to most men than the abstract 'military family' of the Austro-Hungarian military. Of course, the former was constructed around the trope of patriarchal hierarchy: 'The commander is a father and the men are his children', Jan Šindelář wrote in his memoir.[52] Images of soldiers as 'boys', 'children of Prague' or 'children of Brdy' remained a staple in describing military formations long after the war,[53] and in the same way, the image of officers, NCOs or veteran soldiers effectively accommodated the notion of a fatherly authority. Josef Jarkovský returned late from his leave in October 1918, which brought him before his commanding officer – a 'fair and wise' colonel whom he describes using the ideal imagery of perfect patriarchal authority.[54] Similarly, four years earlier, Jan Šmatlán commented upon a 'nice Mr. Corporal', who took care of his unit in a way that reminded him of fatherly care.[55] Later on, František Prudil was 'assigned to two old guys ... like fathers. I was so grateful for all the advice they gave me. How to behave, what to do in combat, how to take cover, how to dig in, how to protect my head in those desperate moments when one has only his little spade and little time'.[56] The same logic of patriarchy also made it into Josef

Ulrych's memoir – initially he 'got a platoon sergeant, an old fatherly type', only to become one two years later when he was assigned to command a platoon of raw recruits who 'ran in my steps like children following their dad'. The same author also commented upon a popular platoon commander's reassignment, saying 'it will be like losing a father for us'.[57] These sentiments became the core source of legitimacy underscoring the highly disproportionate access to resources and power – insofar as the officers, NCOs or generally men higher up in the hierarchy were understood to be 'fathers' of their 'dependents', they inherently possessed a right to the 'patriarchal dividend' because of their 'patriarchal role'. It was the officer's commission in particular that, thanks to the nature of the Austro-Hungarian military hierarchy, made all the difference in this regard, providing the men who were able to attain it with a completely separate path to all kinds of resources, beginning with rations and ending with women, as well as to power in general. For the authorities to be seen as legitimate beneficiaries of these dividends, they had to conform to the generally accepted image of a 'good father' within the context of a 'military family'. Consequently, the way in which soldiers understood and portrayed this image was a key to their understanding of the authorities, who were always confronted with the ideal form; a form seen as a precursor to the top position in the wartime masculine hierarchy.

What characteristics conferred the most legitimacy to wield power, besides the formalized categories of rank and institutional position? In the words of František Skála: 'We particularly respect *Major* Müller ... He is a regular officer, he knows no danger or personal discomfort, and he cares about his soldiers. He feels for each and every one of them. And he is proud to be a Czech, even though he had a German education'.[58] According to František Šmída, 'an officer's authority required ... manly bearing and quick thinking'.[59] It is clear that the ideal authority more or less reflected the hegemonic ideals of wartime manhood, combining both patriarchal themes (fatherly, caring, firm but fair) with such militarized concepts as courage under fire, decisive thinking, commanding skill and general 'manliness'. It is also clear that 'pride in being a Czech' represents a distinctive category that may well have played its role for some of the men, and we will come to this issue later in the chapter. Digging deeper into the discourse of patriarchal authority as imagined by the soldiers, we can see at the core of its legitimacy the willingness of the commanders to share the dangers and hardships of wartime service with their men, or at least to pretend successfully to do so. As noted by Egon Erwin Kisch in November 1914:

> life at the Division HQ seems like a gross crime to me. I cannot say a word against any of the staff officers, as they rarely have the time to eat, but the very number of aides, staff company commanders, signal officers, accounting officers, quartermaster officers, accessory officers, ration officers, supply officers, who all just wander around aimlessly, is just unbelievable. It is these gentlemen who always start shouting whenever they feel the buns with custard are not perfect. Old retired staff officers, who often volunteered

to serve in the frontlines after the war began, don't get rations for days, the men being much, much worse off. But the officers' mess at the division is always like a hotel restaurant.[60]

Not only is the disproportion in accessing dividends exercised more or less publicly here, but the legitimacy of the divisional authorities is undermined both by their sheer distance from the danger zone (which the 'old staff officers' dutifully share with the men) and by their unwillingness to share in hard work with them (which the staff officers at the HQ apparently do, and are therefore exempt from Kisch's scathing criticism). On the other hand, the same author projected an idealized notion of authority into his description of the way in which things were supposedly working in the Serbian army: 'Officers "on the other side" are simple and modest men, the complete opposite of the Austrian gentlemen who only talk to their equals and want to sleep in beds. With the Serbs, officers spend nights with their men in cowsheds'.[61] In the same vein, another author happily (and inaccurately) reports that the German army issues 'the same rations to the men and to the officers'.[62] In fact, the reality behind these claims is inconsequential, as it tells us about the ideal that the men were searching for, projecting it onto the image of 'the other', while missing it deeply in the everyday reality of the Austro-Hungarian army.

When soldiers expected their commanders to share hardships with them, they primarily expected them not to shun the dangers of the frontline. Kisch's diary includes his contemplation of 'an interesting type of war criminal … the regular officer who falls sick every time when there is a battle to be fought, the one who reports to hospital the moment an air of danger surrounds the troops in the trenches, the one who awaits the result of battle safely at the rear'. In Kisch's eyes, 'war only serves these aristocratic shirkers as a lift to a better life, attention and constant care'[63] – in other words, status and the dividends of hegemonic masculinity that are unattainable to the rank-and-file men, even though they were constantly proving their manhood through stoic bravery in the trenches (or at least felt as if they were doing so). As a result, the soldiers had difficulties accepting the officers in question as authority figures because they barely respected them as men. They also felt offended by the injustice they perceived in the way in which wartime reality warped the gender order; it was they who had proven their masculinity in full, with little to no reflection on their standing in the military hierarchy. Whatever hopes they had were buried in the institutional structure of the army, and only a bitter aftertaste remained regarding many of the men given power, such as '*Hauptmann* Totzauer, who shot himself the moment we reached the front lines. Coward. All he could do was slap men around'.[64] The gendered notion of bravery or cowardice is discernible in the fact that many men depict unpopular cowardly officers in feminine terms: 'In the afternoon, a pale officer from another company showed up', recalled Jaroslav Křenek. 'White in the face, he was shaking, and he had obviously sprinkled his own tunic with dirt. Now he reported being buried by a shell, suffering from shock. He was such a wretched, hysterical creature, he was hardly worth a spit on the ground'.[65] '*Herr Hauptmann* told us we were "old women", not soldiers', wrote an artilleryman of k.u.k. Field Artillery Regiment 24 in his diary, 'but when the firing started, he was the first one to run'.[66] Officers who were 'wretched hysterics' and 'old women' themselves were obviously problematic authority figures in an environment that based its own official discourse, with medals, awards and citations, on the supposedly manly attribute of physical bravery. Cowardice destroyed the image of masculinity, and with it all respect for the man's power.

Of course, most of the officers were well aware of this discourse, as they had existed within its realm along with their men. They knew that the easiest way to make men brave in combat is to lead by example. And the higher casualty rate of regular officers in comparison with the other ranks tells us that most of them behaved accordingly, and paid the price, for trying to uphold their authority by following the expected behavioural pattern. There are plenty of examples of these men in soldiers' writings, including those of otherwise highly critical subordinates: 'At that moment, *Hauptmann* Práš charged the wops with his company, actually chasing them all back … They were so afraid of Práš, who was running around like a devil, a revolver in one hand, a sword in the other, shouting at his boys to hold steady'.[67] The image of the ultimate brave father figure, victoriously leading his 'boys', has rarely been better illustrated. As another soldier wrote, 'the intensity of the barrage grew exponentially and the shells were playing havoc in our midst. Our brigade commander, *Generalmajor* Daniel, stood dauntlessly on his spot, smoking cigarettes and eating biscuits'.[68] Josef Slezák has described the above-mentioned leadership by example in a few terse but effective words in his diary: 'Nobody wanted to go forward. The officers had to go first'.[69] Even when the army, on the verge of collapse, was retreating from the Piave to Vittorio Veneto in late October 1918, the principle was still effective: 'And so we went, in the mud, along the line of cars … But what could I do, when even *Leutnant* Kubíček and *Herr Doktor* Kocmut were going on foot? Only march on and let no one see I'd had more than enough'.[70]

The officers' bravery in the face of danger motivated the men to obey their orders, but did not necessarily equal taking chances in search of military glory. Overt eagerness in combat was actually counterproductive, as the men were quick to recognize those who were brave and those who were outright foolish and therefore dangerous to themselves and their units: 'The best officers did not look for adventure and were not trying to get themselves medals, but did their duty and fulfilled even the most dangerous tasks without any complaints'.[71] Military skill, which – from the point of view of the rank and file – roughly translated as the ability to maintain combat-effectiveness while keeping casualties (and the level of action in general) to a minimum, played an important role in the soldiers' assessment of their 'fathers'. Put simply, they were much more open to respecting and obeying those men with whom they felt safe than those whom they suspected of not 'caring' about them, exposing them to the risk of violent death through sheer incompetence.[72]

While soldiers' personal accounts often mention this theme only in a fleeting manner that is not easy to discern, it was obviously important in their assessment of the military authorities, as we can see in the fact that many of them easily accepted the postwar image of general incompetence of the Austro-Hungarian military, both in the individual memoirs and in collections such as Žipek's *Domov za války*. Similarly, in some accounts, men are willing to accept any authority based solely on the perceived ability to ensure their survival in critical situations, regardless of the person's position in the military hierarchy: 'Men, under heavy fire, are running around scared like animals, searching for safety from death. The captain and the other officers have disappeared. No one needs them as our defensive effort is being masterfully directed by the tall *Feldwebel* Bidlo ... In a calm frame of mind, he is quietly scanning the horizon. His orders are dutifully performed, as the men have full confidence in him'.[73] When the last vestiges of confidence crumbled, morale fell along with it, as soldiers lost confidence in the military hierarchy itself: 'The men of the 91st were more angry than usual when disaster struck and casualties happened, telling everyone about the incompetence of their *Major*, adding many bizarre stories of his stupidity as well. It was the same gentleman ... whom I have blamed here for the previous disaster [on the Drina River, 8 September 1914]'.[74]

When, in his diary, František Prudil summarizes the events of a Russian offensive that landed himself and many other soldiers in captivity, he mentions 'a company commander, *Oberleutnant* Šátral', who shot himself when he saw his unit being overwhelmed: 'A young, handsome man, keen on all things soldierly, first in every charge. Even though a German, he was a great leader. What a shame'.[75] Not only does Prudil place military qualities and courage above nationality in terms of importance here – which only proves the complicated dynamic mentioned below – but he also thinks it necessary, in the difficult moment of becoming a POW, to commit to writing information about the 'handsomeness' of the man. In fact, he is far from the only one obsessed with the one particularly gendered aspect of military authority – the male body as a culturally and socially construed physical projection of masculinity. This literal 'embodiment' of manliness was indeed a key to military authority, as it was generally understood to be its archetype, with its form embedded in phrases like 'military bearing' and 'manly shape', and its interesting influence over the way in which the men viewed their superiors.

Simply put, there is a general rule that the better the commander, the more he is described as close to the idealized notion of male physical form. Beauty of the body is merged with the beauty of the perfect uniform, completing the image of a perfect officer and a man, as in the case Poláček's *Major* Klofanda, whose 'black moustache and slender legs in polished high boots' are part of the image his men admire in him – quite nonsensically, regarding the context of the comment. In the same vein, Jaroslav Křenek describes a 'good, reasonable commander' of the regimental depot of his k.u.k. Infantry 42 in a very specific way: 'Dark as resin, with piercing eyes and a chiselled jaw, sitting on black horse'. A popular executive officer of a *Marschbattalion* received the same treatment: 'A tall, muscular guy, a true *Grenzjäger*, red-faced, dressed in a perfect grass-green uniform'.[76] Perhaps the best example of this tendency to equate the ideal of authority with the ideal of the male body, and vice versa, is the memoir of *Oberleutnant* Lirš, ex-k.u.k. Infantry Regiment 28. An officer-school commander was, for him, 'a tough and handsome man ... slender, lively and elegant ... A beautifully sculpted little nose, a pointy jaw ... A true soldier: tough, no-nonsense, stern', while another perfect officer he met had a 'tanned, olive complexion, a true exemplar of physical maleness'.[77] Similarly, the equation of body, character and the respect one commanded often made its way into descriptions of those authorities who were lacking in popularity and, apparently, also in abilities. Examples are provided in the self-confessed anti-Austrian collection edited by Alois Žipek, where emasculating rhetoric often accompanies the image of a hated officer: 'If you mention *Major* Rudolf Fleischer in front any guy who has ever served in the 30th Infantry, they will all vividly remember the hundreds of slappings he distributed during his tenure ... However, Mother Nature was more of a stepmother to him, as it was very difficult to tell if *Herr Major* was a man or a woman'.[78] There are actually a number of memoirs in which an unpopular officer is, at the same time, subjected to a degree of feminizing imagery: 'A person of small stature, bulging eyes, white gloves tied to the bayonet, cleanly shaven'.[79]

All of the above-mentioned characteristics played an important role in Czech soldiers' attitudes to the military authorities and, subsequently, to their service in general. Many of these characteristics tended to be gendered to a certain extent, as well as closely connected to the material conditions of service, while nationality played a mostly supporting role. As one particular image of an ideal commander put it, this 'great guy', also a Czech, first and foremost spared his men 'useless tasks', 'did not make them go where he did not have to', called them 'comrades' and paid for 'a hundred litres of beer' out of his own pocket after a successful storming of Russian positions in January 1916. Only the perfect male body image is missing here. As the author of this image, František Chmela, wrote: 'It was a pleasure to make war with him ... We would all die for our *Hauptmann*'.[80] In addition, it does not seem that these officers were an inherently rare breed – they seem to be quite ubiquitous, at least in the wartime accounts, where the trope of a 'good commander' is more or less on a par with that of the 'arrogant tyrant' who diminished the men's feelings of self-worth and manliness. It seems that it was these 'fatherly' officers who enabled soldiers to surmount the oppressive limits of wartime reality, keeping at least their masculinity intact, as they received respect in exchange for their service. And it was the feeling of being respected as men that made them forget the loss of power and control their masculinity sustained in the process.

The Usual Suspects

Respect is, besides *control* and *power*, the key element of masculinity in a patriarchal society, a reflection of the social capital connected to the patriarchal dividend. As a result, respect for the men (and for their basic identity as *men*) was something the authorities could trade for obedience; on the other hand, disrespecting the men ('unmanning' them) undermined their sense of masculinity, damaging their motivation and morale. When a company of k.u.k. Infantry Regiment 98 received orders to retreat in the summer battles in Galicia in 1915, it ran into reinforcements from another regiment, commanded by an *Oberleutnant*:

> [He] shouts at us, calls us traitors and cowards. Then he pulls a revolver and orders his companies to advance against us with bayonets. When it almost comes to the worst, our colonel shows up, puts his revolver to the *Oberleutnant*'s back, and orders him and his companies to charge against the Russians, shouting angrily after them: 'I'll show you traitors and cowards, goddamit!'[81]

The author's positive reaction to the actions of the colonel is a great example of the fact that although the interwar culture of war remembrance in Czechoslovakia (including many memoirs) would like us to think otherwise, Czech soldiers did not actually prefer to be seen as traitors and cowards, and we may well suspect that this had a lot to do with their feeling of being robbed of respect, as well as their core manliness. However, during the war, the Austro-Hungarian state and its institutions operated as if it was trying to do just that.

Rooted deeply in the premodern era and the ethos of dynastic loyalty, the Austrian and later Austro-Hungarian army always insisted on its supranational character. As *Reichskriegsminister* Edmund von Krieghammer declared in the *Reichsrat* in 1897, defending the troops against German nationalists after the army quelled a nationalist riot in Graz, 'I can assure you … In the army every nationality is equal and equally respected'.[82] Even Conrad von Hötzendorf, the volatile Chief of the General Staff from 1906 until 1917, agreed, writing in 1907 that 'within the army all nations enjoy equal rights'.[83] However, using Conrad as a prime example, it can be argued that the practice of the Army Command was in profound conflict with this depiction, even before the war. In Gunther Rothenberg's analysis, Conrad 'could never understand the power of nationalism and he regarded all opposition … as inspired by the evil machinations of subversive elements'. Disagreeing with many observers in 1913, he wrote to

Helmuth von Moltke: 'We hardly can count on the enthusiastic support of our Slavs'.[84] Along with its longtime Chief of Staff, the Austro-Hungarian army always remained suspicious of certain 'subversive' elements – particularly socialists, Magyars, Czechs, Serbs, Italians and Ruthenes – and carried this suspicion well into the war. The success of the mobilization in July 1914 may have surprised many, but when the initial campaigns hit trouble in early September 1914, many an Austrian officer's mind quickly turned to these 'usual suspects' in search of scapegoats, deservedly or not.[85] Rapid expansion as well as debilitating casualties of the prewar officer corps, steeped in the ideology of supranationalism, led to a hasty incorporation of thousands of reserve officers from a middle-class background – a breeding ground of nationalism,[86] which only exacerbated the entire issue and turned it into a severe problem of morale even before the infamous and much-publicized cases of alleged 'mass desertion' of Czech-dominated units in the spring of 1915. Not only could many of the newly appointed commanders hardly talk to their men, as they had no time – or even intention – to learn their language in an army where more than half of the 330 prewar regiments were officially bilingual or multilingual, thus exacerbating the issue of bizarre communications problems that had plagued the army for years.[87] They had also often suspected their men of disloyalty before they had even met them, as in Bohemia and Moravia, German-speaking middle classes were overrepresented in the reserve officer corps.[88]

The surrender of k.u.k. Infantry Regiment 28 from Prague, in which 98% of soldiers were Czech-speaking, during a Russian offensive in the Carpathians in April of that year became a final turning point on this issue both for the military authorities, for the Austrian-German nationalist politicians and consequently also for the general public. Although the roots of the defeat were much more complicated and consisted in a combination of combat exhaustion, inexperienced replacements, miserable conditions and mistakes by superior commanders that led the unit into an encirclement, the authorities, engaging in the blame game, quickly jumped on the 'treasonous Czechs' bandwagon, which led to an unprecedented and very public punishment of the entire regiment – it was disbanded.[89] While a subsequent investigation actually exonerated the unit from any blame, with the result that it was quietly restored in 1917, these conclusions were never made public, and Czech-speaking soldiers were forever stuck with the public image of 'treasonous cowards'.[90] Meanwhile, the Austro-Hungarian military authorities became, in the words of Richard Lein, 'increasingly hostile and paranoid' in their relationship with their third-largest manpower contingent.[91] Following further failures of Czech-dominated units, the public image of Czechs as 'unreliable' (along with the Serbs, Italians and Ruthenes, i.e. much smaller groups) became a staple trope, particularly in the German and Hungarian press. As Mark Cornwall noted, 'books about the Czechs' treason' were on display in Prague bookshops by 1917.[92] The fact that similar failures often befell units made up of other nationalities, including Germans and Magyars, did not register, as it did not fit the discourse that enabled the shifting of the blame for lack of military success onto the Czechs.

As far as we know, Czech soldiers were very well aware of this discourse being floated around, as they were all more or less involuntarily defined by it – and not in a positive way. As a one-year volunteer of the k.k. Landwehr Infantry Regiment 13 noted: 'Our command took care to make life for all Czech people in uniform as miserable as possible, all the time'. As a result, it only helped them to identify as Czech even more strongly, as they were singled out by the discourse as such: 'It was just because of our nationality. They were saying that a lot of men were deserting to the Russians'.[93] Karel Vaněk had experienced this stereotyping firsthand when talking to his commander in January 1915: 'He told me I was a true Czech soldier: girls, beer, playing cards, without a care for the service. It is supposed to be the same on the battlefield too – the Czechs just make jokes and would not fight for all the gold in the world'.[94] Even those who gave little thought to their national identity beforehand were now repeatedly told where to put themselves on the fabric of the monarchy. It seems that many of Czech soldiers were actually offended by this image: 'The Corps commander … made a long, hateful speech on the disappointing combat record of the 98th Regiment … His speech was full of bile and hatred for everything Czech. He wanted to degrade and humiliate us. You could see the helpless, unbound anger in everyone's eyes'.[95]

The experience of public humiliation is actually a staple of Czech soldiers' war accounts. Immediately after the 28th Infantry Regiment was disbanded, František Šmída had a 'nasty recollection' of a classmate in the officer training school in Obilin, Croatia, who 'had introduced himself to me with a derisive greeting of "hands up", just to let me know his offensive opinion of the Czechs. He considered us cowards, who would throw their arms up in the air the moment they saw the enemy'.[96] It is clear from Šmída's account that he regarded such an opinion as offensive to his military honour. Indeed, the accusation of cowardice struck deep into the very masculine identity of the men, as bravery under fire was an integral part of the military masculinity ideal, and many of them were repulsed by the notion of being called cowards: '"Just look at those fucking Magyar bitches up there"', soldiers of Ferdinand Lirš's battalion shouted when marching through Szeged in late April, 1915. 'We were just passing a military hospital. I looked in the direction mentioned and saw nurses … mockingly raising their arms and laughing at us openly'.[97] Being labelled cowards by *women* clearly hit the men in a particularly sensitive spot, as reflected by the language of the reaction. No wonder, as this was a situation in which women were calling their masculinity into doubt. The fact that this accusation had originated with the military authorities merely added insult to injury, creating a perfect storm of officially degraded manliness. In the words of the same author, they had expected to 'be able to project power and be respected', i.e. to attain the status of full men through their wartime service.⁹⁸ And now Czechs were apparently excluded from this process en masse by means of collective guilt and stereotyping, losing all the respect they had among the general public in many regions of the empire.

Not surprisingly, the general feeling of a decidedly undeserved and apparently institutionalized injustice generated a growing resentment among Czech servicemen towards those authorities whom they considered responsible for the situation, while the morale of the men suffered as well. Difficulties also arose when cooperation with other national groups in the army was involved: 'Even though I'm hungry as hell, I don't want anything from them because of their contempt for the Czechs', wrote the combat medic Augustin Mudrák in his diary after his company, destroyed as a unit during the Brusilov Offensive in August 1916, had been merged with a Hungarian battalion.⁹⁹ Two years later, when army paranoia fed by the activities of the Czechoslovak exiles reached its peak, Alois Dolejší noted in his diary in a resigned tone: 'We cannot speak a word in Czech, otherwise they'll point at us and put their hands up in the air … It's just tiresome, and there's no hope of it getting any better except for death'.¹⁰⁰ The general atmosphere of suspicion also made the men paranoid, and one of the oft-repeated themes in Czech soldiers' writings later in the war and afterwards became a nationalized interpretation of military institutions and their actions, including operational and tactical decisions. One of the typical claims reads:

> Hungarian regiments are being spared … [while] our regiment is being killed out here. The men from the 36ᵗʰ Regiment said the situation was the same there … The neighbouring 19ᵗʰ Hungarian Brigade did not withstand the assault and fled … The retreat of the Magyars was kept secret from us, and we did not get any reinforcements, which was suspicious. The army command obviously needed another excuse to persecute a hated Bohemian regiment.¹⁰¹

Army policy towards the Czechs, perhaps overtly harsh, had created a vicious circle of suspicion on all sides, and opened up a path towards a thoroughly 'nationalized' interpretation of the Czech war experience.

However, the feeling of disrespect many Czech soldiers mentioned when discussing the military authorities did not necessarily originate only from the army's 'paranoia' towards them. Another issue, similarly gendered, is easily identifiable in the way in which soldiers and the army, respectively, understood the disciplinary measures the authorities wielded in order to keep troops in line. The particular problem here was the different ideas concerning what measures were appropriate for disciplining modern, *civilized* men. As already mentioned in Chapter 2, the close connection between a sense of civility and culture on the one hand and manliness on the other was an important element of modern masculine identity. War, perceived often as an anti-cultural phenomenon, threatened to deprive men of their civilized exterior, turning them into animals, nonmen. And

Figure 4.3 A drawing by Karel Rélink of k.u.k. Infantry Regiment 28, entitled 'A Field Punishment for a Lost Can', vividly capturing the oft-abused practice of 'binding' (Karel Rélink, *Album obrazů ze světové války: Utrpení českého vojáka v poli*, Brno, 1922).

it was a similar logic that threatened to kick in regarding traditional methods of military discipline. In the Czech soldiers' accounts in particular, there are not many efforts to deny the army the general authority to enforce discipline – but many object to the methods, as their idea of disciplining modern men with respect, and thus in a manner that kept their manliness intact, clearly differed from everyday army practice.

The Austro-Hungarian army, like most other armies in the early twentieth century, still held steadfastly to the time-honoured tradition of corporal punishment when it came to disciplining men.[102] It is true that the infamous practice of 'running the gauntlet' was abolished in 1855, as were other major forms of physical punishment during the army reform of 1868 that turned the army into a modern reserve force based on (theoretically) general conscription. On the other hand, even after 1868, beatings remained (unofficially) an everyday part of military life, and further punishments were added that targeted not just the soldier's body but also his mind, from suspended leave to *Arrest*, i.e. short-time imprisonment.[103] The only form of corporal punishment officially preserved in the army regulations was 'binding' (*das Anbinden*) and *Spangen* (*das Schliessen in Spangen*). In the former, the soldier's ankles were tied, along with his hands behind his back, and he was subsequently bound to a post or a tree by the wrists and pulled up so that only his toes touched the ground. The army regulations of 1902 stipulated a maximum of two hours for such a punishment. In the latter, the man's right hand was tied to his left ankle for a maximum of six hours.

When the war started in 1914 and the army felt the sudden need to discipline large numbers of reservists in the hands of often inexperienced officers, these punishments became a common occurrence and were used to punish even the slightest offences against the military code. Judging from the soldiers' accounts, the most common pretext for binding a man was that he ate his 'iron ration' can of meat without authorization. Moreover, these officers, not all of whom wielded natural authority with the men, sometimes 'finetuned' these punishments into particularly cruel forms (by lengthening them, for example) or even used corporal punishments that were prohibited by the regulations, like public beatings. After Charles I became emperor, he went on to abolish all forms of corporal punishment in a bid to liberalize the service in June 1917. The Army High Command protested vehemently, pointing to a spike in desertions, and it eventually succeeded in revoking the abolition in the spring of 1918.[104]

In reality, the practice outlined above depended heavily upon the individual commander or even the type of unit in which a soldier served. František Chmela, after being transferred from an artillery battalion to k.u.k. Infantry Regiment 91, complained: 'Everything was really by-the-book here, it was a different type of soldiering, it was infantry. Only then did I come to realize how easy it had been being a cannoneer'.[105] Chmela's company commander with the 91st Regiment was a good example of cruel resourcefulness when it came to the abolition of all corporal punishment in 1917 – he invented a small barbed wire cage, where offenders were forced to stay for hours at a time.[106] Many Czech soldiers found such treatment appalling and tended to lose any respect for the authorities because of it: 'An order was announced in the afternoon that four of the comrades were to be punished by *Oberleutnant* Procházka' – bound for two hours for reporting late to the unit. 'Because of this cruel punishment, *Herr Oberleutnant* lost any remaining love the company had for him'.[107] It seems that with at least some of the formations of the Austro-Hungarian army, moments when 'officers yell and beat men with sticks', were rather common, and the Czech soldiers found it invariably disgusting and disrespectful: 'The way he treated his men, the obscenities ... the cruelty of the way he beat and kicked them, the callousness with which he woke up his batman ... it all made me almost blind with rage'.[108] It seems that in the world of the Austro-Hungarian army during the First World War, negative and positive ways of sustaining motivation clashed to an extent where the resulting conflict potentially damaged the soldiers' morale. [109]

As Christa Hämmerle mentions in her study of the Austro-Hungarian military's ideological background, the army culture of punishment had a specific character. She writes that the idea of the army as a 'school of manliness' was tightly connected to institutionalized 'cultural imperialism', which led the army authorities to repeatedly re-emphasize the way in which 'shabby boys', particularly those from the eastern and southeastern parts of the Empire, 'urgently required strict discipline and education in order to become more civilized'.[110] Although this prejudice was mostly targeted at the often illiterate peasant soldiers from Galicia, Bukovina or the Balkans (mixing class sensibilities with a sense of ethnic superiority common to Austrian elites), it is clear that many officers during the war did not differentiate between ethnic backgrounds, in agreement with *Oberleutnant* Král from Poláček's novel, whose motto was that 'any stupid brute should tremble in the face of an officer's uniform'. Indeed, many a man from a peasant background, used to a patriarchal social structure backed by violence, would be content with such ways, at least to a point. The already mentioned description by a village boy from eastern Bohemia summed up this attitude all too well: 'It is all very strict here … I must learn a lot, do things well, and everyone must obey'.[111] However, even the author of this summary was probably not a big supporter of overt corporal punishment or outright abuse. In fact, looking at the sources, it is clear that most Czech soldiers had a different idea of military discipline from the army they served. Ideally, they expected less beating, vulgar yelling and binding, instead preferring 'a quiet mutual understanding of the precise limits of what needs to be done in order to fulfil one's duty'.[112] Reality not only sometimes made the men angry to the point of rage; they first and foremost thought it generally 'unnecessary, stupid and above all humiliating'.[113] A connection with respect as a part of experiencing one's masculinity is clear to be seen here – Czech soldiers sensed that the army disciplinary methods, often staged as public performances, were further degrading their already besieged manliness. In some recorded cases, the gendered, performative aspect of the punishment is obvious, such as when in October 1917 an entire company was forced to witness 'a disgusting retribution' upon three men, who received twenty-five lashes with a stick on their naked buttocks for eating their 'iron rations': 'An old soldier … a father of three … yelled and fainted. Partly because of the pain, but mostly, for sure, from the anger of such a public humiliation in front of so many teenage boys'.[114] Hardly ever was a symbolic degradation of masculinity performed more effectively than in this particular case.

The Slavic Athenians

The everyday practice of corporal punishment, reproduced under the ideological umbrella of the army's 'cultural imperialism' bent on 'educating' men by all means, did not just 'unman' the men. It seems that Czech soldiers had a particular knack of also interpreting it as a cultural humiliation, since if we have said that the Austro-Hungarian authorities held up 'cultural imperialism' as a guiding idea of their approach to the men, most Czech soldiers held beliefs that were surprisingly similar. Their sense of cultural superiority and subsequent entitlement, i.e. a little 'cultural imperialism' of their own, is obvious in almost every written account of the war. Czechs, as long as they identify as such, invariably thought of themselves as positioned at the very top of the 'pyramid of civilization' among the monarchy's nations, along with the Austrian Germans, and saw the other nationalities sharing the Imperial and Royal uniform with them as culturally inferior. Of course, this attitude was nothing new and was particularly widespread among Czech nationalist intellectuals before the war, who often regarded themselves as self-styled missionaries of civilization among the 'lesser' Slavic peoples. When the Czechs organized the 1912 Slet of the Sokols in Prague, they stylized the capital of Bohemia as a 'Slavic Athens', repeatedly pointing to their leading role in teaching civilization to their backward Slavic brethren and celebrating 'our success and progress in the healthy education and ennoblement of the Slavic people ... This dear Slavic people, whom we wish to lead out of oppression and humiliation, and into the light of learning and freedom'.[115] The sense of cultural superiority was an integral part of Czech national self-definition.

In the wartime diary of Alois Dolejší, there is an almost perfect summary of national stereotypes held by Czech soldiers in general, including a rare reflection of one's own superiority mirrored in the superior, seemingly unconcerned position of the narrator's group – the Czechs themselves: 'There is the German, who is always arguing about some victories. Then there is the Czech, sitting somewhere on his luggage, chatting with one of his own, passing judgment on all that wonderful Babel'. The Germans are at the top right next to the Czechs, the only thing dividing them being their attitude towards the war effort – for the former, it is a subject of emotional investment; for the latter, an object of ironic observation. Following down the order, then, there is a hierarchy of parodic stereotypes of the other, culturally 'inferior' nations of the monarchy:

> The Magyar straddles the sack which serves as his granary, eats bacon dusted in paprika so thick it makes one's hair stand on end, and swallows so loud one gets goosebumps. To make sure it works, he washes it all down with some good shots of rye. But alas, then the army merchant appears on the scene, i.e. the Bosnian, walking from person to person and buying or exchanging whatever could be bought or exchanged for a *kruh* [bread] ... Back in the corner an old Pole sits in prayer, making enormous crosses in the air while on the lookout for things to steal. Then there are three Italians from Trieste, playing cards and being loud as fifty Czechs would be in the process. There is also a guy from Dalmatia, half-naked and hunting for lice, who are bound to be plentiful on him as all the soldiers sitting around him are long gone ... Then there is a Slovene standing by the stove, as they always have to cook something, even if it is just plain water ... And there is a bunch of Slovaks from around Prešov, chasing skirts all the time ... Further back, there are two Romanians talking, one of them smoking a chibouk, the other one chewing tobacco. Then there are the two Ruthenians, sitting

in Turkish style, carving something out of wood ... And finally two Tyrolians, singing and yodelling in the wholly self-absorbed language of theirs.[116]

The sense of cultural superiority is also apparent in the way in which Czech soldiers treat the local populations from the distant frontiers of the monarchy in their writings. While the villages of Galicia and Bukovina are repeatedly treated to such adjectives as 'filthy' and 'smelly', a soldier comments happily on being able 'to breathe fully' in a 'clean' village populated with German colonists somewhere in the Carpathians.[117] In the same spirit, the experience of being transferred to a Polish-dominated regiment to serve with the Poles, Ruthenes and Romanians only creates resentment at being forced to serve with 'such riffraff' that, according to another soldier, 'looks just primitive ... I don't know why'.[118] The Poles in particular are often subjected to the cultural imperialism of the Czechs, being repeatedly described as 'simple people' with little to show in the ways of civilized existence. As one infantryman put it, 'they are Poles, and therefore they are lousy as hell'.[119]

Another case that further proves our thesis about the cultural imperialism of the Czech is the image of Bosnians in Czech soldiers' writings. Josef Váchal did not regard them so much as proof of his superiority as he did project the image of the 'noble savage' onto them: 'Those sons of nature deeply revered anyone who had mastered the mystery of "letters" in a manner that is usually reserved for the most sacred deities'.[120] The Bosnians were often depicted in a manner similar to the concept of 'warrior races' present in West European imperialism.[121] 'Horror stories are circulating about the capture of Monte Meletta', František Skála noted in his diary. 'The Italians were not willing to retreat, so they have sent the Bosnians in. Gave them rum first, so they got drunk, put their rifles aside along with all the equipment, and charged forward armed only with their daggers. Then, in those shallow trenches, they stabbed, cut throats, strangled, yes, even bit their victims to kill'.[122] Jaroslav Vítek held a similar image of the Bosnian regiments: 'They run forward like lions unleashed during bayonet charges, and the wops are terrified of even the idea of facing them and usually run away. So whenever we need to break through, they send the Bosnians in and they *will* break through, for sure'.[123] In Czech soldiers' writings, 'sending the Bosnians in' is an oft-repeated phrase, usually mixed with horror and awe at describing something that does not fit even into the brutalized world of 'civilized' warfare.

While the image of Bosnians bordered on admiration for the 'primitive other', it was the Magyars who bore the brunt of the Czechs' cultural resentment. For many of them, including František Bouška, they were 'not even human', just 'primitives', 'Mongol animals', 'our European Orientals'.[124] For František Skála, 'life with the *honvéd* regiments was completely different. They always shout and yell, they shoot at everything and then always wonder what happened'. In his opinion, the harsh army discipline was not excessive when it came to dealing with the Magyars: 'There is a field gendarme stationed with every platoon, which is something that has long been abolished in our units, as it is not needed'.[125] Many Czech soldiers repeatedly expressed outright hatred towards everything Hungarian, starting with the deeply felt humiliation of being forced to serve in 'backward', 'barbaric' Hungary, while their counterparts from the Hungarian regiments enjoyed the beauty of 'civilized' Bohemia. The very fact that the army had actually gone through with its prewar plan to transfer the depots of some supposedly 'unreliable' units to other parts of the monarchy (including a number of regiments from Bohemia, whose 'cadres' swapped positions with several Hungarian regiments) in late 1914 and early 1915, only added insult to the injury of the perceived administrative injustice Czech soldiers felt they suffered at the hands of the army. Not only were they subjected to collective punishment and their loyalty openly questioned, but now, as a result, a further distance was put between them and their loved ones, while the hated 'barbarians' (i.e. the Magyars) were being transferred to their place at home. It was all the more hurtful as many Czech soldiers thought of their Hungarian comrades-in-arms in decidedly negative terms regarding their combat abilities. Invariably, Hungarians are portrayed by them as mediocre soldiers at best, with Hungarian units the ones usually blamed for causing retreats, losing positions the Czechs had previously fought bravely for or being forced to retake with heavy casualties later on.[126] The perceived cowardly nature of the frequently ironized 'knightly Magyar nation', referred to as such by at least two authors,[127] is a clear rallying cry to the sense of injustice and emasculation caused by the army policies towards Czechs, who felt there were others much less manly in the Austro-Hungarian military hierarchy.

Returning to the notion of cultural superiority felt by many Czech soldiers, it is easy to see how incompatible this was with the military's concept of discipline. The idea that they were the most civilized, cultured men in the army carried along with it – in the minds of the soldiers at least – the right to be disciplined accordingly, and corporal punishment of all sorts hardly fitted the picture. Not only did the authorities not respect their expectations, adhering to their traditional notion of keeping the 'stupid brutes' at bay, but in addition, led on by their paranoia of the 'treacherous Czechs', they focused their disciplinary measures, both formal and informal, on Czech soldiers in particular. 'A soldier's life in Olomouc (Olmütz) compared to Bochnia was like heaven and hell', remembered a Czech infantryman after being transferred to a Polish regiment. 'In Olomouc, it wasn't so bad after all. In Bochnia, slapping, beating, kicking and other delights were always around the corner for you. And Czechs were always the rebels, they thought … to be kept on a tight leash'.[128] 'Slapping, beating, kicking' were precisely the disciplinary methods the Czechs resented, as they often thought that these punishments were good only for 'uncivilized' ethnic groups, but not for themselves. 'One lieutenant constantly kicks them in anger, pokes them with his stick, hurls the worst and most vulgar epithets at them', Jaroslav Vítek remembered a Polish regiment marching through Galicia. 'Those people are poor and miserable, degraded and enslaved to such an extent that they would be willing to be slaughtered like a calf right on the spot. Czechs and Germans would never accept such treatment. This is only possible with the Poles'.[129] As another soldier reflected, 'this is not the way to train people who are supposed to shed blood for someone', *people* here being synonymous with civilized people, Czechs (or Germans) refusing to be 'degraded and enslaved'.[130]

František Šmída, who served in two Croatian regiments during the war, included a short reflection at the end of his diary, wondering 'if a Czech soldier – a thinking philosopher ... could ever understand such a sense of discipline' as shown by the 7th Bosnian-Herzegovinian Infantry Regiment, 'obeying orders and obediently marching back to the position, without rest and hungry' in the last days of October 1918.[131] A Czech soldier was a 'thinking' person, i.e. he was too civilized according to Šmída. Czech soldiers did not necessarily disagree with the notion of 'stupid brutes', even though they were generally disgusted by the methods it often brought upon the others. What they hated most, however, was the fact that they too were seen as such, viewing the disciplinary measures as a projection of this unwarranted attitude, and correspondingly regarding the authorities as guilty of cultural degradation.

Perhaps the best summary of how Czech soldiers viewed themselves and what they expected from the military authorities as a consequence comes from Jaroslav Šindýlek and his short essay in the veterans' magazine *Kamarádství* published in 1937:

> The Czech soldier had to be understood by his officer. He could not be harmed and wronged all the time, because he could think for himself and had a certain pride and faith in his own judgment ... During the war, when the officers and the general command only followed orders from Vienna, no one could blame the Czech soldier that he had no enthusiasm for the fatherland and the House of Habsburg ... [The authorities] did not even try to improve things in this regard, only punished more, indulged in slander, and constantly underestimated us.[132]

The last sentence is particularly poignant in terms of our analysis – the Czech soldiers gradually lost all respect for the authorities because they thought they were not shown any respect themselves. They were punished in a way unfit for men of their cultural refinement, while they were publicly labelled as cowards even though they fought (or so they thought) better than most.

What resulted was a deep ideological conflict between the 'children' and the 'fathers' in the Austro-Hungarian military, at least as far as Czech soldiers were concerned. Couched in the terms of John Lynn's theory, the army authorities tended to rely upon traditional, coercive forms of compliance, while the men who we have discussed here mostly expected (or even demanded in their writings) a predominantly normative approach based on a respect for their active consent. The clash between these two approaches led the army and its Czech subordinates onto a gradually divergent path of mutual misunderstanding.[133] Recalling Karel Poláček, we may well agree that the paranoia and apparent contempt the authorities often expressed towards the Czechs had indeed led to a burning sense of 'dignity and civil rights' to be awakened. As a result, many soldiers felt not only war-weariness, but also a gradual decline in consent and estrangement from any sense of loyalty they may well have held at the beginning of the war, with their sustaining motivation and morale suffering accordingly. The issue of the conflict was not the war and its meaning; it generally focused on the men and their position within the structures engaged in the war, as well as the terms of their 'social contract' that had led them to give up the dividends of their masculinity (power, control, freedom of action). In fact, it seems that the conviction that they deserved more respect and better treatment than most was firmly rooted in the Czech soldiers' feeling that they should have more control over themselves, because they were full, 'civilized' men, not slaves. As a result, harsh discipline hit them straight at the heart of their masculinity.

Soldiers into Czechs

Influenced by the thesis of 'national indifference' as postulated by historians such as Pieter Judson and Tara Zahra early in the twenty-first century,[134] Rudolf Kučera once wrote that while it is open to debate as to whether the thesis fits well with our knowledge of general society in Bohemia or Austria, the Austro-Hungarian Common Army indeed represents a truly 'indifferent' social space with regard to nationality, a space that only gradually became contested by various nationalities. Indeed, he claims that at the beginning of the war, the key dividing line defining group loyalties in the army was not nationality, but class, 'a demarcation line of material want, dividing the officers who are provided for on the one hand and the men who are materially deprived on the other'. Only after the first campaigns and an ever-deepening rift in supply conditions, he says, did the Czech men in uniform start to see themselves as 'Czechs' first and foremost. As a result, a 'universal paradigm' was formed that replaced the class-based dichotomy of officers/men with a nationalized worldview, interpreting everything (including material conditions) in national terms.[135]

While the national 'indifference' to the military social space in Austria-Hungary is open to debate, maybe not in theory but certainly in practice, we may well agree with Kučera's thesis of gradual shift towards full, politicized national self-identification caused by the war. Indeed, while supply conditions indeed played an important role, as we will see in Chapter 5, war exhaustion described in Chapter 2, or sense of personal self-worth and institutional pressures described here were equally important. It may be argued that the Austro-Hungarian army actually succeeded, at least initially, in replacing the men's original group loyalties with those of its own, reflecting the peculiarities of the military hierarchy. This process may also be explained through shifts in the gender order and the process of militarizing hegemonic masculinity during the first weeks of the war.[136] Subsequently, the increasingly disastrous supply situation at home and at the front played a key role in destroying soldiers' morale, and interpreting these hardships in national terms was an obvious route to take.[137] Nevertheless, for the soldiers to define themselves in national terms, they had to overcome their initial 'national indifference', whatever its original levels, and identify themselves as members of a national group. Put simply, for the Czechs to feel culturally superior and subsequently degraded, they first had to feel that they were *Czech*, and it seems it was the army that played an unfortunate self-defeating role in this process of 'nationalizing' itself.

The traditional view, actually supported by the Army High Command itself during the war, claims that 'the armed forces slowly became infected by nationalism' during the war because of their growing reliance on reserve officers, which brought 'a substantial degree of apathy towards the war effort'. However, the process was not one-sided.[138] The army increasingly began to view everything through the prism of nationalism, 'poisoning the patriotic atmosphere' of the early days of the war, while its lower-echelon command structure was rife as much with aggressive German nationalism as the rank and file supposedly was with its Slavic counterpart, with the resulting tensions projecting themselves onto the military hierarchy and command structure in various unfortunate ways.[139] In the words of Laurence Cole, Austria-Hungary lost 'the battle for hearts and minds' of its own population by implementing often unnecessary harsh measures, among other factors by 'distinguishing crudely between allegedly "loyal" and "disloyal" nationalities and ... [by] "Germanizing" policies', which 'placed the state in a major crisis of legitimacy' from late 1917 onwards.[140] Regarding the particular policy towards political dissent, another author has claimed it to be 'expensive and counterproductive ... helping to undermine social cohesion, traditional gender roles, and, ultimately, the legitimacy of the state itself ... particularly in Slav and Italian communities'.[141]

Literally the same may be true with regard to both the self-conscious and the potential Czechs in the military during the war – their loyalty was publicly questioned, with many a Czech soldier branded a 'Czech traitor' even before he had had the time to fully realize he was actually a member of a specific group defined as 'Czech soldiers'. They were often selected for collective disciplinary measures or outright punishments solely because of being identified as Czechs, and for the same reason their gender identity, based on a perception of their own worth, came under attack even more than it normally would have in the conditions of mass industrial war. This pressure pushed many Czech soldiers towards adopting the same optics, even though they may have had been far from this position at the beginning of the war. As a result, a dormant civic identity, when present (as in the case of middle-class, educated, often politically aware men), was awakened or, when originally missing, gradually came into being. The authorities, the war and ultimately the monarchy itself gradually lost any legitimacy they had, and the sense of identification with a group other than the army grew, while such groups were increasingly defined in linguistic or even national terms and their agency gradually divorced from the overall war effort. As a part of the same process, everything concerning the individual or the group then came to be viewed through a national prism – material situation, administrative and disciplinary measures, and operational decisions. Only coercion and the deep-seated sense of obedience kept most men fighting on until the very end.[142]

Of course, this national filter was used in dealing with the authorities even fairly early on in the war, although it was usually considered secondary to other qualities back then. As already mentioned, as early as 1915, František Skála includes 'pride in being Czech' in his picture of an ideal officer. A year later, the ex-Sokol František Šmída wrote that he valued 'anti-German feelings' in his brother officers first of all, with 'soldierly qualities, friendship, and character' only coming second.[143] However, also in 1915, František Prudil mentions the fact that the 'handsome officer' was a German, even though only as a side-note, as military and masculine qualities were more important to him in a man. In fact, many accounts follow the same logic – the authors feel obliged to mention the officer's nationality, even though they apparently do not care much about it. 'A very agreeable character he was, forty years of age, a reserve officer, therefore a bit more civil. A true German, but that I do not mind', Alois Dolejší wrote as late as September 1918.[144] With him, 'civility' still has the upper hand over nationality. František Skála would seem to agree when he reported on his experience on a training course for telephone operators in early 1915: 'An *Oberleutnant* from the 18th Infantry was the commander. A German, but nice enough. He spoke very quietly, but still could keep proper order and discipline'.[145]

Following Skála's phrasing, it therefore appears that 'German' usually equates with a character that is '*not* nice' enough. Here, in a fashion rather typical of many of the writings, there is no purpose for mentioning nationality other than for it to be *mentioned*. Similarly, language is often mentioned as a secondary qualifier at best, bearing little importance to the outcome of the story, as in Josef Slezák's poetic effort from July 1916: 'Horzinek was the name / visit us he indeed did / In Czech he spoke, and tame / at first our fears grew thin … But it was the only shtick / that good about him was / As we quickly learned / all of his crazy thoughts'.[146] Obviously, the officer's willingness to speak Czech was still of less importance than his moral and soldiery qualities when it came to judging him as authority; on the other hand, it was still important enough for the author to record it as a positive trait.

It seems that, especially early on in the war, more often than not, the perceived nationality of the authorities played only a supporting role that assisted the men in their initial orientation vis-à-vis a commander. The ultimate judgement of any authority was a much more complex issue and generally depended on the treatment soldiers received, as well as how much it corresponded with their perception of themselves as men in uniform. If the authorities respected soldiers as individuals as well as a group (when defined as 'Czechs'), fulfilling the ideal requirements of patriarchal authority through their approach to discipline, their military abilities, considerate exercise of power and privilege, as well as through their masculine appearance, their nationality was rarely an issue. If they failed in this regard, nationality tended to become one of the defining characteristics of 'otherness', as occurred in the case of the above-mentioned *Hauptmann* Horzinek, who quickly gained the nickname 'Polish dog' from his men.[147] Even soldiers' interwar writings, which were generally more prone to outright nationalist logic, frequently betray a prioritizing of attitude over nationality: 'It may well have been by pure chance, but of all the officers I came to know more closely during the war, the Germans were always the most tactful and considerate men, while Czechs tended to treat the men in harsh, arrogant, or somewhat boorish manner'.[148]

Apparently, it was indeed respect for one's 'dignity and civil rights' that ultimately took precedence. And it was this area in which the army ultimately failed to sustain the Czech soldiers' morale the most, and it was this area that injured their sense of manliness as they experienced it. While many of them subsequently adopted national optics, it was only a consequence. At the same time, the power dynamics of the hierarchy of masculinities shook the men's identity to the core, creating new instabilities and new paths for renegotiating one's position in the new, wartime structure of (masculine) military institutions, with all the consequences regarding the so-called patriarchal dividend (power, control, resources); the results regarding soldiers' motivation were deeply ambivalent. Sometimes it actually seems as if the army authorities worked hard towards making the situation even worse for Czech men in particular. They did not show them any of the respect they rightly or wrongly expected for their sacrifices, and quickly went on to treat them as cowards and traitors, diminishing their manliness even further, strengthening or even creating a national identity in the process. After all, as Josef Váchal wrote in his memoir, 'the Austrian soldier's woes resulted' from 'miserable logistics' and 'bad treatment'.[149]

Notes

Part of this chapter has been published before in Czech; see Jiří Hutečka, 'C. a k. armádní autority a morálka českých vojáků, 1914–1918', in *Léta do pole okovaná. 1915: noví nepřátelé, nové výzvy*, eds Jaroslav Láník and Tomáš Kykal (Prague, 2017), 278–92. Its fleshed-out form appears here courtesy of the editors.

1. Karel Poláček, *Podzemní město* (Prague, 1994 [1937]), 34.
2. Ibid., 50, 55, and 95.
3. Ibid., 47.
4. Ibid., 64.
5. Ibid., 60 and 62.
6. Marshall, *Men against Fire*, 44.
7. Shils and Janowitz, 'Cohesion and Disintegration in the Wehrmacht in World War II', 196; see also Stouffer et al., *The American Soldier*, vol. 2, 126–27; Holmes, *Acts of War*, 340; or Watson, *Enduring the Great War*, 108, 139.
8. See Connell, *Masculinities*, 55–57; see also Connell and Messerschmidt, 'Hegemonic Masculinity', 847–853. For a similar understanding of gender relations, see Joseph Pleck, 'Men's Power with Women, Other Men, and Society: A Men's Involvement Analysis', in *Men's Lives*, eds Michael S. Kimmel and Michael A. Messner (2nd edition, New York, 1992), 5–12; see also Lynne Segal, *Slow Motion: Changing Masculinities, Changing Men* (London, 1990). For a similar argument in a historical perspective, see Michael Roper and John Tosh, 'Introduction', in *Manful Assertions: Masculinities in Britain since 1800*, eds Michael Roper and John Tosh (London, 1991), 8–9.
9. For the sake of brevity, it is assumed here that the conflict involves two specific forms of a single wartime hegemonic masculinity. However, there is also the possibility that the 'officer masculinity' and that of the 'other ranks' may well be interpreted as two distinctly separate masculinities. See Connell, 'Masculinity, Violence, and War', 129; or Marcia Kovitz, 'The Roots of Military Masculinity', in *Military Masculinities*, 8–9.
10. See Manfried Rauchensteiner, *Der Tod des Doppeladlers: Österreich-Ungarn und der Erste Weltkrieg* (Graz, 1993), 44.
11. For casualties, see Deák, *Beyond Nationalism*, 75 and 194. The crisis of command, particularly in the infantry formations where the casualties were heaviest during the first months of the war, is easily ascertained in many Czech soldiers' personal writings. For example, Egon Erwin Kisch repeatedly summarizes the heavy toll the war took on the officer corps of his k.u.k. Infantry Regiment 11 on the Serbian front. As he noted on 2 October 1914, the last surviving captain in the whole regiment (field battalions) was wounded and, by the end of the month, 'only three officers remained with the regiment in the field who could claim continuous service with the regiment from the very beginning' a mere three months ago. Kisch, *Vojákem pražského sboru*, 121 and 148.
12. Quoted in Rothenberg, *The Army of Francis Joseph*, 186.
13. Deák, *Beyond Nationalism*, 194.
14. Slezák, *Paměti Josefa Slezáka k I. světové válce*, vol. 2, 53; a week later, Slezák claims the same even more bluntly: 'We have not enough officers'. See ibid., 62.
15. For numbers, see Deák, *Beyond Nationalism*, 194 and 201.
16. For a thorough discussion of this issue, see Schmitz, *'Als ob die Welt aus den Fugen ginge'*, 47–50; also Rothenberg, *The Army of Francis Joseph*, 218.
17. Deák, *Beyond Nationalism*, 194–195. For the sake of comparison, even the class-obsessed Prussian army allowed exceptions (even if rarely used) and even introduced a stop-gap measure that circumvented the problem during the war – the noncommissioned rank of *Feldwebelleutnant*. See Watson, *Enduring the Great War*, 121–122.

18. Laška, *Pochod hladu Albanií*, 37.
19. Neumann, *Válčení civilistovo*, 21.
20. Váchal, *Malíř na frontě*, 18 and 13.
21. Neumann, *Válčení civilistovo*, 21 and 10.
22. Lirš, *S Osmadvacátníky za světové války*, 17.
23. Šmída, *Vzpomínky z vojny*, 21.
24. Holmes, *Acts of War*, 38–51; Watson, *Enduring the Great War*, 56–57.
25. Kühne, 'Comradeship', 236.
26. Neumann, *Válčení civilistovo*, 88.
27. Křenek, *Vzpomínky na vojnu v Albanii*, 6.
28. František Cihelna, 'Učitelské oddělení u 75. Pluku', in *Pětasedmdesátníci vzpomínají*, 38.
29. Šmída, *Vzpomínky z vojny*, 21.
30. Joanna Bourke came to a similar conclusion regarding Great Britain. In her opinion, it was particularly teachers and 'professional elites' who were hit hardest by these shifts in the gender hierarchy, and while she identifies this issue primarily with a 'fundamental shift in the balance of power between the sexes' in general society, we may well argue that the same was also true in the hierarchy of military masculinities. See Bourke, *Dismembering the Male*, 23 and also 171–209. In fact, there is plenty of evidence of this development in Bohemian and Moravian wartime society. For example, the recollections of a number of Czech-speaking teachers in Alois Žipek's collection – edited with the purpose of demonstrating Austria-Hungary to be a cruel dictatorship – often show nothing other than a slow humiliation of a specific, nationalistic and vocal social group of middle-class intellectuals, who are hit hard both by wartime shortages and inflation at home, and by the status upheaval they experience in the army. Not surprisingly in such a collection, they all interpret the perceived 'oppression of the Czech intelligentsia and teachers' solely in national terms, trying to paint themselves as 'national martyrs'. See *Domov za války*, particularly vol. 3 and 4. Citation from František Mikulášek, 'Po druhé v Karpatech', ibid., vol. 5, 193.
31. Neumann, *Válčení civilistovo*, 90.
32. For all the above, see Kisch, *Vojákem pražského sboru*, 224–26, diary entries from January 1915.
33. Ibid., 225, diary entry from 10 January 1915.
34. Neumann, *Válčení civilistovo*, 104.
35. Skála, *Válečný deník*, 9.
36. At the beginning of the war, constant craving and easy access to 'luxury' enjoyed by even junior officers was criticized by a number of senior commanders as hurtful to the morale of troops. See Schmitz, *'Als ob die Welt aus den Fugen ginge'*, 40–42.
37. Sperling, *Český důstojník na frontách monarchie*, 129, diary entry from 15 September 1918.
38. Diary of Jan Janošík, 19 December 1915.
39. Černý, *Moje záznamy ze světové války*, 64–65.
40. Dolejší, *Válečné zápisky z první světové války*, 216, diary entry from 6 July 1918.
41. See Duffett, *The Stomach for Fighting*, 69.
42. For a comparison in the case of the German army and the British army, see Watson, *Enduring the Great War*, 124–130; for other armies in other eras, see also Holmes, *Acts of War*, 231–240.
43. Šmída, *Vzpomínky z vojny*, 97.

44. Skála, *Válečný deník*, 15; and Slezák, *Paměti Josefa Slezáka k I. světové válce*, vol. 5, 113.
45. The diary of Jan Janošík, 19 December 1915; see also Morávek, *Špatný voják*, 201. For further evidence of growing resentment among the troops towards officers' privilege during the final year of the war, see, for example, Šmída, *Vzpomínky z vojny*, 133; or Tříska, ed., *Zapomenutá fronta*, 89–90.
46. Watson, *Enduring the Great War*, 114.
47. Kühne, 'Comradeship', 245.
48. Hämmerle, 'Back to the Monarchy's Glorified Past', 158.
49. Quoted in Rothenberg, *The Army of Francis Joseph*, 30.
50. See also Kučera, *Rationed Life*, 107.
51. As a consequence of this process, the longest-serving Habsburg emperor is subjected to various epithets in many a soldier's memoir: 'the cruel old man' (Šefl, *Paměti domobrance 28. pluku z války světové 1914–1918*, 9) or 'the old Pandrhola' (Ladislav Wagner, 'Černé neštovice', in *Domov za války*, vol. 3, 336). The emperor's body is unceremoniously described as a 'corpse' by one of the men attending the funeral, (Antonín Zoglmann, 'Na pohřbu Františka Josefa I', in *Domov za války*, vol. 3, 418). There are many similar examples of a damaged father–son relationship between the soldier and the emperor. However, there are also Czechoslovak Legion veterans who use the same logic, only transposing it onto the first President of Czechoslovakia, Tomáš G. Masaryk, denoting him as 'the father Masaryk' and describing him as the highest patriarch. See, for example, Šlesingr, *Legionáři*, 59.
52. Šindelář, *Proti vlastní vůli*, 88.
53. See, for example, Kisch, *Vojákem pražského sboru*, 115, diary entry from 25 September 1914. 'The Children of Prague' was a traditional nickname for k.u.k. Infantry Regiment 28, while 'the children of Brdy' was used in Hájický, 'Křížová cesta Čsl. vojska – z mých zápisků ze Srbska', 1.
54. Jarkovský, 'Kronika ze světové války', 92.
55. Jan Šmatlán to his parents, 29 October 1914, in *Zapomenuté hlasy*, 9.
56. Jurman, ed., *Legionářská odyssea*, 10–11.
57. Ulrych, 'Moje zápisky', 28, 71 and 62.
58. Skála, *Válečný deník*, 125.
59. Šmída, *Vzpomínky z vojny*, 76 and 28.
60. Kisch, *Vojákem pražského sboru*, 172, diary entry from 21 November 1914.
61. Ibid., 210, entry from 19 December 1914.
62. Dolejší, *Válečné vzpomínky z první světové války vojína Dolejše*, 118, diary entry from 1 November 1917.
63. Kisch, *Vojákem pražského sboru*, 176, diary entry from 26 November 1914. For another example, see Černý, *Moje záznamy ze světové války*, 79 and 89. In his memoir, the infantryman Jan Šindelář calls the deep dugouts men had to build for the company and battalion headquarters, the *Heldenkeller* (heroes' dugouts). Šindelář, *Proti vlastní vůli*, 95.
64. Skála, *Válečný deník*, 239.
65. Křenek, *Vzpomínky na vojnu v Albanii*, 170.
66. Chmela, *Vzpomínky z 1. světové války*, 10.
67. Jarkovský, 'Kronika ze světové války', 23.
68. Kápar, *Cestou kamenitou*, 40.
69. Slezák, *Paměti Josefa Slezáka k I. světové válce*, vol. 1, 32.

70. Dolejší, *Válečné vzpomínky z první světové války vojína Dolejše*, 312.
71. Skála, *Válečný deník*, 223.
72. For a comparison, see Watson, *Enduring the Great War*, 112–21.
73. A description of a Russian raid on the Gallician Front in October 1915; Skála, *Válečný deník*, 103.
74. Kisch, *Vojákem pražského sboru*, 186, diary entry from 13 December 1914.
75. Jurman, ed., *Legionářská odyssea*, 18.
76. Křenek, *Vzpomínky na vojnu v Albanii*, 12 and 79.
77. Lirš, *S Osmadvacátníky za světové války*, 10 and 76.
78. Viktor Flaišer, 'Důstojníci a oficíři u 30. střel. pluku', in *Domov za války*, vol. 4, 105.
79. Křenek, *Vzpomínky na vojnu v Albanii*, 7.
80. Chmela, *Vzpomínky z 1. světové války*, 21–22.
81. Skála, *Válečný deník*, 35.
82. Quoted in Rothenberg, *The Army of Francis Joseph*, 130.
83. Quoted in ibid., 148.
84. Both quotations in ibid., 144 and 170.
85. Schmitz, *'Als ob die Welt aus den Fugen ginge'*, 69–75.
86. For the 'nationalizing of the officer corps' through the incorporation of reserve officers, see ibid., 60; Cornwall, *The Undermining of Austria-Hungary*, 31; Rothenberg, *The Army of Francis Joseph*, 184.
87. On the complicated use of languages in the Austro-Hungarian army and the massive headaches it was causing to everyone involved, see Schmitz, *'Als ob die Welt aus den Fugen ginge'*, 28–33; or Tamara Scheer, 'Habsburg Languages at War: "The Linguistic Confusion at the Tower of Babel Couldn't Have Been Much Worse"', in *Languages and the First World War: Communicating in a Transnational War*, eds Julian Walker and Christophe Declerq (London, 2016), 62–78.
88. Speaking in relative terms, the ratio of German-speaking to Czech-speaking reserve Officers was more than 6 to 1 in 1910, as career in the corps was apparently more popular with Bohemian and Moravian German-speaking populations. See Deák, *Beyond Nationalism*, 180–81; see also Koldinská and Šedivý, *Válka a armáda v českých dějinách*, 240–48.
89. Lein, *Pflichterfüllung oder Hochverrat*, 53–201.
90. The way in which the Austro-Hungarian authorities, heavily influenced by their own stereotypes, interpreted the whole affair subsequently enabled them to introduce a heavy-handed approach to those Czech politicians they had long identified as subversives, such as Karel Kramář or Alois Rašín, who were imprisoned, charged with high treason and sentenced to death (the sentence was never carried out). See Mark Cornwall, 'Traitors and the Meaning of Treason in Austria-Hungary's Great War', *Transactions of Royal Historical Society* 25, no. 1 (2015): 129–31. For a Hungarian stereotype of the Czechs as 'traitors', which formed during the war and that viewed every unit from Bohemia or Moravia as a group of potential deserters, see Ferenc Pollmann, 'Die Ostfront des "Grossen Krieges" – aus ungarischer Perspektive', in *Jenseits des Schützengrabens*, 102.
91. Lein, 'The "Betrayal" of the k.u.k. Infantry Regiment 28', 347.
92. Cornwall, *The Undermining of Austria-Hungary*, 33. For the Austro-Hungarian military stereotyping of 'unreliables', see also ibid., 19–20; and Mark Cornwall, 'Disintegration and Defeat: The Austro-Hungarian Revolution', in *The Last Years of Austria-Hungary: A Multi-national Experience in Early Twentieth-Century Europe*, ed. Mark Cornwall

(2nd revised edition, Exeter, 2002), 174; or Rothenberg, *The Army of Francis Joseph*, 183–184.
93. Opletal, *Anabáze hanáckého medika*, 13, diary entry from 21 October 1914.
94. Diary entry from 18 January 1918. Vaněk, *Charašó pán, da?*, 29.
95. Skála, *Válečný deník*, 15.
96. Šmída, *Vzpomínky z vojny*, 24–25.
97. Lirš, *S Osmadvacátníky za světové války*, 24.
98. Ibid., 30.
99. Mudrák, *Bojoval jsem za císaře pána*, 46.
100. Dolejší, *Válečné vzpomínky z první světové války vojína Dolejše*, 258, diary entry from 28 August 1918.
101. Skála, *Válečný deník*, 36–37. The k.u.k. Infantry Regiment 36 was another Czech-dominated unit (95% Czech-speaking), based in Mladá Boleslav (Jungbunzlau) in Bohemia, which suffered from collective punishment after a supposedly purposeful lacklustre combat performance during the battle at Siniewa in May 1915. See Reiter, 'Der Untergang des IR 36', 36.
102. For a general comparison with other armies over time, see, for example, Darius M. Rejali, *Torture and Democracy* (Princeton, 2007), 298–300.
103. See Christa Hämmerle, '"… dort wurden wir dressiert und sekkiert und geschlagen … Zum Drill und dem Disziplinarstrafrecht und Soldatenmisshandlungen im Heer (1866 bis 1914)"', in *Glanz – Gewalt – Gehorsam*, 31–54.
104. See Cornwall, 'Morale and Patriotism in the Austro-Hungarian Army', 177–78; see also Rothenberg, *The Army of Francis Joseph*, 203. For a specific First World War comparison, see, for example, Watson, *Enduring the Great War*, 58–60 (for the British and German armies, respectively).
105. Chmela, *Vzpomínky z 1. světové války*, 17.
106. Ibid., 20.
107. Slezák, *Paměti Josefa Slezáka k I. světové válce*, vol. 1, 23.
108. Šrámek, *Paměti z první světové války Josefa Šrámka z Ústí nad Labem*, 6, diary entry from 13 October 1914. For another example, see Kisch, *Vojákem pražského sboru*, 131.
109. As argued by Hannes Leidinger, there was an obvious – and officially denied – connection between harsh discipline and the abnormally high suicide rate in the prewar Austro-Hungarian army (fifteen times higher than in the general population, twice as much as in the German and five times higher than in the French and the British armies). See Hannes Leidinger, 'Suizid und Militär: Debatten – Ursachenforschung – Reichsratinterpellationen 1907–1914', in *Glanz – Gewalt – Gehorsam*, 337–58. For a study of suicide in prewar Austria in general, see Hannes Leidinger, *Die Bedeutung der Selbstauslöschung: Aspekte der Suizidproblematik in Österrreich von der Mitte des 19. Jahruhnderts bis zur Zweiten Republik* (Innsbruck, 2012).
110. Hämmerle, 'Back to the Monarchy's Glorified Past', 160–61.
111. Jan Šmatlán to his parents, 19 December 1914, in *Zapomenuté hlasy*, 18.
112. Tříska, ed., *Zapomenutá fronta*, 77.
113. Kisch, *Vojákem pražského sboru*, 64, diary entry from 29 August 1914.
114. Jaroš, 'Pochod benátskou rovinou až k Piavě', in *Domov za války*, vol. 4, 470.
115. Quoted in Claire Nolte, 'All for One! One for All! Federation of Slavic Sokols', in *Constructing Nationalities in East-Central Europe*, eds Pieter M. Judson and Marsha L. Rozenblit (New York, 2004), 135.

116. Dolejší, *Válečné vzpomínky z první světové války vojína Dolejše*, 103, diary entry from 5 September 1917.
117. Diary of Jana Janošík, entry from 27 September 1916.
118. Ulrych, 'Moje zápisky', 29; Černý, *Moje záznamy ze světové války*, 34.
119. Bouška, *Zápisky ze světové války*, 27.
120. Váchal, *Malíř na frontě*, 109.
121. See, for example, Heather Streets, *Martial Races: The Military, Race and Masculinity in British Imperial Culture, 1857–1914* (Manchester, 2004), 87–156.
122. Skála, *Válečný deník*, 180.
123. Vítek, *V cizích službách*, 166.
124. Boušek, *Zápisky ze světové války*, 17; Jaroš, 'Pochod benátskou rovinou až k Piavě', in *Domov za války*, vol. 4, 470; Rélink, *28. pluk 'Pražské děti'*, 65.
125. Skála, *Válečný deník*, 139.
126. See, for example, Lirš, *S Osmadvacátníky za světové války*, 52; Rélink, *28. pluk 'Pražské děti'*, passim; Šefl, *Paměti domobrance 28. pluku z války světové 1914–1918*, 41; Wagner, *S českým plukem na ruské frontě*, 135; Ladislav Wagner, 'Rozvrat', in *Domov za války*, vol. 5, 98.
127. Skála, *Válečný deník*, 35–36; and Rélink, *28. pluk 'Pražské děti'*, 50.
128. Leopold Menšík, '1918', in *Domov za války*, vol. 5, 104.
129. Vítek, *V cizích službách*, 256.
130. Pokorný, 'Vzpomínky z první světové války', 8.
131. Šmída, *Vzpomínky z vojny*, 141.
132. František Šindýlek, *Po rozpuštění býv. p. pl. 36*, Kamarádství 7–8 (1937): 122–23.
133. Lynn, *Bayonets of the Republic*, 21–24; for a contemporary analysis of the issue, see also Charles Kirke, 'Group Cohesion, Culture, and Practice', *Armed Forces & Society* 35, no. 4 (2009): 745–53.
134. See Pieter Judson, *Guardians of the Nation: Activists on the Language Frontiers of Imperial Austria* (Cambridge, 2006); see also Tara Zahra, 'Imagined Noncommunities: National Indifference as a Category of Analysis', *Slavic Review* 69, no. 1 (2010): 91–119.
135. Rudolf Kučera, 'Entbehrung und Nationalismus: Die Erfahrung tschechischer Soldaten der österechisch-ungarischen Armee 1914–1918', in *Jenseits des Schützengrabens*, 136–37.
136. See also Matthew Stibbe, 'The Internment of Political Suspects in Austria-Hungary during the First World War: A Violent Legacy?', in *Gender and Modernity in Central Europe*, ed. Agatha Schwartz (Ottawa, 2010), 215.
137. See also Cornwall, 'Morale and Patriotism in the Austro-Hungarian Army, 1914–1918', 188–90.
138. Ibid., 175.
139. Cornwall, *The Undermining of Austria-Hungary*, 20.
140. Cole, *Military Culture and Popular Patriotism in Late Imperial Austria*, 112–13.
141. Stibbe, 'The Internment of Political Suspects in Austria-Hungary during the First World War', 217.
142. In the words of Laurence Cole, 'military traditions and dynastic loyalty potentially worked at a deeper level of consciousness than the national antagonisms of daily politics'. As a consequence, the deeply ingrained feeling of loyalty kept the majority of the disaffected in the ranks until late in the war, in most cases until the very end of October 1918. See Cole, *Military Culture and Popular Patriotism in Late Imperial Austria*, 153.

143. Šmída, *Vzpomínky z vojny*, 76.
144. Dolejší, *Válečné vzpomínky z první světové války vojína Dolejše*, 287, diary entry from 28 September 1918.
145. Skála, *Válečný deník*, 10.
146. Slezák, *Paměti Josefa Slezáka k I. světové válce*, vol. 3, 120.
147. Ibid., vol. 3, 91.
148. Neumann, 'Válčení civilistovo', 94. There are even some stories in the otherwise thoroughly 'nationalized' collection of memoirs edited by Alois Žipek: 'There were many officers who were liked by both Germans and Czechs. I remember one *Oberleutnant* Kunz from the 5th Company, where I had several friends who openly admitted: "While our commander is a German, we would not exchange him for anything'." See Viktor Flaišer, 'Důstojníci a oficíři u 30. střel. pluku', in *Domov za války*, vol. 4, 105. Even here, though, the officer's nationality is an important point of orientation.
149. Váchal, *Malíř na frontě*, 217.

Chapter 5

VENUES OF MANLINESS
Home

Husbands and sons and lovers; everywhere
They die; War bleeds us white.
Mothers and wives and sweethearts, – they don't care
So long as He's all right.

—Siegfried Sassoon, *Their Frailty*[1]

In early April 1918, with Russia out of the picture for good, German offensives on the Western Front losing their initial momentum and American troops finally starting to trickle into the trenches, the First World War in France and Belgium entered its decisive phase. At the same time, the Austro-Hungarian army was building up its strength for a final effort to push through the Entente lines on the Piave River in northern Italy, while the French, British, Serbian and Greek troops were preparing to do the same with the positions of the Central Powers in the Macedonian mountains. It was at this largely forgotten front, specifically at the Albanian port of Durazzo (Durrës) deep in its rear on the Adriatic coast, where a *Feldpostkarte* (field postcard) addressed to *Zugsführer* (sergeant) Pavel Zeman, serving as an accountant with the local Austro-Hungarian headquarters, arrived:

> Dear dad! Many heartfelt hugs and kisses from us. No mail has arrived today. There is nothing new out here. We have nice weather again. Are you getting mail from me alright? And the papers? I'll be sending you a small box tomorrow again! Write as soon as you can let me know you are back, I can hardly wait to hear. Love and kisses, Máŕa and Milda.[2]

On a small piece of hard paper addressed to her husband, Marie Zemanová, an accountant's wife from Olomouc summarized with striking efficiency the most common themes of family correspondence in wartime. All of the field cards she wrote to her husband during that summer, more than one hundred in total over the course of four months, are structured in the same way, and many phrases tend to be repeated almost verbatim in each and every one of them. While 'many heartfelt kissed and hugs', 'are you getting mail from me' or 'there is nothing new out here' almost feel like obligatory pieces of bourgeois correspondence rituals learned through years of schooling that had formed a middle-class housewife, many of these 'filler' phrases also betrayed love, affection, anxiety, the agony of waiting, eagerness for news, solidarity both emotional and material, and emotional dependency that made her message an all-important piece of non-news – telling her husband not to worry while expressing loving concern for his wellbeing.[3]

The relationship between the soldiers and the 'home front' during the First World War has stirred some discussion in the historical profession. Authors such as Paul Fussell, George Mosse and Samuel Hynes concluded that not only was the war the breaking point in the emergence of 'modern consciousness', but that it also created a deep dividing line across the whole society, one that divided the men at the front from the rest of the society.[4] According to the thesis that became more or less the dominant interpretation of the 'war experience' during the 1980s, the war created a rift between the two groups, one that only deepened over time. It was supposedly based on a mutual inability to understand each other's experience, fuelled by the fact that the men at the front found themselves unable to communicate their 'war experience' and subsequent disillusionment in a language accessible to those outside of their group. This theory of negative interaction between the front and the hinterland soon became a target of criticism that also helped to dismantle the idea of the two social spaces as gendered opposites, i.e. masculine front and feminine home. Authors such as Michael Roper, Jessica Meyer and Maureen Healy concluded that the front and the rear were not emotionally separate spaces by any means, and that they represented two parts of a symbolic continuum that encompassed the whole wartime society.[5] As Carol Acton puts it in her study of grieving in wartime: 'Contrary to this version of the home/front binary, letters written by soldiers reveal a reliance on a shared narrative of sorrow with family and friends at home in order express grief and negotiate loss at the front'.[6] Benjamin Ziemann has shown an 'increasing emotional dependence on wives and sweethearts' in the letters written by German soldiers, while Stéphane Audoin-Rouzeau concluded in his study of French trench newspapers that 'by 1915 … [home] is the most frequent topic discussed in the newspapers [and] its importance grew ever greater as time passed'.[7] In the case of Austria-Hungary, Christa Hämmerle reached similar conclusions.[8] Also, while the gendered social geography of the war was actually felt by many as a lived experience – even if it was a grossly inaccurate construct at best – the idea of home as an idealized symbolic space was an intrinsic part of soldiers' existence.

If there were barriers between them and their loved ones at home, their dynamic was much more complicated than the simple picture painted by the original narrative of this relationship.[9]

In Czech soldiers' personal accounts, including their communications with home, there are indeed many examples where soldiers paint 'the rear' in a negative light. We have already discussed the gendered view of the two separate social spaces of war, which was also a part of the official discourse. The same discourse sometimes attempted to make the men forget home altogether and, perhaps in the name of combat-effectiveness, persuaded them that their only purpose now was to fulfil their manly destiny on the field of battle. 'You have left your families, you have become soldiers', a military chaplain preached to the massed formations of three replacement battalions of k.u.k. Infantry Regiment 98 in August 1914, just before they left for the front. 'Be soldiers and nothing else! Forget all ties you have with your homes!' However, the success of such a motivational speech was open to dispute. As a member of the audience noted in his diary: 'It left us with a horrible impression'.[10]

There are also many instances when vain efforts to communicate one's experience in a way both comprehensible and personally palatable are mentioned by the authors (see Chapter 6). Some of the men even go on to intellectualize this problem into a broader feeling of alienation, which resembles some of the 'war poets' analysed by Paul Fussell or Samuel Hynes, such as Siegfried Sassoon. The linguist František Jílek-Oberfalcer stated that, after one year of war, he already felt alienated from the people at home, belonging more to 'the authenticity of life' at the front, and wrote to a friend: 'Ah, you civilians! What do you know about war? You make politics, read daily newspapers, and follow army reports. We drill day and night, make war, and don't care about politics'.[11] The feeling of alienation is particularly obvious in a number of postwar memoirs, such as the one written by another intellectual-turned-soldier, the radical leftist poet Stanislav Kostka Neumann: 'I came from the rocks of Albania and Macedonia, strong of faith and rash with words. I had little understanding for the quiet and the cautious. For this reason, I stopped visiting [poet-friends in Brno] early on'.[12] However, memoirs tend to reflect postwar disillusionment with the situation (social or political) of the young republic, projecting it all the way back into the war years in the same way that many treat the issue of loyalty to the monarchy. As a result, historians need to be careful in interpreting especially the most radical judgements of the home front contained in recollections and memoirs.

But while there were indeed those who felt the 'home front' had little understanding for them and that the hinterland was – in the words of Jaroslav Vítek – 'the place where people get rich on everything' to the detriment of the soldiers, it is obvious that for most of the Czech soldiers, the everyday experience of soldiering at the front and the affairs and developments at home were part of the one and only axis of their personal identity and existence.[13] More often than not, home represented a central point of their being, a beacon that made it possible for them to orient themselves and survive in the maelstrom of war.[14] Home and their loved ones, as an idea, an image stuck in time, was a key that made sense of their dreary everyday existence: 'I feel I have been sentenced and condemned by the world to destiny's remorseless claws', wrote the infantry officer František Šmída in his diary in March 1917. 'I thought of home, of my parents, who were the only ones who have always had understanding for me'.[15] Images of home made time pass faster in the trenches as well as in hospitals. The *Landsturm* infantryman Jan Sýkora, 'in spiritual solitude and partially undisturbed peace' on watch on a Galician night, felt his thoughts 'fly ... far away, to my loved ones, to whom I was sending the warmest greetings deep in my mind'.[16] 'I'm really bored, nothing to do. Thinking of home', Josef Slezák confided in his diary in November 1917 while in Jaroslaw in Galicia.[17]

For Slezák, as for many others, home, mother and girlfriend were, often through charms that bore a symbolic connection to them, the subject of final thoughts before entering combat: 'I prayed, then kissed the picture my mother gave me, and the second one, a photo of my dear Mařenka ... [and] in a resigned mood, awaited further orders'.[18] Home as an idea was also the beacon of all men wounded and dying, at least in the words of those who had left an account of their final moments: 'A sapper was dying in a desolate plum orchard by the road ... He was a Czech, and he gave his final thoughts to his native village. I know he saw it flooded with the golden October sunlight of the Indian summer, I am sure he saw his garden basking in that yellow light ... He saw himself, wandering among the fallen leaves, and had no other wish than to be there ... Back home!'[19] When describing combat situations, men often mentioned 'cries and yells of the wounded, calling to their loved ones' or 'the names of their parents, wives, or children'.[20] Weighed down by these sensory reports, the same authors often go on to picture their own home, the way they had always remembered it. For example, when Josef Klejna describes the disastrous crossing of the Drina River on 9 September 1914, he mentions 'a dying soldier, pulled downriver, into the unknown' and 'calling for help: Help! Help! My beloved wife, my children ..." Hearing that, my mind quickly drifted to you, my beloved children'.[21]

It is the diary of Josef Klejna where we find another image connected to the idea of home in a fashion that is also typical of personal accounts – a brief remembrance whenever an anniversary or a holiday comes around. In his case, a particularly poignant moment occurs on his birthday, 27 November 1914: 'One year ago I was so happy ... And now? My beloved wife, child and sister are sleeping the eternal dream ... They have left me with my pain, and those little orphans of mine to bring up. And what happened – I had to leave them to their fate and follow the uncertain paths of destiny'.[22] A wedding anniversary caused *Landwehr* infantryman Václav Poláček to reminisce about home even in the attack line somewhere on the Vistula: 'Lying in a potato field, writing this. I'm thinking about the ten-year anniversary of our marriage. What a nice memory'. Far from being a 'soldier and nothing else', he clearly saw himself remaining a part of the world he had left behind. Although removed physically from its midst, he still felt a strong emotional attachment to it: 'God, please, save me for my family'.[23] The most emotionally charged anniversary came, not surprisingly, with the coming of Christmas, a holiday seen above else as a time when families and friends should be together. Soldiers were both creative and sentimental when they came to celebrate the holiday with their new 'military family'. However, even in this context, the ritual of reminiscence over people and things left behind played a key role: 'I thought about my family, but the memory made me sick', wrote František Černý in his diary at Christmas in 1915. 'Every year, I tried to come up with some joyful surprise for my family. But today, I did not even know if I would make it till the evening'.[24] Emotionally charged memories of home could be brought to the surface even by seemingly innocuous images, such as the sight of an unknown *Hauptmann* saying goodbye to his fiancée at a train station somewhere in Tyrol: 'One of the fellow-travellers in our car, perhaps remembering how he had bid farewell to his mother, wife, children or perhaps a fiancée, wipes tears flowing like a stream down his cheeks and onto his shirt with his scarf'.[25] Egon Erwin Kisch was surprised to see his comrades from the k.u.k. Infantry Regiment 11, when they 'suddenly fell silent and sad, and started to talk about their families' as soon as they had time to sit down for a while and roll some cigarettes. He only discovered later that the wives of many of the men worked in a tobacco factory – and, according to their husband's memories, no one could roll a cigarette the way they did.[26]

The examples above tell us clearly that home and loved ones – wives, children, parents – were an inseparable part of soldiers' everyday existence. In fact, it would hardly be an exaggeration to say that most of the men were, in their minds, at least partially back home most of the time. Besides the acute feeling of one's mortality, the threat of emotional loneliness mentioned in Chapter 3 also came into play. While building ties of comradeship may well have helped to alleviate the worst symptoms, it seems that for many, the memories of home and the idealized images of a 'perfect past' were the last line of defence. In the words of Bohumil Sperling, a cadet in a heavy artillery regiment, 'only here, in all that desolation and loneliness, one finally appreciates all the relatives and acquaintances he ever had. Only here does he fully remember his home, even if that home was the last of all hellholes in the world. Where is my home?'[27]

Besides the emotions inherently attached to the idea of home, men often also remembered it for other characteristics. Not surprisingly, these tended to reflect their personal situation at the given moment: 'Whoever would have thought that when there is some free time and three or four of us meet in a small room, we talk about ethics or aesthetics, or something similarly abstract and distant, well, he would be mistaken', noted Bohuslav Hála in his diary turned into a memoir of the Eleventh Battle of the Isonzo.

> The key elements of any reminiscing were: good food, coffeehouses, railways, big houses, girls, those beautiful years of student life, full of joy and free of care ... filled with the tender smell of unclouded naïveté, interwoven with the magic of girls' locks and spring songs of girls' eyes ... So many memories flew back home, of quiet evenings under the gaze of bright charming little eyes, of those beautiful quiet evenings with hands pressing against each other, with all those soft kisses.[28]

Good food, coffee, leisure, houses, girls' locks and eyes, the pleasures of youth – in other words, a poetic version of the 'bread, warmth, and sex' – reflected soldiers' attitude to the world and were as important characteristics of home as loving wives, children and mothers.

As a consequence of its importance for soldiers' emotional existence, the idea of home formed an important part of their sustaining motivation. At Christmas in 1916, Augustin Mudrák felt depressed and demoralized, but it was the memory of home and the hope of returning there that kept him going in the end:

> Crouched in a frozen trench, hungry and exhausted, pain, suffering and desolation all around me. Dirty military rags crawling with nasty insects are burning me alive, and there is no relief in sight. Only death is the last hope of redemption. No! I want to live, I want to live a life full of beauty, among the people I love! I am young and full of life. The soil of your fathers awaits you to dig a plough in its bosom, so you can pass onto your descendants not a smaller, but a larger house and a family lot.[29]

This sort of 'motivation by home' revolved around the desire to fulfil one's patriarchal social role, a desire rooted in the actor's position in the prevailing gender order. The image of home (the 'idea' of it) therefore reflects this order, and 'home' constructed as such has an indispensable role in the construction of soldiers' masculine identity. Answering the question about the nature of this role is the primary goal of the following chapter, where the 'idea of home' will be confronted with the imperfect reality as perceived by the men through correspondence or during infrequent leaves. In particular, we will look closely at the consequences the resulting conflict had for the morale and motivation of Czech-speaking troops.

The Connection

Agreeing to the claim that home was a key, albeit physically distant presence in soldiers' lives, we first need to assess the options they had in crossing that distance. Fundamental to this assessment is the army postal service, the *Feldpost*. 'Estimates of the volume of mail conveyed to and from the front indicate that the war-related exchange of letters not only became immensely popular', Christa Hämmerle wrote about the outreach of this institution in wartime Austria-Hungary, 'but also developed into what could be described as a mass cultural phenomenon that affected *all* classes of society'.[30] As a consequence, war brought the practice of regular correspondence down the social ladder, from the upper and upper-middle classes to basically anyone whose relatives or friends were sent to the front. Mail as a communication device – virtually the only one able to sustain contact over long distances and timeframes – became an ever-present factor of essential importance for the soldiers' morale. 'Write as often as you can' is perhaps the most common phrase occurring in soldiers' letters home.[31] 'I guess you have no idea how happy I am upon receiving every letter from you, how much pleasure and joy it brings to me', Jan Šmatlán wrote to his parents in December 1914. 'I always read them many times over'.[32] Quarrels over who wrote more often and why the other side had gone quiet for a while are a key feature of every written dialogue: 'Mařenka, you at least write to me. Oh dear, I can hardly wait to receive a line or two from you people', wrote desperate *Landwehr* infantryman František Šrámek. 'Have you all forgotten about me?'[33] Interruptions in the flow of correspondence often traumatized the men in a way that was comparable to the loss of a comrade, and they tended to use the same vocabulary when commenting on it.[34]

The emotional dependence upon news from home is one of the endemic topics in the majority of the diaries. 'Mail has arrived, and many cried because of the memories of home it brought', wrote a cadet in k.u.k. Infantry Regiment 73 in August 1914.[35] Vladislav Květoň was clear about the importance of mail as a connection to the world outside of war: 'Mail, postcards and letters coming, that was our only joy, it was our connection to life, to parents, siblings, friends and the world'.[36] For the artilleryman Bohumil Sperling, mail was primarily a way 'to satisfy spiritual hunger', while Jan Morávek saw it as 'a breath of the Paradise we have been thrown out of', one that had always made him 'sad and sentimental'.[37] Many accounts actually tell us that the need to communicate with home increased in proportion to how bad the soldier's immediate situation was. Augustin Mudrák described a moment during a Russian preparatory barrage in the spring of 1916, when he pulled a bundle of old letters from his jacket pocket and 'read each one of them again' while crouching under fire. He describes it as 'keeping myself entertained'; however, it is hard to overlook the fact that he had chosen, as a tool of his 'entertainment', the window to 'normalcy' that correspondence represented in the minds of the frontline recipients.[38] Perhaps the most observant definition of the importance of everyday connection with home for soldiers' wellbeing comes from the diary of František Šmída, where he almost invokes the trope of the incommunicability of the combat soldier's experience: 'Those who have never experienced a military campaign, who have never been to the field of battle, can never fully appreciate the importance of the mail a soldier

Figure 5.1 'In the Trenches. Gifts from Home.' A wartime postcard bringing home the message of how important mail and especially packages of useful supplies are for the soldiers' wellbeing and morale, 1915 (Museum of Eastern Bohemia, Hradec Králové).

receives. It is the only comfort, consolation and morale boost, the only connection to the world we have left behind, living like outlaws ever since'.[39]

On the same page as the statement just quoted, we also find Šmída's final note: 'I cannot complain – I have been receiving two field cards a day on average, as well as two or three letters a week'.[40] Thus, in the relative calm of a reserve position on the Eastern Front in the spring of 1917, an average middle-class junior officer in the infantry (somewhat arbitrarily, Šmída is used here as an archetype) would receive about forty or fifty brief postcards as well as about ten letters a month, along with the welcome addition of several 'little boxes' with foodstuffs and other goods, which many soldiers received from their families on a more or less regular basis. Their frequency was, of course, directly proportional to the family's social status and economic situation – the lower-class urban population was unable to send these even early in the war, while middle-class families living in the country such as the Šmídas, or those with connections and purchasing power strong enough to operate on the black market, such as the Zemans mentioned in this chapter's introduction, could do so as late as 1918. Even if *Oberleutnant* Šmída's social status and education are taken into account, admitting that his communication rate with the home front was probably above average because of a combination of ease, habit and social pressure, it is obvious that the sheer amount of mail that soldiers sent and received was staggering. And, surprisingly, this massive amount of mail was, for the most part, successfully delivered to the recipients on a regular basis. The 2,800 employees of the k.u.k. military postal service, staffing more than 500 field post offices and 200 depot offices, sometimes dealt with more than nine million packages a day. In his diary, Josef Slezák repeatedly places the time it took letters from his mother to reach him in the positions near Caré Alto (above Trento in the Italian Alps) at between six and seven days.[41]

Military postcards were the most common type of shipment, and the government had 655,696,314 of them printed during the war *in Cisleithania alone*.[42] It is hardly surprising that the army postal service suffered from being regularly overburdened and the military authorities repeatedly brought up a plan to introduce a postal charge to alleviate the problem (letters up to 200 grams were free of charge) or suspended the service for a while when the danger of a collapse was imminent. While the former measure was never introduced because of the public uproar it generated whenever it was brought up, the latter, while thoroughly unpopular, was used on a regular basis in areas of strategic importance, usually during a build-up for an offensive or other large-scale operations, i.e. in the moments when soldiers were more keen than any other time to *communicate* their situation to their families. The consequence of this clash between soldiers' needs and operational secrecy was the infamous military field card, preprinted with a short message in all the languages of the monarchy: 'I am in good health and doing well'. Men were banned from adding anything but the address to the message, but at least were given the means to let their loved ones know they were alive.[43] From this specific example as well as from the outstanding effort required to deliver the sheer volume of letters, cards, and packages, it is clear that the Austro-Hungarian authorities were fully aware of the importance mail had for the morale of the troops, and went to great lengths to keep it going even in the

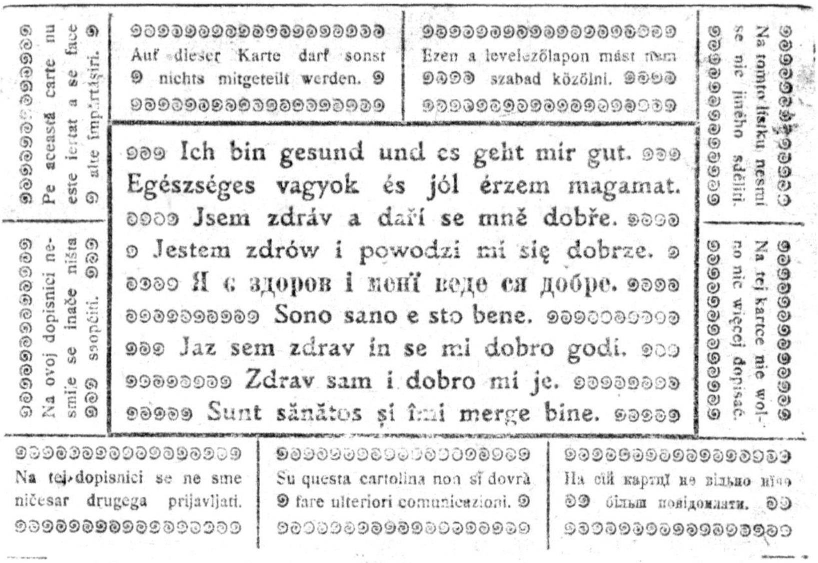

Auf dieser Karte darf sonst nichts mitgeteilt werden.

Ezen a levelezőlapon mást nem szabad közölni.

Pe această carte nu este iertat a se face alte împărtășiri.

Na tomto lístku nesmí se nic jiného sdělit.

Ich bin gesund und es geht mir gut.

Egészséges vagyok és jól érzem magamat.

Jsem zdráv a daří se mně dobře.

Jestem zdrów i powodzi mi się dobrze.

Я є здоров і менї веде ся добре.

Sono sano e sto bene.

Jaz sem zdrav in se mi dobro godi.

Zdrav sam i dobro mi je.

Sunt sănătos și îmi merge bine.

Na ovoj dopisnici ne smije se inače ništa saopćiti.

Na tej kartce nie wolno nic więcej dopisać.

Na tej dopisnici se ne sme ničesar drugega prijavljati.

Su questa cartolina non si dovrà fare ulteriori comunicazioni.

На сій карті не вільно нїчо більш повідомляти.

Figure 5.2 'I am in good health and doing well.' A military-issue postcard given to soldiers when all other types of messages to their loved ones were banned because of operational necessity (Military History Institute, Prague).

worst possible conditions. As a result, the idea of home was never completely out of reach for the vast majority of the soldiers.

Huge quantities and the sheer size of the army's effort notwithstanding, mail also made the life of the military command complicated in terms of quality. Fears of military secrets being spilled by men putting them on paper, the morale of the population being damaged by those demoralized or merely frank in their descriptions of modern combat, or of loyalty being undermined by the airing of subversive thoughts – all these created the desire and need for tight regulation of the very contents of soldiers' private messages. Describing specific geographical locations was prohibited, as was identifying any military units or criticizing military decisions or even the monarchy's war effort in general.[44] To enforce these regulations and to gain at least partial insight into the private thoughts of the rank and file, the Army High Command quickly introduced a sophisticated system of wartime censorship of all inbound (i.e. front to hinterland) correspondence overseen by the War Surveillance Office *Kriegsüberwachungsamt* (KÜA). The only way to avoid this measure was to have packages or letters sent via comrades going home on leave. As early as August 1914, Egon Erwin Kisch noted that the letters written by his comrades, including lively descriptions of imaginary 'bloody skirmishes and dangers overcome … will not, in all probability, reach their destination, because the censorship is tight'.[45] However, besides selected samples, suspected subversives and all Austro-Hungarian POWs, the majority of the censoring effort was actually carried out by the units themselves, where officers were responsible for the careful screening of the letters of their men, while their correspondence was vaguely controlled by their immediate superiors.[46] It seems that at least in some cases, the censors were rather tolerant of indirect criticisms of their own efforts, as shown by the example of a letter received by the parents of Jan Janošík, where their son complains: 'Dear parents, please receive my cordial greetings. I cannot write what I should be writing, because all the letters are read and searched before they go out'.[47]

Censorship theoretically also covered outbound (i.e. from the hinterland to the front) correspondence, but its very volume made it such a gargantuan task that the KÜA focused its attention on random samples and selected areas of particular strategic or political importance, such as industrial agglomerations. Instead, the contents as well as the form of correspondence became a target of a propaganda campaign to make it closely follow the official discourse. For example, one of the key messages of the government-subsidized collections of soldiers' letters, the 'letters from the front', was the joy soldiers experienced when receiving mail. 'We look forward to the letters from our loved ones and wait', one of the letters told its readers in an obvious effort to encourage the civilian population to increase their efforts and to raise the morale of the men.[48]

These collections, as well as examples of letters, real or fabricated, published in the daily press, were selected precisely because of their adherence to the official discourse, which also included the gendered discourse of the war. In their understanding of wartime society, it was the women who were primarily responsible for supporting the sons, husbands and brothers in their traditional 'masculine task' of defending the fatherland, and because it was supposedly the women who populated the 'home front', the task of doing so through letters was seen as overwhelmingly theirs. The image of a 'good soldier's wife' was combined here with the traditional middle-class ideal of a corresponding woman, acquiring patriotic connotations and responsibility for army morale in the process.[49] As mentioned by Christa Hämmerle, this 'gender coding' of the communications between home and the front found its apogee in the established institution of so-called *Liebesgaben*, anonymous packages made by women at home and delivered to random soldiers for selected holidays. Practised mostly in the first years of the war, the purpose of this effort was to sustain the bond between the front and the hinterland, and – in the background – to strengthen the notion of 'true wartime womanhood', proving itself by expressing support for the fighting men.[50]

One such package is described in detail in the diary of Bohuš Adamíra, who received it for Christmas in 1915, near Rovereto in Italy: 'And we've got a *Liebesgabe*. A slice of cheese, a piece of bacon, four packs of cigarettes, two blocks of chocolate and two cans of sardines'.[51] At the same time, a few hundred kilometres away in Serbia, Karel Suchý received his own *Liebesgabe* and, reflecting the soldier's need for 'bread', commented upon its contents: 'Much better than last year. We have got five cigars each and twenty cigarettes, everyone got one lighter, a needle, patent buttons, a notebook and a pipe, but not everyone got that one. And there were also five packs of candy for us to share'.[52] It may well be true that Christmas of 1915 was actually an improvement in terms of fulfilling a soldier's needs, as the contents of the packages received by k.u.k. Infantry Regiment 11 in late November 1914 elicited the following comment from Egon Erwin Kisch: 'I was looking forward to some cigarettes ... [Instead], I have got warm underwear, mostly knitted and useless in the field, things like ornamental gloves with a fancy hem, braces ... mittens large enough for baby elephants, knee pads for storks and stuff like that'. Ignoring the bitter irony of Kisch's entry, it is clear that he indeed saw war as a gendered enterprise, projected onto a gendered space, and *Liebesgaben* were a reflection of ideal wartime womanhood constructed around 'joyous' and happy support for the men at the front: 'Things that girls knitted during evenings full of joy and boredom to make themselves feel important ... I have been getting used to the lack of cigarettes for weeks now ... If one of those kind souls sent me a ten-pack of them, I would marry her immediately'.[53]

The Message

Turning our attention back to the military post as a primary communication link between soldiers and the discursively feminized space of home, we should consider the way in which its contents were shaped by the masculine identity of the men. One of them, platoon commander František Loubal, summarized what he had read in the letters of his men while censoring them:

> There was a lot of poetry and some comedy in there too. Some of the letters were complete family secrets. There was plenty of new, unforeseen knowledge as well. Many of those dirty, ragged bastards ... surprised me by the tenderness of their words to their wives or children. Another drew the first lines of a future family tragedy, threatening his wife with not just a beating but even murder when he came home, because he had learned of her infidelity. Single men often tried to convince their sweethearts that their love was never ending, and warned them against getting too close with one or another rival who was somehow still managing to avoid being drafted. There was a considerable amount of poetry in those letters home, as well as a great deal of rudeness and cynicism. Some did not even try to hide their politics, which peeped out now and then behind a scant covering of words. A few of them were actually very careless in this regard.[54]

Loubal's recollection may well serve us as a rough analysis written by a first-line censor, and while ignoring the author's sense of class superiority expressed in his contempt for the 'dirty, ragged bastards', it gives us some basic idea of the themes that the soldiers' correspondence consisted of: emotional expressions of love, jealousy, efforts to keep relationships working over a long distance and (prohibited) criticism of wartime conditions. Most of these themes are connected to emotional ties to home, and these ties are subsequently based on a gendered understanding of one's own role and one's own immediate position in the process of masculinity. In Loubal's picture, there are fathers, husbands or lovers communicating exclusively with women, as if there was no one else to communicate with.

It may be surprising that Loubal completely ignores one other typical communication model – that of a son writing to his parents, mostly (and not surprisingly; see above) to a mother. The mother, as argued by Michael Roper, is one of the key categories in understanding both soldiers' correspondence and their emotional world, a category that is again thoroughly gendered. In Roper's view, one's relationship with one's mother and communication with her were the key points of emotional orientation in a soldier's life.[55] Looking at the sources, Czech soldiers were hardly different from their British counterparts: the relationship with the 'mum' (*matička*) or even 'little mum' (*maminečka*) is often a guiding thread going through many a soldier's personal account. The diaries of Josef Slezák, Josef Ulrych and Josef Kápar are the most typical examples here; however, a warm and deeply personal relationship with mothers is obvious in other diaries as well as in the soldier's correspondence: 'Dear mum! If only I could tell you how much I love you, I would do it today', Bedřich Václavek wrote. 'Living far away from you, I have finally realized that your love is the only one that is unconditional and stands by a man always and in every situation'.[56] In his diary, Jaroslav Havlíček reflected on 'an image of the good old warmth' of a home he 'couldn't forget': 'Mum always used to take us on her lap and sing the old, moving song "Cradle Me, Oh My Dear Mother" … full of that sad, touching maternal kindness'.[57] Similarly, the usual trope of dying more often than not includes a call not only to home and the loved ones, but specifically to the mother: 'Mamma!', 'Mother!' 'Mutter!' or 'my beloved mum!'[58]

What soldiers generally expect from their mothers is to keep the gender order as it should be by fulfilling the above-mentioned image of an unconditionally loving caregiver, crying with every parting and tearfully embracing her son when he comes back home. František Šmída, for example, is clearly disappointed that 'surprisingly, my mother did not cry' when he was leaving for the front for the first time.[59] Consequently, when Josef Kápar describes the image of regiments leaving for the train stations at the beginning of the war, the gender order is kept upright – 'mothers' hearts are being broken', 'wives feel their marriages being torn apart' and 'fathers are going grey'.[60] Such a thoroughly gendered structure of mourning, with two feminine and one masculine form of existence being specified, hints at the important difference soldiers had in their relationship to each of their parents. While mothers were expected to offer support, care and emotions, and represented the whole family to an extent, the image of the fathers were bound by traditional patriarchal masculinity, a distant authority figure offering quiet, stoical support from the background. In Kápar's words, the father was 'the standard bearer of all values', and when he cries it is an unwelcome surprise, while his 'mom prays for me and thinks of me'.[61]

It is therefore the mutual social positioning of the author and his counterpart that defines the way in which text of an account is 'coded', and shapes the communication as well as the emotions and topics involved. It is through these that it is possible to analyse the way in which soldiers experienced their masculinity, as is obvious even from the very limited number of correspondence collections analysed for the purposes of this study. One of the most gendered tendencies is the above-mentioned practice of communicating differently with feminine and masculine counterparts respectively. Letters addressed to fathers, brothers or friends, i.e. *men* from the perspective of social definition, are usually written in a sober, quasi-realistic tone. Authors tend to be more sincere and blunt, and even shift towards naturalism. Also, if possible, they try to communicate their experience as *manly*, even aggrandizing their own experiences to closely reflect the general picture of a stoical warrior. Thus, when Rudolf Wagner wrote a letter addressed to his father, he went to great lengths in describing the reality of the Brusilov Offensive in the summer of 1916:

> On day three we were supposed to attack, to make an *Angriff* [assault]. So our guns started their *Trommelfeuer* [barrage] … They were firing from quarter to two till eight o'clock in the evening, without interruption … It was a drumming that shook the earth to the core. The Russians were not quiet either, sending shrapnel after shrapnel as well as many shells, right in the middle of the village where we were quartered. We could not take cover, everyone was crouching in his own hole, which does not help much against artillery.[62]

From the same sector of the front, only two weeks later, Emil Marek reported to his brother: 'I was lucky to make it, it was really bad the things that went on here. I would not wish you to go through anything like that, you know. Everyone who does not have to be here should consider himself lucky. But it's alright, only no cigarettes'.[63] While the author points towards the implied horrors of war in his message, at the end he seems to provide reassurance that he is still coping with it and keeping a calm head, the only important deprivation being a lack of cigarettes. The need to present oneself in a stoical manner is also obvious in an anonymous letter written in April 1916 and addressed to the author's brother in Prague, a reply to a message that the soldier's wife had suffered a stroke. Even in such a desperate and difficult moment, he still tries to keep his emotions suppressed as much as humanly possible: 'Dear brother, please make all the arrangements, everything that's necessary, and please let me know any developments in her sickness. Being so far away, your letter upset me a lot, and I cannot write any further. Please, my dear brother, do not leave me and my little children, the situation is really serious for me now'.[64]

While communication of men with other men is usually directed towards down-to-earth, no-nonsense stoicism, men's communication with women (mothers, wives, sweethearts, sometimes sisters or other relatives) is typified by its comforting character. 'Work here is not that hard', 'I went through some critical hours … [but now] we are expecting to be relieved any minute' or 'I am well and in good health, it's like you would expect in the army, ample food and everything' – these are examples of rather typical statements to be found in some of the letters.[65] The strategy of self-censorship, which was apparently common in communications with the feminine counterpart, is well described in a letter by the poet and writer Fráňa Šrámek, addressed to his wife in 1918. He asks her to correct a verse in one of his poems that he had sent her two years earlier, 'changing the second stanza into: The white of a shrapnel cloud / lured the spark in your eye, etc. I did not want to frighten you, so I did a little "cover up" there, you know'. The title of the poem was *On the Banks of the Isonzo*.[66] An even more perfect example is a short 'report' from Jan Janošík in a letter to his parents (i.e. primarily his mother; see below) on 1 July 1916: 'I am well so far. Otherwise, nothing of note happens here'. However, his diary says that just before the letter was written, his unit had been thrown into the midst of the Brusilov Offensive, lost three-quarters of its numbers in a series of battles, and the author himself mentions that he himself had several 'close calls' with death.[67] In a similar way, when Egon Erwin Kisch sent his diary recording of the first few months of the war back home, he went on to write a letter to his mother where he says: 'I was in danger from time to time, but I always miraculously escaped, and now I am very well indeed. We are stationed in a beautiful coastal area and life in the country, close to nature, does wonders for my nerves'.[68] His sincere effort to calm his mother's fears is obvious, as if he knew she would need such support before reading his relatively candid account of combat on the Serbian front.

As shown by these examples, soldiers did not try *absolutely* to hide the reality of war from their female audience. They obviously did not expect women to be that isolated from the world of war and were aware of the danger of too much insincerity, which could ultimately harm their agenda, as it would cross the threshold into the realm of the simply unrealistic and unbelievable. They found a solution in not denying the danger of their duty, but putting it firmly in the past tense. Put simply, they attempted to persuade their womenfolk that while service *is* dangerous, as everybody knew, the danger was now gone and there was no longer any reason to worry. This logic then enabled them, for example, to be surprisingly naturalistic in describing sights at the front: 'My dear wife and children!', Antonín Kyšperský wrote from Italy in August 1917. 'Thank you for your card … I am alright as well, as of now, but there is a nauseating smell from all the corpses that were left unburied, because for five days and nights both sides threw everything they had at each other in heavy gunfire. We are expecting to be relieved soon, and I can tell you, I can hardly wait for the moment'.[69] Gunfire and its consequences – the dead – are not denied, but firmly situated in the past, as something that is finished. While the message is serious enough, the danger is over.

Denying danger was not only unrealistic, but perhaps also somewhat undesirable with regard to the construction of wartime masculinity. This construction was based upon the idea of fulfilling the 'manly duty' of military service – and the ability to sustain one's calm in the face of mortal danger was an integral part of this. Also, facing this danger laid claim to emotional support from home. As the poet Jan Kotrba complained in a letter to Bedřich Václavek after being seriously wounded: 'I have been writing things like "just a scratch, does not hurt" for three weeks, just to calm my parents down'. In fact, he tells his friend, his leg wound is 'horrible' and now he feels he is lacking the support he had expected: 'The result: they actually believed me and make light of it. Was I disappointed in my belief that true love can read between the lines?'[70] Is it possible that the author tried so hard to hide the true nature of his injuries that he ultimately felt that he was not pitied and perhaps not sufficiently appreciated as a wounded fighting man?

Fitting the picture of wartime masculinity could also be achieved by a strategy opposite to denial – by 'improving' reality. For example, Ferdinand Lirš mentions a soldier's letter addressed to the man's parents from the frontline in Carinthia:

> Please excuse the gap since my last letter. There was some heavy, brutal fighting. We're currently fighting the wops, but also black, colonial troops. Those blacks do not spare anyone ... We fought bravely, like lions. The wops were bombing us ... We were really scared. Then, the enemy charged our positions. Horrible moments of killing and maiming followed, our guys were falling in droves, moaning and groaning in pain ... But in the end we prevailed. I'm wounded in the leg, but it's just a scratch ... Please, write to me soon and send some nice food too ... [Signed], Venca.[71]

Venca's heroism in survival, used here to support his claim for 'some nice food', looked impressive enough; however, as Lirš claims in his memoir, the sector of their XI Battalion of k.u.k. Infantry Regiment 28 had been absolutely quiet since the unit arrived at the front.

The same effort to boost one's masculine status through a warrior-like image was witnessed by Egon Erwin Kisch in a businessman's household in Písek, where the author was spending his final night before joining his regiment in July 1914:

> His wife was worried that her husband would have to go to war with the *Landsturm*. He made sure she kept those thoughts alive by deliberately clumsy, fake efforts to calm her, only to brag that he was a warrior after all and to strengthen her love through anxiety. I had the unpleasant task of both consoling the wife and, with respect to the man, pushing forward his agenda of the mortal danger that awaited him.[72]

Confirmation of the man's social identity becomes the key issue of the communication here, reflecting the shift in the wartime discourse of masculinity and laying claim to emotional attachment and support from the female counterpart. It was probably a similar logic that caused Ladislav Rezek to write the following to his girlfriend: 'I will leave it all to destiny. I calmly expect the worst, as there is nothing else here to expect ... I don't know if my cards are bothering you, as I can feel displeasure from your last few letters ... I'm not one to be obtrusive'.[73] The dynamics of stoical masculinity are closely connected to the expected reciprocity in kind – most probably in enthusiastic admiration and support. When it does not come, the feeling of being wronged seems to have been hard to swallow, as was the unfulfilled (and perhaps unspoken) craving for intimacy and emotional support that was also one of the key functions of wartime correspondence.

The Performance

Letters and field cards were the primary space where the men could express their emotions and receive much-needed positive emotional impulses. It was one of the ways by which 'the dirty, ragged bastards' managed to survive the war emotionally, the other being comradeship.[74] However, the fact that correspondence was a socially accepted medium for expressing and receiving emotions was not the sole reason for it to be of fundamental importance for both the men's motivation and masculine identity. In the list of themes he found interesting in the letters of his subordinates, the 'censor' František Loubal also mentioned 'future family tragedies', like those threats of murder when a soldier suspected his wife of being unfaithful to him. He also includes men 'trying to convince their sweethearts' of their love and sending warnings against possible rivals. These examples of jealousy and potential romantic conflict may well be defined as an effort to exercise one's masculine power and control, seriously weakened by the distance and time spent away from home, over a partner or a household, where the man was still expected to be the head. The effort to keep or re-establish the level of control that the traditional gender order ascribes to the masculine element was also not limited only to sexual discipline as the most obvious manifestation of masculine power over women. It covered a much broader economic and social context, one that was closely connected to the construction of modern masculinity and the notion that it needed to be exercised over various parallel 'arenas' at once.

According to John Tosh, the experience of *modern* masculinity is rooted in the way in which it is socially performed. In his research, he identifies several 'venues' of such performance, Masculinity needs to be performed effectively in these fields in order for an individual to be able to claim hegemonic status successfully. These venues are the home and family, work and so-called homosocial institutions, i.e. the public space.⁷⁵ In addition to these venues, Sonya Rose, in her study of soldiers' voting rights in prewar Great Britain, suggested adding 'a fourth venue of masculine performance, the military'.⁷⁶ Within the context of the radical militarization of hegemonic masculinity in wartime, as was the case in Austria-Hungary during the First World War, we may very well agree with her suggestion. The logic of performing masculinity in several venues at once of course poses a key problem. First, lack of success in one of the venues places the individual's identification with the hegemonic ideal in jeopardy. Second, the virtual incompatibility of those venues makes effective performance in all of them all the time impossible. It was difficult to be a good father and a breadwinner within the venue of the home, while at the same time effectively performing the role of a 'public man' in bars, pubs and other spaces of male sociability, as those roles not only required different sets of psychosocial skills and attitudes, but were often directly contradictory. In the same way, to be a good soldier fulfilling his masculine duty to obey and serve, and to be the true 'head of a household', was even more difficult in practical terms. However, for hundreds of thousands of men (including Czechs) between 1914 and 1918, this uphill battle was their daily social reality. Hegemonic masculinity, which de facto co-opted the military as its primary venue at least for the duration of the war, faced a permanent conflict that repeatedly endangered the very core of the men's sense of manliness – while war gave them the chance to acquire or defend their masculine status through the role of a warrior, this role made their life in all the other venues, particularly at work and home, massively complicated. Suddenly it was very difficult to direct, control and feed the socially dependent actors they had left at home. Put simply, even the best of warriors were in constant danger of being poor fathers, husbands or sons, constantly experiencing the threat of completely losing control over the 'home' venue of their social being.

The above-mentioned jealousy and general insecurity in long-distance romantic relationships may therefore be interpreted as a manifestation of this conflict, as men were worried about their ability to discipline and control their female partners and their sexuality, which, according to many authors, is what the gender order and the dominant position of masculinity is mostly about.⁷⁷ Soldiers did not see their wives and sweethearts only as idealized 'angels' and sources of much-needed emotional support. As the traditional image of femininity discussed in Chapter 2 also included weakness in the face of temptation and an inherently sexualized nature, doubts and distrust were often quick to creep into their minds. As a result, female infidelity is one of the primary themes of discussion regarding home in most of the soldiers' personal accounts, as well as in postwar fiction. The lingering suspicion that his wife is cheating on him, and his inability to overcome this suspicion are the key traits of the main character in the semi-biographical war novel written by Rudolf Vlasák.⁷⁸ Karel Rélink, in his half-witty and probably half-fictional memoir of service in the only surviving battalion of the k.u.k. 28ᵗʰ

Infantry, mentions one 'Franta Flinta, a firmly devoted newlywed', who 'could not keep himself from repeated bouts of jealousy, when his mind started to draw vivid pictures of his wife's remarkable bosom, whose defence was left to the very limited abilities of his mother'.[79]

Even if one finds it difficult to believe Rélink's account, there is an almost perfect example of this issue in the wartime diary of Josef Slezák. Over five volumes, one can witness an ongoing, slightly obsessive and in all probability rather typical process, during which the author quickly feels like losing control over the sexual discipline of his 'beloved Mařenka'. At first, they are promising each other absolute fidelity and Slezák reassures himself that 'she was sincere, that's for sure'. However, shortly after being mobilized, Slezák starts to be suspicious, noting that 'she may have been dating that night', only for them to repeat the mutual promise 'to be faithful unto death'.[80] Even so, in September 1914, when he spends some time reminiscing, he not only recalls his 'mother, and whether she's doing well', but also 'my beloved, whether she's faithful'.[81] In July 1915, when he finally gets his first leave, he is 'terribly disappointed with the news I got from friends, that my beloved girl had been unfaithful to me in Králova Lhota, which she denied'.[82] Even though the whole issue might have emanated from pure slander, as often happened, the author began to see his relationship with 'Mařenka' as being over: 'I did not go to Králova Lhota', he noted when he returned from another leave, this time in the autumn of 1916. 'Because I have heard some not very nice things about my ex-girlfriend', he added, unwilling to witness the consequences of his inability to exercise control over a woman whom he considered guilty of 'not keeping her pledge'.[83] Still, as late as November 1918, he remembered her as a 'dear girl' from time to time, particularly in moments of emotional crisis.[84]

Effective exercise of power and discipline over women went hand in hand with the use of violence. 'You didn't tell me that Anča was taking lessons', Jan Horálek wrote to his mother from Dalmatia in May, 1916. 'Is she seeing some dude? I'll break his legs'.[85] As František Loubal noted, violence, 'even murder', was often directed against women and this would have probably been a frequent argument in many families. The diary of Jaroslav Vítek contains a soldier's monologue on the topic of a woman who got out of his control:

> I wasn't due to go home ... Oh God, I was so looking forward to see her again, as we hadn't seen each other for a long time ... My wife was a good woman. I ran all the way from the train, I actually ran, impatient and eager. It was four in the morning, the house was locked. I knock, and nothing happens ... So I run upstairs to my apartment, I knock, my wife asks: 'Who's there?' I responded, then I hear confusion and whispers, and bad feeling starts to come over me ... Then a half-naked soldier runs out of the place – a Magyar! I didn't know what to do at that moment, I took a cane, my wife knelt before me and pleaded with me, her hands clasped, and I beat her and beat her ... I beat the person who meant everything to me.

In the end the man forgave his wife 'because I was not free of sin myself'; however, he would still prefer not to have been a witness to his own failure as a husband and a man: 'If only I hadn't seen it'.[86] Regarding this story, it is worth noting that the author thought it important to tell the audience that the soldier in his apartment was 'a Magyar', which only lends further support to the argument that the transfer of Hungarian regiments' reserve battalions to Bohemia in exchange for the reserve battalions of some Czech-dominated units was a particularly irritating administrative measure. Ever since then, the image of a Magyar enjoying the suspected compliance of their wives and girlfriends became a staple of Czech soldiers' accounts, a veritable nightmare that manifested itself in stories like this one.[87]

Of course, soldiers' efforts to sustain control and power over women at home were not limited to sexuality; they encompassed the notion of the household as a whole. Mainly those men whose idea of home was synonymous with a farm or a family business (i.e. where it blended with the venue of work) found the fact that they had had to leave everything and join the army deeply traumatizing, as it made the conflict between two parts of their social identity as men all the more acute. Those working in agriculture felt particularly torn in 1914, as the war had begun at the end of July when the agricultural season peaked: 'There are no words to describe how I felt in those early days', Josef Slezák recalled in the introduction to his diary. 'Just the thought! Harvest coming, just bought a young horse, and suddenly, I'm leaving all that to my old, sick mother'.[88] 'So many able-bodied men had to leave their homes when the harvest was on', František Kylar despaired years after the war.[89] The conflict between the reconstructed, militarized version of hegemonic masculinity and the traditional identity of a good farmer remained ongoing throughout the war, undoubtedly worsening with the deteriorating economic situation that was already felt even in rural areas as early as 1916.[90] 'Recalling home, I don't know where my head is. So much work to be done there, and I'm here, in this faraway land', Josef Zeman complained in a letter to his brother in August 1917.[91] In July 1918, Josef Slezák received 'a long letter from home' that 'upset me a lot': 'Mother is writing again about a harvest leave, that she cannot do it alone, and pleads for me to come home. She says everyone is getting a leave, and thinks I just don't want to come home'.[92] The resulting emotional disturbance competed here with a crisis of masculine identity, where the notion of being a good farmer and a good son went against the enforced manly duty of military service: 'If only I could be at home and help too'.[93]

When men left for war, households were not left desolate, but moved under the complete control of women. The only male help many of them received after the war started in earnest was from older relatives or neighbours, and many were forced to become independent farmers, saleswomen or businesswomen. As Jan Janošík's sister Marie wrote with pride: 'Imagine, I am the head of the household now, for example, today we've been shovelling manure. And in the evening I put on a dress and go out as if nothing has changed'.⁹⁴ The newly discovered social and economic independence the mass of women experienced for the first time during the war, here in perfect symbiosis with an effort to preserve one's notion of femininity, ran completely counter to the views many men held. For them, it was difficult to imagine that a woman could be fully independent, be successfully in charge of the family budget or even a farm or a business. Many actually doubted even their basic abilities and thought that the only way in which things could be made to work would be when they themselves returned back to the venue to perform their part: 'Is your heating really on, *madame*?' Fráňa Šrámek wrote to his wife when she fell ill with a cold in November 1915. 'I think it is time for my firm hand to intervene, along with my booming voice, isn't it?'⁹⁵ Similarly, the diary of Jan Tříska is filled with doubts concerning whether 'a lonely mother caring for a child' would be able to take care of a family shop 'in disintegrating Vienna with all the rationing'. And even though his wife more than proves that, with some help from grandparents who took care of their little daughter, she is indeed up to the task, Tříska still repeatedly worries about 'my brave and lonely Boženka', 'so young and vulnerable'. His worries were only exacerbated towards the end of the war, when the social and economic situation in the monarchy's capital became increasingly desperate, to the extent that he 'cannot protect Božena' from the 'upcoming revolution'.⁹⁶ Ironically, military service with all its discursive notions of protection conflicted here with the author's personal need to protect his family; being a social 'protector' clashed with the primary need to be an individual one. Understandably, this conflict was damaging to Tříska's sustaining motivation, which rapidly deteriorated during 1918, and leaving Vienna at the end of his last leave in August of that year seemed to be an exercise in self-denial.

The shifting sands of the gender order at the home front, with women taking over large parts of the economy including the role of breadwinners, did not stop some men from trying to reconcile the two venues of their masculinity by directing their households from a distance. However, their efforts were bound to fail not only because of the distance and time lag itself, but also because of the growing barrier of misunderstanding caused by the fast-changing conditions in the hinterland, which were becoming radically different from anything the men had known or could have imagined.⁹⁷ An outstanding example of this process may be found in a series of short letters sent home by a South Bohemian craftsman-turned-*Landsturm* infantryman, Václav Poláček, to his wife in late 1917 and early 1918. While her notes leave us with the strong impression that the family was gravely missing his economic output and the war economy had hit them hard from the beginning, making them increasingly dependent on small-time agriculture, gardening and Mrs. Poláčková's short-time work, Poláček still keeps to his notion of how the family worked when he left in 1914, becoming more and more cut off from reality. Thus, in late 1917, he repeatedly asks his wife to oil a power-drill he has left in his workshop, complains that he 'does not get any news' from her or the family, which makes him 'all sullen', and repeatedly dwells on the school grades of their two children and on the fact that they do not send him any letters. In March 1918, he places great emphasis on inquiring about a family photograph that he has received, wondering why the children have 'wooden shoes' and almost berating his wife for the fact that: 'Mařka has no warm tights …? Wasn't the picture taken in the middle of winter?' In the last preserved letter, written in April 1918, he actually seems to realize that his family 'must be badly suffering … from a hard and sad life'. However, in the search for the reason for this situation, he completely ignores the crumbling economy of the home front, focusing solely on his own perceived all-importance as a breadwinner, claiming that the reason for their distress was that 'you dearly miss your provider'.[98] It seems as if the author is trying to reassure himself as well as his wife that he still *is* the provider and that all the trouble would be gone if only he could come home.

Similarly missing the point with regard to the wartime reality at home, Jan Čundrle, a teacher from Moravia and, since October 1914, a POW in Russia, also deals with the crisis of his performance in the 'home' venue with a vain effort to 'perform' over distance. He repeatedly urges his wife, busy with their three children and battling an increasingly difficult economy, to send him more money and more new clothes, and becomes troublesome when his demands are not met either because of difficult communications between Siberia and Moravia or the sheer inability of the family to meet them. Ignorant of the situation at home, he still insists upon being the one who directs the education and upbringing of the children, particularly the boys: 'Let them enjoy their childhood', he writes in August 1918.[99] Meanwhile, Josefa Čundrlová manages the household with an increasingly steady hand, reporting to her husband as early as in June 1917: 'Everything is the same here, I'm managing things as we always did together, perhaps even better'. Her pride in her ability to overcome the difficulties in her new role is obvious, and it was a direct blow to her husband's ability to perform in a venue where it seemed he was no longer needed. Mrs Čundrlová's sigh that 'the kids need their dad' probably helped only to a certain degree.[100] Two years later, in the summer of 1919, Jan Čundrle was a member of the Czechoslovak Legion for more than a half a year and still looking for ways to get home. However, messages from his wife had indeed signalled that he would be coming back to a wholly different family from the one he left behind, where he had served as the 'head' and the breadwinner: 'Over time I've got used to doing everything by myself', Josefa Čundrlová wrote proudly in July. 'I can hardly think of any task that I'd be sharing with you … But here you are, and you are – *our everything!*'[101] While the reassurance of strong emotional attachment is still there, the self-confident young woman he was bound to find at home was a decidedly different person from the passive, caring housewife he had left in 1914. Because of the conflict between the military and domesticated forms of masculinity and the virtual inability to perform both effectively, he had lost a large amount of power and control, and possibly also his claim to hegemonic masculinity.

The fact that men understood the change that was happening in their 'home' venue very well is illustrated, for example, in the correspondence of Fráňa Šrámek with his wife, where the poet ironically calls her 'Mrs Changed'. Here, the use of irony seems to be a way of hiding his own insecurity arising from the perceived loss of control:

> How the iron era has changed you! I hope you have not become one of those serious women, God forbid! I hope you haven't made yourself an example of all the virtues? That would ... make me worried about coming home. I can imagine it, standing at the door reading a sign: 'Returnees from the field are to be advised of our radical change. Please make yourselves comfortable with it!'[102]

The very need for such a defence mechanism implies that despite Šrámek's proclaimed understanding later on, it was not easy for him to admit his own inability to control one of the key venues of masculine performance.

If the claim that war brought two separate venues of masculinity into an insoluble conflict is true, then wartime correspondence may well be a narrow bridge that connected those two venues and at least enabled their coexistence. Besides that, *Urlaub* (furlough) was another way that made the arrangement work at least partially. Understandably, this is a favourite theme in the vast majority of the soldiers' accounts. While mail is usually represented as an object of hope in an everyday context, leave fulfilled a similar function when it came to weeks, months or even years. In the same way, the periodicity of incoming mail was one of the basic timeframes in a soldier's life, and the same is even more true when it comes to leave – for example, many diaries are not structured around the traditional framework of a calendar, but rather around the author's periods of leave, with many soldiers skipping their 'diary duty' when they were at home. Using a metaphor, it may be said that the planet soldiers inhabited did not rotate around the sun, but around leave permits. 'Everyone is talking about leave', Josef Slezák wrote in the summer of 1918. 'It is our only hope'.[103] Augustin Mudrák was 'unbelievably happy' when, in the autumn of 1916, he was told that the men like him who had not yet been on leave since the beginning of the war would be allowed to 'start one the next morning by boarding a train. The night feels endless, I can hardly wait'.[104] Based on the personal accounts available, long periods without leave were quite frequent, particularly during the first half of the war, and had an obviously negative effect on the soldiers' morale and motivation: 'To be away from home for such a long time is just too horrible. It feels like a punishment. I have requested leave three times already, but it's not possible to get one, it's worse than jail. Twelve months in the field and no *Urlaub* in sight!'[105] Complaints such as this are easily found in almost every source, but the situation

Figure 5.3 'Auf Urlaub!' ('On Leave!') A propaganda image of the military hero's homecoming, promising the men to maintain or even improve their position in the gender order (Regional Museum in Olomouc).

in the Austro-Hungarian army never reached the seriousness of the crisis in the French army in the summer of 1917, when the disastrous Nivelle Offensive gave the final impetus to a 'mutiny' of sorts among the frontline troops, where the main complaint of the 'mutineers' revolved around the injustices in the leave distribution system.[106]

For many soldiers, the primary function of leave was not only to re-establish ties with loved ones in person, but also to return or at least come as close as possible to what they imagined, idealized and cherished as the notion of 'normalcy'. Taken from the point of view of basic existence, it is usually represented by things such as a clean, soft bed, clean underwear, undisturbed sleep, a bath or basic comfort in general, i.e. things that were in decidedly short supply at the front and immediately behind the front. 'My greatest wish was to get leave to Prague, have a good bath, have a good meal, dress nicely and see my loved ones', Egon Erwin Kisch noted in his diary in October 1914.[107] In the same way, Jan Tříska starts every one of his leaves in Vienna with a trip to a barber, then to a laundry, only after which he 'could hug my dear Božena' and 'live once again like a human being!'[108] This almost ritual cleansing off of the dirt, blood and 'war paint' (uniform) was a rather typical way to start a leave, it seems.

'Becoming human again' was actually a gendered process par excellence, as it returned the individual back to his civilized, traditionally manly form. Later on, he could start to re-adopt those behavioural patterns that would support this change and therefore also his masculine identity. Being home was the best moment for soldiers to try to re-establish the gender order in their household, reacquiring power and control over its inner as well as outer goings-on, and at least for a while performing their domesticated masculinity. Their momentous return to the 'manly tasks', the roles that had been taken over by women while they were in the army, in a situation where their sense of masculinity was constantly under threat and they felt almost feminized by war, represented a sort of escape back to the known – the prewar, 'normal' gender order, where everything was as it should be. Leave was a way to reconcile the venues of war and home for a moment, to 'repair' the broken hegemonic masculinity. According to many soldiers' accounts, men often spent their leave doing whatever had made them 'domesticated men' in peacetime – they did the hard work,[109] worked in the fields,[110] repaired houses, took over the family business for a while (if it was still in business) or re-established their authority in general. They also fulfilled their marital sexual 'duties'. František Mikulášek recalled his comrades' stories told on a train that took them back to the front in late 1917:

> When their work was done, they went to the little stream, sat in the shadow of a tree, and, wow – that was a ride! It's like the first weeks after the wedding, or even like when one was standing in a girl's room for the first time, or making out in a passageway. The blood is boiling and you feel – no wonder – that you're twenty again and this is your first time with a girl!

Using the same example, with the same group of narrators sharing their stories to kill time, one of the men reports how he 'ploughed the field and sowed it', another 'repaired a roof', another one 'was helping his wife at home and went to an exam with his son' and the others mostly 'spent their leave with toil and hard work', i.e. all of them were more or less performing their 'normal' masculine roles at home.[111]

This performance was made up not only of the role of a husband (and the sexual, economic and power responsibilities it entailed), but also of the role of a father. Fatherhood was always, to a certain extent, an 'invisible' but important part of modern masculinity, and in the case of Czech soldiers of the First World War, it was no different.[112] Their accounts are often filled with touching images of parental love towards – because of the age of the men – babies and young children. Almost endemic is their acute sensibility to fatherhood in connection with death and dying. František Šmída, himself childless, was shocked by the death of a popular *Hauptmann* during a training exercise and had nightmares for several weeks where the man's 'six orphans' played the main role: 'I saw a sad orphan looking for his dad … with a picture in his tiny hand. Then came another one, and another, and suddenly I was surrounded by a drove of crying orphans, pleading with me in a terribly sad and moving way. I always woke up drenched in sweat and horrified'.[113] Reflecting on his own role as a father of two, Josef Klejna was depressed by the sight of bodies near the Serbian border in 1914: 'It was a long row, healthy and good men just a few days ago, many of them had left a wife and children back home'.[114] František Černý even observed that, in his opinion, fatherhood entailed an increased risk at the front: 'Every time someone gets hit, it's a guy who is a father of four to eight back in Bohemia'.[115] The conflict between being a good father and a good soldier was obvious from the first days of the war: 'Tomorrow in the morning, I have to say goodbye to you my dear children, and to go fight against Serbia', Josef Klejna starts his 'diary of a father', dedicated to his children. 'Please pray for me so I may come back uninjured, and will be able to take care of you once again'.[116]

Obeying the manly duty to serve makes it impossible to be a good father for Klejna, which is all the more painful as his wife had died in childbirth a few months before the war (and his baby son was about to die a month after he was conscripted). Václav Doleljší faced the same issue in his diary (again, one that is also dedicated to his children): 'My dear and beloved children, when will I see you again? If only I could see you, I am sure that it would stop me from going over [the top]'.[117] Many men tried to perform their role of fathers over distance, or at least tried to make up for their absence when they were home on leave, which further reflects the untold but ever-present importance of fatherhood for the men's morale – and the difficulty it faced over a long-term conflict. The anonymous soldier from the above-mentioned recollection, who 'went to an exam with his son', was in fact symbolically restoring his fatherhood and, with it, his masculinity that was damaged by wartime pressures. The negative consequences of distant fatherhood are – besides the issues of jealousy and marital fidelity – also one of the key themes in the novel *Vojáci císařovi* by Rudolf Vlasák, while vain efforts to restore paternal authority from a POW camp near Moscow are a staple in the communications between Jan Čundrle and his family.

Of course, the disruption of the bond between a father and his children was not limited to the simple dimension of eroded masculinity in the 'home' venue. It was palpably difficult in emotional terms, as it usually entailed painful feedback from the children themselves. The men's inability to do anything about it led them to doubt their masculinity and any possible 'dividend' the war may have brought, which was damaging to their motivation and morale. Letters such as the one received by Ferdinand Vařík from his anxious daughter in March 1915 were undoubtedly hard to read: 'Are you well yet? Just please, daddy, come back soon. I can hardly wait for you'.[118] Adolf Vraspír received a similar heart-wrenching plea from his children: 'Dear dad, we are always thinking of you, what you're doing, what will be … Dad, please, come home, we will take care of you ourselves. All the daddies are coming home, only you are not, and it makes us very sad. Bye, and see you soon'.[119] Jarka, the four-year-old nephew of Karel Vaněk, inadvertently touched on a raw nerve of the conflict between the disparate arenas of modern masculinity when he quickly changed his mind over his father's military service: 'He misbehaves, saying again and again that he cannot wait to have his dad back home', Vaněk's sister-in-law wrote in January 1915:

> During the mobilization, he was so happy that his 'dad is a soldier, he has a gun and eats out of a tin cup', but now he is sad that there's no one to tell him stories … At the beginning, he prayed every day for his daddy to come home, but it's impossible to make him do it now, he cries in protest. Says he's 'prayed enough already, and as daddy isn't coming, and the Lord doesn't listen, he won't ask no more'.[120]

The war-induced inability to perform masculinity properly at home was present on both a symbolic and emotional level of existence, but perhaps the most damning problem the war brought about was the issue of the material wellbeing of soldiers' families. We have already hinted at the problem of missing breadwinners on a symbolic level, but within the context of the gradually crumbling war economy of Austria-Hungary, it tended to have dire consequences, upon which men often reflected in their accounts. While the men tried to re-establish their presence at home during their brief spells of leave, they could not possibly make up for the fact that their families had missed their economic output year in, year out. When the situation in the Cisleithanian hinterland started to deteriorate, many families quickly lost their economic ground. By 1917, those of a lower- and even middle-class background without their own means of subsistence (i.e. living in the cities and towns) were suffering from near-starvation, as daily rations, when available, were getting more meagre by the day – only 230–300 grams of bread for workers by the end of the year.[121] As a result, starvation, cold due to massive shortages of coal and wood, and scarcity of most goods of everyday consumption became a defining trait of experiencing the latter stages of the First World War in the Bohemian lands. Bohemia itself, being the most industrialized and urbanized of the imperial lands besides Lower Austria, was hit particularly hard, but the situation was bad in the rural areas as well, suffering from the ever-increasing requirements of the state agencies responsible for keeping the supply system from collapsing altogether.

Men were able to perceive the problems their families faced through correspondence, the inability of their relatives to send any 'packages' as they usually did in the first months of the war and, ultimately, through leave. This was a particularly depressing experience late in the war and, combined with the army's apparent tendency to distribute leave more often in order to sustain morale in 1917 and 1918, it was a double-edged sword in terms of soldiers' motivation. As František Pavel remembered after the war in September 1918, 'the frontlines suffered from a lack of supplies, but back here, in the hinterland … there was just nothing'.[122]

Many saw Vienna as a measure of social and economic decline, as after the de facto armistice and peace in the East, most military transports to and from

Bohemia and Moravia had to pass through the capital. 'The city did not look very nice, the general shortage of everything was blatantly obvious', František Šmída noted when passing through in July 1918.[123] However, coming home was no better. As early as February 1917, Jaroslav Vítek described his arrival in Česká Skalice as a depressing experience: 'Česká Skalice is a sad place now. Anxiety and poverty is all around. The children are weak, the women are worried'.[124] In such a situation, coming home may have turned into a harrowing experience that only further reminded the men of their inability to take care of their families:

> How sad is the chapter of the diary I am forced to write! It deals with the destitution and suffering of those I love the most. I do not care much about the horrible sufferings of life in war, when a man has to withstand things that no animal would. A soldier would quietly lower his back, wipe the sweat from his face, curse a bit, and even withstand a beating from time to time, if only he knew that his loved ones had no idea and did not have to suffer and starve themselves. But if he comes home and instead of happy, rosy-cheeked children and a healthy-looking, happy wife, he finds there skinny, hungry shadows and a worn-out, tormented, worried woman with eyes blood-red from constant crying, it hurts, it hurts so damn much … People should try and empathize with the state of mind of such a man, a father of a family, who has spent a year and a half in a far-away land, seen all the horrors of battle, and now, when he comes home, he sees he was not the only one suffering and that even the little ones, who have never hurt anyone or done anything wrong, are suffering as well.[125]

The feeling that his masculinity is being degraded at the front is something the author is willing to accept. However, the fact that he sees it subverted in his home is almost too much for him. The only possible outcome of this perceived inability to resolve the conflict was deep disillusion and demoralization, with sustaining motivation decreasing with every piece of news from home. National identity and ethnicity is hardly mentioned in this context, and probably did not matter, as the problem crossed language barriers. 'He curses everything military. Where is that fighting spirit, so typical of the Germans?', Alois Dolejší asks in his diary, describing a dialogue he had with a German-speaking 'Corporal Šulc from Vienna' on a train taking them both back to the front. In his own words, Šulc was cutting his leave short, returning to his unit in order not to 'eat out his family' by staying with them. 'Hunger and poverty are destroying everything' was his final judgement.[126] He was not alone, as many soldiers' accounts reflect the same sentiment. In the words of another soldier travelling to the front: 'Here it's bad … But when you see your wife and kids toil away in vain and starve, you see them drink ground acorns instead of coffee, eat ground reeds instead of flour, use reeking dirt instead of gravy, you get so angry that you would punch just about anyone in sight'.[127]

The slowly disintegrating Austro-Hungarian war economy did not pose merely the problem of feeding the armies; from mid 1917 at the latest, these armies, while often on the brink of starvation, were supported more or less to the detriment of the civilian population – be it the Italian population between the Isonzo and the Piave after the successful breakthrough at Caporetto in November 1917 or the population of Cisleithania proper, where the situation particularly in the cities was nearing disastrous levels, feeding both revolutionary ideas and fears of them.[128] The Army High Command was very well aware of the fact that this issue was hurting the troops' morale in a particularly sensitive way, but was unable to do much about it: 'Morale is being damaged … especially by the conditions in the hinterland' read a report of a staff officer inspecting the XX Corps of the 10th Army in September 1918. 'Again and again one hears complaints among the officers or in the ranks about the total disorganization of the hinterland and the inability of the government to remedy the economic and political misery'.[129] The beleaguered manliness of Austro-Hungarian soldiers was being struck at in such a way that many men started to see the situation as an impossible choice between various venues of masculinity, as well as between various competing loyalties. Consequently, thousands of them became susceptible not only to political radicalization, either socialist or nationalist, but also to an outright desire to 'get out' and preserve themselves for the future (their own or that of their families) in the ever-growing ranks of deserters, the 'green cadres' operating throughout the hinterland.[130] And even those whose motivation sustained them enough to stay in the ranks were becoming thoroughly demoralized by their dilemma, as in their eyes, monarchy lost all its legitimacy through economic incompetence that was all too obvious and that encroached upon their families more and more each day.

Home as a symbolic as well as a real space played a key role in the way in which Czech soldiers understood, structured and experienced their wartime service. Without it, they would probably not be able to survive the war emotionally. Their experience more or less revolved around the idealized notion of home and nostalgia for it, as well as around the way in which they perceived the difference between this ideal and the reality. Czech soldiers' personal accounts confirm that there was indeed no 'chasm' of misunderstanding between the 'home front' and the men in the trenches. Both sides repeatedly encountered communication barriers, with civilians (often women) having difficulties or lacking the willingness to disclose the nature of change at home, and men lacking the language or the willingness to describe the horrors of modern warfare. However, it is obvious that the emotional survival of the troops, as well as their loved ones, depended to a large extent on their ability to cross these barriers and reach the 'others'. Through mail or through infrequent leave soldiers were able to draw important, gender-safe support more easily and with less experimenting than from the construct of wartime comradeship, as there was a much clearer agreement on its proper gender coding, which was closely related to the notion of normalcy. The sense of normalcy was closely related to the notion of home as one of the key venues of masculinity. Manliness, which is a highly performative construct based on active enactment of control and power, was supposed to rule this venue or support it in several important areas, which laid claim to the hegemonic masculine status of the given individual.

Subverting the men's ability to enact power and control meant a direct threat to their sense of manliness, which led many men to attempt to assert this manliness even over distance, through their letters or in person during the short periods they spent at home on leave. These efforts were directed towards either re-establishing normalcy or at least creating the semblance of it.[131] They were often less than successful – women's sexual discipline and children's upbringing were areas where failure was frequent, and the men's fears of disintegration of the patriarchy consequently increased. A female author committed this contemporary nightmare to paper after the war when she wrote with much flair and oversimplification:

> Women were getting social support for their husbands and sons who went to war. There is a lot of money among the people. When the cruel moment of farewell was forgotten and the welfare check arrived, many faces lit up, particularly with the man far, far away. As one woman noted to another on the street: 'If I'd only known that I'd be getting so much for that bastard, I wouldn't have sold the pig'. Some women even have no idea what to do with so much money and so much freedom. Their farms make a good living, and the money is for them to spend … There were also others, we have heard about them even out here in the country, who were spending their welfare money with soldiers in pubs in Kroměříž [Kremsier], singing a sort of a wartime anthem: 'God preserve, God protect / Our welfare and the war / Better than those beasts of ours / Is all the money in the world'.[132]

In this rather typical warning against too much change in the gender order, which invariably ends up in debauchery and anarchy, the author, at the end, goes on to assure the reader that most women actually behaved respectably during the war, i.e. fulfilled their roles as good wives and mothers. Presumably it was the women of the city and the town who got dangerously out of control because of the war and war policies, while the women in the countryside remained 'proper'. This conservative warning against too much feminine freedom aptly reflects Maureen Healy's conclusion about postwar Austria, where large segments of society harboured fears of 'brutalized', violent soldiers coming home, while many of the soldiers saw the 'fatherless society' they found at home as 'unleashed', and thought it necessary to restore control (and their power) quickly.[133] It seems that Czech society was no different, which further supports our claim that Czech men experienced the same feelings of danger and insecurity when it came to wartime social developments.

Consequently, the home venue of masculinity was just another social space where soldiers' masculinity was gradually degraded and compromised, turning them from active players into passive observers at best. It is also here where the process is perhaps the most obvious, defined by the dilemma of impossible options – being a soldier and a warrior, as the official wartime discourse that men initially accepted had required, or being a husband, a breadwinner, a father. We may well assume that this was perhaps the most depressing dilemma that men, and not just Czechs, faced during the war. In their specific case, though, it may well have led to a willingness to accept anything that seemed even remotely hopeful in terms of ending the conflict and getting them home, where they would 'just live with my family' and restore their manliness on the most basic level.[134] Desertion might have been one such solution, albeit a rather desperate one. Statistics show a close correlation between the economic situation in the hinterland and the desertion rate in the Austro-Hungarian army, which reached the debilitating level of almost a quarter of a million men being absent without leave at one time in mid 1918.[135] A safer and much harder to quantify way involved one's own body as the ultimate tool: 'If only I got that lucky hit, so I could get back to you', an unknown soldier wrote to Ludmila Vaňková in December 1915.[136] A friend of her namesake Karel Vaněk tried to share a similar plan with him in May of that year, with the same motivation – home: 'I will not stand this for long. I'll put one in myself at the first possible instance, well enough so that they cannot send me back, and I will be with my wife. She will love me even with a limp'.[137] And in his diary, Josef Slezák too always cited the hard-to-control desire to live, eat well and be close to home as the primary motives for the three times he supposedly shot himself during the war.[138]

Notes

1. Siegfried Sassoon, 'Their Frailty', in *The War Poems* (London, 1983), 90. First published in the *Cambridge Magazine*, 8 December 1917.
2. Marie Zemanová to Pavel Zeman, 9 April 1918, The Zeman Letters, Vlastivědné muzeum v Olomouci, sbírka 'Novodobé dějiny – Odboj', acquisition number 67/2016.
3. For the way in which prewar education shaped the style and basic framework of wartime correspondence, see the analysis by Martha Hanna, 'A Republic of Letters: The Epistolary Tradition in France during World War I', *American Historical Review* 108, no. 5 (2003): 1338–61; or by Andreea Dancila, 'Les lettres privées publiques: Un genre épistolaire ambigu des Roumains de Transylvanie dans la Première Guerre mondiale', *Revue des Études Slaves* 88, no. 4 (2017): 743–56.
4. For the First World War as the birthplace of 'modern consciousness', see Modris Eksteins, *Rites of Spring: The Great War and the Birth of the Modern Age* (London, 1989). See also Paul Fussell, *The Great War and Modern Memory* (London, 1975); Samuel Hynes, *A War Imagined: The First World War and English Culture* (London, 1992); George L. Mosse, *Fallen Soldiers: Reshaping the Memory of the World Wars* (Oxford, 1990).
5. Roper, *The Secret Battle*, particularly 6–8; Jessica Meyer, *Men of War: Masculinity and the First World War in Britain* (London, 2009); and Healy, *Vienna and the Fall of the Habsburg Empire*. For similar criticism, see also Bourke, *Dismembering the Male*, 21;

Stéphane Audoin-Rouzeau and Annette Becker, *1914–1918: Understanding the Great War* (London, 2002), 35–36; or Michael Roper, 'Maternal Relations: Moral Manliness and Emotional Survival in Letters Home during the First World War', in *Masculinities in Politics and War*, 296. On the other hand, Frederic Rousseau argues that a certain barrier and mutual inability to understand indeed existed between the front and the rear. See Rousseau, *La guerre censurée*, 261–63.

6. Carol Acton, *Grief in Wartime: Private Pain, Public Discourse* (Basingstoke, 2007), 114.
7. Ziemann, *War Experiences in Rural Germany*, 117–18; Audoin-Rouzeau, *Men at War*, 128.
8. Hämmerle, *Heimat/Front*, 55–84.
9. For example, Stéphane Audoin-Rouzeau pointed to an interesting contrast between specific and abstract images of the home front in two chapters of his book, entitled 'The Hated Home Front' and 'The Fascination of the Home Front', respectively. While in the former he described a generally negative image of the abstract 'rear' (represented by the press and other stereotypes such as noncombatants or rear-echelon troops), in the latter he analysed the positive view trench newspapers usually held of specific individuals at home, particularly those known to the men in person (mothers, fathers, siblings, friends). The 'rear' was therefore a generalized stereotype, while 'home' (situated in the rear, of course) was a place of hope. See Audoin-Rouzau, *Men at War*, 92–154.
10. Bouška, 'Zápisky ze světové války', 4, diary entry from 9 August 1914.
11. Letter from August 30, 1915, quoted in Dagmar Blümlová, '"… Ale vojna je tak úžasná věc, že ztraví celého člověka": Velká válka v životě a díle jazykovědce Františka Jílka-Oberfalcera', in *Armáda, společnost a první světová válka: Sborník příspěvků z vědecké konference konané v Jihočeském muzeu v Českých Budějovicích dne 8. listopadu 2002* (České Budějovice, 2003), 14.
12. Neumann, *Bragožda*, 37.
13. Vítek, *V cizích službách*, 200.
14. Tables in Appendix I in Alexander Watson's seminal work on soldiers' morale also point to the importance of 'home' for the men's emotional survival. See Watson, *Enduring the Great War*, 236–37.
15. František Šmída's diary entry from 1 March 1917, written in Posiecz, Poland. Transcribed in Šmída, *Vzpomínky z vojny*, 79.
16. Sýkora, 'Tarnavka – Obrázek ze světové války', 8.
17. Slezák, *Paměti Josefa Slezáka k I. světové válce*, vol. 5, 37.
18. Ibid., vol 1, 33.
19. Morávek, *Špatný voják*, 151.
20. Slezák, *Paměti Josefa Slezáka k I. světové válce*, vol. 1, 45; Mudrák, *Bojoval jsem za císaře pána*, 89.
21. Klejna, *Voják – zajatec – legionář*, 43, diary entry from 13 September 1914.
22. Ibid., 54.
23. Poláček, *Zápisky Václava Poláčka ze světové války*, 47.
24. Černý, *Moje záznamy ze světové války*, 68.
25. Šindelář, *Proti vlastní vůli*, 154.
26. Kisch, *Vojákem pražského sboru*, 32, diary entry from 13 August 1914.
27. Sperling, *Český důstojník na frontách monarchie*, 27, diary entry from 14 June 1916.
28. Hála, 'Vzpomínka na 11. sočskou bitvu', 59–60.
29. Mudrák, *Bojoval jsem za císaře pána*, 59.

30. Christa Hämmerle, '"You Let a Weeping Woman Call You Home?" Private Correspondences during the First World War in Austria and Germany', in *Epistolary Selves*, 153, emphasis in original.
31. 'Write me often and send newspapers', written by František Škoda to his wife on 26 September 1914, represents a typical example. *Zapomenuté hlasy*, 91.
32. Jan Šmatlán to his parents, 19 December 1914, in *Zapomenuté hlasy*, 18. This is confirmed, for example, by Fráňa Šrámek in a letter to his wife, written on 14 August 1915: 'You make me so happy through the letters you send me'. Fráňa Šrámek, *Listy z vojny: Výbor z korespondence 1915–1918* (Prague, 1956), 6.
33. František Šrámek to his daughter Marie, not dated (probably late 1917), in *Když naši dědové bojovali a umírali*, 29. Fráňa Šrámek's correspondence with his wife, or Jan Čundrle's with family, contain further evidence of the same (see the Jan Čundrle Papers, currently in the Čundrle Family Private Collection).
34. On the importance of mail in a soldier's life, see Roper, *The Secret Battle*, 5–6; see also Holmes, *Acts of War*, 88–89. Frederic Rousseau described correspondence as 'a vital life-line between two worlds'. See Rousseau, *La guerre censurée*, 39.
35. František Petržíla's diary, 21 August 1914, in *Zapomenuté hlasy*, 55.
36. Květoň, *Vzpomínky z první světové války*, 16.
37. Sperling, *Český důstojník na frontách monarchie*, 27, diary entry from 14 June 1916; Morávek, *Špatný voják*, 130.
38. Mudrák, *Bojoval jsem za císaře pána*, 39.
39. František Šmída's diary entry from 4 March 1917, in Posiecz, transcription in Šmída, *Vzpomínky z vojny*, 83.
40. Ibid.
41. Slezák, *Paměti Josefa Slezáka k I. světové válce*, vol. 4, 31.
42. See Frederic Patka, 'Auch das war die Feldpost. Episoden aus dem dienstlichen Alltag der k.u.k. Feldpost 1914–1918', in *Studien und Dokumente zur Österreichisch-Ungarischen Feldpost im Ersten Weltkrieg*, eds Joachim Gatterer and Walter Lukan (Vienna, 1989), 55–75; see also Paul Höger, 'Das Post- und Telegrafenwesen im Weltkrieg', in *Studien und Dokumente zur Österreichisch-Ungarischen Feldpost*, 43–48.
43. For a short summary on the workings of the k.u.k. military mail service, see Hämmerle, '"You Let a Weeping Woman Call You Home?"', 153–54.
44. Ibid., 154–56.
45. Kisch, *Vojákem pražského sboru*, 25, diary entry from 10 August 1914.
46. For details on wartime censorship in Austria-Hungary, see Gustav Spann, 'Zensur in Österreich während des 1. Welt Krieges 1914–1918' (Ph.D. dissertation, Vienna: University of Vienna, 1972); see also Bernd Ulrich, 'Feldpostbriefe im Ersten Weltkrieg – Bedeutung und Zensur', in *Die Rekonstruktion des Kriegsalltags als Aufgabe der historischen Forschung und der Friedenserziehung*, ed. Peter Knoch (Stuttgart, 1989). On the specifics regarding POWs, see Rachamimov, *POWs and the Great War*, 135–60; for an example of using collections of the censorship office for a thorough research of attitudes expressed in soldiers' letters, see Hanák, 'Die Volksmeinung während des letzten Kriegsjahres in Österreich-Ungarn', 58–66.
47. Jan Janošík to his parents, 3 September 1914.
48. *Listy našich vojáků*, vol. 3, 30.
49. See Hämmerle, '"You Let a Weeping Woman Call You Home?"', 156; also see Hämmerle, *Heimat/Front*, 56–58.

50. For 'gender coding' of *Liebesgaben*, see Hämmerle, '"You Let a Weeping Woman Call You Home?"', 142–47. For the image of the same in German-written Austrian newspapers and with German-speaking soldiers, see ibid., 148–59.
51. Diary of Bohuš Adamíra, entry from 25 December 1915, in *Když naši dědové bojovali a umírali*, 66.
52. 'Karel Suchý of the military railways' to his wife Hana, 24 December 1915, in *Zapomenuté hlasy*, 100.
53. Kisch, *Vojákem pražského sboru*, 181, diary entry from 27 November 1914.
54. František Loubal, 'V Haliči po průlomu u Gorlice r. 1915', in *Domov za války*, vol. 2, 393.
55. Roper, *The Secret Battle*, 6, 24–25, 45–118. See also Roper, 'Maternal Relations', passim.
56. Václavek to his mother, 6 and 8 March 1917, quoted in Kábová, *Bolestná cesta od věřícího mládí k přijetí zkonkrétněného světa*, 33, footnote 28.
57. Quoted in Taudyová, 'Válečná milostná korespondence Jaroslava Havlíčka', 102.
58. For quotes, see Šindelář, *Proti vlastní vůli*, 45 and 125; Tříska, ed., *Zapomenutá fronta*, 96; and Ulrych, 'Moje zápisky', 40; and also many others.
59. Šmída, *Vzpomínky z vojny*, 16.
60. Kápar, *Cestou kamenitou*, 25.
61. Ibid. Similarly, for Ferdinand Lirš, the father is the one who is supposed to be comforting a crying mother. See Lirš, *S Osmadvacátníky za světové války*, 14. Interestingly, though, images of fathers are surprisingly rare in most soldiers' accounts, and it seems that Michael Roper's thesis on generally 'absent' fathers also fits the Czech case. According to Roper's estimate, for example, only about 8% of surviving British soldiers' correspondence comprise letters to or from fathers, which roughly corresponds with the modest sample used here (Roper, *The Secret Battle*, 60). As an explanation, Roper offers the plausible thesis that this situation does not necessarily reflect emotionally inadequate relationships between soldiers and their fathers, but rather the fact that letter-writing as well as keeping a journal or a diary were traditionally understood to be *feminine* forms of communication, based on behaviour culturally defined as *feminine* – introspection, verbosity, ability to express emotions (for the letter as a form of communication coded as feminine, see, for example, Steedman, 'A Woman Writing a Letter', 111–33). On the other hand, the father–son relationship (or any other relationship between men reflecting modern Western masculinity) is traditionally much less verbose and is rather oriented towards joint activity (work, sport, entertainment), which makes for a difficult transposition into the textual form of a letter or a diary entry. To pick a representative example from our sources, we may look at the diary of Josef Ulrych, who often mentions his 'mum', while his 'dad' is to be found only once in the whole diary (Ulrych, 'Moje zápisky', 74), except the moment when Ulrych learns and reacts to his death (at 85 and 91). His reaction is therefore surprising, at least within the context of the diary, as he is utterly devastated ('Oh, what a horrible misfortune!'), and it forms the basis for his subsequent depression and disillusionment. Ulrych obviously loves his father; he just does not mention him in his diary, even at the very beginning when the author leaves home for war – Ulrych pictures the moment in a thoroughly gendered way, and the family is represented here only by the crying mother (at 25–27). However, in the way in which he pictures his father, he is more than typical, proving the validity of Roper's argument even outside of Great Britain.
62. Rudolf Wagner to his father, 21 June 1916, in *Zapomenuté hlasy*, 103–4.

63. Emil Marek to Josef Marek, 5 July 1916, ibid., 104.
64. Anonymous, 15 April 1916, ibid., 102.
65. Jan Kudrnáč to his wife, 8 April 1916, and Antonín Kyšperský to his wife, 23 August 1917, both ibid., 102 and 109. For 'I am well', see Adolf Vraspír to his wife, 25 April 1918, Adolf Vraspír papers, private collection of Dr Eva Horová.
66. 20 April 1918, in Šrámek, *Listy z vojny*, 165.
67. See Jan Janošík diary, in Jan Janošík papers.
68. Egon Erwin Kisch in a letter to his mother, 30 August 1914, in Kisch, *Vojákem pražského sboru*, 67.
69. Antonín Kyšperský to his wife, 25 August 1917, in *Zapomenuté hlasy*, 104.
70. Jan Kotrba to Bedřich Václavek, 6 August 1916, quoted in Kábová, *Bolestná cesta od věřícího mládí k přijetí zkonkrétněného světa*, 42, footnote 54.
71. Lirš, *S Osmadvacátníky za světové války*, 135.
72. Kisch, *Vojákem pražského sboru*, 10–11, diary entry from 1 August 1914.
73. Ladislav Rezek to Marie Šrámková, 17 August 1916, in *Když naši dědové bojovali a umírali*, 30.
74. The war experience has been defined in several recent works as a process of a more or less desperate search for lost intimacy with parents, spouses and children. See Roper, *The Secret Battle*, 33; Michael Roper, *Maternal Relations: Moral Manliness and Emotional Survival in Letters Home during the First World War*; also Michael Roper, 'Slipping out of View: Subjectivity and Emotion in Gender History', *History Workshop Journal* 59, no. 1 (2005): 57–73; or Crouthamel, *An Intimate History of the Front*, 2–4.
75. Tosh, 'What Should Historians Do with Masculinity?', 184–87.
76. Sonya O. Rose, 'Fit to Fight but Not to Vote? Masculinity and, Citizenship in Britain, 1832–1918', in *Representing Masculinity*, 132.
77. Deborah Harrison, 'Violence in the Military Community', in *Military Masculinities*, 79.
78. See Rudolf Vlasák, *Vojáci císařovi* (Prague, 1932).
79. Rélink, *28. pluk 'Pražské děti'*, 256.
80. Slezák, *Paměti Josefa Slezáka k I. světové válce*, vol. 1, at 2, 8, 12 and 14.
81. Ibid., 48.
82. Ibid., vol. 2, 82.
83. Ibid., vol. 3, 92.
84. Ibid., vol. 5, 123.
85. Jan Horálek to his mother, 12 May 1916, in *Zapomenuté hlasy*, 103.
86. Vítek, *V cizích službách*, 210.
87. It is worth noting that, as can be seen above, men usually employed decidedly double-standard thinking when discussing sexuality. For example, while they often discussed, albeit indirectly, their sexual exploits in Hungary, they feared and at the same time despised the same behaviour in women back home. Jaroslav Vítek's story quoted here continues with another soldier's monologue, describing how 'something similar happened to him' when he came home unexpectedly on leave to find his wife in bed with a local hotel owner. The story ends with the narrator's summary: 'I did not speak to my wife, did not say goodbye, and went to my ex-girlfriend in Mladá Boleslav, where I spent the rest of my leave'. Vítek, *V cizích službách*, 212.
88. Slezák, *Paměti Josefa Slezáka k I. světové válce*, vol. 1, 3.
89. Kylar, 'Vzpomínky z vojny', 34.
90. In his study of the Bohemian Crown Lands during the war, Ivan Šedivý wrote that

the first crisis hit the rural areas of the country as early as 1915. However, most of the personal accounts used here suggest that a serious lack of supplies (i.e. the moment when there were not enough foodstuffs even for the producers themselves) did not appear for the first time until 1916. Yet, judging the specific impact of the ever more intensive requisitioning of the life of individual producers is extremely difficult, as it greatly depended on their ability to hide parts of production and to trade on the black market. See Šedivý, *Češi, České země a Velká válka*, 233–36. For personal accounts, see, for example, Slezák, *Paměti Josefa Slezáka k I. světové válce*, vol. 3, 77 and 87. On page 102 of the same volume of his diary, there is a typical example of the difference between the producers and the rest of society later in the war. The author is, according to his notes at least, able to stay in a convalescent centre in Česká Lípa for a long time because he bribes the commanding officer with some flour for his family. According to this story, in the summer of 1917 flour was a rare commodity even for a k.u.k. *Oberleutnant*, while Slezák, coming from a farming background, was still able to trade it freely for favours. For other similar examples, see Bohuslav Brožek, 'Bouřnými dny', in *Domov za války*, vol. 3, 129–41; František Jaroš, 'Na dovolené', ibid., vol. 4, 228–32; Karel Vyhlídal, 'Kus tragedie českého učitele za války', ibid., 280–84; or Venda M. Gajová, 'Z mého zápisníku', ibid., 210–19.
91. Josef Zeman to Martin Zeman, 1 August 1917, in *Zapomenuté hlasy*, 108.
92. Slezák, *Paměti Josefa Slezáka k I. světové válce*, vol. 5, 66.
93. Jan Čundrle to his wife, 19 May 1918.
94. Marie Janošíková to Jan Janošík, 16 March 1916.
95. Fráňa Šrámek to his wife, 6 November 1915, in Šrámek, *Listy z vojny*, 13.
96. Tříska, ed., *Zapomenutá fronta*, 34, 76, 110 and 114.
97. For a similar example from an Austrian middle-class setting, with slightly different dynamics, see the analysis of a large collection of wartime correspondence between Christl Lange and Leopold Wolf by Christa Hämmerle: Hämmerle, '"You Let a Weeping Woman Call You Home?"', 157–75; for another analysis of a couple's correspondence in wartime Austria, see Ines Rebhan-Glück, '"Wenn wir nur glücklich wieder beisammen wären…" Der Krieg, der Frieden und die Liebe am Beispiel der Feldpostkorrespondenz von Mathilde und Ottokar Hanzel (1917/18)' (Master's thesis, Vienna: University of Vienna, 2010).
98. Poláček, *Zápisky Václava Poláčka ze světové války*, 77.
99. Jan Čundrle to his father-in-law, 18 August 1918, Jan Čundrle Papers, Čundrle family private collection.
100. Josefa Čundrlová to her husband, 20 June 1917, ibid.
101. Josefa Čundrlová to her husband, 19 July 1919, ibid.
102. Fráňa Šrámek to his wife, 9 December 1915, in Šrámek, *Listy z vojny*, 16; for the 'Mrs. Changed' letter, see Šrámek to his wife, 24 December 1915, ibid., 20.
103. Slezák, *Paměti Josefa Slezáka k I. světové válce*, vol. 5, 79.
104. Mudrák, *Bojoval jsem za císaře pána*, 52.
105. Jan Horálek to his mother, Františka Horálková, 12 May 1916, in *Zapomenuté hlasy*, 102. While it may seem surprising, home leave may well have been dangerous. During those two or three weeks, they tended to lose focus as well as many of the habits needed to survive in the trenches (for example, the life-and-death ability to judge where an incoming shell would land according to the sound it made), and their minds were usually slow to adjust when coming back to the life-threatening environment of the front. 'One month

after returning here, and I'm still back home in my mind', Josef Janošík wrote in his diary on 21 July 1918. The promise of getting leave was also dangerous: 'I am really nervous and itchy', Jaroslav Vítek wrote before Christmas in 1917. 'I am thinking of Bohemia, of home, of my friends there ... I do not care about anything, even the mines that the Italians are throwing at us' (Vítek, *V cizích službách*, 193). As František Skála noted: 'I knew many cases of people who were wounded or killed after returning from leave. The intensity of thoughts and recollections made them absent-minded, which made them less alert. The consequences were dire' (Skála, *Válečný deník*, 236). For some particular examples, see ibid., 101; or Šindelář, *Proti vlastní vůli*, 184. Thus, while leave could have improved a soldier's motivation to remain in the service in the long term, it may have been damaging to his combat-effectiveness or even survival in the short term.

106. On the 'French mutinies' of 1917, see, for example, André Loez, *14–18: Les rufus de la guerre. Une histoire des mutins* (Paris, 2010); see also Leonard V. Smith, '"War and Politics": The French Army Mutinies of 1917', *War in History* 2, no. 2 (1995): 180–201; Denis Rolland, *La grève des tranchées* (Paris, 2005); André Loez and Nicolas Marlot, eds, *Obéir/désobéie. Les mutinieries de 1917 en perspective* (Paris, 2008).
107. Kisch, *Vojákem pražského sboru*, 138, diary entry from 24 October 1914.
108. Tříska, ed., *Zapomenutá fronta*, 52. 'Wash, de-louse, shave' was a motto of Jaroslav Vítek every time he came home on leave; see Vítek, *V cizích službách*, 195.
109. See, for example, the diary of Josef Slezák, including the periods of leave that followed an injury. He also frequently (and successfully) requested leave 'for sowing' in 1916 and 1917, which may have lasted up to six weeks and was designed to fulfil his 'head of the household' duty back at the family farm (and to support the weakened production of food crops). See Slezák, *Paměti Josefa Slezáka k I. světové válce*, passim.
110. See, for example, Tříska, ed., *Zapomenutá fronta*, 57, 74–77.
111. Fr. Mikulášek, 'Po druhé v Karpatech', in *Domov za války*, vol. 5, 187–88.
112. Regarding the concept of fatherhood in Czech-speaking middle-class society in Bohemia, see Jitka Kohoutová, 'Konstrukce otcovské identity v 19. století: aspekt otce-živitele v rodinách české intelektuální buržoazie', in *Konstrukce maskulinní identity v minulosti a současnosti*, 175. For a more general summary on fatherhood in the West, see Trev Lynn Broughton and Helen Rogers, *Gender and Fatherhood in the Nineteenth Century* (New York, 2007); Michael E. Lamb, ed., *The Father's Role: Cross-Cultural Perspectives* (Hillsdale, 1987), John Nash, 'Historical and Social Changes in the Perception of the Role of the Father', in *The Role of the Father in Child Development*, ed. Michael E. Lamb (4th edition, New York, 2004), 65–87; or Tosh, *A Man's Place*, 79–101.
113. Šmída, *Vzpomínky z vojny*, 71.
114. Klejna, *Voják – zajatec – legionář*, 51, diary entry from 2 November 1914.
115. Černý, *Moje záznamy ze světové války*, 88.
116. Klejna, *Voják – zajatec – legionář*, diary acknowledgements, 26 July 1914, 38.
117. Václav Doležal to his wife, Anna, inserted as a part of his diary. Not dated, probably around Christmas 1915. Private collection of Martin Čihák.
118. 'Mařka' in a letter to Ferdinand Vařík, 19 March 1915, in *Zapomenuté hlasy*, 95.
119. Letter to Adolf Vraspír, not signed, 27 September 1916. Private collection of Eva Horová.
120. Diary entry from 4 January 1915, in Vaněk, *Charašó pán, da?*, 26.
121. Rauchensteiner, *Der Tod des Doppeladlers*, 548. Compare with the situation and survival strategies of Slovak families during the war in Gabriela Dudeková, 'Strategie prežitia

v mimoriadnej situácii: Vplyv Velkej vojny na rodinu na území Slovenska', *Forum Historiae* 3, no. 1 (2009): 1–19.
122. František Pavel, 'Z Francie domů', in *Domov za války*, vol. 5, 528.
123. Šmída, *Vzpomínky z vojny*, 129. On the images of social decay men witnessed in Vienna late in the war, see also Šindelář, *Proti vlastní vůli*, 151–52; Vítek, *V cizích službách*, 199–200; Dolejší, *Válečné vzpomínky z první světové války vojína Dolejše*, 229; or Tříska, ed., *Zapomenutá fronta*, 75–77.
124. Vítek, *V cizích službách*, 208.
125. Jaroš, 'Na dovolené', in *Domov za války*, vol. 4, 228.
126. Dolejší, *Válečné vzpomínky z první světové války vojína Dolejše*, 230, diary entry from 25 July 1918.
127. Fr. Mikulášek, 'Po druhé v Karpatech', in *Domov za války*, vol. 5, 188.
128. For a general summary of the Austro-Hungarian war economy and its evolution during the war, see, for example, Juraj Křížek, 'Die Kriegswirtschaft und das Ende der Monarchie', in *Die Auflösung des Habsburgerreiches*, 43–52. On Bohemia and Moravia specifically, see Šedivý, *Češi, České země a Velké válka*, 244–69.
129. Quoted in Cornwall, 'Morale and Patriotism in the Austro-Hungarian Army, 1914–1918', 189.
130. For a general overview on this issue, see Plaschka, Haselsteiner and Suppan, *Innere Front*, 81–89. For specific examples of Slovak and Croatian troops, see Beneš, '"Zelené kádry" jako radikální alternativa pro venkov na západním Slovensku a ve středovýchodní Evropě 1917–1920', 21–30; and Bogumil Hrabak, *Dezerterstvo, Zeleni Kadar i prevratana anarhija u Jugoslavenskim zemljama 1914–1918* (Novi Sad, 1990). See also Rothenberg, *The Army of Francis Joseph*, 211, for the massive security issue these 'green cadres' have become for Austria-Hungary during the final year of the war. However, Austria-Hungary was not alone in this predicament – by the end of 1917, up to 100,000 Italian 'deserters and draft-dodgers were hiding in the interior of the country' from the ever-increasing brutality of both the war and the Italian war regime. See Mark Thompson, *The White War: Life and Death on the Italian Front, 1915–1919* (London, 2008), 275.
131. Alon Rachamimov identified the desire to establish some semblance of 'bourgeois normalcy' in the German POW cross-dressing practices. See Rachamimov, 'The Disruptive Comforts of Drag', 374.
132. Gajová, 'Z mého zápisníku', 211.
133. See Maureen Healy, 'Civilizing Soldier in Postwar Austria', in *Gender and War in Twentieth-Century Eastern Europe*, 47–69; see also Healy, *Vienna*, 258 ff. For a similar situation in France, see Mary Louise Roberts, *Civilization without Sexes: Reconstructing Gender in Postwar France, 1917–1927* (Chicago, 1994); for Great Britain, see Susan Kingsley Kent, *Making Peace: The Reconstruction of Gender in Interwar Britain* (Princeton, 1993).
134. Quoted in Klejna, *Voják – zajatec – legionář*, 4.
135. Lein, 'The Military Conduct of the Austro-Hungarian Czechs in the First World War', 542; see also Rauchensteiner, *Der Tod des Doppeladlers*, 546–51.
136. Anonymous letter addressed to Ludmila Vaňková, 27 December 1915, in *Zapomenuté hlasy*, 101.
137. Diary entry from 1 May 1915, in Vaněk, *Charašó pán, da?*, 66.
138. Slezák, *Paměti Josefa Slezáka k I. světové válce*, vol. 1, 80–88; vol. 2, 62; vol. 3, 77–80.

Chapter 6

MANLINESS UNDER FIRE
Combat and the Body

Then a big Turkish shell knocked me arse over head,
And when I woke up …
… well I wished I was dead.
Never knew there was worse things than dyin'.
—Eric Bogle, *And the Band Played Waltzing Matilda*[1]

Images of combat situations usually represent the climactic moments of soldiers' narratives, often balancing on the edge of the surreal: 'Shell after shell is coming. Exploding in the rocks around here gives them even more devastating power. Whatever is missed by the iron is hit by sharp-edged rocks.' Such was Jaroslav Vítek's description of a night counterattack on the Carso during the Eleventh Battle of the Isonzo in early September 1917:

> The lieutenant's *'Vorwärts!'* is heard and motivated by his revolver, we run forward … The night ceases to be night, as the frontline is alive with the blinding light of searchlights and flares, and machine-guns barking constantly. The night's long, I think it will never end. We get some chow at midnight, but then nothing for the rest of the day. The sun is beating down on our steel helmets, the thirst is unbelievable … Death reaps a good harvest … Evening – it's dark again, I hear the familiar cling-clang of marching troops … At midnight our guns start to pour heavy fire onto the Italian trenches. Shells are wreaking terrible havoc, one feels really uneasy. I would be happy to disappear into the ground. After half an hour or so they move the barrage further forward. Orders are being passed in a whisper – 22nd Regt.: attack up front; 57th in reserve. Suddenly, vicious rifle and machine-gun fire erupts, supported by hand-grenades. The 22nd advances.[2]

However, even the mechanized, industrial conflict was not free of more intimate and perhaps even more disconcerting experiences of combat violence: 'Then our side started to run and the brown woolly hats of the Russians appeared under the trees', Karel Vaněk wrote in his description of a Russian attack in May 1915:

> One of ours shoots a Russian in the chest from only a few feet away, while another Russian pierces our guy's throat with a bayonet ... Everybody's gone animal, eyes bulging out, foaming at the mouth ... Then a rifle butt breaks through a window and I'm staring at a bayonet, with a crimson red face and angry voice behind it: 'Ty strílal a to ja tebe ubiju!' [If you shoot, I'll kill you!] ... It would be easy to shoot him in the face, but it's difficult to pluck up the courage to kill a fellow human face to face ... He didn't find it either.[3]

Many men focused on the particularly discomforting images of the physical effects of modern weaponry: 'The assembly point which the first waves as well as the reserves used as a springboard to cross the Piave has turned into a slaughterhouse', Jan Tříska commented in his diary with a mixture of fascination and dread:

> It was hard to believe what could be seen there. Dismembered, mutilated bodies of men and animals, torn limbs hanging from tree stumps, crushed skulls, open bloody stomachs with intestines flowing out – the horror was beyond the worst nightmare and the smell was nauseating. The place was hell. The men found it difficult to navigate their carts through the sea of corpses and limbs. Getting into position ... was a bloody eternity.[4]

Whichever perspective we take to look at the history of warfare, there is always only one ultimate raison d'être for everything we see – combat. In war, violence is the primary tool of forcing one's own will upon the opposing side. As Carl von Clausewitz had already noted, it is impossible to study war without acknowledging this very fact:

> Kind-hearted people might of course think there was some ingenious way to disarm or defeat an enemy without too much bloodshed ... It is a fallacy that must be exposed ... It would be futile – even wrong – to try and shut one's eyes to what war really is from sheer distress at its brutality ... War is thus an act of force to compel our enemy to do our will.[5]

While there seem to be a fair proportion of 'kind-hearted people' among the historians who study war, particularly those who do so from a cultural or social perspective, it is impossible to deny that even modern war is anything other than a highly developed and organized form of armed violence.[6] War is about people dying, people killing, and human bodies being used to destroy and be destroyed, to inflict suffering and to suffer. Consequently, as has already been noted, 'the violence of war inevitably takes us back to a history of the body'.[7] Therefore, any analysis of the way in which Czech soldiers experienced their wartime service in the ranks of the Austro-Hungarian military would be insincere and, indeed, methodologically flawed if it did not take into account the way they saw, felt and interpreted combat and the clash of bodies it entailed.

To be able to get through the above-described experiences and stay immediately effective as combat soldiers, men had to bring up specific coping mechanisms and sets of motivations that were radically different from those that sustained them in the service in the long term. It is what John Lynn defines as 'combat motivation' in his theory, a tip of the motivational pyramid necessary to make it work towards the ultimate goal: fighting. It is the realm where the above-described logic of long-term influences, interests and loyalties ceases to work, and the individual's mind starts to function on the simplest of levels. Primary group, immediate individual interest in survival, stress and primeval emotions – most of all fear – are brought to the surface and almost exclusively decide the outcome of one's behaviour, be it 'fight', 'flight' or a stunned inability to move and act.[8] In terms of military psychology, the battlefield is a place where combatants 'quickly lose much sense, not just of the overall strategic situation, but also of almost anything that happens beyond the small group of men they can actually hear and see'.[9] And, it may be added, they did not hear or see that much, as the battlefields of the First World War were mostly the epitome of S.L.A. Marshall's 'empty battlefield', where thousands lived and killed each other without ever seeing each other. Even artillery observers, usually placed in the best position of observation available, had trouble surmounting the problem: 'It's all desolate around here … Only guns and rifles firing tell you there are humans somewhere'.[10]

As a result, the study of combat is an analytical minefield where the very stress of the situation causes difficulties in interpretation, notwithstanding the sensory overload and memory lapses these situations usually entail. As noted by Josef Šefl in his memoir, the very attempt to *remember* something as psychologically intensive and emotional as combat is extremely problematic: 'It seems to me that recollections of fighting are like fast trains on a main railway, one following another at speed'.[11] The inherently chaotic nature of these events makes it necessary for the survivors to make sense of them by introducing some sort of order into their recollections, i.e. to create a structured narrative that would be at least a bit meaningful. Indeed, the ability of language to capture reality and express its perceived meaning becomes crucial here. The problem was, as a generation of historians following in the steps of Paul Fussell argued, that language was often inadequate to the task. Inability to communicate one's experience was not an issue specific to British 'war poets' – a number of Czech soldiers also expressed the same feeling in their accounts. For example, Josef Slezák thought that 'those who have not tried [combat] can never imagine or understand the way it affects people'.[12] When František Prudil tried to describe a sudden outburst of combat, he found himself lost for words: 'Well, I will not try to write more, as it is not possible to express in words, and if I had not experienced it myself, had not been through it, I would not have believed how much a man can endure and do when necessary'.[13] It was not just 'ordinary', albeit well-educated middle-class men who fell silent in the face of indescribable violence. Even such a master of words as the journalist Egon Erwin Kisch had to surrender. 'My talents are not enough to tell what happened to us this Friday', he wrote with resignation the night after yet another failed attempt of the Austro-Hungarian forces to cross the Drina River.[14] What the historian Eric Leed once described as 'cultural sources of meaning', a tool necessary for language to process and describe reality through reference to previous experience, blatantly failed here. In the pre-1914 world, there was nothing that would provide the template for a description of modern warfare.[15]

Killing

If combat is the essence of war, then the essence of combat is, in the words of Joanna Bourke, 'not dying, but killing'.[16] The ultimate goal of every soldier is not to die, but to kill every opponent who does not submit to his will immediately and willingly. And while killing in war is ubiquitous, as proven by the statistics, it is surprisingly rare in soldiers' writings, where even secondhand accounts of killing such as the one noted by Karel Vaněk are few and far between. It actually seems that killing, and writing about it, was a cultural taboo for many, and this taboo was at work across time and space. While there are men who, in their accounts of combat service, described killing in detail – and Joanna Bourke chose precisely these to support the sweeping and overstated argument in her book that modern soldiers indeed enjoyed face-to-face killing – historically, most soldiers do not dwell on the issue too much, as is clear from reading the work of authors such as Richard Holmes.[17] Regarding the First World War itself, the French historian Stéphane Audoin-Rouzeau has noted a 'reticence on the reality of battle', 'the majority of combatants avoiding the subject in their letters and newspapers. The taboo was broken [only] on occasions'.[18] Leonard Smith agreed, writing that 'actual killing is surprisingly elusive in Great War testimonies. Millions died; very few indeed seemed to have killed'.[19] Similarly, in the case of German soldiers, Jason Couthamel noted that while 'the experience of suffering and, strangely, even the "beauty" of war could be conveyed … the act of killing and the graphic details of combat remained taboo'.[20] This conclusion may be applicable to the majority of Czech soldiers' accounts too – while passive suffering is the key theme of many of their writings, they also have no qualms contemplating the ambivalent aesthetics of war, be it 'the beautiful spectacle of shells landing on the bridge [over the Isonzo at Tolmin] or in the river' or the 'at once beautiful and horrific spectacle' of shrapnel explosions at night over the Serbian position on the Drina a few years earlier.[21] They only rarely mention a personal experience of killing though, be it in correspondence, diaries or memoirs.

Killing is perhaps the biggest taboo one encounters while reading Czech soldiers' personal accounts of the First World War. While in correspondence, self-censorship may well be the obvious motivation for this reticence, it is still difficult to explain why even the instances where the narrator is not the killer (or, obviously, the victim) are relatively rare. To some extent, we may well agree that 'beyond the discursive constructs, the relative silence on killing has something to do with how men actually died in the Great War' – being hit by artillery or mown down in the murderous killing zones of machine guns.[22] Based on the statistics of wounds, about three-quarters of casualties were caused by artillery, about 15% by bullets (including machine guns), 2% by hand-grenades, less than 2% by poison gas, and less than 0.5% by cold steel (bayonets, knives and sabres).[23] There was little space for personalized killing in modern warfare.

However, in an effort to explain the taboo regarding the one-fifth of the killings not caused by long-range weaponry, attention has to be turned to the 'discursive elements' mentioned in the quotation by Leonard Smith above. In his interpretation, these elements revolved around the narrators' effort to 'present themselves, in effect, as the heirs to renaissance humanism – rational, self-conscious, morally autonomous beings' that were above killing fellow humans and would prefer to think the same about their comrades.[24] It is open to discussion as to whether this conclusion is applicable to the French case that Smith uses; however, it seems that a similar cultural construct may well be applicable to many Czech soldiers. On the other hand, in analysing their personal writings, other motivations for the 'discursive silence' also need to be taken into account.

It seems that for many Czech soldiers it was not just the psychological barrier that made them unable to admit to the audience they had expected for their texts, as well as to themselves, that they were indeed willing to kill, personally participated in killing or even killed directly. In memoirs in particular, it is easy to identify a whitewashing effort to 'correct' one's own war record so that it seems less 'guilty' of fighting on the wrong side, i.e. for the Habsburg monarchy. Denial of killing 'brother Slavs', particularly Russians, is especially common, rendering direct accounts of killing on the Eastern Front almost nonexistent in Czech soldiers' writings. While it is obvious that *someone* had to do all the killing and that the regiments with German, Hungarian or Polish majorities would not have managed to do all the fighting, Czech authors in general always find a way to excuse at least themselves from the process. A simple and rather typical solution is to be found for example in the memoirs of an infantryman of k.u.k. Infantry Regiment 54, Vladimír Soušek, whose primary efforts during the Gorlice Offensive in 1915 had apparently consisted of a self-conscious refusal to target Russians and then hiding in barns and cellars.[25] Augustin Mudrák also interpreted the war in pan-Slavic terms: 'Why should we, Slavs, kill each other? I have not shot at a Russian yet, and I have to get out of here at all costs, so I do not have to'.[26] 'I did not shoot' is an almost classical *topoi* in a large number of accounts, almost resembling the controversial thesis by S.L.A. Marshall about most men being culturally unaccustomed and therefore unwilling to kill. The only difference here is that Czech veterans were proud of the fact and even made a point of it in their memoirs sometimes.[27]

There are also some diaries that work more or less in the same way when it comes to recording the author's participation in violence. For example, František Bouška starts his diary with the claim that he considers himself to be an 'antimilitarist and a Sokol', and vows to 'never kill anyone' the moment he is mobilized.[28] In the diary of František Černý, there is a rather typical example of the way in which such a vow could be executed: 'I was shooting too, but I sincerely have no idea where my bullets went. It did not cross my mind for even a second to try and hurt anybody'. His excuse was bordering on the humanism that Leonard Smith had identified in French soldiers: 'I knew very well that there were men in those trenches, men with families like me. Maybe not with families, but with worried parents. Therefore, I only shot when I had to'.[29] In this way, Augustin Mudrák fired at the Russians only after a villain in the form of a 'warrant officer ... a German Jew' had intervened.[30] However, even the humanism of František Černý had its limits, and these limits seemed to be lifted when the killing ceased to be personal and could be interpreted as self-defence. Describing a moment when his unit came under accurate Russian artillery fire, he added: 'Afterwards, we were watching carefully for any enemy in our vicinity. The moment we saw someone ... we made them pay dearly [by calling in their own artillery] ... I was no fan of shooting at people who did me no harm, not at all. But that one time, I was really angry at them'.[31]

In the reality of combat, one of the key reasons for overcoming any moral qualms is often the stress itself or, more particularly, the way in which action, including operating weapons, works in terms of coping with such stress. The moment men come under fire, firing one's own weapon, on target or not, effectively or not, is one of the few things they can do besides charging the enemy or running away. And while charging forward usually needs to be induced by a further impetus (an officer's order), running away is problematic not only because of loyalty to comrades or fears of punishment, but also because it may involve leaving cover and turning one's back to the source of danger. In such a situation, firing a shot or two, or a whole magazine, may indeed serve as a welcome relief. Karel Vaněk agreed with this theory in his diary: 'Explosions of one's own rifle give a feeling of safety to a man'.[32] Also, when the unit of Egon Erwin Kisch came under heavy Serbian fire, responding in kind was their first reaction, which Kisch almost felt a need to apologize for: 'What else should we have done than fire, fire, fire? Only then did the idea to take cover hit us'. When he finally found some weak cover behind a body of one of his dead comrades, his stress level peaked, forcing him into more action: 'I started to quell my feelings of fear, horror and desperation by repeatedly loading and firing my rifle. My movements got quicker and quicker, and suddenly I realized I was only cocking and pulling the trigger again and again for a while, aiming at a pile of rocks where the Serbs were hiding – but I had forgotten to load a new magazine'.[33] Later, when his company was retreating back to the Drina River, he noted similar behaviour in everyone around. The officers ordered covering fire whenever the unit moved further back, but because they had not bothered to explain the order to their men, 'our people thought danger was imminent and were terrified. They were firing like maniacs, giving it everything, keeping their heads down as much as possible in the process'.[34] In these instances, the men were excused from trying to kill by the very fact that they could not help themselves from reacting.

It is in Kisch's diary where we also find one of the few descriptions of personal involvement in combat going beyond general, impersonal, sometimes almost literary phrases like 'our rifles mowed the Russian ranks down and our bayonets were thrust into the hearts of those who made it into our trenches' – when it comes to fighting, there usually is an emphasis on the passive voice.[35] 'We have advanced about twenty metres', Kisch reported in his diary on 16 September 1914:

> Close combat with bayonets is unavoidable ... I charge one of them from the side. I'm only a step away from him when he notices me. He wants to shoot me, but I step on his rifle. He jumps up and goes for my eyes, then, suddenly, lets me go with a cry. Private Patočka of my squad has bayonetted him in the back. Frenzied and wild-eyed, the Serb turns to face his new foe, just as Private Dejmek buries his bayonet into the man's stomach. He sinks down ... We're all panting heavily.[36]

But even in this account, the fortunes of war (or of interpretation?) rescue the author, who is one step away from killing another human being, finding someone else to do the job – and that only in the defence of the author's life. František Petržíla came a step closer to admitting that he had killed, attempting to describe his part in combat a month earlier in the same area, even though he also felt language was failing him: 'When we got only a few steps from them, suddenly we heard a cry: "Na nůž!" [Bayonets!] What happened then is impossible to describe, as the things that took place are too terrible to tell. I just took my rifle at the barrel and, using it as a club, I absentmindedly bludgeoned everything around'.[37] In another example, the artillery observer Bohumil Sperling had a much easier job in describing his killing of the enemy – for him, the 'enemy' were miniature, somewhat comical figures seen through the lens of binoculars, and his weapon was a heavy 305 mm mortar: 'Today I chased Italian cars, but with little success. Most of them made it to safety, but it was a comedy indeed, I had to laugh at their fear. I think there was no reason to be afraid of us'.[38] He clearly tries to build up a case for himself, in which his efforts are just a harmless exercise, unable to hit anyone in any case. In the same way, while Josef Klejna came tantalizingly close to admitting having killed, the power of the cultural taboo still kept his hold over him, even though his diary leaves little doubt over what had happened in the Serbian trench on the Kolubara in November 1914: 'I jump into the trench. A Serb jumps at me with a rifle in his hands, bayonet fixed. A shot is fired, but he misses. I aim my bayonet high and ---'. And then comes the ultimate discursive silence.[39]

The logic of 'killing before being killed', which Klejna uses as a narrative vehicle, justifying the untold ultimate act, is directly mentioned in the only example of killing by the author himself that is to be found in our sample of soldiers' personal accounts. It is Karel Vaněk, the usually brusque, curt and self-conscious future writer, who could not 'pluck up the courage to kill a fellow human face to face' in the quote above, who had no qualms about killing from a distance as an act of revenge, even though he still had to help himself by dehumanizing the opponent as much as possible. In his diary, he presents a lengthy description of killing a Russian sniper at the Dukla Pass in the Carpathians in April 1915:

> It needs to be known that you are just a pawn, a figurine, and this whole thing is a comedy, so stop it, or … I load a dum-dum; you have no idea that I have my carbine aimed well at the shadow by that tree … That's you! There's a flash on your side, and someone cries out on ours … You son of a bitch! … I've got you, you son of a bitch! Boom! 'Oh honey, ain't you shooting no more?'[40]

The intimate, almost erotic relationship between the shooter and his target is actually present at several other instances in Vaněk's diary, such as when he is finally captured in Galicia in May 1915: 'We stand in front of each other, embarrassed like lovers after sinning for the first time'.[41] The 'first sin' here is the mutual death threat, and the metaphor sheds some light on the way in which killing may have been understood by the soldiers – as a deeply intimate act that should remain untold in the same way erotic 'sins' stay with the participants either because of the perceived immorality of it or the inability to properly communicate the feelings that accompany such an act. However, Vaněk is the only one in our sample who comes close to the tendency to eroticize the violence that has been described in literature with regard to soldiers of other modern wars.[42]

Fear

Looking back to the problem of fear, the sources confirm that it is indeed the most important emotion of the battlefield. In fact, fear – as opposed to acts of violence carried out by the author – is present in almost every personal account, even of those men who have rarely come close to danger. Although fear is traditionally considered to be an 'unmanly' emotion, it does not seem that Czech soldiers felt any trouble expressing it, particularly in diaries and memoirs. 'It felt like a prison, anxiety and fear were running high', František Černý wrote in a reserve trench in the Carpathians at the end of 1915. When his company finally moved into a second line trench, their anxiety worsened even further: 'We were so nervous that we did not even feel hungry, even though our stomachs had been empty for days. I could not stop thinking that this time, it was our turn to die'.[43] František Prudil, who had served in Galicia half a year earlier, 'hardly cared about anything else than how it would all end … My stomach ached at the thought of whether I would get out of this alive or what'.[44] Egon Erwin Kisch actually considered it much worse to *go back* into combat than to go there for the first time: 'Those who have already been there are worse off, because they know what it is like'. The worst part, for him, was the waiting before action starts: 'It makes you really anxious'. On the other hand, he found the combat itself somewhat more palatable in terms of stress, as there is little time to think and there is something to do: 'When one is already in the water, it doesn't feel that cold, and it's the same with being under fire. It's the feeling *before* one gets there that makes men quiver with fear'.[45]

The fact that Czech soldiers were afraid in combat is hardly surprising. What is interesting, though, is the *meaning* they ascribed to their fears. As Sabine Haring noted in her 'sociological-emotional' analysis of k.u.k. Infantry Regiment 27 from Graz (a 94% German-speaking unit) and its combat experiences on the Eastern Front in the autumn of 1914, 'fear as an emotion is hardly ever conceptualized or even mentioned in the sources presented', and even though she is able to identify several indirect instances of its presence, it is (particularly in official narratives such as the regimental history, but also in personal accounts) generally interpreted as an obstacle on the way to ultimate bravery and courage, or, sometimes, as further proof of the moral deficiency of those who could not overcome it.[46] Fear, it seems, is being constructed here as a sort of a litmus paper of the ultimate qualities of military masculinity – courage, bravery, loyalty to comrades. It is a test of manliness, a tool that makes possible the traditional interpretation of combat itself, which is traditionally seen as the ultimate proving ground of masculinity.[47] Without fear, such a test would not make sense, as fear is the primary obstacle to be pushed away.

The fact that men understood the close connection between fear and their masculine identity is obvious in many instances, such as when Jaroslav Vítek wrote just before the start of the fateful Piave offensive:

> The suffocating atmosphere of anxiety affects us all, the feeling of a storm coming. It depresses even the hardiest men, revives almost forgotten images of past horrors, evokes nightmares, undermines manliness, and takes away any urge to live … Our sergeant's spirit is broken. I try in vain to restore some manly attitude in him, he is just too afraid of the coming offensive. He has been in the field since the very beginning, he has been wounded twice, and he is afraid … He does not sleep well, he had a dream that he was seriously wounded and was dying in horrible pain. He is always looking at a photograph of his wife and children, kissing it, almost crying every time.[48]

Besides the image of an experienced soldier on the verge of collapse, rather typically being afraid not only of dying but also of the manner in which he may die, Vítek also conceptualizes fear as an 'unmanly' emotion that needs to be overcome in order to reach the state of 'manliness' that apparently reflects the wartime ideal of hegemonic masculinity. In other words, a soldier – and it is not without importance that it is not the author, but someone else – faces an inner conflict with his fears, one that he has to win if he wants to be seen as a man. Consequently, this psychological victory would also make him an effective soldier, which tells us a lot about the way in which masculinity is interconnected with the notion of war and violent conflict, where the former makes the latter psychologically sustainable.[49] This is also the reason why soldiers are always afraid to think too much, as noted by Kisch before an attack on the Drina in September 1914: 'Just do not think'.[50] To think meant to be afraid, and to be afraid meant to make a mistake, get killed, fail comrades – and fail the test of manliness. In this way, František Skála was able to pass the test in Galicia in June 1915:

> Before entering combat for the first time, one feels a cold shiver all over his back. When the smoke had cleared, the order was given to attack at speed ... We had only just started running when the bullets started to fly towards us ... My arteries were pulsating like crazy, my heart wanted to jump out of my chest, my mouth was gasping for more air to supply my racing lungs. My legs moved mechanically. I lost sense of space, time or events. Spiritual numbness set in ... Then my survival instinct took over. Not cowardly fear, but cold calculation that saw me through.[51]

In Skála's view, he passed the test and became what society wanted him to be – a brave, courageous, manly soldier and a man.

Overcoming fear in combat is therefore as much a real effort as it is a performance of masculine quality, and combat violence is the tool that gives it the primary impetus. The nature of the violence itself does not seem to be that important here – as Joanna Bourke mentioned in her 'cultural history of fear' and as mentioned above, modern combat is most fearsome when it produces passivity and denies men any chance of either active confrontation or just simple escape. The relief of action is often both impossible and meaningless on a battlefield where death comes from distance or above, and running away means exposing oneself to even more danger. Consequently, the soldiers are forced to wait, trying not to go mad in their inability to act, and not to think 'doom is coming' with every incoming shell, as Josef Ulrych once did.[52] While men turned into passive objects may feel that their masculinity is being compromised, it has little consequence in relation to the meaning of the fear they experience. The fear is still there, it is real and it has to be overcome in order to pass the test. As such, fear becomes a tool that enables men to reconstruct their masculinity around the new circumstances of the modern battlefield – to avoid construing manliness around the active (i.e. combat, which also carries along the taboo of killing) and embracing the passive (overcoming fear, 'getting through'). It may be said that, at least in the case of Czech soldiers and their masculine identity, war became a mass variant of the duel, a public performance of masculinity based on the ability to vanquish one's fear of pain and dying.[53] It is as if the soldiers agreed with Clausewitz, who had actually claimed – at a time when the duel was understood to be the perfect test of one's masculine honour among the elites – that 'war is nothing more than a duel on an extensive scale'.[54] Similarly to the duel, combat is a ritualized form of both violence and masculinity, which is reflected in the fact that it is usually the high point of any narrative of war experience – although, as Leonard Smith rightly pointed out in his definition of combat as a sacrum of the battlefield narrative, one that ushers men into a new, liminal state of being, there is no way to make sure that this moment in the narrative is either a definitive turning point or that the resulting state is for good. In modern war in particular, combat is terrifyingly repetitive, and men are never sure that they will not be killed or will not run away and fail the test the next time.[55]

There is plenty of evidence that the interpretation of combat as ritualized masculinity was not peculiar to Jaroslav Vítek. When František Šmída describes his efforts to rally his second in command so that he would be able to stand watch at a dangerous forward position on a nearby mountain in the Alps, his words are as follows: 'I had to use all my talents for him to man up'. The cadet in question did 'man up' at the end (with the help of a bottle of rum), which elicited Šmída's comment: 'He stayed there as long as everyone else, and was a hero, as were all the men who went through that baptism of fire'.[56] The 'manly heroism', i.e. heroism as an integral part of the idea of manliness, was confirmed here by a 'baptism of fire', itself a term out of a propaganda pamphlet advertising the militarized masculine discourse. Its substance, however, was not any active heroism – it was a thoroughly passive act of 'staying' alone in an exposed and dangerous position, prescribed by the way the job of artillery observer was practiced in reality. Even so, it still retained its transformative power connected to one's manliness.

The language of 'baptism by fire', which pointed to the ritual, transformative notion of combat, is often to be found in soldiers' writings. Josef Rezek, an infantryman of k.u.k. Infantry Regiment 18, defined his first combat experience as such, as did František Čapek of k.u.k. Infantry Regiment 13.[57] The ritual importance of combat to one's sense of self-worth and masculinity is also obvious from the retelling of Jan Tříska's diary: 'Deep down inside he was not sure how he would react – would he possess enough courage, would he keep his calm? He could hardly wait for the ultimate test of his character and manhood'.[58] Ferdinand Lirš was much less poetic in his description of another test of bravery he passed when an Italian air raid surprised him in the middle of an outdoor shower with no time to find cover: 'There may well be some people who, in my place, would have needed a change of underpants'. In the next sentence, he makes sure the reader knows both the result of the test and its consequence for his identity: 'But not me. I was, after all, a self-composed soldier'.[59] Again, it is worth noting the sheer passivity of this test of manhood. Also, here more than anywhere else, it is clear that the very nature of the test was not important. If in the eighteenth and nineteenth centuries it had been possible to prove one's honour and masculinity by firmly 'receiving' the opponents' fire from a few steps away, it may not be surprising that one might have done so also by quietly standing, half-naked and covered in soap, in a wooden box, with heavy bombs falling around.

Czech soldiers do not see combat solely as a test of individual masculinity – they somewhat surprisingly also interpreted it as a group test. Here the evidence clearly contradicts the clichéd image of the 'passive Czech', a 'Švejk' who waits only for the right moment to desert to the enemy.[60] It seems that many men, while gradually exhausted by physical suffering at the front and at home, and disillusioned by the attitude the army increasingly held towards them, were also proud of their units and their battle records. Even František Černý, the self-proclaimed 'anti-militarist and Sokol', mentioned a moment in his diary when 'that one time', he got 'carried away' by a defensive effort of his regiment in Galicia: 'We fought like dragons, and this time even I was firing like crazy … The Russians got a thorough thrashing from us that day'.[61] František Bouška found it hard to hide pride in his unit, the 98th Infantry, and its combat record during the retreat from Galicia in September 1914: 'The regiment went through a lot … We were always covering the retreat of the others … They also read us an order of the day, which commended our XI Corps'.[62] The theory of war as a duel is further supported by the ever-popular emphasis many authors placed on the contrast between the bravery of themselves and their comrades, and the cowardice of the obviously 'unmanly' enemy. In the latter stages of the war in particular, the Italians bore the brunt of this treatment. While Czech soldiers had great respect both for the landscape of their country and for the sheer industrial power of their artillery and particularly the air force, Italians as soldiers were treated with disdain. For Bohumil Sperling, they were 'dirty cowards' who 'ran like hell' at Caporetto, and František Skála repeatedly asserted that 'the value of the Italian infantry is low'. For František Šmída, the Italian rank-and-file men were 'convinced inside that the *Austriaco* was a better man and victory could therefore only come to his side'. He saw this as the primary reason why the morale of the Italian troops had always seemed so low to him in comparison with the Austro-Hungarian army.[63] Thoughts such as these paved the way for the Italians to be, in the eyes of many of their opponents, emasculated and even feminized. As Šmída noted in another instance: 'I did not see any anxiety or fear in the local womenfolk … Today, I actually think that if the Italian men were as brave as their women, the war would have been over two years earlier'.[64] Under this judgement, not only were Italian men degraded to a subordinate level vis-à-vis their women; the Austro-Hungarian soldiers, including the Czechs, were proven to be the victors of the duel and their manliness was secured, which was obviously important to many of them. As Jan Sýkora summarized his experience of the bloody 'battles of the frontiers' in Galicia in 1914, Czech soldiers' qualities were not supposed to be open to doubt: 'The k.k. Landwehr Infantry Regiment 30 from Vysoké Mýto [Hohenmauth in German] … How did it fight? Like a thousand ancient heroes … Without guns, without machine guns, without any trenches, they stood there and kept the numerically superior enemy from advancing by their own bodies. And it was a Czech regiment – a Czech one!'[65]

The idea that the ability to suppress fear is a proof of manliness, a test that some pass and some fail, some obviously being 'more men' than others, seems to have been not only an integral part of the official discourse, which used it for propaganda purposes, but was apparently also part of the way in which many Czech soldiers experienced their own masculinity. In their case, it was rarely connected to the official discourse of imperial patriotism; however, the very core of the idea, namely that *men* have to prove their manhood in the 'duel' that is war by overcoming their fears, remained an integral part of their thinking. Thanks to this, they were actually able to reconcile their need to fulfil their gender role on the battlefield while keeping an interpretative distance from the potential taboo of killing. 'Fighting like a dragon' could therefore mean passive survival, 'staying' in place and keeping the enemy from advancing 'by one's own body', and it was still manly and heroic; there was no need to go into the psychologically uncomfortable detail of what 'fighting like a dragon' meant in terms of combat reality. This discourse enabled men to accommodate their desperate need for proof by 'baptism of fire' into the reality of modern warfare, where they were mostly relegated to the status of pure objects of destruction rather than its executors – they still had fear as a test, which helped them keep their elementary notion of bravery, and therefore masculinity, intact.

This interpretation is bound to find expression in the attitudes combat soldiers held towards those men who, while in uniform, were not 'lucky' enough to participate in the 'baptism of fire'. In any war, but in a modern one in particular, mixing the categories of 'men conscripted' and 'men deployed in combat' is highly problematic. With regard to the Austro-Hungarian military, the official statistics listed 8,420,000 men drafted by the end of 1917. Between 1914 and the end of 1917, 4,010,000 of these men had 'left the armed services' for various reasons (780,000 dead, 1,600,000 missing, 500,000 invalid or other medical reasons, 130,000 passing the age bracket of 52 years, 400,000 re-employed in the war industry and 600,000 discharged for other reasons).[66] It is difficult, using these crude statistics, to judge what percentage of drafted men did actually engage in combat during the war. In her study of wartime Vienna, Maureen Healy argues for counting all the dead and 'most of those who became invalid' as the only groups it may be safely assumed to have had 'combat experience'.[67] However, even this may not be correct, as many of those men died or were discharged for various reasons not connected to combat (i.e. disease), in the same way as many of the 'missing' (i.e. mostly POWs) were members of support units captured in mass surrenders on the Eastern Front (for example, the surrender of the fortress of Przemysl in March 1915 alone brought 120,000 men into captivity, with auxiliary personnel undoubtedly constituting a substantial part). On the other hand, there may well be a large number of those who served in combat before 'making it' into the other groups mentioned above. If we disregard all these qualifications out of sheer lack of precise numbers, it may be assumed that about 2,800,000 men (the majority of the dead, the missing and the invalided) had passed through combat service by the end of 1917 (34% of the total conscripted) before being discharged one way or another. Of the 4,410,000 men remaining in service by the end of 1917, 1,560,000 were listed with domestic security details and support services in the hinterland. This leaves 2,850,000 men officially serving with field units; however, even this number included a substantial quantity of auxiliary personnel.[68]

Taking a hint from a more statistically covered conflict thirty years later, further help may be accrued from Samuel Stouffer and his sociological work on the Second World War. He had estimated that during the final stages of the conflict, 'less than half of the men [of the U.S. army] present in Europe could be counted to be in combat at any one time'.[69] While it is obvious that an army in the mid 1940s required more substantial logistical support than one in the late 1910s,[70] Stouffer's estimate, combined with the statistics above, may give some support to an educated guess that about half of the 4,410,000 men (excluding the 1,560,000 officially deployed in the hinterland plus a further 700,000) were engaged in combat operations of some sort. Combined with the above estimate of combat experience among the men already discharged, we may guess that out of the men who had entered the Austro-Hungarian military service by the end of 1917, about 4,950,000 (59%) experienced some sort of combat. It also seems that during 1918, the percentage of units deployed in combat was steadily decreasing because of the increasing need for providing domestic security and also because of the inability of the army to move and provide for the troops effectively. According to Istvan Déak, only a quarter of the field army was actually defending the lines on the Piave and in the Balkans in October 1918 as a result of this.[71]

However, the statistical exercise above, while helpful, does not tell us a lot about the way in which men actually saw their war experience. As is typical in the history of warfare, most of the members of noncombat units, even though they never saw an enemy or came under fire, would still swear that their war was, indeed, a *war* with all the attributes, including combat.[72] Looking at the Czech soldiers' personal accounts, this tendency seems to be confirmed, and it closely reflects the logic of combat being seen as the ultimate 'test of manliness'. In fact, the statistical divide described above has, from the standpoint of masculine identity, created a specific variant of a hierarchy of masculinities. The division that ran across the otherwise unified notion of militarized hegemonic masculinity in wartime distinguished between men who were seen as 'frontline' soldiers and those who were not, with the latter understood to lose some of the claim they had on the symbolic benefits and dividends of hegemonic masculinity. And it is this division that is very well reflected in the sources, adding another piece into the mosaic of the soldiers' gendered worldview.

The way in which frontline soldiers treat those they perceive as the *Etappenschweine* (literally 'depot swine') in their writings is, on the surface, defined primarily by the disparity between them doing 'all the work' that men are supposed to do in war, while the 'others' receive all the benefits in terms of food and shelter. Consequently, as the nickname suggests, their attitude is generally negative: 'The worst ones were and are those who were never at the front'.[73] In the eyes of Egon Erwin Kisch, the 'Etappenschweine' were 'men who had hardly ever heard a rifle shot'.[74] And as another soldier added:

> How many days we were without chow, exhausted by marching day and night, constantly in danger and under enemy fire, while they were having all the fun. They were playing musical instruments, singing, lying in the shadows, chow always ready. They were playing games, dancing, and generally doing whatever they could to entertain themselves, while heavy fighting was raging for hours and thousands were dying ... And these guys would undoubtedly claim that they were at the front all the time.[75]

It is the last sentence that conveys anger at the fact that the men who did not share the suffering of frontline service would be able to claim the social capital, including the position at the top of the wartime gender hierarchy, and this further supports our argument that combat was indeed seen as a 'sacred space', an ultimate test that no one should be allowed to bypass in their claims to hegemonic masculinity.[76]

In Kisch's diary, there are several complaints about:

> accountant officers, cooks, field kitchen coach drivers *e tutti quanti*, collecting Serbian rifles, knives, shrapnel casings, shell fragments, spent cases and other remnants of 'their attack' [in a conquered Serbian trench]. They will be sending all that back home ... and will decorate their apartments with this war loot, turning them into military museums, and will go on telling their awestruck compatriots many a heroic story of theirs. Meanwhile, the only thing a real combat warrior will bring home is rheumatism or a hole somewhere in his body.[77]

According to this interpretation, the 'real combat warrior' is clearly the sole embodiment of the true military masculinity that the official discourse repeatedly celebrated and the public more or less venerated. The 'collectors' in Kisch's story are, in his view, trying to swindle their way into any possible (mostly symbolic) privilege that the status at the top of the wartime gender hierarchy may entail. Within this context, it is hardly surprising that many Czech veterans of Austro-Hungarian service insisted on calling themselves 'frontline soldiers' or 'frontline warriors' after the war – for them, the term was an important element of their masculine identity, one that they repeatedly used to support their claims for 'full masculinity' in the otherwise ideologically hostile republican society.[78]

Bodies of Men

The above-quoted passage from Kisch's diary presents us with an example where the 'warrior's' body is turned into a relic of wartime masculinity. For the warrior who comes home 'with rheumatism or a hole in his body', it is the ultimate evidence, a symbolic space where masculinity is played out through 'badges of courage' in the form of wounds and aches. The discourse of proving one's manliness through 'making it through' combat is performed here directly on the masculine physical form, i.e. on the soldier's body. Interpreting wounds in this way, bodily deformations resulting from combat experience are not necessarily a negative intrusion into the *complete* state of the male body; on the contrary, the painful experience is interpreted as positive *outward sign* of masculinity. Of course, there were limits to the ways in which the body could be 'transformed' and still work as a symbol of true manliness, as noted by a comrade of Karel Vaněk: 'Of course, you mustn't be wounded too much, like disfigured or mutilated or something, so you don't scare people'.[79] As noted by Sabine Kienitz in her study of the social (re)construction of manliness of war invalids in postwar Germany, devastating wounds always threatened to turn men into emasculated 'war eunuchs', because the body has always been a key constitutive part of masculine identity as well as a performative space, connected to masculinity through a complicated network of meanings.[80] Tellingly, what the same comrade was promising to Vaněk in the case that he managed to avoid being 'wounded too much' was both concern and romantic (in a soldier's view, sexual) interest of women, as a 'proper wound' would make him 'a true man' in their eyes.

Of course, the problem was that a soldier in a modern war has little to no control over *what* kind of wound he might sustain and whether he will survive being hit at all (and what the quality of his survival will be like). And, as everyone knew, there were innumerable, often nightmarish ways in which the body could be mutilated. Images of these are actually a staple of all personal accounts, particularly diaries and memoirs, and in stark contrast with the discussion of combat itself, the authors often do not hesitate to go into even the most horrifying detail.[81] As much as they find these sights repulsive and shocking, they seem to hold a deep fascination for them.[82] Thus, Jaroslav Křenek, while horrified, describes in great detail 'a wounded soldier, hit by a shrapnel, whose head was turned into a mass of raw, live meat with just one eye staring out'.[83] Similarly, while Augustin Mudrák is shocked by the sight of a field kitchen blown to pieces when lunch issue was in full swing, he still goes on to describe the details in a

Figure 6.1 'A reaper in the school for the disabled soldiers.' One of a series of postcards promising the men to keep their masculinity and status in the workforce, even if their body is permanently damaged, 1915 (Museum of Eastern Bohemia, Hradec Králové).

disgusted fascination: 'A horrible sight it was … fourteen horribly mutilated corpses. Poor bastards with their heads torn off, collected pieces of bodies neatly stacked in a pile. I recognize a fellow countryman, Hlavica, among them … he is lying there completely torn apart. Agitated and almost crying, I went back to the trenches'.[84] This is the same Augustin Mudrák who sends home postcards with photographs of dead Russian soldiers. The artilleryman Bohumil Sperling's

Figure 6.2 'Silent Heroism.' The positive side of a soldier's disability in wartime propaganda, postcard, 1915 (Museum of Eastern Bohemia, Hradec Králové).

description of an accident at one of the heavy howitzers of his battery also went into graphic detail: 'Lieutenant Pfob ... had his head torn off by the chin. Lots of blood all around, with pieces of brains, an eye, nose, and teeth mixed in. It was his 19th birthday. It's really sad. That's war'.[85] And finally, Egon Erwin Kisch saw 'a hundred scenes of misery' when commencing an assault on the Drina, scenes he does not hesitate describe in gruesome detail later on: 'crushed bones', 'bits of skin hanging from a face' or 'streams of blood'. Only later does it all seem to become too much for him, and he settles for a generalized phrase appearing in agonizing repetition: 'the unforgettable horrific images'.[86]

It actually seems as if this is the very first encounter with the effects of modern weaponry upon the human body, when the men's fascination with the sights reaches its peak. When Karel Vaněk encountered 'his' first dead, several dozen Russian soldiers heaped in a trench, he defines it as a 'terrible sight', but then goes to great length in describing 'torn off arms, crushed heads, headless torsos, heads without the rest of the body, all mixed up with chunks of meat, viscera and dirt'.[87] Josef Slezák captured the feeling well when he described the moment when the train carrying his unit to the front for the first time passed 'the first train with the wounded. We wanted to see them so much, but we were not allowed to leave the train', he noted with disappointment.[88] And when he and his comrades finally met some wounded on the march from the train terminus, they 'caught our special attention': 'It had a bad effect on every one of us, seeing so many young men mutilated and covered in blood'.[89]

While rookies felt both shocked and mesmerized by their first encounter with bodily destruction, for veteran soldiers it was only a painful reminder of things that were always just around the corner for them. They often feared not death itself, but its potential form – too often had they witnessed men suffering in pain for hours or even days, and experience told them that there was no way to ensure they would not suffer a similar fate. This was confirmed by contemporary psychiatry, which agreed that 'the men's primary fear was not death but mutilation'.[90] Michael Roper, in his study of the emotional world of British soldiers during the First World War, argues that gruesome images of extremely violent death which men were forced to witness in the trenches served not only as a reminder of one's own mortality, but also as an accelerator of 'powerful irrational feelings … [that] could threaten psychic disintegration', ultimately rooted in 'the most primitive and profound anxiety of the baby that it had no secure physical boundary to differentiate its "inside" from "outside"'.[91] Similarly, while Leonard Smith borrows a part of his explanation from a cultural history by Carolyn Bynum, arguing that 'hell and damnation … had been for centuries depicted in terms of fragmentation of the body', he also agrees that 'at a psychological level, annihilating the body meant annihilating the physical line demarcating the self from the outside world, a primary form of human knowledge'.[92] Putting these observations in terms of contemporary science of physiology, Stefanos Geroulanos and Todd Meyers quote Kurt Goldstein's theory of self-actualization where the individual organism itself constantly strives for wholeness, but only realizes so at the moments of acute loss (a physical injury) when the disastrous alternative becomes all too obvious. Taking their argument further, this physiological state, creating acute sense of fear and panic, may be seen as the source of the psychological reaction to the threat of bodily destruction closely witnessed in others.[93]

One way or another, this primeval, literally *embodied* fear of physical disintegration was closely reflected in the language Czech soldiers employed in describing the way in which artillery fire – responsible not only for most of the wounds, but also for a majority of the most horrible ones – affected their psyche. 'A terrible feeling … just thinking about when it will hit *you* and tear you to pieces', František Bouška noted the discomforting context of being shelled.[94] Jan Morávek summarized how exploding shells made him feel in a telling way: 'The sheer noise of the explosion and the air pressure tore your entrails inside out'.[95] According to Roper, the 'tearing entrails inside out' was not just a metaphor, but a projection of an 'irrational fear', triggering deep-set 'primitive' panic reactions buried in soldiers' subconscious.[96] 'The knowledge that at any second I may well be turned into one such shapeless bundle of green rags and torn tissue gave me not just strength, but it made me almost fly', Bohuslav Hála recalled his feelings after witnessing the gruesome effects of Italian artillery barrage before the Eleventh Battle on the Isonzo.[97]

Remembering the above-mentioned argument about the body being a constitutive part of masculine social as well as individual, psychological identity, it is hardly surprising that the sight of the catastrophic destruction of other men's bodies – the 'nameless dread', as Michael Roper has called it – painfully reminded any observer of his inability to ensure even the basic physical integrity of his own body and, along with it, his own masculinity. 'A head here … an arm there … A festering shred of something over there, right next to a part of what used to be a human leg', Josef Ulrych described a sappers' dugout after suffering a direct hit by a heavy shell. 'When it was all being collected into bags, they could not tell which was whose. Just horrible, blown up limbs and human bodies'.[98] The author finds the sudden nonexistence of the elementary boundary between the body of one man and that of another thoroughly shocking, as does Jaroslav Vítek when he describes a burial of some decomposing corpses, noting with disgust the fact that they were 'falling apart like mud' when moved, lacking any of the youthful strength, firmness and beauty that characterized the idealized masculine body of a warrior.[99] Similarly, Jan Šindelář's account of infantry advancing through artillery barrage ended up focusing on 'many a comrade, hit mid-stride by an exploding shell, disappearing in front of our eyes. The only thing left of him was unidentifiable remains of a human body spread all over the place'.[100] As argued by Geroulanos and Meyers, contemporary physiology concluded that it was 'the individual patient and his norms' that played the decisive role in setting the terms of physiological reactions to injury, and the reality of modern warfare threatened to destroy that individuality at a whim, along with all its norms, including gender.[101] The sudden metamorphosis of a man into *unidentifiable* remains was therefore the ultimate loss of power and control men encountered during the war; it was the final, definitive subversion of their manliness. It was, literally, its *embodiment*, as in confrontation with modern firepower, men lost control over the *shape* and *form* of their own physical being, unable to influence its future fate by whatever they did. And as the body was the core symbolic space where masculinity was always performed *and* experienced, catastrophic destruction caused the disintegration of a man not only in physical terms, but also in symbolic and social terms. 'He was no longer a guy, but a mystery with a wound for a face', Vladislav Vančura described the fate of the main character in his war novel, the village idiot František, after he was disfigured by a shell fragment. 'He became a gaping wound' was the telling summary of his metamorphosis by war that had once promised him full social manhood.[102]

Particularly destructive, in symbolic terms, were injuries suffered in the area of sexual organs, which presented the emasculating power of war in the most specific terms possible, with men being painfully aware of the consequences for both their life *and* social identity: 'One of them … is limping directly towards us', František Skála described one wounded soldier in the process of evacuation from a first line trench after a Russian artillery barrage:

He complains bitterly: 'My dear friend, I'm done for. I'll never taste a woman again. What made me a man is gone, shot off'.[103] Not accidentally, Jan Šindelář juxtaposed his recollection of a similar situation with the youth and impeccable physical masculinity of the man in question: 'Next to me in the car lies the seriously wounded Corporal P ... a fair, black-haired, well-built boy from Romania. The poor bastard has been hit by a shell fragment in the stomach, and his manhood is gone, too'.[104]

In their personal writings, soldiers conceptualized not only the destruction of the body as such, but also the possibility of losing control of one's being as a consequence. Egon Erwin Kisch thought of wounds as directly connected to the horror of losing the layers of culture and civilization that, as seen in Chapter 2, also defined modern masculinity: 'Now you are crossing [the Drina River] as well, only to end up, in a few minutes, over there in the state of those men – brutalized, mutilated, groaning, an animal. They were the wounded'.[105] The inability to control one's reaction to pain is a well-established topic in many of the sources, reflecting the author's effort to keep the façade of stoic masculinity as intact as possible: 'I am in pain, too. Every little stone causes me indescribable pain, but I do not make a sound', František Skála wrote in his diary, trying to prove his stoicism in a rather obvious way.[106] Later on he noted: 'The injured body is a lifeless mass, depending on the help of others'.[107] As such, its 'owner' has no control over it, and as the body is an integral part of his masculinity that emphasizes control, activity and independence, his masculinity comes under serious threat. He, through his damaged body, becomes an object, exposed to arbitrary external intervention. And what was particularly depressing in wartime was that this intervention often came in the form of female nurses or even senior medical personnel, whose actions may well have caused pain and further subsequent endangerment of the men's masculinity through their 'unmanly' reactions to it.[108] The traditional hierarchy of the *active* and *passive* actor in the gender order is turned upside down, with the remnants of masculine identity disappearing in the fog of the fact that a man is becoming dependent not only on the support and care, but, worse, on the expertise of women.

The worst moments of losing control came when the body started to behave as if independent of the mind, which may have happened not only during combat, but also, as a consequence of post-traumatic stress disorder, years after the war was over: 'Suddenly ... I hit the ground, on pure survival instinct', Jan Morávek recalled an afternoon walk in Prague in the early 1920s. 'Something like a shell exploded right next to me ... It was a streetcar running over something. But my nerves yielded to the alertness of my senses, still tuned to the long forgotten horrors of the battlefield. People turned their heads, watching me in sympathy'. The same author remembered waking up in the middle of the night, on the floor, taking cover against 'some noise that sounded like the distant clatter of a machine gun'.[109] As in the case of physical wounding, the body becomes a

Figure 6.3 The gruesome reality of bodily destruction in modern warfare, a military hospital in the town of Czernowitz, Bukovina, 1915 (Museum of Eastern Bohemia, Hradec Králové).

foreign object here, one that functions independently of his will, which damages the individual's masculine identity, as without an obedient, functioning, well-sculpted and controlled body, manliness is an incomplete, deformed shell.

The theme of losing control over one's body is an important reflection of the wider issue that troubled men throughout their wartime service, one already mentioned in each of the preceding chapters. It was an issue that, over time, seriously undermined the men's morale and motivation to be effective soldiers, year in, year out, and sometimes may have even opened their minds to alternative loyalties that presented them with a way out. That issue, typical in modern warfare, was the inability not only to make active decisions on every level of existence; it entailed a complete inability to influence one's physical existence through specific actions, behaviour, skills or abilities. In the static, industrialized war of 1914–1918, all of these traditionally masculine qualities usually had little value when it came to survival. In fact, we may paraphrase the title of Rudolf Kučera's book on the often emasculating experience of the *rationed life* of the working classes in the Bohemian hinterland and argue that for the men who left their homes and went on to become combat soldiers, the process they were facing was more of a *rationed death*.

In modern warfare, this 'ration' was distributed along more or less democratic lines and in complete disregard of the traditional idea that in war it is the best men who come out on top and survive thanks to their masculine qualities: 'Here, the biggest weakling may kill an athlete, or the biggest idiot the finest spirit of Europe', Karel Vaněk observed. 'There is no heroism out here. Everything's scared, cowardly, hapless, and crazy'.[110] This fact was another reason why fear itself became the proving ground of manliness – due to the prevalence of death by artillery, a soldier's survival skills ended with the ability to guess the right direction and timing of an incoming shell, or the trajectory and effective range of machine-gun fire. And even if a man mastered these instincts over time, death and dying was still absurdly random, bereft of manly heroics. There are many instances where men died or survived on a whim of fate. On 24 September 1914, Egon Erwin Kisch recorded a chat with a machine gunner in a dugout, after which the man left 'to take a leak by the road'. Suddenly a shell hit, 'the ground shook, the air whirled around, my cap flew away from my head and my face was covered in an avalanche of dirt … The sergeant … was lying there with his head crushed … and behind him, stuck deep in the ground, an intact heavy shell'. The shell was a dud, which ensured Kisch's survival; however, in a bizarre twist of fate, on its way into the mud, it took a trajectory directly through the space occupied, at that very moment, by the sergeant's head. Later on, in October of the same year, a direct hit by artillery massacred an officers' dinner party, killing several men and maiming others. Three days later, Kisch was waiting by a battalion headquarters dugout with a message when 'suddenly a bullet flew by me' and hit the *Major* 'in the chin and shoulder' while he was talking to other officers.[111] František Křížek recalled that he had once discovered a soldier's body at the bottom of a latrine: 'I think he was answering the call of nature, was shot and fell down'.[112] Jan Šindelář summarized the men's feelings about modern warfare, writing in his memoir: 'No one knows and no one will ever know who killed whom. Not people, but machines operated by them, kill with mathematical accuracy, kill from the distance, kill even when the victim cannot see them … There is no good or evil at work here'.[113] He could well have added that there was no bravery or cowardice, manliness or unmanliness either.

As mentioned above, according to John Lynn, emotions, particularly fear, are the key element of soldiers' combat motivation. Fear in combat had many faces, many of them closely related to the men's gender identity. As a consequence, the very idea of true manliness in Czech soldiers' writings generally entailed the notion of passive, stoic survival, while active heroics were often seen as morally problematic, nonsensical, or outright impossible. Of course, this concept was closely related to the primary group. As long as the group subscribed to the notion of stoic survival, its members were encouraged to sustain any suffering by the feeling of loyalty to their comrades.[114] And, as masculinity is both an internalized construct and a social experience, the group was indeed an all-important factor in the process of gendered combat motivation – in the end, men were first and foremost judged by other men, and their ability to perform in the 'duel' of modern war was important as long as it was important for the group. When the group failed, through casualties or general exhaustion, men were left without the important social imperative to fight on.

The body played an important role in this process, as it served as the primary space where masculinity was performed in combat, with ambiguous consequences for the men's motivation. On the one hand, the body may have been the ultimate 'evidence of manliness' when damaged 'properly' in combat; however, in modern warfare, the potential damage to men's bodies tended to be both random and 'improper', generating substantial 'embodied' fears of wounds that were both dehumanizing and emasculating. This fear, which several authors see as the reflection of a psychologically or culturally motivated fear of bodily disintegration, was perhaps the most gendered fear of all. First, it applied directly to the body as the constitutive element of masculine identity; second, it generated a feeling of loss of control and power that was typical of the wartime masculine experience, this time concerning the inability to control the fate and shape of one's own *male* form. This horrifying, intimate, deeply felt fear rose to the surface under fire, directly influencing – and gendering – the men's combat motivation.

Ironically, the body was not only an object of the men's fears, but also a possible source of hope. As mentioned by Joanna Bourke, men in wartime 'used their bodies to evade perilous situations … By feigning illness or incapacity … some men attempted to avoid exposure to the horrific physical risks' of the frontlines.[115] Within the context of our argument here, the body could actually help the men to become active subjects again, acting as a path to restore one's control and power over one's fate. Ironically, while the body was the most sensitive symbolic space where manliness could be threatened in war, it was also its ultimate line of defence. In Joana Bourke's definition, it was 'the last remaining thing [a soldier] could claim as his own'.[116] It was a space that men could hope to control, even long after they had lost control over everything else in their lives. As such, again, the importance of the body as a space for the soldiers' masculine identity cannot be overstated, which also further emphasizes the painful dimension of combat when it came to reshaping bodies.

The use of one's body in order to escape the (bodily) dangers of combat and, at the same time, regain some elementary control is as common a theme in Czech soldiers' writings as it is in those of their British counterparts studied by Joanna Bourke.[117] Strategies vary, but they all include the body being reshaped to obtain the one desirable result: medical discharge, or at least delay in being sent to the front. There are numerous examples in Žipek's ideologically motivated collection, where men try to escape conscription by either pretending to be medically unfit or causing their bodies to be so (by injecting or consuming various substances, intentionally contracting venereal disease, scalding, burning, etc.). Whatever the method, the result was a direct effort to keep one's life situation under control using one's body, in an effort to avoid a situation that would gradually deprive most men of all the control and power they had ever had.

For those who ended up in the army, self-mutilation was a preferred path to regain control through one's body, especially in the early stages of the war when the medical personnel did not have enough experience in identifying these acts. If their diaries (edited after the war) are to be believed, Augustin Mudrák stabbed himself twice in his forearm with a bayonet, and Josef Slezák shot himself three times over the course of the war. On the Piave in 1918, Jan Tříska witnessed two Hungarian *honvéd* soldiers shooting each other's legs, something that two soldiers of k.u.k. Infantry Regiment 75 could not force themselves to do on the Kolubara in 1914. Similarly, according to his diary, Josef Ulrych became so desperate that he considered cutting himself with an axe, only to relinquish it, realizing that he 'cannot do this to myself. Oh God, it would hurt!'[118] There was also a rather more passive way of restoring control over one's fate through the body – purposefully allowing the enemy to do the job. During the Battle of the Piave, the above-mentioned Jan Tříska, 'in the hope of finally getting into a quiet, tranquil, clean hospital in the rear', stuck out both his legs from a foxhole in the midst of a heavy machine-gun barrage, only to retract them 'half an hour later' without sustaining even a scratch, feeling both disappointed and ashamed.[119] The *Tausendguldenschuss* (a 'blighty wound' in the British soldiers' parlance) was the subject of many men's dreams, but leaving it all to chance as Tříska did was something probably only the most desperate ones tried – the risks were too high. In our sample, only Jan Šlesingr mentions similar behaviour when he 'climbed out of the trench in the midst of heavy fire', but in his case, he claimed disregard not only for his body, but even for his life.[120] The desperate need to reclaim control over one's life – by ending it – reached its ultimate level here, as in our interpretation suicide was the most radical and final act of regaining power, one that can be defined as a desperate effort in masculine redemption.

Besides self-inflicted wounds, the most common and apparently the most preferred method of evading frontline service (if not any service at all) with the use of one's body was feigning various illnesses or systemic disabilities. In particular, postwar accounts, both fiction and nonfiction, are filled with examples of men trying to picture themselves as true malingerers – one only has to recall the numerous examples populating the pages of the most famous Czech war account of all, Jaroslav Hašek's *The Good Soldier Švejk*.[121] Of course, in the postwar interpretation, malingering was a true manly effort to avoid 'collaboration' with the 'hated Austria', as the plentiful examples in Žipek's collection would present it. Ideology aside, this interpretation may have reflected the inherent 'manliness' of these actions in the fact that the men took control over their fate back into their own hands, and the more they felt disillusioned by the war and its unfulfilled promises (including those in the field of gender), the more they were probably willing to believe that this was indeed so.

As a result, if one was to base his or her opinion of the issue solely on Žipek's collection, it would seem that military hospitals in the hinterland were filled only with malingering Czechs.[122] However, such images were not a postwar speciality. Looking closer at the sources that originated at the time of the war itself, from time to time we encounter moments of deep demoralization and desperation, leading to efforts to evade further service by forcing one's body to do things that might save it from the threat of destruction – František Chmela, exhausted both in body and mind by the winter in the Carpathians, repeatedly searches for raw bacon with the intention of using it – along with some water from a puddle – to induce, in vain, a case of dysentery.[123] Josef Slezák, recuperating from a supposedly self-inflicted wound (he only added the information that *all* his wounds were self-inflicted into his diary *after the war*) in a hospital in Hradec Králové late in 1914, cryptically mentions what seems like an effort to prolong his stay there by feigning dysentery for a while.[124] František Bouška successfully feigned a case of sciatica during the same winter, which allowed him more frequent periods of rest from hard work in the trenches: 'It was hardly heroic, but I did not care', he admitted in a complete rebuttal of the official discourse of masculine wartime heroism. While many – unlike Bouška, who was apparently always keen on limiting his duty to a minimum – may have subscribed to the discourse at the beginning of the war, frozen trenches on the monarchy's frontier and constant shelling by Russian guns tended to change their views of their own masculinity as well as the duty that it conditioned.[125] The author's body, along with the broader symbolic system of masculine identity that had encompassed it, was being deformed, mangled and twisted, taken further away from the discursive ideal, and the ideal was quickly losing its legitimacy. Ironically, it was the body that often became a last line of defence against the feeling of one's masculinity to be not only besieged, but utterly subverted. It was a vehicle of real or feigned protest – a protest that aimed at restoring at least a *feeling* of being in control.

Notes

1. Eric Bogle, *And the Band Played Waltzing Matilda* (Sydney: Larrikin Music Pty Ltd., 1971).
2. Vítek, *V cizích službách*, 158–59.
3. Vaněk, *Charašó pán, da?*, 73, diary entry from 13 May 1915.
4. Tříska, *Zapomenutá fronta*, 106.
5. Carl von Clausewitz, *On War*, eds Michael Howard and Peter Paret (Princeton, 1989), 75–76.

6. 'The history of warfare – particularly academic and scholarly history, but also traditional military history – is all too often disembodied ... [the result is] an unacceptable way of sanitizing war'. Stéphane Audoin-Rouzeau and Annette Becker, *1914–1918: Understanding the Great War* (London, 2002), 14.
7. Ibid., 15.
8. See Lynn, *The Bayonets of the Republic*, 36.
9. Leonard V. Smith, *The Embattled Self: French Soldiers' Testimony of the Great War* (Ithaca, 2007), 35. For a summary, see Holmes, *Acts of War*, 136–75.
10. Sperling, *Český důstojník na frontách monarchie*, 45, diary entry from 19 August 1917. Similarly, Josef Váchal had volunteered for a forward observation post in order to 'see at least one defender of his country doing his task, shooting and fighting'. He left thoroughly disappointed, seeing nothing, only trenches: 'I looked for him in vain'. Váchal, *Malíř na frontě*, 94.
11. Šefl, *Paměti domobrance 28. pluku z války světové 1914–1918*, 30.
12. Slezák, *Paměti Josefa Slezáka k I. světové válce*, vol. 1, 45.
13. Jurman, ed., *Legionářská odyssea*, 15.
14. Kisch, *Vojákem pražského sboru*, 115, diary entry from 25 September 1914.
15. Leed, *No Man's Land*, X. On the discontinuity between the reality and language in the First World War, see also Fussell, *The Great War in Modern Memory*, 3–35; and Hynes, *A War Imagined*. For the author's take on the issue, using a specific case study of J.R.R. Tolkien's work, see Jiří Hutečka, 'Literární dílo jako odraz válečného prožitku? J.R.R. Tolkien a Pán prstenů', in *Mezi Martem a Memorií: Prameny osobní povahy k vojenským dějinám 16. – 19. století*, ed. Vítězslav Prchal (Pardubice, 2011), 133–149.
16. Joanna Bourke, *An Intimate History of Killing: Face-to-Face Killing in Twentieth Century Warfare* (London, 1999), 1.
17. Holmes, *Acts of War*, 376–93.
18. Audoin-Rouzeau, *Men at War*, 67.
19. Smith, *Embattled Self*, 90. Smith rightly disagrees with Joanna Bourke's conclusion that men found violence fascinating, particularly when it came to its individual, personal form of close combat. See Bourke, *An Intimate History of Killing*, 3–4.
20. Crouthamel, *An Intimate History of the Front*, 71.
21. Ulrych, 'Moje zápisky', 53; Morávek, *Špatný voják*, 133.
22. Smith, *Embattled Self*, 90.
23. Estimates based on French and German statistics for the period between 1914 and 1917, quoted in Benjamin Ziemann, 'Soldiers', in *Brill's Encyclopedia of the First World War*, eds Gerhard Hirschfeld, Gerd Krumeich, and Irina Renz (Leiden, 2012), vol. 1, 119. John Keegan's estimates based on the British army are fairly similar, with about 70% of all wounds being caused by artillery, less than 30% by bullets and less than 1% by bayonets. See John Keegan, *The Face of Battle* (London, 1976), 269. Richard Holmes has reached slightly different numbers in his research, though, with 58.51% of all losses caused by artillery, 38.98% by bullets, 2.19% by explosives and hand grenades, and 0.32% by bayonets. See Holmes, *Acts of War*, 210.
24. Smith, *Embattled Self*, 91.
25. Soušek, *Z Olomouce na perské hranice*, 24–36.
26. Mudrák, *Bojoval jsem za císaře pána*, 21.
27. Marshall, *Men against Fire*, 51.
28. Bouška, 'Zápisky ze světové války', 1.

29. Černý, *Moje záznamy ze světové války*, 81. František Skála supposedly thought exactly the same: 'I know for sure that even if someone steps in my way, I will not shoot or stab. For me, the fear for my own life cannot surpass the fear of killing a fellow man'. Skála, *Válečný deník*, 20.
30. Mudrák, *Bojoval jsem za císaře pána*, 18.
31. Černý, *Moje záznamy ze světové války*, 75–76.
32. Diary entry from 22 February 1915, in Vaněk, *Charašó pán, da?*, 39. For the way in which men behave under fire, see David Marlowe, 'The Human Dimension of Battle and Combat Breakdown', in *Military Psychology: A Comparative Perspective*, ed. Richard A. Gabriel (London, 1986), 7–24; see also Arnold M. Rose, 'The Social Psychology of Desertion from Combat', in *Motivating Soldiers: Morale or Mutiny*, ed. Peter Karsten (New York 1998), 250–265; Frederick J. Manning, 'Morale, Cohesion, and Esprit de Corps', in *Handbook of Military Psychology*, eds Reuven Gal and A. David Mangelsdorff (Chichester, 1991), 453–70.
33. Kisch, *Vojákem pražského sboru*, 46, diary entry from 17 August 1914.
34. Ibid., 90, diary entry from 10 September 1914.
35. Sýkora, 'Tarnavka – Obrázek ze světové války', 6.
36. Kisch, *Vojákem pražského sboru*, 105–6, diary entry from 16 September 1914.
37. The diary of František Petržíla, in *Zapomenuté hlasy*, 43.
38. Sperling, *Český důstojník na frontách monarchie*, 116, diary entry from 29 September 1917.
39. Klejna, *Voják – zajatec – legionář*, 53, diary entry from 25 November 1914.
40. Vaněk, *Charašó pán, da?*, 61–62, diary entry from 26 April 1915.
41. Ibid., 73, diary entry from 13 May 1915.
42. See, for example, Tracy X. Karner, 'Engendering Violent Men: Oral Histories of Military Masculinity', in *Masculinities and Violence*, ed. Lee H. Bowker (Thousand Oaks, 1998), 197–232. In *Understanding the Great War*, Stéphane Audoin-Rouzeau and Annette Becker mention the surprising similarity between the way in which violence and sexuality are treated in historical writing, calling the process 'academic puritanism' that ends up 'disembodying' and 'sanitizing' certain areas of historical experience, particularly the moments when it comes to the body. It is worth considering that soldiers may well have suffered from the same inhibitions as the professional historians who came after them. See Audoin-Rouzeau and Becker, *Understanding the Great War*, 14.
43. Černý, *Moje záznamy ze světové války*, 68–69.
44. Jurman, ed., *Legionářská odyssea*, 13.
45. Kisch, *Vojákem pražského sboru*, 80, diary entry from 7 September 1914.
46. Haring, 'K.u.k. Soldaten an der Ostfront im Sommer und Herbst 1914', 85.
47. Leo Braudy, *From Chivalry to Terorrism: War and the Changing Nature of Masculinity* (New York, 2003), xvi.
48. Vítek, *V cizích službách*, 265–66.
49. John Horne took this argument here even further and, referring to Clausewitz, defined war as 'masculinity by other means'. See John Horne, 'Masculinity in Politics and War in the Age of Nation-states and World Wars, 1850–1950', in *Masculinities in Politics and War*, 31.
50. Kisch, *Vojákem pražského sboru*, 105, diary entry from 16 September 1914.
51. Skála, *Válečný deník*, 20.

52. Ulrych, 'Moje zápisky', 62. See also Joanna Bourke, *Fear: A Cultural History* (London, 2005), 201.
53. Christopher Forth sees the duel as an ideal, individualized form of masculine violence, and agrees with Robert Nye that modern warfare is its democratized variant applied to the masses, where honour is not a matter of individual bourgeois identity, but rather collectively identified with the nation, and that the nation is then subjected to war as a collective test. Also, as Nye pointedly shows in the case of France and Ute Frevert for Germany, the beginning of the First World War rendered the widely popular social ritual of duelling obsolete almost overnight – there was no need to prove one's masculinity in a duel when one could do so on the socially preferred field of battle. See Forth, *Masculinity in the Modern West*, 118–21; Nye, *Masculinity and Male Codes of Honor in Modern France*; and also Frevert, *Men of Honour*. For a further comparison, particularly with Italy, Britain and the United States, see the essays in Pieter Spierenburg, ed., *Men and Violence: Gender, Honor, and Rituals in Modern Europe and America* (Columbus, 1998). Unfortunately, there is no similar study on duelling in Austria; however, it is known that in the prewar years, this social practice was generally limited to the army officer corps and that it died away with the start of the war as well. See Deák, *Beyond Nationalism*, 126–38.
54. Clausewitz, *On War*, 75.
55. See Smith, *Embattled Self*, 34–58.
56. Šmída, *Vzpomínky z vojny*, 124.
57. Recollection of Josef Rezek, in *Když naši dědové bojovali a umírali*, 39; diary of František Čapek, not dated, probably June 1915.
58. Tříska, ed., *Zapomenutá fronta*, 34.
59. Lirš, *S Osmadvacátníky za světové války*, 244.
60. Zückert, 'Memory of War and National State Integration', 116–18; see also Hutečka, 'Kamarádi frontovníci', 240–46.
61. Černý, *Moje záznamy ze světové války*, 83.
62. Bouška, 'Zápisky ze světové války', 24.
63. Sperling, *Český důstojník na frontách monarchie*, 116, diary entry from 23 October 1918; Skála, *Válečný deník*, 189; Šmída, *Vzpomínky z vojny*, 130.
64. Šmída, *Vzpomínky z vojny*, 140.
65. Sýkora, 'Tarnavka – Obrázek ze světové války', 1.
66. Statistics quoted in Healy, *Vienna and the Fall of the Habsburg Empire*, 264.
67. Ibid.
68. Again, statistics quoted in ibid.
69. Stouffer et al., *The American Soldier*, vol. 2, 231.
70. See Holmes, *Acts of War*, 76–78. For a general overview, see Martin van Creveld, *Supplying War: Logistics from Wallenstein to Patton* (Cambridge, 1977); see also John A. Lynn, ed., *Feeding Mars: Logistics in Western Warfare from the Middle Ages to the Present* (Boulder, 1993).
71. Deák, *Beyond Nationalism*, 201–2.
72. For further information, see Holmes, *Acts of War*, 77–78.
73. Vítek, *V cizích službách*, 23.
74. Kisch, *Vojákem pražského sboru*, 213.
75. Slezák, *Paměti Josefa Slezáka k I. světové válce*, vol. 2, 65
76. Tellingly, a number of the men who made it into the ranks of the 'depot swine' during their service were all but happy to exchange the uncertain (and mostly symbolic)

'benefits' of the status of a frontline soldier for the much more real certainties of the life in the rear. See, for example, Josef Váchal after his redeployment to the 'paradise' of the *'Fassungstelle'* (Váchal, *Malíř na frontě*, 236) or the main character of a fictionalized memoir included in Žipek's collection: 'Back here, behind the front, we enjoyed life in spite of all the death ... In spite of all those at the front. For the next several months ... I have become what the poor bastards were jealously calling an *Etappenschweine*'. See F. Horečka, 'Bojování civilistovo', in *Domov za války*, vol. 3, 369.

77. Kisch, *Vojákem pražského sboru*, 144.
78. The best example here may be the veterans' biweekly magazine *Kamarádství*, published 1932 to 1938. Also, many memoirs hold the same view; for a perfect example, see Šindelář, *Proti vlastní vůli*.
79. Vaněk, *Charašó pán, da?*, 18, diary entry from 20 September.
80. Sabine Kienitz, *Beschädigte Helden: Kriegsinvalidität und Körperbilder 1914–1923* (Paderborn, 2008), 238–85. See also Sabine Kienitz, 'Die Kastrierten des Krieges: Körperbilder und Männlichkeitskonstruktionen im und nach dem Ersten Weltkrieg', *Zeitschrift für Volkskunde* 95, no. 1 (1999): 63–82; and Sabine Kienitz, 'Das Ende des Männlichkeit? Zur symbolischen Re-Maskulinisierung der Kriegskrüppel im Ersten Weltkrieg', in *Männlich. Weiblich: Zur bedeutung der kategorie Geschlecht in der Kultur*, eds Christel Köhle-Hezinger, Martin Scharfe, and Rolf Wilhelm Brednich (Münster, 1999), 181–89. See also Carden-Coyne and Doan, 'Gender and Sexuality', 100.
81. As a particularly extreme example, we may point to the memorial collection edited by Alois Žipek. As its admitted purpose was to summarize the sufferings of Czechs in their wartime service for the monarchy, it does not spare its readers any detail when it comes to graphic descriptions of this suffering. For a typical example, see a soldier's recollection of the Battle of Caporetto: 'A theatre of horrors: several men rolling about in pain in a pool of blood, fingers, two noses, a chin and three pieces of ear lying about ... [Another moment:] Two men were killed, their heads blown to smithereens all over the ravine. One had just a horrible bloodied stub for a throat sticking out of his coat, while all the other guy had left of his head was a left gum with a row of yellow teeth'. Antonín Zoglman, 'Po průlomu u Tolmína', in *Domov za války*, vol. 4, 245.
82. Stéphan Audoin-Rouzeau identified the same tendency of 'horrified fascination' in trench newspapers published by French soldiers during the war. See Audoin-Rouzeau, *Men at War*, 78.
83. Křenek, *Vzpomínky na vojnu v Albanii*, 172.
84. Mudrák, *Bojoval jsem za císaře pána*, 58.
85. Sperling, *Český důstojník na frontách monarchie*, 100, diary entry from 6 June 1918.
86. Kisch, *Vojákem pražského sboru*, 81 and 104, diary entries from 8 and 15 September 1914.
87. Vaněk, *Charašó pán, da?*, 71, diary entry from 8 May 1915. For further examples, see the diary of František Petržíla, in *Zapomenuté hlasy*, 51–52; Váchal, *Malíř na frontě*, 93; or Vítek, *V cizích službách*, 150, among others. An exception to the rule can be found in the short memoir of Josef Rezek, who still mentions 'the horrible, unforgettable impression' that 'the first wounded made upon me', even adding that 'I cried, I'm not ashamed to admit', but steers away from any details. Josef Rezek, 'Recollections', in *Když naši dědové bojovali a umírali*, 38.
88. Slezák, *Paměti Josefa Slezáka k I. světové válce*, vol. 1, 18.
89. Ibid., 30.

90. Watson, *Enduring the Great War*, 28. For a similar conclusion, see also Holmes, *Acts of War*, 209–11.
91. Roper, *The Secret Battle*, 248 and 260.
92. Smith, *Embattled Self*, 76–77; Smith quotes Carolyn W. Bynum, *The Resurrection of the Body in Western Christianity, 200–1336* (New York, 1995).
93. Geroulanos and Meyers, *The Human Body in the Age of Catastrophe*, 201–5.
94. Bouška, 'Zápisky ze světové války', 30.
95. Morávek, *Špatný voják*, 105.
96. Roper, *The Secret Battle*, 249.
97. Hála, 'Vzpomínka na 11. sočskou bitvu', 67.
98. Ulrych, 'Moje zápisky', 42.
99. Vítek, *V cizích službách*, 156.
100. Šindelář, *Proti vlastní vůli*, 53.
101. Geroulanos and Meyers, *The Human Body in the Age of Catastrophe*, 316–18.
102. Vančura, *Pole orná a válečná*, 128.
103. Ibid., 57.
104. Šindelář, *Proti vlastní vůli*, 54.
105. Kisch, *Vojákem pražského sboru*, 83, diary entry from 10 September 1914.
106. Skála, *Válečný deník*, 254.
107. Ibid., 258.
108. Ibid., 261; see also Slezák, *Paměti Josefa Slezáka k I. světové válce*, vol. 3, 72.
109. Morávek, *Špatný voják*, 204–5.
110. Vaněk, *Charašó pán, da?*, 39, diary entry from 22 February 1915.
111. Kisch, *Vojákem pražského sboru*, 113, 124 and 125.
112. František Křížek, 'Z válečných zkušeností chudého vojáka', 193–203, in *Domov za války*, vol. 3, 194.
113. Šindelář, *Proti vlastní vůli*, 186.
114. On the importance of group loyalty in combat motivation, see Stouffer et al., *The American Soldier*, vol. 2, 136–38.
115. Bourke, *Dismembering the Male*, 76.
116. Ibid., 81.
117. For a comparison of self-inflicted wounds in the German army, see Benjamin Ziemann, 'Verweigerungsformen von Frontsoldaten in der deutschen Armee 1914–1918', in *Gewalt im Krieg: Ausübung, Erfahrung und Verwegierung von Gewalt in Kriegen des 20. Jahrhunderts*, ed. Andreas Gestrich (Münster, 1996), 108–110.
118. Mudrák, *Bojoval jsem za císaře pána*, 21; Slezák, *Paměti Josefa Slezáka k I. světové válce*, vol. 1, 88; vol. 2, 64–65; and vol. 3, 77; Tříska, ed., *Zapomenutá fronta*, 100; Jan Flíček, 'Na Kolubaře', in *Pětasedmdesátníci vzpomínají*, 72; Ulrych, 'Moje zápisky', 109.
119. Tříska, ed., *Zapomenutá fronta*, 101.
120. Šlesingr, *Legionáři*, 18.
121. Ironically, while the army was always redefining its discourse of 'able-bodied' men to be able to conscript as many as possible, some men did whatever they could to make their body 'un-able', be it through physical harm or merely an inspired pretence. In this race, malingerers were gradually cornered, as exemplified by the case of the writer Eduard Bass, who had spent most of the war in military hospitals trying to find a way to a medical discharge. By the end of 1917, he noted in his memoirs, it was clear that the army has lowered its physical requirements so much that even men of poor health

(or ability to feign it) found it difficult to avoid frontline service. See Eduard Bass, *Moje kronika* (Prague, 1985).
122. An excellent example of this trope is to be found in Eduard Bass's memoir: 'Everyone was completely healthy in that hospital, there was just one sick person – the Chief Medical Officer. He was sick in the mind'. Bass, *Moje kronika*, 98.
123. Chmela, *Vzpomínky z 1. světové války*, 24.
124. Slezák, *Paměti Josefa Slezáka k I. světové válce*, vol. 1, 83.
125. Bouška, 'Zápisky ze světové války', 34.

Conclusion

In the previous chapters, we have witnessed the way in which the First World War induced changes in the masculine identity of men conscripted into the ranks of the Austro-Hungarian military. Each particular chapter enabled us to see one specific area, a symbolic space where masculinity was challenged, contested and often changed under pressure, always facing the spectre of the loss of power and control – the prime masculine qualities. In the supreme irony of wartime gender shifts, the war that had promised men the possibility of attaining or retaining the status of hegemonic masculinity threatened to take away the very core that constituted it, offering little in exchange for the accompanying miseries. From the point of view of soldiers' masculinity, therefore, the war of 1914–18 was one immense, collective disappointment and shock.

When the war came in 1914, the social geography defining the symbolic space of Austro-Hungarian society quickly aligned with the official discourse, presenting as a fact the dichotomy of the feminine 'hinterland' and the masculine 'front'. Consequently, the masculine 'part' of this dichotomy was also redefined around the newly militarized notion of masculine identity, influenced both by the officially presented image of wartime manliness and by the influential 'residual elements' deeply ingrained in the prewar culture. These shifts were both officially promoted *and* experienced on the individual level. Military masculinity was elevated to the status of the hegemonic form of manliness in wartime society, with both the hierarchies of masculinities and paths leading to the 'patriarchal dividend' reflecting the process, making it all the easier for men to accept their new role. In particular, men who had been disadvantaged in the original peacetime hierarchy because of their age, economic or social status had comparatively little to lose (not having careers, families or a substantial property) and much to gain (status, prestige and favour) from following the trajectory of these shifts, while those who already occupied a hegemonic social position were more or less bound to follow just to be able to keep it. The resulting quick and calm mobilization of the army units in the Bohemian Crown Lands mirrored the strong initial motivation of the troops. While this motivation clearly reflected some immediate factors such as fear of punishment and the expectation of a short war (or no war at all), the social pressure of everyone around doing their duty and the notion of the duty itself were clearly rooted in the general understanding of a man's obligations in wartime. Czech-speaking troops, while not overly enthusiastic, were perfectly content to heed this call. It did not take more than a few months for many to begin to doubt their judgement, encountering the many deep conflicts between the expectations and the reality that the war had brought about on several fronts.

Not only did the real war not end 'before the plums were ripe' or, at worst, before Christmas; its very dehumanized, industrial reality, with the deluge of fire and steel facing the men and forcing them to dig in quickly, confounded any expectations or notions that may have promised them confirmation of their masculine status. The war turned men-active actors into men-passive victims. The constant lack of food, shelter and basic comforts, along with the neverending threat of randomly dispensed death, brought them to the verge of physical and mental exhaustion. Space and time gradually lost shape, along with the same process regarding one's own being, which instead of a living, healthy, civilized man increasingly came to resemble previously marginalized forms of masculinity – cultureless, uncivilized barbarians, wild animals without any control over their needs or destiny, dehumanized machines without any trace of humanity in them. What resulted was a deeply felt sense of subverted manliness, an unmanning accompanied by loss of power over everything, starting with one's own body and sexuality, which threatened the men with dangerous experimentation and the potential for homosexual practices inherent in the all-male environment of the army, as traditional, 'manly' heterosexual behaviour was either impossible due to the inaccessibility of women, strictly regulated or rife with plentiful threats in itself.

Sexual contacts between the soldiers and (particularly) local women were seen, by society as well as by many of the men themselves, as a reflection of moral decline and social decay, as well as further evidence of devalued masculinity. In the sources, casual sex is almost always a matter of 'the others', while the author retains the moral high ground. On the other hand, heterosexual contacts became an obsession with the men, seen not just as a fulfilment of their physical needs, but also as proof of one's masculinity. As a result, sexuality is seen as a symbolic space of restoring power over femininity, and women are inherently seen as truly feminine, weak, passive and often thoroughly sexualized objects. However, this image came into stark contrast with reality, where women increasingly encroached upon the traditionally masculine spheres, including the very spatial core of wartime masculinity – the 'frontline' (i.e. the army), which was seen as the last stronghold of masculinity and gender exclusivity in the whirlwind of social change. The female trespassers upon the gender boundaries even ended up wearing the same uniforms as the men, serving as the *hilfskräfte* in large numbers in the latter stages of the war. Looking at the soldiers' personal accounts, it is obvious that they quickly became a symbolic object of fear, further pointing towards the loss of social control the men felt they were experiencing. As a result, many ended up projecting further masculine qualities onto the women, including supposedly aggressive sexual behaviour. From the point of view of the men, the war was deeply compromising to their subjective experience of manliness by the very way it blurred the once-clear social boundaries of dominant masculinity and subordinate femininity, rendering their motivation to continue to fight dangerously unstable.

The homosocial environment of the army, where soldiers spent years in intimate physical coexistence, had always threatened the codes of masculine morality with its borderline homoerotic connotations, and the Austro-Hungarian army was no different. We may also speculate as to whether it induced further fears of losing control over one's erotic or even sexual affinities. The symbolic concept of comradeship, which clearly developed its basic outlines during the war, served the men to keep these fears at bay by creating a framework that enabled intimate relations as well as 'feminine' qualities to be accommodated within the broader notion of masculinity. The process made it possible to incorporate several patterns of wartime social as well as psychological practice, such as the eroticization of the male body, cross-dressing, physical intimacy, emotionality and open emotional dependence on other men, as well as all the traditionally feminized mundane tasks of everyday life. This reconstruction of wartime masculinity actually supported the proper functioning of primary groups, traditionally seen as the key factor in sustaining men's motivation over long periods of military service.

When it came to sustaining motivation, perhaps the most essential connection with our gender analysis manifested itself in the soldiers' relationship with the military authorities. The key role was played here by the seismic shifts in the wartime hierarchies of masculinities, originally reflected in the way in which army life restructured groups of men into separate classes regardless of their previous economic or social status, which led to a class victory of the lucky few to be elevated, and the disillusionment of many who felt degraded and commanded by men they saw as inferior. The class distinction between the enlisted men and the officers also created a deep resentment, as it rarely reflected the supposed values of 'true' masculine qualities of men in wartime. While many of these issues were common in several armies throughout the war, one that seems to have been specific to Czech soldiers related to the gradually increasing feeling of the unjust, degrading treatment the men who were seen as Czech received from the hands of the military authorities. Emanating mostly from the politically motivated and somewhat inherent distrust the military authorities harboured towards anything and anyone Czech, this attitude, often very public, appearing in full when the first blame-games and searches for scapegoats started early in the war, actually led many soldiers to complain of disrespect towards their (sometimes unwilling, but still real) sacrifice. And, as their sacrifice defined them as true men in wartime, they saw their manliness being painfully diminished in the process, with a detrimental impact on their loyalty, which was based on fulfilling their masculine duty. The issue was exacerbated even further by ideological conflict between the army authorities and many of the Czech-speaking soldiers over the nature of discipline, in which the authorities followed their notion of 'cultural imperialism', pressing for traditional, both formal and informal, corporal punishment. Czech soldiers often saw themselves as the most civilized members of the Austro-Hungarian cultural milieu, and the practice of such punishments only deepened their growing discontent.

The steep decline in morale typical of the final year of the war was not just a consequence of a general disillusionment with the army and its failed hierarchies; it owed even more to the massive deterioration of both the economy and the supply system in Austria-Hungary. While the lack of 'bread' hit the men hard by itself, it played an even more systemic role when acting through another symbolic arena of masculinity – the home. Being a sum of several key 'venues' of masculine performance expected of a true man (family, work, economic existence), home placed the men before an unsolvable dilemma – how to be a good father, husband, son and breadwinner, and to fulfil one's masculine duty to the state in war *at the same time*. The worsening economic situation in the Austrian part of the monarchy made this issue increasingly pressing, and the consequences for the men's morale were devastating. What made the situation even worse was the fact that home served as a beacon of hope the men held dearest, even if it was only an idealized image reflecting their inner longing for normality. This image was indispensable for the men's emotional survival and any changes to it were generally disapproved of by them. Particularly difficult to swallow were shortages in provisions caused by economic distress and shifts in the distribution of power caused by wartime necessities, especially the fact that while the men were away, women did all the work, made all the decisions and had all the control over the family, its economy, as well as themselves and their bodies. Men saw these processes as further evidence of the unmanning the war had brought upon them, rendering them unable to act and leaving their sense of masculinity thoroughly subverted. As a result, their faith in the legitimacy of the war and the state itself was shattered. Although they often tried to restore 'normalcy' in the domestic power relations from a distance, it was an impossible effort and their role as the main actor in the matters of home management gradually fell apart. Both mail and the institution of home leave were limited as tools, unable to do more than offer brief nostalgic peeks into moments of 'gender normality', where men could keep the semblance of being still in control, positioned in the central position of all social, economic and power relations in the family.

The need for masculine performance on the field of battle, which was essential for fulfilling the requirements of militarized hegemonic masculinity, was, of course, a factor that was stressful by itself. Combat and violence were always at the very core of this performance, but in Czech soldiers' accounts, their attitude towards violent action and killing amounted to a cultural as well as ideological taboo. While it is clear that even the authors themselves participated in their fair share of violent encounters on the battlefield, they staunchly refused to mention any details beyond the fact of these events actually happening. As a result, images of combat presented in personal accounts largely consisted of passive survival. Under this trope, soldiers turn into victims, pure objects of external forces, bereft of anything that traditionally constitutes military masculinity. As a result, control slips out of the men's hands, and if combat was to remain the ultimate proof of manliness, it had to undergo a symbolic reinterpretation, one that resembled a duel on a mass scale; a duel as a trial of courage that is designed around one's ability to ignore fear. This new courage was the new, modern test of manliness, primarily based on the power to *stay* – not, as the traditional mode of courage would be, the power to *act*. However, staying was made difficult by the nature of modern warfare, particularly by the fact that the key part of its character is the ever-present, permanent danger of catastrophic and dehumanizing destruction of one's body. It is as invariably connected to the modern nature of combat as the fear of it is interwoven into the texture of modern masculinity, making it a key issue in soldiers' combat-effectiveness. In this context, fear was literally 'embodied' in the images of masculine forms, symbolic spaces essential for the modern understanding of manliness, being horrifically destroyed, reshaped and maligned all around. Personal accounts reveal not only fear of one's mortality, but also deep-seated anxiety regarding the potential loss of control and power over the most basic essence of manliness – a man's body, be it dead or still alive. In soldiers' eyes, this body was the final bastion of their already hard-pressed, shaken, compromised and degraded masculine identity – and through combat, it became an object of fear itself. Beyond their body, there was nothing left for men to control; there was no manliness left in war. It is actually fully understandable, in this context, as to why men used their body as the primary tool to regain control and at least some power, at least for a short period of time. They did it either in a symbolic manner, by feigning illnesses or wounds, or directly through the body itself, reshaping it by self-wounding in order to remove themselves from the 'masculine' space of the frontline for a while or for good.

At the beginning, the men in our sample felt that war, while an unwelcome event not worthy of enthusiasm, did at least conform to their notion of masculinity in some way, which helped them to make sense of it and consent to the state's demand for them to join in. However, instead of entrenching or improving their position in the gender order, it only dismantled, deformed and altered their sense of masculinity. It is clear that these pressures helped to erode the soldiers' motivation to fight on, and while they may not have played the most obvious, primary role, they were important background factors, resurfacing from time to time in the thought and writing of the men in the trenches, influencing both their subjective experience of masculinity as well as, consequently, the social practices that shaped this experience.

If we turn our attention back to the questions asked at the beginning of this book, it seems possible to argue successfully that part of the answer to what enables men to endure years of industrial warfare is to be found in a gender analysis of their experience. The primary sources tell us that gender considerations, while often hidden in the background of more pressing and obvious matters, are always on the soldiers' minds, influence the way in which they understand their situation and help to define the conditions for their consent or rejection. Based on our analysis, it is still open to debate as to whether these considerations are supportive of soldiers' morale and motivation in general or not. However, it is obvious that gender cannot be skipped over in any effort to understand these categories, and 'gendering of military history', while adhering to the constraints of historicity, agency and differentiation, is indeed a useful category of analysis. In other words, the way in which an individual experience the masculine identity is tightly linked to the nature of the conflict; henceforth, the experience, attitude and the ultimate consent or discontent reflect the dynamics of this relationship.

In the case presented here, we have seen that the prewar military culture was steeped deep in the notion of war as manly business, and it is possible to paraphrase and concur with Laurence Cole's argument that it 'offers part of the explanation as to why the Habsburg military machine kept fighting for longer than some observers expected'.[1] While some men might have been 'coerced into war', for the most part it seems that even self-admitted Czechs, who would generally not see it as 'their' conflict, were perfectly willing to fulfil their duty. Their initial consent was deeply bound to their sense of manliness and the desire to keep it. Consequently, the same effort to keep one's masculinity as intact as possible played a similarly important role in soldiers' motivation during the war. However, over the course of the long conflict, the subjective experience of masculinity, under pressure from massive shifts in the social reality, increasingly diverged from masculinity as understood on the level of cultural patterns and discourses. The inability to keep the two layers of masculine existence working together led many men to develop negative attitudes towards the war effort. The institutions sustaining this effort – the army and the Habsburg state – gradually lost most of their legitimacy, while men ceased to see any purpose or meaning in the war itself, and their consent was constantly withering away. By mid 1918, coercion had become the overriding motivational factor for the vast majority of them. Particularly after the disastrous experience of the Battle of the Piave, most Czech soldiers seem to have entered a vegetative state of sorts in terms of their morale – all hopes of a quick victory, understood almost exclusively in terms of a quick ending to the war, were lost; consent to further military action, which had promised to end the war, was gone; and the new identities, long-simmering under the increasingly brittle façade of the old army and fuelled by total disillusionment, rose to the surface.² For all intents and purposes, in the eyes of Czech soldiers as well as most of the others in the Austro-Hungarian uniform, the war was over in June 1918.

An important question that is worth addressing at the end of our analysis is whether the above-described experience of men at war was in some way specifically different for the men who saw themselves as Czechs. The answer is not simple, as many of the above-mentioned conflicts of identity emanated from the universal notion of gender identity in early twentieth-century European culture, and may be seen as common to most of the soldiers who served through the First World War. While all of the issues described here at length are indeed men-specific, it is difficult to ascertain which ones may have been Czech-specific. As Alexander Watson pointed out regarding the example of combat effectiveness, 'allegedly society-specific qualities identified by historians as beneficial to resilience were often common human responses to stress'.³ On the other hand, John Lynn is right when he criticizes the notion of a universal soldier, and this criticism is as well founded with regard to global cultures and histories as it is with regard to the First World War, as awareness of multiplicity and diversity of historical experience are key parts in an effort to understand it.⁴ Compared to manifold other cases, Czech-speaking troops were similar in some areas and specific in others. While they faced similar (often wildly variable) levels of exposure to frontline dangers and were attached to their home as any other soldiers were, they did not share the same levels of logistical support as Benjamin Ziemann's rural Germans, nor did they find much escape in any religion. Instead, urban or even industrial background brought them fear for the wellbeing of their loved ones, while their education and cultural background offered them readily available secular ideologies such as socialism or, more importantly, nationalism. They could hardly rely on the respite of furloughs, as the Austro-Hungarian army issued these only sparingly in the first years of the war – between 1914 and 1916, two weeks once a year were a general standard even for the soldiers from a rural background. In 1917, the situation changed radically in a belated effort to keep the men's morale up, but at that moment, it only helped to bring many a soldier into the midst of the economic disaster that was their home at the time. They feared punishment as well, but theirs had been always tinted with a notion of collective guilt of a 'suspect minority'. Being conscripts or reserve officers at best, they did not share the value system of gentlemanly honour that carried along the majority of the professional officer class as described by Martin Schmitz; on the other hand, they were often proud adherents to their own concepts of social hierarchy that (in their own eyes) set them apart from the other minorities in the army and made them susceptible to further resentment of its practices. And, finally, being gendered as men made many of these specifics all the more painful.

The wartime crisis of gender identified throughout this book had obviously influenced Czech soldiers' morale and was especially damaging to their attitude to the Austro-Hungarian military authorities and the state they represented. This attitude was primarily fomented in reaction, as its original loyalty bordering on indifference towards the war was transformed by the suspicions the army command had traditionally harboured towards Czechs (and other minorities), the ones it fell back on when the war did not go according to plan. True or not, Czech-speaking soldiers quickly felt themselves to be singled out as a group, suspected of disloyalty or outright treason, while still expected to shed blood for the monarchy.[5] The perceived lack of respect, unworthy of fighting men who bring sacrifice to the state even though they see little reason in it, is an endemic theme in most personal accounts of the war and is clearly connected to the soldiers' sense of masculine self-worth. What is evident as well is the fact that these feelings tended to be shared and harboured in groups, turning their interest and agency against the powers that be. In this sense, it is obvious that the Austro-Hungarian army command, for the most part, blatantly failed in motivating Czechs to be more enthusiastic about its cause – its attitudes and actions were actually damaging their loyal, somewhat hopeful consent to the point where only coercion and automated, blind obedience to authority remained alone in the structure of the men's motivation. Then, battlefield chaos or a combat crisis was all that was needed to sever the brittle ties of imposed discipline – and a surrender or even active desertion could well be seen as a moment of taking back control over one's (masculine) fate.

It is a great irony that the image of a 'disloyal Czech' may provide a prime example of a self-fulfilling prophecy, as the Army High Command's suspicions ultimately fuelled precisely those attitudes it sought to eradicate from the ranks. And while coercion and the strong tradition of duty still managed to keep a large proportion of the men in line until the very end, an ever-increasing number of Czech-speaking men gave up on it, on the war and on the monarchy itself much earlier, taking back control in any way they could. The wartime practices of institutional bullying, paranoia and harsh discipline dispensed on men defined by their language made them increasingly conscious, even painfully aware – and constantly reminded – of their nationality. Being singled out (negatively) as members of a group, the disillusionment described above made them identify with the group through the shared feeling of humiliation and (often gendered) degradation. The fact that they were increasingly denominated as 'Czechs' only strengthened their national self-identification along with the attached attitudes of betrayed cultural superiority, while parallel wartime social and economic pressures made them lose faith in the legitimacy of the same monarchy they felt was turning against their interests, both individual and collective.

While imperial loyalty and national self-identification were hardly at odds in July 1914, the moment Czech-speaking officers and men were singled out in this way, these categories got on a collision course. The army, led by its own fears of national subversion that turned into a mild paranoia as early as late

1914, ended up inadvertently subverting the essential sense of their masculine self-worth, pushing them towards national identity that was already available and fostered by the Czech political and intellectual elites for decades. Of course, national self-identification was not the only alternative to the ailing monarchy that was available to either soldiers or the general population. Class, regional or local identities were also playing havoc with the loyalty to the state in the later stages of the war, as attested by both the 'military strikes' and mutinies of 1918, the existence of 'green cadres' and many other forms of 'military resistance'. As one historian put it, at the beginning, nationalism was only one of the options available, while 'others were socialists or, later, Communists, whose chief loyalty was to the labour movement rather than to their nationality. Anti-Habsburg sentiments in the Slav and Italian parts of the empire were thus often overborne by dynastic, religious, or class loyalties, and it was only gradually that national identity won out'.[6] This victory had much to do with the way in which the Austro-Hungarian military command pursued its 'minority policy', furthering the deep disillusionment with one's masculinity gradually destroyed in a war that once promised to edify it. Thus, in the end, Austria-Hungary may have lost support of these troops because it failed them as *men*.

Notes

1. Cole, *Military Culture and Popular Patriotism in Late Imperial Austria*, 314.
2. For the general context of the Austro-Hungarian army and its morale after the Battle of the Piave, see Rothenberg, *The Army of Francis Joseph*, 214–15; Rauchensteiner, *Der Tod des Doppeladlers*, 579–81; or Cornwall, *The Undermining of Austria-Hungary*, 406–7.
3. Watson, *Enduring the Great War*, 7.
4. See Lynn, *Battle*, xiv–xv.
5. See Schmitz, *'Als ob die Welt aus den Fugen ginge'*, 88–90. For a similar case of discrimination leading to a collapse of loyalty, Schmitz quotes the case of Italian-speaking soldiers from the Trentino region. See also Oswald Überegger, *Der andere Krieg: Die Tiroler Militärgerichtsbarkeit im Ersten Weltkrieg* (Innsbruck, 2002), 270. With regard to the 'frontier minorities' such as Tyroleans or Ruthenes, numerous authors argue that by 1918, many wanted peace at any cost.
6. Stibbe, 'The Internment of Political Suspects in Austria-Hungary during the First World War', 215.

BIBLIOGRAPHY

Primary Sources

Archives

Central Military Archives – Military Historical Archives in Prague

Sbírka historických prací, kart. 7: V.P. Hájický, *Křížová cesta Čsl. vojska – z mých zápisků ze Srbska* (manuscript).
Sbírka historických prací, kart. 7: Jan Sýkora, *Tarnavka – Obrázek ze světové války* (manuscript).
Sbírka osob II, Pozůstalost Bohuslava Hály, Vzpomínky: *Vzpomínka na 11. sočskou bitvu* (typescript).

Literary Archive – Memorial of National Literature

Fond František Langer, inv. č. 12952.

State District Archive in Olomouc

Fond Janošík Jan, pplk. v. v.

State District Archive in Havlíčkův Brod

Sbírka soudobé dokumentace okresu Havlíčkův Brod, sign. D7A, Diary of František Čapek (manuscript).

Regional Museum in Olomouc

Sbírka 'Novodobé dějiny – odboj', č. 67/2016, The Zeman Family Letters.

Regional Museum in Dobruška – Archival Collections

Jarkovský, Josef, *Kronika ze světové války od roku 1/2 1915 do 4/9 1919* (manuscript), sig. XIV/300.
Slezák, Josef, *Paměti Josefa Slezáka k I. světové válce*, (manuscript, 5 vols), unprocessed.
Ulrych, Josef, *Moje zápisky, 1893–1922*, (manuscript, 1922), CD-ROM 115.

Private Collections

Private collection of Eva Horová: wartime correspondence of Adolf Vraspír.
Private collection of Jan Janošík: wartime diary and correspondence of Josef Janošík.
Private collection of Martin Čihák: wartime diary of Václav Doležal.
Private collection of the Čundrle family: wartime family correspondence of Jan Čundrle.
Private collection of the Holec family: wartime diary of František Bouška, *Zápisky ze světové války 1914–1920 a z čsl. revolučního vojska na Rusi*.

Published Primary Sources

Bass, Eduard. *Moje kronika*. Prague, 1985.
Blümlová, Dagmar, ed. '"…Ale vojna je tak úžasná věc, že ztráví celého člověka": Velká válka v životě a díle jazykovědce Františka Jílka-Oberpfalcera'. In *Armáda, společnost a první světová válka: Sborník příspěvků z vědecké konference konané v Jihočeském muzeu v Českých Budějovicích dne 8. listopadu 2002*. České Budějovice, 2003, 13–16.
Brod, Max. *Život plný bojů*. Prague, 1994.
Černý, František. *Moje záznamy ze světové války*. Prague, 2014.
Chmela, František. *Vzpomínky z 1. světové války*. Týn nad Vltavou, 2014.
Dolejší, Alois. *Válečné vzpomínky z první světové války vojína Dolejše z Nového Strašecí*, edited by Dagmar Neprašová. Brno, 2014.
Habrman, Gustav. *Mé vzpomínky z války: Črty a obrázky o událostech a zápasech za svobodu a samostatnost*. Prague, 1928.
Hašek, Jaroslav. *Osudy dobrého vojáka Švejka za světové války*. 4 vols. Prague, 1921–1923.
——. *The Fateful Adventures of the Good Soldier Švejk during the World War*. Translated by Zdeněk Sadloň and Emmit Joyce, 3 vols. London, 1997.
Jaroš, Karel. *Z turecké armády do britského zajetí*, edited by Petr Havel. Prague, 1995.
John, Jaromír. *Listy z vojny, jež psal svému synovi*. Prague, 1917.
Jurman, Oldřich, ed. *Legionářská odyssea. Deník Františka Prudila*. Prague, 1990.
Kaiser, Alois L. *Od Piavy ke Komárnu*. Prague, 1931.
——. *Voják statečný. Fragment posledního nápotu třistaleté armády*. Prague, 1930.
Kamarádství: List válečných, převratových a současných dějů, Prague, 1932–1938.
Kápar, Josef. *Cestou kamenitou*. Prague, 1922.
Kisch, Egon Erwin. *Vojákem pražského sboru*. Prague, 1965.
Klejna, Josef. *Voják – zajatec – legionář*, edited by Michaela Mrázová. Velké Přílepy, 2014.
Kolman, Jaroslav. *Cassiovy listy*. Prague, 1921.
Konečný, Miloš, ed. *Když naši dědové bojovali a umírali v 1. světové válce*. Vlkov, 2014.
Křenek, Jaroslav. *Vzpomínky na vojnu v Albanii*. Jihlava, 1924.
Krulichová, Milada, and Milan Jankovič, eds. *Zapomenuté hlasy: korespondence, deníkové záznamy a kresby z první světové války*. Hradec Králové, 1986.
Květoň, Vladislav. *Vzpomínky z první světové války*. Prague, 1995.
Kylar, František. 'Vzpomínky z vojny: Válečné paměti 1917–1918'. In *Rodové paměti v Kunčicích*, edited by Alois Kněžek and Emil Vondrouš. Ústí nad Orlicí, 2006, 34–54.
Laška, Jan. *Asinara*. Prague, 1928.
——. *Pochod hladu Albanií (Z Niše do Valony)*. Prague, 1920.
Lirš, Ferdinand. *S Osmadvacátníky za světové války*. Prague, 1936.
Listy našich vojáků. Co nám píší z bojiště. 5 vols. Prague, 1915.

Morávek, Jan. *Špatný voják*. Prague, 1929.
Mudrák, Augustin. *Bojoval jsem za císaře pána*, edited by Jiří Červenka. Brno, 2011.
Neumann, Stanislav Kostka. *Bragožda a jiné válečné vzpomínky*. Prague, 1928.
———. 'Válčení civilistovo'. In *Spisy Stanislava K. Neumanna*. Prague, 1976, 7–115.
Opletal, Bedřich. *Anabáze hanáckého medika, 1914–1920*. Prague, 1998.
Peerz, Rudolf. *Vlast volá! Slovo k obyvatelstvu Rakouska-Uherska*. Vienna, 1916.
Pětasedmdesátníci vzpomínají. Z pamětí účastníků světové války. Jindřichův Hradec, 1936.
Poláček, Jaroslav, ed. *Zápisky Václava Poláčka ze světové války a ze života v Hojkově*. Jihlava, 2011.
Poláček, Karel. *Hrdinové táhnou do boje*. Prague, 1994.
———. *Podzemní město*. Prague, 1994.
Rélink, Karel. *28. pluk 'Pražské děti': Osmadvacátníci, veselí kluci, ve válečné vichřici*. Prague, 1932.
Sassoon, Siegfried. *The War Poems*. London, 1983.
Šindelář, Jan. *Proti vlastní vůli: z deníku bojovníka první linie, 1914–1918*. Prague, 1932.
Skála, František. *Válečný deník, 1914–1918*. Kyšperk, 1937.
Šlesingr, Jan. *Legionáři*. Olomouc, 2005.
Šmída, František. *Vzpomínky z vojny 1914–1919*, edited by Miroslav Kobza. Olomouc, 2014.
Soušek, Vladimír. *Z Olomouce na perské hranice: Vzpomínky ze světové války*. Brno, 1930.
Sperling, Bohumil. *Český důstojník na frontách monarchie: válečný deník*, edited by Leonard Hobst. Brno, 2003.
Šrámek, Fráňa. *Listy z vojny. Výbor z korespondence 1915–1918*. Prague, 1956.
———. *Žasnoucí voják: povídky z vojny*. Prague, 1924.
Šrámek, Josef. *Paměti z první světové války Josefa Šrámka z Ústí nad Labem, 1914–1918*. Brno, 2007.
Šuláková, Ladislava, ed. 'Vzpomínky z první světové války'. *Malovaný kraj. Národopisný a vlastivědný časopis Slovácka* 6, no. 1 (2002): 8–9.
Tonar, František, ed. *Válečný deník: Český voják bojující v Rakousko-uherské armádě na východní frontě za 1. světové války*. Brno, 2008.
Tříska, Jan F., ed. *The Great War's Forgotten Front*. New York, 1998.
———. ed. *Zapomenutá fronta: vojákův deník a úvahy jeho syna*. Prague, 2001.
Váchal, Josef. *Malíř na frontě: Soča a Italie 1917–18*. Prague, 1996.
Vančura, Vladislav. *Pole orná a válečná*. Prague, 1966.
Vaněk, Karel. *Charašó pán, da? Zápisky všelijakého vojáka, 1914–1919*. Prague 2013.
Vítek, Jaroslav. *V cizích službách: deník ze světové války*. Česká Skalice, 1937.
Vlasák, Rudolf. *Vojáci císařovi*. 2 vols. Prague, 1932.
Wagner, Karel. *S českým plukem na ruské frontě*. Prague, 1936.
Žipek, Alois, ed. *Domov za války: Svědectví účastníků*, 5 vols. Prague, 1929–1931.

Secondary Sources

Aaslestad, Katherine, Karen Hagemann and Judith Miller, eds. *Gender, War and the Nation in the Period of Revolutionary and Napoleonic Wars: European Perspectives*. Philadelphia, 2007.
Acton, Carol. *Grief in Wartime: Private Pain, Public Discourse*. Basingstoke, 2007.

Adams, Michael C.C. *The Great Adventure: Male Desire and the Coming of World War I.* Bloomington, 1990.
Addison, Paul, and Angus Calder, eds. *Time to Kill: The Soldier's Experience of War in the West, 1939–1945.* London, 1997.
Arkin, William, and Lynne R. Dobrofsky. 'Military Socialization and Masculinity'. *Journal of Social Issues* 34, no. 1 (1978): 151–68.
Ashworth, Tony. *Trench Warfare 1914–1918: The Live and Let Live System.* Basingstoke, 1980.
Audoin-Rouzeau, Stéphane. *Men at War, 1914–1918: National Sentiment and Trench Journalism in France during the First World War.* Oxford, 1992.
Audoin-Rouzeau, Stéphane, and Annette Becker. *1914–1918: Understanding the Great War.* London, 2002.
Bakhtin, Mikhail. *Rabelais and His World.* Bloomington, 1985.
Bederman, Gail. *Manliness and Civilization: A Cultural History of Gender and Race in the United States, 1880–1917.* Chicago, 1995.
Beneš, Jakub. 'The Green Cadres and the Collapse of Austria-Hungary in 1918'. *Past & Present* 236, no. 1 (2017): 207–41.
———. '"Zelené kádry" jako radikální alternativa pro venkov na západním Slovensku a ve středovýchodní Evropě 1917–1920'. *Forum Historiae* 9, no. 2 (2015): 20–34.
Benko, Juraj. 'Vojnová sociálizácia mužov v armáde, v zajatí a v legiích (1914–1921)'. *Forum Historiae* 3, no. 1 (2009): 1–14.
Berding, Helmut, Klaus Heller and Winfried Speitkamp, eds. *Krieg und Erinnerung. Fallstudien zum 19. und 20. Jahrhundert.* Göttingen, 2000.
Black, Jeremy. *Rethinking Military History.* London, 2004.
Bláha, Filip. *Frauenkörper im Fokus: Wahrnehmung zwischen Strasse und Turnplatz in Prag und Dresden vor dem Ersten Weltkrieg.* Frankfurt am Main, 2013.
Blom, Ida, Karen Hagemann and Catherine Hall, eds. *Gendered Nations: Nationalisms and Gender Order in the Long Nineteenth Century.* Oxford, 2000.
Boháč, Zdeněk. 'Wilhelm Winkler, Die Totenverluste der öst.- ung. Monarchie nach Nationalitäten: Die Altersgliederung der Toten. Ausblicke in die Zukunft. Wien 1919'. In *Československý statistický věstník I.* Prague, 1920, 59–80.
Boisserie, Etienne. *Les Tchèques dans l'Autriche-Hongrie en guerre (1914–1918).* Paris, 2017.
Bordiugov, Genadii. 'The First World War and Social Deviance in Russia'. In *Facing Armageddon: The First World War Experienced*, edited by Hugh Cecil and Peter Liddle. London, 1996, 539–53.
Bourdieu, Pierre. *La domination masculine.* Paris, 1998.
Bourke, Joanna. *Dismembering the Male: Men's Bodies, Britain, and the Great War.* London, 1996.
———. *Fear: A Cultural History.* London, 2005.
———. *An Intimate History of Killing: Face-to-Face Killing in Twentieth Century History.* London, 1999.
———. 'New Military History'. In *Palgrave Advances in Modern Military History*, edited by Matthew Hughes and William J. Philpott. London, 2006, 258–80.
Bradley, John F.N. *The Czechoslovak Legion in Russia, 1914–1920.* Boulder, 1991.
Braudy, Leo. *From Chivalry to Terrorism: War and the Changing Nature of Masculinity.* New York, 2003.
Broughton, Trev Lynn, and Helen Rogers. *Gender and Fatherhood in the Nineteenth Century.* New York, 2007.

Bynum, Carolyn W. *The Resurrection of the Body in Western Christianity, 200–1336*. New York, 1995.
Canning, Kathleen. 'The Body as Method? Reflections on the Place of the Body in the Gender History'. *Gender & History* 3, no. 2 (1999): 499–513.
Carden-Coyne, Ann, and Laura Doan. 'Gender and Sexuality'. In *Gender and the Great War*, edited by Susan R. Grayzel and Tammy M. Proctor. Oxford, 2017, 91–114.
Chauncey, George, Jr. 'Christian Brotherhood or Sexual Perversion? Homosexual Identities and the Construction of Sexual Boundaries in the World War One Era'. *Journal of Social History* 19, no. 2 (1985): 189–211.
Citino, Robert M. 'Military Histories Old and New: A Reintroduction'. *American Historical Review* 112, no. 4 (2007): 1070–90.
Clark, Christopher. *Sleepwalkers: How Europe Went to War in 1914*. London, 2012.
Cole, Laurence. 'Differentiation or Indifference? Changing Perspectives on National Identification in the Austrian Half of the Habsburg Monarchy'. In *Nationhood from Below: Europe in the Long Nineteenth Century*, edited by Maarten van Ginderachter and Marnix Beyen. Basingstoke, 2012, 96–119.
———. *Military Culture and Popular Patriotism in Late Imperial Austria*. Oxford, 2013.
———. 'Questions of Nationalization in the Habsburg Monarchy'. In *Nations, Identities and the First World War*, edited by Nico Wouters and Laurence van Ypersele. London, 2018, 191–221.
Cole, Laurence, and Daniel L. Unowsky, eds. *The Limits of Loyalty: Imperial Symbolism, Popular Allegiances, and State Patriotism in the Late Habsburg Monarchy*. Oxford, 2007.
Connell, R.W. 'The Big Picture: Masculinities in Recent World History'. *Theory and Society* 5, no. 2 (1993): 597–623.
———. *Masculinities*, 2nd edition, Berkeley, 2005.
———. 'Masculinity, Violence, and War'. In *Men's Lives*, edited by Michael S. Kimmel and Michael A. Messner, 3rd edition. Boston, 1995, 125–130.
Connell, R.W., and James D. Messerschmidt. 'Hegemonic Masculinity: Rethinking the Concept'. *Gender and Society* 19, no. 6 (2005): 829–59.
Cornwall, Andrea, and Nancy Lindisfarne. 'Dislocating Masculinity: Gender, Power, and Anthropology'. In *Dislocating Masculinity: Comparative Ethnographies*, edited by Andrea Cornwall and Nancy Lindisfarne. London, 1994, 34–37.
Cornwall, Mark, 'Austria-Hungary and "Yugoslavia"'. In *A Companion to World War I*, edited by John Horne, Oxford. 2012, 369–85.
———. 'Disintegration and Defeat: The Austro-Hungarian Revolution'. In *The Last Years of Austria-Hungary: A Multi-national Experience in Early Twentieth-Century Europe*, edited by Mark Cornwall, 2nd edition. Exeter, 2002, 167–96.
———. 'Morale and Patriotism in the Austro-Hungarian Army'. In *State, Society, and Mobilization in Europe during the First World War*, edited by John Horne. Cambridge, 1997, 173–92.
———. 'The Spirit of 1914 in Austria-Hungary'. *Prispevki za novejšo zgodovino* 55, no. 2 (2015): 7–21.
———. 'Traitors and the Meaning of Treason in Austria-Hungary's Great War'. *Transactions of Royal Historical Society* 25, no. 1 (2015): 113–34.
———. *The Undermining of Austria-Hungary: The Battle for Hearts and Minds*. London, 2000.
Crouthamel, Jason. *An Intimate History of the Front: Masculinity, Sexuality, and German Soldiers in the First World War*. New York, 2014.

Dancila, Andreea. 'Les lettres privées publiques: Un genre épistolaire ambigu des Roumains de Transylvanie dans la Première Guerre mondiale'. *Revue des Études Slaves* 88, no. 4 (2017): 743–56.

Dangl, Vojtech. *Armáda a spoločnosť na prelome 19. a 20. storočia*. Bratislava, 2006.

Das, Santanu. 'Kiss Me, Hardy: Intimacy, Gender, and Gesture in First World War Trench Literature'. *Modernism/Modernity* 9, no. 1 (2002): 51–74.

———. *Touch and Intimacy in First World War Literature*. Cambridge, 2005.

Davidson, Roger, and Lesley A. Hall, eds. *Sex, Sin and Suffering: Venereal Disease and European Society since 1870*. London, 2001.

Davie, Maurice R. *The Evolution of War: A Study of its Role in Early Societies*. New Haven, 1929.

Deák, István. *Beyond Nationalism: A Social and Political History of the Habsburg Officer Corps, 1848–1918*. Oxford, 1990.

Deak, John. 'The Great War and the Forgotten Realm: The Habsburg Monarchy and the First World War'. *Journal of Modern History* 86, no. 2 (2014): 336–80.

Deist, Wilhelm. 'The Military Collapse of the German Empire: The Reality behind the Stab-in-the-Back Myth'. *War in History* 3, no. 2 (1996): 186–207.

Demetriou, Demetrakis Z. 'Connell's Concept of Hegemonic Masculinity: A Critique'. *Theory and Society* 30, no. 2 (2001): 337–61.

Dinges, Martin. '"Hegemoniale Männlichkeit": ein Konzept auf dem Prüfstand'. In *Männer – Macht – Körper: Hegemoniale Männlichkeiten vom Mittelalter bis heute*, edited by Martin Dinges. Frankfurt am Main, 2005, 7–33.

Domansky, Elizabeth. 'Militarization and Reproduction in World War I Germany'. In *Society, Culture and the State in Germany, 1870–1930*, edited by Geoff Eley. Ann Arbor, 1996, 427–63.

Du Picq, Ardant. *Battle Studies: Ancient and Modern Battle*. Translated by John N. Greely and Robert C. Cotton. New York, 1920.

Dudeková, Gabriela. 'S Bohom za kráľa a vlasť? Problém lajality a bojovej morálky radového vojaka vo Veľkej vojne'. In *Vojak medzi civilmi, civil medzi vojakmi: Pocta Vojtechu Danglovi*, edited by Gabriela Dudeková and Elena Mannová. Bratislava, 2017, 163–96.

———. 'Stratégie prežitia v mimoriadnej situácii: Vplyv Veľkej vojny na rodinu na území Slovenska'. *Forum Historiae* 3, no. 1 (2009): 1–19.

Dudeková Kováčová, Gabriela. 'The Silent Majority: Attitudes of Non-prominent Citizens at the Beginning of the Great War in the Territory of Today's Slovakia'. *Revue des Études Slaves* 88, no. 4 (2017): 699–720.

Duffett, Rachel. *The Stomach for Fighting: Food and the Soldiers of the Great War*. Manchester, 2012.

Earle, Rebecca. 'Letters, Writers and the Historian'. In *Epistolary Selves: Letters and Letter-Writers, 1600–1945*, edited by Rebecca Earle. Aldershot, 1999, 1–14.

Ehrenreich, Barbara. *Blood Rites: Origins and History of the Passions of War*. London, 1997.

Eksteins, Modris. *Rites of Spring: The Great War and the Birth of the Modern Age*. London, 1989.

Elias, Norbert. *On the Process of Civilization*. Dublin, 2012.

Ellis, John. *Eye Deep in Hell: Trench Warfare in World War I*. Baltimore, 1976.

Englander, David. 'Discipline and Morale in the British Army, 1917–1918'. In *State, Society and Mobilization in Europe during the First World War*, edited by John Horne. Cambridge, 1997, 125–43.

Engle, Jason C. '"This Monstrous Front Will Devour Us All": The Austro-Hungarian Soldier Experience, 1914–1915'. In *1914: Austria-Hungary, the Origins, and the First Year of World War I*, edited by Günter Bischof, Ferdinand Karlhofer and Samuel R. Williamson. New Orleans and Innsbruck, 2014, 145–64.

Epkenhans, Michael, Stig Förster and Karen Hagemann, eds. *Militärische Erinnerungskultur: Soldaten im Spiegel von Biographien, Memoiren und Selbstzeugnissen*. Paderborn, 2006.

Esposito, Fernando. 'Über keinem Gipfel ist Ruh. Helden- und Kriegertum als Topoi medialisierter Kriegserfahrungen deutscher und italienischer Flieger'. In *Der Erste Weltkrieg im Alpenraum/La Grande Guerra nell' arco alpino: Erfahrung, Deutung, Erinnerung / Esperienze e memoriam*, edited by Hermann J.W. Kuprian and Oswald Überreger. Innsbruck, 2006, 73–90.

Fellner, Fritz. 'Der Krieg in Tagebüchern und Briefen: Überlegungengen zu einer wenig genützten Quellenart'. In *Österreich und der Grosse Krieg 1914–1918: Die andere Seite der Geschichte*, edited by Klaus Amann and Hubert Lengauer. Vienna, 1989, 205–13.

Ferguson, Niall. *The Pity of War*. London, 1998.

Ferguson, R. Brian. 'Explaining War'. In *The Anthropology of War*, edited by Jonathan Haas. Cambridge, 1990, 26–55.

———. 'Introduction: Studying War'. In *Warfare, Culture, Environment*, edited by R. Brian Ferguson. Orlando, 1984, 11–39.

———. 'A Paradigm for the Study of War and Society'. In *War and Society in Ancient and Medieval Worlds: Asia, the Mediterranean, Europe, and Mesoamerica*, edited by Kurt A. Raaflaub and Nathan Rosenstein. Cambridge, 2001, 389–437.

———. 'Violence and War in Prehistory'. In *Troubled Times. Violence and Warfare in the Past*, edited by Debra L. Martin and David W. Frayer. Amsterdam, 1997, 321–55.

Fialová, Ludmila, Pavla Horská et al. *Dějiny obyvatelstva českých zemí*. Prague, 1998.

Forth, Christopher E. *Masculinity in the Modern West: Gender, Civilization and the Body*. London, 2008.

Forth, Christopher E., and Bertrand Taithe, eds. *French Masculinities: History, Culture, and Politics*. London, 2007.

Freud, Sigmund. 'Aktuální poznámky o válce a smrti'. In *Sebrané spisy Sigmunda Freuda*, vol. 10: *Spisy z let 1913–1917*. Prague, 2002, 277–302.

———. 'Mimo princip slasti'. In *Sebrané spisy Sigmunda Freuda*, vol. 13: *Mimo princip slasti a jiné práce z let 1920–1924*. Prague, 1999, 7–58.

———. 'Proč válka?' In *Sebrané spisy Sigmunda Freuda*, vol. 16: *Spisy z let 1932–1939*. Prague, 1998, 15–26.

Frevert, Ute. 'Das Militär als Schule der Männlichkeiten'. In *Männlichkeiten und Moderne. Geschlecht in den Wissenskulturen um 1900*, edited by Ulrike Brunotte and Rainer Herrn. Bielefeld, 2008, 57–76.

———. *Emotions in History – Lost and Found*. New York, 2011.

———. *'Mann und Weib, und Weib und Mann': Geschlechter-Differenzen in der Moderne*. Munich, 1995.

———. *Men of Honour: A Social and Cultural History of the Duel*. Cambridge, 1995.

———. *Nation in Barracks: Modern Germany, Military Conscription, and Civil Society*. Oxford, 2004.

Fučík, Josef. *Generál Podhajský*. Prague, 2009.

———. *Osmadvacátníci: spor o českého vojáka Velké války*. Prague, 2006.

———. *Piava 1918*. Prague, 2001.

——. *Soča (Isonzo) 1917*. Prague, 1999.
Fuhs, Burkhard. 'Fliegende Helden: Die Kultur der Gewalt am Beispiel von Kampfpiloten und ihren Maschinen'. In *Gewalt in der Kultur*, edited by Rolf W. Brednich and Walter Hartinger. Passau, 1994, 705–720.
Fussell, Paul. *The Great War and Modern Memory*. London, 1975.
Galandauer, Jan. *2. 7. 1917. Bitva u Zborova. Česká legenda*. Prague, 2002.
——. 'Československé legie a jejich komemorace'. In *Česká společnost za velkých válek 20. století: pokus o komparaci*, edited by Jan Gebhart and Ivan Šedivý. Prague, 2003, 293–312.
——. 'O struktuře české historické paměti'. *Historie a vojenství* 45, no. 2 (1996): 132–36.
——. 'Wacht am Rhein a Kde domov můj: Válečné nadšení v Čechách v létě 1914'. *Historie a vojenství* 45, no. 5 (1996): 22–43.
Gat, Azar. *War in Human Civilization*. Oxford, 2006.
Gerber, Marjorie. *Vested Interests: Cross-Dressing and Cultural Anxiety*. New York, 1992.
Geroulanos, Stefanos, and Todd Meyers. *The Human Body in the Age of Catastrophe: Brittleness, Integration, Science and the Great War*. Chicago, 2018.
Gilmore, David D. *Manhood in the Making: Cultural Concepts of Masculinity*. Yale, 1991.
Goldstein, Joshua. *War and Gender: How Gender Shapes the War System and Vice Versa*. Cambridge, 2001.
Goodman, Dena. *The Republic of Letters: A Cultural History of the French Enlightenment*. New York, 1994.
Gray, J. Glenn. *The Warriors: Reflections on Men in Battle*. New York, 1959.
Grayzel, Susan R., and Tammy M. Proctor, eds. *Gender and the Great War*. Oxford, 2017.
Guilaine, Jean, and Jean Zammit. *The Origins of War: Violence in Prehistory*. Oxford, 2001.
Hagemann, Karen. '"Heroic Virgins" and "Bellicose Amazons": Armed Women, the Gender Order and the German Public during and after the Anti-Napoleonic Wars'. *European Historical Quarterly* 37, no. 4 (2007): 507–27.
Hämmerle, Christa. 'Back to the Monarchy's Glorified Past? Military Discourses on Male Citizenship and Universal Conscription in the Austrian Empire, 1868–1914'. In *Representing Masculinity: Male Citizenship in Modern Western Culture*, edited by Stefan Dudink, Karen Hagemann, and Anna Clark. New York, 2007, 151–68.
——. 'Desertion vor Gericht. Zur Quellenproblematik von Militärgeschichtsakten am Beispiel der k.(u.)k. Armee 1868–1914/18'. *Wiener Zeitschrift zur Geschichte der Neuzeit* 8, no. 2 (2008): 33–52.
——. '"…dort wurden wir dressiert und sekkiert und geschlagen": Zum Drill und dem Disziplinarstrafrecht und Soldatenmisshandlungen im Heer (1866 bis 1914)'. In *Glanz – Gewalt – Gehorsam. Militär und Gesellschaft in der Habsburgermonarchie (1880 bis 1918)*, edited by Laurence Cole, Christa Hämmerle, and Martin Scheutz. Essen, 2011, 31–54.
——. '"Es ist immer der Mann, der den Kampf entscheidet, und nicht die Waffe": Die Männlichkeit des k.u.k. Gebirgskriegers in der soldatischen Erinnerungskultur'. In *Der Erste Weltkrieg im Alpenraum/La Grande Guerra nell' arco alpino: Erfahrung, Deutung, Erinnerung /Esperienze e memoriam*, edited by Hermann J.W. Kuprian and Oswald Überreger. Innsbruck, 2006, 35–60.
——. *Heimat/Front: Geschlechtergeschichte/n des Ersten Weltkriegs in Österreich-Ungarn*. Vienna, 2014.
——. 'Opferhelden? Zur Geschichte der k.u.k. Soldaten an der Südwestfront'. In *Krieg in den Alpen. Österreich-Ungarn und Italien im Ersten Weltkrieg (1914–1918)*, edited by Nicola Labanca, Oswald Überegger. Vienna, 2015, 155–80.

———. 'Von den Geschlechtern der Kriege und des Militärs: Forschungseinblicke und Bemerkungen zu einen neuen Debatte'. In *Was ist Militärgeschichte?*, edited by Thomas Kühne and Benjamin Ziemann. Paderborn, 2000, 229–62.

———. '"You Let a Weeping Woman Call You Home?" Private Correspondences during the First World War in Austria and Germany'. In *Epistolary Selves: Letters and Letter-Writers, 1600–1945*, edited by Rebecca Earle. Aldershot, 1999, 152–82.

———. 'Zur Relevanz des Connell'schen Konzepts hegemonialer Männlichkeit für "Militär und Männlichkeit/en in der Habsburgermonarchie (1868–1914/18)"'. In *Männer – Macht – Körper: Hegemoniale Männlichkeiten vom Mittelalter bis heute*, edited by Martin Dinges. Frankfurt am Main, 2005, 103–21.

Hanák, Péter. 'Die Volksmeinung während des letzten Kriegsjahres in Österreich-Ungarn'. In *Die Auflösung des Habsburgerreiches: Zusammenbruch und Neuorientierung im Donauraum*, edited by Richard G. Plaschka and Karl-Heinz Mack. Munich, 1970, 58–66.

Hanks, Bryan. 'Constructing the Warrior: Death, Memory and the Art of Warfare'. In *Archaeology and Memory*, edited by Dušan Boric. Oxford, 2010, 121–37.

Hanna, Martha. 'A Republic of Letters: The Epistolary Tradition in France during World War I'. *American Historical Review* 108, no. 5 (2003): 1338–61.

Haring, Sabine A. 'K.u.k. Soldaten an der Ostfront im Sommer und Herbst 1914: Eine emotionssoziologische Analyse'. In *Jenseits des Schützengrabens. Der Erste Weltkrieg im Osten: Erfahrung – Wahrnehmung – Kontext*, edited by Bernard Bachinger and Wolfram Dornik. Innsbruck, 2013, 65–86.

Harrison, Deborah. 'Violence in the Military Community'. In *Military Masculinities: Identity and the State*, edited by Paul R. Higate. Westport, 2003, 71–90.

Havel, Petr. 'K otázce bojové morálky českých vojáků v počáteční fázi první světové války'. In *Od Sarajeva k velké válce/Ab Sarajewo zum Grossen Krieg*. Prague, 1995, 47–55.

Healy, Maureen. 'Civilizing Soldier in Postwar Austria'. In *Gender and War in Twentieth-Century Eastern Europe*, edited by Nancy M. Wingfield and Maria Bucur. Bloomington, 2006, 47–69.

———. *Vienna and the Fall of the Habsburg Empire: Total War and Everyday Life in World War I*. Cambridge, 2004.

Herwig, Holger H., ed. *The Outbreak of the World War I*. Boston, 1997.

Higate, Paul R., ed. *Military Masculinities: Identity and the State*. Westport, 2003.

Higonnet, Margaret E., and Patrice L.-R. Higonnet. 'The Double Helix'. In *Behind the Lines: Gender and the Two World Wars*, edited by Margaret R. Higonnet, Jane Jenson, Sonya Michel and Margaret Collins Weitz. New Haven, 1987, 31–50.

Hirschfeld, Gerhard, Irina Renz and Gerd Krumeich, eds. *Brill's Encyclopedia of the First World War*. 2 vols. Leiden, 2014.

Hirschfeld, Magnus. *Sittengeschichte des Weltkrieges*. 2 vols. Leipzig, 1930.

Höger, Paul. 'Das Post- und Telegrafenwesen im Weltkrieg'. In *Studien und Dokumente zur Österreichisch-Ungarischen Feldpost im Ersten Weltkrieg*, edited by Joachim Gatterer and Walter Lukan. Vienna, 1989, 23–54.

Holmes, Richard. *Acts of War: The Behavior of Men in Battle*. New York, 1985.

Hooper, Charlotte. 'Masculinist Practices and Gender Politics: The Operation of Multiple Masculinities in International Relations'. In *The 'Man' Question in International Relations*, edited by Maryška Zalewski and Jane Pappart. Boulder, 1998, 31–47.

Horne, John. 'Masculinity in Politics and War in the Age of Nation-States and World Wars,

1850–1950'. In *Masculinities in Politics and War: Gendering Modern History*, edited by Stefan Dudink, Karen Hagemann and John Tosh. Manchester, 2004, 22–40.

Hrabak, Bogumil. *Dezerterstvo, Zeleni Kadar i prevratana anarhija u Jugoslavenskim zemljama 1914–1918*. Novi Sad, 1990.

Hutečka, Jiří. 'Kamarádi frontovníci: maskulinita a paměť první světové války v textech československých c. a k. veteránů'. *Dějiny-teorie-kritika* 9, no. 2 (2014): 231–66.

———. 'Literární dílo jako odraz válečného prožitku? J. R. R. Tolkien a Pán prstenů'. In *Mezi Martem a Memorií. Prameny osobní povahy k vojenským dějinám 16. – 19. století*, edited by Vítězslav Prchal. Pardubice, 2011, 133–49.

———. 'Militární maskulinita jako koncept historického bádání'. In *Konstrukce maskulinní identity v minulosti a současnosti: Koncepty, metody, perspektivy*, edited by Radmila Švaříčková-Slabáková, Jitka Kohoutová, Radmila Pavlíčková, Jiří Hutečka et al. Prague, 2012, 36–47.

Hutečka, Jiří, and Radmila Švaříčková-Slabáková, 'Od genderu k maskulinitám'. In *Konstrukce maskulinní identity v minulosti a současnosti: Koncepty, metody, perspektivy*, edited by Radmila Švaříčková-Slabáková, Jitka Kohoutová, Radmila Pavlíčková and Jiří Hutečka. Prague, 2012, 9–20.

Hynes, Samuel. *A War Imagined: The First World War and English Culture*. London, 1992.

Jansen, Christian, ed. *Der Bürger als Soldat. Die Militarisierung europäischer Gesellschaften im langen 19. Jahrhundert: ein internationaler Vergleich*. Essen, 2004.

Jefferson, Tony. 'Subordinating Hegemonic Masculinity'. *Theoretical Criminology* 6, no. 1 (2002): 63–88.

Judson, Pieter. *Guardians of the Nation: Activists on the Language Frontiers of Imperial Austria*. Cambridge, 2006.

———. *The Habsburg Empire: A New History*. Cambridge, 2016.

Kábová, Hana. 'Bolestná cesta od věřícího mládí k přijetí zkonkrétněného světa (Bedřich Václavek a první světová válka, 1914–1918)'. In *Armáda, společnost a první světová válka: Sborník příspěvků z vědecké konference konané v Jihočeském muzeu v Českých Budějovicích dne 8. listopadu 2002*. České Budějovice, 2003, 22–64.

Karner, Tracy X. 'Engendering Violent Men: Oral Histories of Military Masculinity'. In *Masculinities and Violence*, edited by Lee H. Bowker. Thousand Oaks, 1998, 197–232.

Keegan, John. *The Face of Battle*. London, 1976.

Keeley, Lawrence H. *War before Civilization*. New York, 1996.

Kent, Susan Kingsley. *Making Peace: The Reconstruction of Gender in Interwar Britain*. Princeton, 1993.

Kienitz, Sabine. 'Body Damage: War Disability and Constructions of Masculinity in Weimar Germany'. In *Home/Front: The Military, War and Gender in Twentieth Century Germany*, edited by Karen Hagemann and Stefanie Schüler-Springorum. Oxford, 2002, 181–204.

———. 'Die Kastrierten des Krieges: Körperbilder und Männlichkeitskonstruktionen im und nach dem Ersten Weltkrieg'. *Zeitschrift für Volkskunde* 95, no. 1 (1999): 63–82.

Kienitz, Sabine. *Beschädigte Helden: Kriegsinvalidität und Körperbilder 1914–1923*. Paderborn, 2008.

———. 'Das Ende des Männlichkeit? Zur symbolischen Re-Maskulinisierung der Kriegskrüppel im Ersten Weltkrieg'. In *Männlich. Weiblich: Zur bedeutung der kategorie Geschlecht in der Kultur*, edited by Christel Köhle-Hezinger, Martin Scharfe and Rolf Wilhelm Brednich. Münster, 1999, 181–89.

Kimmel, Michael S. *The History of Men: Essay on the History of American and British Masculinities*. New York, 2005.

King, Anthony. 'The Existence of Group Cohesion in the Armed Forces: A Response to Guy Siebold'. *Armed Forces & Society* 33, no. 4 (2007): 638–45.

——. 'The Word of Command: Communication and Cohesion in the Military'. *Armed Forces & Society* 32, no. 4 (2006): 493–512.

King, Jeremy. *Budweisers into Czechs and Germans*. Princeton, 2002.

Kirke, Charles. 'Group Cohesion, Culture, and Practice'. *Armed Forces & Society* 35, no. 4 (2009): 745–53.

Knežević, Jovana. 'Prostitutes as a Threat to National Honor in Habsburg-Occupied Serbia during the Great War'. *Journal of the History of Sexuality* 20, no. 2 (2011): 312–35.

Knoch, Peter. 'Kriegsalltag'. In *Die Rekonstruktion des Kriegsalltags als Aufgabe der historischen Forschung und der Fridenserziehung*, edited by Peter Knoch. Stuttgart, 1989.

Kohoutová, Jitka. 'Konstrukce otcovské identity v 19. století: aspekt otce-živitele v rodinách české intelektuální buržoazie'. In *Konstrukce maskulinní identity v minulosti a současnosti: Koncepty, metody, perspektivy*, edited by Radmila Švaříčková-Slabáková, Jitka Kohoutová, Radmila Pavlíčková and Jiří Hutečka. Prague, 2012, 174–83.

Koldinská, Marie, and Ivan Šedivý. *Válka a armáda v českých dějinách: Sociohistorické črty*. Prague, 2008.

Kovitz, Marcia. 'The Roots of Military Masculinity'. In *Military Masculinities: Identity and the State*, edited by Paul R. Higate. Westport, 2003, 1–14.

Kramer, Alan. 'Recent Historiography of the First World War (Part I)'. *Journal of Modern European History* 12, no. 1 (2014): 5–27.

——. 'Recent Historiography of the First World War (Part II)'. *Journal of Modern European History* 12, no. 2 (2014): 155–74.

Krejčí, Jaroslav. *The Paths of Civilization: Understanding the Currents of History*. Basingstoke, 2004.

Kronenbitter, Günther. 'Die k. u. k. Armee an der Südwestfront'. In *Krieg in den Alpen. Österreich-Ungarn und Italien im Ersten Weltkrieg (1914–1918)*, edited by Nicola Labanca and Oswald Überegger. Vienna, 2015, 105–27.

——. *'Krieg im Frieden': Die Führung der k.u.k. Armee und die Grossmachtpolitik Österreich-Ungarn, 1916–1914*. Munich, 2003.

Křížek, Jaroslav. *Češti a sovětští rudoarmějci v sovětském Rusku 1917–1920*. Prague, 1955.

Křížek, Juraj. 'Die Kriegswirtschaft und das Ende der Monarchie'. In *Die Auflösung des Habsburgerreiches: Zusammenbruch und Neuorientierung im Donauraum*, edited by Richard G. Plaschka and Karl-Heinz Mack. Munich, 1970, 43–52.

Kučera, Rudolf. 'Entbehrung und Nationalismus: Die Erfahrung tschechischer Soldaten der österechisch-ungarischen Armee 1914–1918'. In *Jenseits des Schützengrabens. Der Erste Weltkrieg im Osten: Erfahrung – Wahrnehmung – Kontext*, edited by Bernard Bachinger and Wolfram Dornik. Innsbruck, 2013, 121–38.

——. 'Muži ve válce, válka v mužích. Maskulinity a světové války 20. století v současné kulturní historiografii'. *Soudobé dějiny* 19, no. 4 (2011): 549–62.

——. *Rationed Life. Science, Everyday Life and Working-Class Politics in the Bohemian Lands 1914–1918*. New York, 2016.

Kühne, Thomas. 'Comradeship: Gender Confusion and Gender Order in the German Military, 1918–1945'. In *Home/Front: The Military, War and Gender in Twentieth Century*

Germany, edited by Karen Hagemann and Stefanie Schüler-Springorum. Oxford, 2002, 233–54.

———. 'Männergeschichte als Geschlechtergeschichte'. In *Männergeschichte – Geschlechtergeschichte: Männlichkeiten im Wandel der Moderne*, edited by Thomas Kühne. Frankfurt am Main, 1996, 7–30.

———. *The Rise and Fall of Comradeship. Hitler's Soldiers, Male Bonding and Mass Violence in the Twentieth Century*. Cambridge, 2017.

Kuprian, Hermann J.W. 'Heimatfronten: Soziale und Wirtschaftliche Verhältnisse in Österreich-Ungarn'. In *Krieg in den Alpen: Österreich-Ungarn und Italien im Ersten Weltkrieg (1914–1918)*, edited by Nicola Labanca and Oswald Überegger. Vienna, 2015, 208–38.

Lamb, Michael E., ed. *The Father's Role: Cross-Cultural Persepctives*. Hillsdale, 1987.

Lamprecht, Gerald. *Feldpost und Kriegserlebnis: Briefe als historisch-biographische Quelle*. Innsbruck, 2001.

Laquer, Thomas. *Making Sex: Body and Gender from the Greeks to Freud*. Cambridge, 1990.

Latzel, Klaus. 'Vom Kriegserlebnis zu Kriegserfahrung: Theoretische und methodische Überlegungen zur erfahrungsgeschichtlichen Unterschung von Feldpostbriefen'. *Militärgeschichtliche Mitteilungen* 56, no. 1 (1997): 1–30.

Leed, Eric J. *No Man's Land: Combat and Identity in World War I*. New York, 1979.

Leidinger, Hannes. *Die Bedeutung der Selbstauslöschung: Aspekte der Suizidproblematik in Österreich von der Mitte des 19. Jahruhnderts bis zur Zweiten Republik*. Innsbruck, 2012.

———. 'Suizid und Militär: Debatten – Ursachenforschung – Reichsratinterpellationen 1907–1914'. In *Glanz – Gewalt – Gehorsam: Militär und Gesellschaft in der Habsburgermonarchie (1880 bis 1918)*, edited by Laurence Cole, Christa Hämmerle and Martin Scheutz. Essen, 2011, 337–58.

Leidinger, Hannes, and Verena Moritz. *In russischer Gefangenschaft: Erlebnisse österreichischer Soldaten im Ersten Weltkrieg*. Vienna, 2008.

Lein, Richard. 'The "Betrayal" of the k.u.k. Infantry Regiment 28: Truth or Legend?' In *Prague Papers on the History of International Relations*. Prague, 2009, 325–48.

———. 'The Military Conduct of the Austro-Hungarian Czechs in the First World War'. *The Historian: A Journal of History* 3, no. 2 (2014): 518–49.

———. *Pflichterfüllung oder Hochverrat? Die tschechischen Soldaten Österreich-Ungarns im Ersten Weltkrieg*. Vienna and Berlin, 2011.

———. 'A Train Ride to Disaster: The Austro-Hungarian Eastern Front in 1914'. In *1914: Austria-Hungary, the Origins, and the First Year of World War I*, edited by Günter Bischof, Ferdinand Karlhofer and Samuel R. Williamson. New Orleans and Innsbruck, 2014, 95–126.

Lenderová, Milena. *A ptáš se knížko má: Ženské deníky 19. století*. Prague, 2008.

Lipp, Anne. *Meinungslenkung im Krieg: Kriegserfahrungen deutscher Soldaten und ihre Deutung 1914–1918*. Göttingen, 2003.

Little, Roger W. 'Buddy Relations and Combat Performance'. In *The New Military: Changing Patterns of Organization*, edited by Morris Janowitz. New York, 1964, 195–223.

Lloyd, Genevieve, *Man of Reason: 'Male' and 'Female' in Western Philosophy*. Minneapolis, 1984.

Loez, André. *14–18. Les refus de la guerre: Une histoire des mutins*. Paris, 2010.

Loez, André, and Nicolas Marlot, eds. *Obéir/désobéir: Les mutineries de 1917 en perspective*. Paris, 2008.

Lynn, John A. *Battle. A History of Combat and Culture.* Boulder, 2003.
——. *The Bayonets of the Republic: Motivation and Tactics in the Army of Revolutionary France, 1791–94.* Urbana, 1984.
——. 'The Embattled Future of Academic Military History'. *Journal of Military History* 61, no. 4 (1997): 777–89.
——. ed. *Feeding Mars. Logistics in Western Warfare from the Middle Ages to the Present.* Boulder, 1993.
Malešević, Siniša. *The Sociology of War and Violence.* Cambridge, 2010.
Manning, Frederick J. 'Morale, Cohesion, and Esprit de Corps'. In *Handbook of Military Psychology*, edited by Reuven Gal and A. David Mangelsdorff. Chichester, 1991, 453–70.
Marek, Jindřich. 'Beránci, lvi a malé děti: Nekonečný spor o českého vojáka v letech 1. světové války'. *Historie a vojenství* 63, no. 1 (2014): 94–113.
——. *Pod císařskou šibenicí: čeští vojáci na křižovatkách roku 1918.* Cheb, 2005.
Marlowe, David. 'The Human Dimension of Battle and Combat Breakdown'. In *Military Psychology: A Comparative Perspective*, edited by Richard A. Gabriel. London, 1986, 7–24.
Marshall, S.L.A. *Men against Fire: The Problem of Battle Command.* New York, 1947.
Meyer, Jessica. *Men of War: Masculinity and the First World War in Britain.* London, 2009.
Mitchell, Reid. 'The GI in Europe and American Military Tradition'. In *Time to Kill: The Soldier's Experience of War in the West, 1939–1945*, edited by Paul Addison and Angus Calder. London, 1997, 304–16.
Moran, Lord. *The Anatomy of Courage.* London, 1945.
Moss, Mark. *Manliness and Militarism: Educating Young Boys in Ontario for War.* Oxford, 2001.
Mosse, George L. *Fallen Soldiers: Reshaping the Memory of the World Wars.* Oxford, 1990.
——. *The Image of Man: The Creation of Modern Masculinity.* New York, 1996.
——. *Nationalism and Sexuality: Respectability and Abnormal Sexuality in Modern Europe.* New York, 1985.
Nash, John. 'Historical and Social Changes in the Perception of the Role of the Father'. In *The Role of the Father in Child Development*, edited by Michael E. Lamb, 4th edition. New York, 2004, 65–87.
Nečasová, Denisa. 'Dějiny žen či gender history? Možnosti, limity, východiska'. *Dějiny – teorie – kritika* 3, no. 1 (2008): 81–102.
Nelson, Robert L. 'German Comrades – Slavic Whores'. In *Home/Front: The Military, War and Gender in Twentieth Century Germany*, edited by Karen Hagemann and Stefanie Schüler-Springorum. Oxford, 2002, 69–86.
Nolte, Claire. 'All for One! One for All! Federation of Slavic Sokols'. In *Constructing Nationalities in East-Central Europe*, edited Pieter M. Judson and Marsha L. Rozenblit. New York, 2004, 126–140.
——. 'Ambivalent Patriots: Czech Culture in the Great War'. In *European Culture in the Great War. The Arts, Entertainment, and Propaganda, 1914–1918*, edited by Aviel Roshwald and Richard Stites. Cambridge, 1999, 162–75.
——. *The Sokol in the Czech Lands to 1914: Training for the Nation.* Basingstoke, 2002.
Norton-Cru, Jean. *Témoins: Essai d'analyse et de critique des souvenirs de combattants édités en francais de 1915 à 1928.* Paris, 1929.
——. *War Books: A Study in Historical Criticism.* San Diego, 1976.
Nye, Robert A. 'Concluding Remarks'. In *French Masculinities: History, Culture, and Politics*, edited by Christopher E. Forth and Bertrand Taithe. London, 2007, 232–41.

———. 'Kinship, Male Bonds, and Masculinity in Comparative Perspective'. *American Historical Review* 105, no. 5 (2000): 1656–66.
———. *Masculinity and Male Codes of Honor in Modern France*. Oxford, 1993.
———. 'Western Masculinities in War and Peace'. *American Historical Review* 112, no. 2 (2007): 417–38.
Orwell, George. *Down and Out in Paris and London*. London, 1933.
Patka, Frederic. 'Auch das war die Feldpost: Episoden aus dem dienstlichen Alltag der k.u.k. Feldpost 1914–1918'. In *Studien und Dokumente zur Österreichisch-Ungarischen Feldpost im Ersten Weltkrieg*, edited by Joachim Gatterer and Walter Lukan. Vienna, 1989, 55–75.
Paulová, Milada. *Dějiny Maffie*. 2 vols. Prague, 1937.
Phillips, Kathy J. *Manipulating Masculinity: War and Gender in Modern British and American Literature*. London, 2006.
Pick, Daniel. *War Machine: The Rationalization of Slaughter in the Modern Age*. New Haven, 1993.
Pichlík, Karel. *Čeští vojáci proti válce, 1914–1918*. Prague, 1961.
Plaschka, Richard G. *Cattaro-Prag: Revolte und Revolution, Kriegsmarine und Heer österreich-Ungarns im Feuer der Aufstandsbewegung vom 1. Februar und 28. Oktober 1918*. Graz, 1963.
———. *Matrosen, Offiziere, Rebellen: Krisenkonfrontationen zur See 1900–1918*. 2 vols. Vienna, 1984.
———. 'Serbien und die Balkankriege als Motivationselemente in der österreichisch-ungarischen Armee'. In *Nationalismus – Staatsgewalt – Widerstand: Aspekte nationaler und sozialer Entwicklung in Ostmittel- und Südeuropa*, edited by Horst Haselsteiner et al. Vienna, 1985, 232–45.
———. '"… a střílet nebudem!" Ein Modellfall zur Frage der Auswirkung der Balkankriege auf Österreich-Ungarn'. In *Nationalismus – Staatsgewalt – Widerstand: Aspekte nationaler und sozialer Entwicklung in Ostmittel- und Südeuropa*, edited by Horst Haselsteiner et al. Vienna, 1985, 246–52.
Plaschka, Richard G. Horst Haselsteiner and Arnold Suppan, *Innere Front. Militärassistenz, Widerstand und Umsturz in der Donaumonarchie 1918*. 2 vols. Vienna, 1974.
Pleck, Joseph. 'Men's Power with Women, Other Men, and Society: A Men's Involvement Analysis'. In *Men's Lives*, edited by Michael S. Kimmel and Michael A. Messner, 2nd edition. New York, 1992, 4–33.
Pollmann, Ferenc. 'Die Ostfront des "Grossen Krieges" – aus ungarischer Perspektive'. In *Jenseits des Schützengrabens. Der Erste Weltkrieg im Osten: Erfahrung – Wahrnehmung – Kontext*, edited by Bernard Bachinger and Wolfram Dornik. Innsbruck, 2013, 87–104.
Prchal, Vítězslav, ed., *Mezi Martem a Memorií: Prameny osobní povahy k vojenským dějinám 16. – 19. století*. Pardubice, 2011.
Procházka, Zdeněk et al. *Vojenské dějiny Československa, vol. 2: 1526–1918*. Prague, 1986.
Pytlík, Radko. *Osudy a cesty Josefa Švejka*. Prague, 2003.
Rachamimov, Alon. 'The Disruptive Comforts of Drag: (Trans)Gender Performances among Prisoners of War in Russia, 1914–1920'. *American Historical Review* 111, no. 2 (2006): 368–72.
———. *POWs and the Great War: Captivity on the Eastern Front*. London, 2002.
Rajšp, Vincenc, ed. *Isonzofront 1915–1917: Die Kultur des Erinnerns*. Vienna, 2010.

Ratajová, Jana. 'Gender history jako alternativní koncept dějin'. In *Dějiny žen aneb Evropská žena od středověku do poloviny 20. století v zajetí historiografie*, eds. Kateřina Čadková, Milena Lenderová and Jana Stráníková. Pardubice, 2006, 19–32.

Rauchensteiner, Manfried. *Der Tod des Doppeladlers: Österreich-Ungarn unde der Erste Weltkrieg*. Graz, 1993.

———. *The First World War and the End of the Habsburg Monarchy*. Vienna, 2014.

Rejali, Darius M. *Torture and Democracy*. Princeton, 2007.

Rhoades, Michelle K. 'Renegotiating French Masculinity: Medicine and Venereal Disease during the Great War'. *French Historical Studies* 29, no. 2 (2006): 293–327.

Robb, John. 'Violence and Gender in Early Italy'. In *Troubled Times. Violence and Warfare in the Past*, edited by Debra L. Martin and David W. Frayer, Amsterdam, 1997, 111–44.

Roberts, Mary Louise. *Civilization without Sexes: Reconstructing Gender in Postwar France, 1917–1927*. Chicago, 1994.

Rolland, Denis. *La grève des tranchées*. Paris, 2005.

Roper, Michael. 'Maternal Relations: Moral Manliness and Emotional Survival in Letters Home during the First World War'. In *Masculinities in Politics and War: Gendering Modern History*, edited by Stefan Dudink, Karen Hagemann and John Tosh. Manchester, 2004, 295–315.

———. *The Secret Battle: Emotional Survival in the Great War*. Manchester, 2009.

———. 'Slipping out of View: Subjectivity and Emotion in Gender History'. *History Workshop Journal* 59, no. 1 (2005): 57–73.

Roper, Michael, and John Tosh, eds. *Manful Assertions: Masculinities in Britain since 1800*. London, 1991.

Rose, Arnold M. 'The Social Psychology of Desertion from Combat'. In *Motivating Soldiers: Morale or Mutiny*, edited by Peter Karsten. New York, 1998, 250–65.

Rose, Sonya O. 'Fit to Fight But Not to Vote? Masculinity and Citizenship in Britain, 1832–1918'. In *Representing Masculinity: Male Citizenship in Modern Western Culture*, edited by Stefan Dudink, Karen Hagemann and Anna Clark. New York, 2007, 131–50.

Rothenberg, Gunther E. *The Army of Francis Joseph*. West Lafayette, 1976.

Rousseau, Frederic. *La guerre censurée: Une histoire des combattants européens de 14–18*. Paris, 1999.

Rousseau, Jean-Jacques. *Émile, ou De l'éducation*. Paris, 1762.

Scheer, Tamara. 'Habsburg Languages at War: "The Linguistic Confusion at the Tower of Babel Couldn't Have Been Much Worse"'. In *Languages and the First World War: Communicating in a Transnational War*, edited by Julian Walker and Christophe Declerq. London, 2016, 62–78.

———. *Zwischen Front und Heimat: Österreich-Ungarns Militärverwaltungen im Ersten Weltkrieg*. Frankfurt, 2009.

Schilling, René. *Kriegshelden: Deutungsmuster heroischer Männlichkeite in Deutschland, 1813–1945*. Paderborn, 2002.

Schmale, Wolfgang. *Geschichte des Männlichkeit in Europa (1450–2000)*. Vienna, 2003.

Schmitz, Martin. *'Als ob die Welt aus den Fugen ginge': Kriegserfahrungen österreichisch-ungarischer Offiziere 1914–18*. Paderborn, 2016.

Schönberger, Bianca. 'Motherly Heroines and Adventurous Girls'. In *Home/Front: The Military, War and Gender in Twentieth Century Germany*, edited by Karen Hagemann and Stefanie Schüler-Springorum. Oxford, 2002, 87–113.

Schulte, Regina. 'The Sick Warrior's Sister: Nursing during the First World War'. In *Gender Relations in German History: Power, Agency and Experience from the Sixteenth to the Twentieth Century*, edited by Lynn Abrams and Elizabeth Harvey. London, 1996, 121–41.
Schulze, Wilfred. 'Ego-Dokumente: Annäherung an den Menschen in der Geschichte? Vorüberlegungen für die Tagung "EGO-DOKUMENT"'. In *Ego-Dokumente: Annäherung an den Menschen in der Geschichte*, edited by Wilfred Schulze. Berlin, 1996, 11–30.
Scott, Joan W. 'Gender: A Useful Category of Historical Analysis'. *American Historical Review* 91, no. 5 (1986): 1053–75.
Sedgwick, Eve K. *Between Men: English Literature and Male Homosocial Desire*. New York, 1985.
Segal, Lynne. *Slow Motion: Changing Masculinities, Changing Men*. London, 1990.
Seidl, Jan. *Od žaláře k oltáři: Eampcipace homosexuality v českých zemích od roku 1867 do současnosti*. Brno, 2012.
Shils, Edward, and Morris Janowitz. 'Cohesion and Disintegration in the Wehrmacht in World War II'. In *Military Conflict: Essay in the Institutional Analysis of War and Peace*, edited by Morris Janowitz. Beverly Hills, 1975, 177–220.
Siebold, Guy L. 'The Essence of Military Group Cohesion'. *Armed Forces & Society* 33, no. 2 (2007): 286–95.
———. 'Key Questions and Challenges to the Standard Model of Military Group Cohesion'. *Armed Forces & Society* 37, no. 3 (2011): 448–68.
Silverman, Kaja. *Male Subjectivity at the Margins*. London, 1992.
Sked, Alan. *Decline and Fall of the Habsburg Empire, 1815–1918*. London, 1989.
Smith, Leonard V. *Between Mutiny and Obedience: The Case of the French Fifth Infantry Division during World War I*. Princeton, 1994.
———. *The Embattled Self: French Soldiers' Testimony of the Great War*. Ithaca, 2007.
———. '"War and Politics": The French Army Mutinies of 1917'. *War in History* 2, no. 2 (1995): 180–201.
Spierenburg, Pieter, ed. *Men and Violence: Gender, Honor, and Rituals in Modern Europe and America*. Columbus, 1998.
Spilker, Rolf, and Bernd Ulrich, eds. *Der Tod als Maschinist: Der industrialisierte Krieg 1914–1918*. Bramsche, 1998.
Steedman, Carolyn. 'A Woman Writing a Letter'. In *Epistolary Selves: Letters and Letter-Writers, 1600–1945*, edited by Rebecca Earle. Aldershot, 1999, 111–33.
Stegmann, Natali. *Kriegsdeutungen – Staatsgründungen – Sozialpolitik: Der Helden- und Opferdiskurs in der Tschechoslowakei, 1918–1948*. Munich, 2010.
———. 'Soldaten und Bürger. Selbstbilder tschechoslowakischer Legionäre in der Ersten Republik'. *Militärgeschichtliche Zeitschrift* 1, no. 1 (2002): 25–48.
Stengers, Jean, and Anne van Neck. *Masturbation: The History of a Great Terror*. Basingstoke, 2001.
Stergar, Rok. 'Hrana na bojiščih 1. svetovej vojne: izkušnje slovenskih vojakov'. *Prispevki za novejšo zgodovino* 55, no. 2 (2015): 22–53.
Stibbe, Matthew. 'The Internment of Political Suspects in Austria-Hungary during the First World War: A Violent Legacy?'. In *Gender and Modernity in Central Europe*, edited by Agatha Schwartz. Ottawa, 2010, 203–18.
Stone, Norman. *The Eastern Front 1914–1917*. London, 1998.

Stouffer, Samuel A. et al. *The American Soldier*. 2 vols, Princeton, 1949.
Strachan, Hew. *The First World War*. New York, 2003.
——. *The First World War*. Volume 1: *To Arms*. Oxford, 2001.
Streets, Heather. *Martial Races: The Military, Race and Masculinity in British Imperial Culture, 1857–1914*. Manchester, 2004.
Šedivý, Ivan. *Češi, české země a Velká válka 1914–1918*. Prague, 2001.
——. 'Česká historiografie vojenství 1989–2002'. *Český časopis historický* 100, no. 4 (2002): 868–901.
——. 'Legionáři a československá armáda 1918–1938'. In *České země a Československo v Evropě XIX. a XX. století: Sborník prací k 65. narozeninám prof. Dr. Roberta Kvačka*, edited by Jindřich Dejmek and Josef Hanzal. Prague, 1997, 209–230.
——. 'Legionáři a mocenské poměry v počátcích ČSR'. In *Moc, vliv a autorita v procesu vzniku a utváření meziválečné ČSR (1918–1921)*, edited by Jan Hájek, Dagmar Hájková, František Kolář, Vlastislav Lacina, Zdenko Maršálek and Ivan Šedivý. Prague, 2008, 16–28.
Taudyová, Hana. 'Válečná milostná korespondence Jaroslava Havlíčka'. *Historie a vojenství* 52, no. 1 (2003): 94–105.
Taylor, A.J.P. *The Habsburg Monarchy, 1809–1918*. London, 1948.
Theweleit, Klaus. *Male Fantasies*. 2 vols. Cambridge, 1987–1989.
Thompson, Mark. *The White War: Life and Death on the Italian Front, 1915–1919*. London, 2008.
Tiger, Lionel. *Men in Groups*. London, 1969.
Tosh, John. 'Domesticity and Manliness in the Victorian Middle Class: The Family of Edward White Benson'. In *Manful Assertions: Masculinities in Britain since 1800*, edited by Michael Roper and John Tosh. Oxford, 1991, 44–72.
——. 'Hegemonic Masculinity and the History of Gender'. In *Masculinities in Politics and War: Gendering Modern History*, edited by Stefan Dudink, Karen Hagemann and John Tosh. Manchester, 2004, 41–58.
——. *A Man's Place: Masculinity and the Middle-Class Home in Victorian England*. 2nd edition. London, 2007.
——. 'Middle-Class Masculinities in the Era of the Women's Suffrage Movement, 1860–1914'. In *English Masculinities, 1660–1800*, edited by Tim Hitchcock and Michele Cohen. London, 1999, 103–27.
——. 'The Old Adam and the New Man: Emerging Themes in the History of English Masculinities, 1750–1850'. In *English Masculinities, 1660–1800*, edited by Tim Hitchcock and Michele Cohen. London, 1999, 217–38.
——. 'What Should Historians Do with Masculinity? Reflections on Nineteenth-Century Britain'. *History Workshop Journal* 38, no. 1 (1994): 179–202.
Überegger, Oswald. *Der andere Krieg: Die Tiroler Militärgerichtsbarkeit im Ersten Weltkrieg*. Innsbruck, 2002.
——. 'Krieg als sexuelle Zäsur? Sexualmoral und Geschlechterstereotypen im kriegsgesellschaftlichen Diskurs über die Geschlechtskrankheiten. Kulturgeschichtliche Annäherungen'. In *Der Erste Weltkrieg im Alpenraum/La Grande Guerra nell' arco alpino: Erfahrung, Deutung, Erinnerung /Esperienze e memoriam*, edited by Hermann J. W. Kuprian and Oswald Überreger. Innsbruck, 2006, 351–66.
——. 'Politik, Nation und Desertion: Zur Relevanz politisch-nationaler und ideologischer Verwigerungsmotive für die Desertion österreichisch-ungarischer Soldaten im Ersten Weltkrieg'. *Wiener Zeitschrift zur Geschichte der Neuzeit* 8, no. 2 (2008): 109–19.

Ulrich, Bernd. *Die Augenzeugen: Deutsche Feldpostbriefe in Kriegs- und Nachkriegszeit*. Essen, 1997.
——. 'Feldpostbriefe im Ersten Weltkrieg – Bedeutung und Zensur'. In *Die Rekonstruktion des Kriegsalltags als Aufgabe der historischen Forschung und der Friedenserziehung*, edited by Peter Knoch. Stuttgart, 1989, 40–83.
——. 'Kampfmotivationen und Mobilisierungsstrategien. Das Beispiel Erster Weltkrieg'. In *Töten im Krieg*, edited by Heinrich von Stietencron and Jörg Rüpke. Freiburg, 1995, 399–419.
Van Creveld, Martin. *Fighting Power. German and US Army Performance, 1939–1945*. London, 1983.
——. *Supplying War. Logistics from Wallenstein to Patton*. Cambridge, 1977.
Von Clausewitz, Carl. *On War*, edited by Michael Howard and Peter Paret. Princeton, 1989.
Watson, Alexander. *Enduring the Great War: Combat, Morale and Collapse in the German and British Armies, 1914–1918*. Cambridge, 2008.
——. 'Mutinies and Military Morale'. In *The Oxford Illustrated History of the First World War*, edited by Hew Strachan. Oxford, 2014, 191–203.
——. *Ring of Steel: Germany and Austria-Hungary in World War I*. New York, 2014.
Westbrook, Stephen D. 'The Potential for Military Disintegration'. In *Combat Effectiveness. Cohesion, Stress and the Volunteer Military*, edited by Sam C. Sarkesian. Beverly Hills, 1980, 244–278.
Wette, Wolfram, ed. *Der Krieg des kleinen Mannes: Eine Militärgeschihcte von unten*. Munich, 1992.
Wingfield, Nancy M. 'The Battle of Zborov and the Politics of Commemoration in Czechoslovakia'. *East European Politics & Societies* 4, no. 2 (2003): 654–81.
——. 'The Enemy Within: Regulating Prostitution and Controlling Veneral Disease in Cisleithanian Austria during the Great War'. *Central European History* 46, no. 3 (2013): 568–98.
——. *The World of Prostitution in Late Imperial Austria*. Oxford, 2017.
Wingfield, Nancy M., and Maria Bucur, eds. *Gender and War in Twentieth-Century Eastern Europe*. Bloomington, 2006.
Winkler, Wilhelm. *Die Totenverluste der öst.- ung. Monarchie nach Nationalitäten: Die Altersgliederung der Toten. Ausblicke in die Zukunft*. Vienna, 1919.
Winter, Dennis. *Death's Men: Soldiers of the Great War*. London, 1978.
Winter, Jay, ed. *The Cambridge History of the First World War*, 3 vols. Cambridge, 2014.
Woollacott, Angela. '"Khaki Fever" and its Control: Gender, Class, Age and Sexual Morality on the British Home Front in the First World War'. *Journal of Contemporary History* 29, no. 2 (1994): 325–47
Zahra, Tara. 'Imagined Noncommunities: National Indifference as a Category of Analysis'. *Slavic Review* 69, no. 1 (2010): 91–119.
——. *Kidnapped Souls: National Indifference and the Battle for Children in the Bohemian Lands, 1900–1948*. Ithaca, 2008.
Ziemann. Benjamin. 'Soldiers'. In *Brill's Encyclopedia of the First World War*, edited by Gerhard Hirschfeld, Gerd Krumeich and Irina Renz. Leiden, 2012, vol. 1, 118–28.
——. 'Verweigerungsformen von Frontsoldaten in der deutschen Armee 1914–1918'. In *Gewalt im Krieg: Ausübung, Erfahrung und Verweigerung von Gewalt in Kriegen des 20. Jahrhunderts*, edited by Andreas Gestrich. Münster, 1996, 99–122.
——. *War Experience in Rural Germany*. Oxford, 2007.

Zückert, Martin. 'Antimilitarismus und soldatische Resistenz: Politischer Protest und armeefeindliches Verhalten in der tschechischen Gesellschaft bis 1918'. In *Glanz – Gewalt – Gehorsam: Militär und Gesellschaft in der Habsburgermonarchie (1880 bis 1918)*, edited by Laurence Cole, Christa Hämmerle and Martin Scheutz. Essen, 2011, 199–220.

——. 'Der Erste Weltkrieg in der tschechischen Geschichtsschreibung 1918–1945'. In *Geschichtsschreibung zu den böhmischen Länder im 20. Jahrhundert: Wissenschaftstraditionen, Institutionen, Diskurse*, edited by Christiane Brenner, Erik K. Franzen, Peter Haslinger and Robert Luft. Munich, 2006, 61–75.

——. 'Memory of War and National State Integration: Czech and German Veterans in Czechoslovakia after 1918'. *Central Europe* 4, no. 2 (2006): 111–21.

Unpublished Theses

Hois, Alexandra. 'Weibliche Hilfskräfte in der österreichisch-ungarischen Armee im Ersten Weltkrieg'. Master's thesis. Vienna: University of Vienna, 2012.

Pazdera, David. 'Češi v první světové válce (Pokus o vymezení válečného prožitku českých vojáků rakousko-uherské armády od mobilizace a nástupu k jednotce po příchod na frontu)'. Master's thesis. České Budějovice: University of České Budějovice, 1997.

Rebhan-Glück, Ines. '"Wenn wir nur glücklich wieder beisammen wären…": Der Krieg, der Frieden und die Liebe am Beispiel der Feldpostkorrespondenz von Mathilde und Ottokar Hanzel (1917/18)'. Master's thesis. Vienna: University of Vienna, 2010.

Reiter, Christian. 'Der Untergang des IR 36: Der "Verrat" der tschechischen Soldaten im Gefecht bei Siniewa 1915'. Master's thesis. Vienna: University of Vienna, 2008.

Spann, Gustav. 'Zensur in Österreich während des 1. Welt Krieges 1914–1918'. Ph.D. dissertation. Vienna: University of Vienna, 1972.

Musical Recordings

Bogle, Eric, *And the Band Played Waltzing Matilda*. Sydney: Larrikin Music Pty Ltd., 1971.

The Clash, 'The Call Up'. CBS-Epic, 1980.

INDEX

Acton, Carol, 182
Adamíra, Bohuš, 120, 191
Ajdovščina (Haidenschaft, Slovenia), 95
Albania, 70, 115, 124, 147, 181, 183
alcohol, 43, 49, 104n31, 122, 167
Alps, 62–63, 70, 73–74, 120, 189, 229
animals, 1, 123, 127
antisemitism, 128, 224
artillery, 20, 31, 42, 48, 66–70, 93, 151, 156, 164, 185–187, 221, 229, 235
    effects of, 71–75, 83, 87n108, 194, 223–225, 230, 237–239, 241, 245n23
Asinara (island off Sardinia), 121, 123
Aswhorth, Tony, 11
Audoin-Rouzeau, Stéphane, 72, 182, 212n9, 222
Austria-Hungary (general), 1, 10, 30, 37–39, 43, 54, 85, 133–134, 145, 170–171, 187, 198, 243, 258–259
    economy, 4, 7, 64, 87, 101, 200–202, 207–209, 211, 254, 257– 258
    language policies, 1
    militarization, 14, 33–34, 56n21,
    minorities, 2, 3, 51, 257–259
Austro-Hungarian Army (general), 1–2, 40, 66, 131–132, 145–146, 148, 151, 159, 173, 230
    10th Army, 64, 209
    III Army Corps, 37
    VIII Army Corps, 30
    IX Army Corps, 30
    XI Army Corps, 230
    XX Army Corps, 209
    3rd Division (*Edelweis*), 74
    18th Division, 74
    19th Infantry Brigade (Hungarian), 162
    Army High Command (*Armeeoberkommando*, AOK), 2, 4, 37, 51, 145, 164, 171, 190, 209, 258
    casualties, 64, 135, 145–146, 156–157, 160, 168, 174n11, 223, 242
    democratic nature, 147
    disciplinary practices, 14, 76, 87, 103n13, 143, 162–173, 254, 258
    Honvéd (territorial army of Hungary), 145, 167, 243
    k.k. Landsturm Infantry Regiment 22, 92
    k.k. Landwehr Infantry Regiment 4, 65
    k.k. Landwehr Infantry Regiment 7, 107n7
    k.k. Landwehr Infantry Regiment 13, 39, 42, 161, 229
    k.k. Landwehr Infantry Regiment 30, 135, 231
    k.u.k. Bosnian-Herzegovinian Infantry Regiment 7, 169
    k.u.k. Dragoon Regiment 10, 83
    k.u.k. Field Artillery Regiment 24, 31, 156
    k.u.k. Field Artillery Regiment 27, 48
    k.u.k. Infantry Regiment 3, 74
    k.u.k. Infantry Regiment 8, 41, 127
    k.u.k. Infantry Regiment 11, 33, 39, 174n11, 185, 192
    k.u.k. Infantry Regiment 18, 36, 62, 74, 134, 172, 229
    k.u.k. Infantry Regiment 27, 227
    k.u.k. Infantry Regiment 28, 3–4, 51–2, 73, 103n8, 158, 160, 161, 163, 196, 199

k.u.k. Infantry Regiment 35, 4
k.u.k. Infantry Regiment 36, 23n24, 103n8, 162, 178n101
k.u.k. Infantry Regiment 42, 115
k.u.k. Infantry Regiment 53, 44
k.u.k. Infantry Regiment 54, 223
k.u.k. Infantry Regiment 57, 40, 219
k.u.k. Infantry Regiment 73, 187
k.u.k. Infantry Regiment 75, 4, 36, 44, 105n39, 119, 243
k.u.k. Infantry Regiment 79, 68
k.u.k. Infantry Regiment 88, 28n83, 37–38, 43, 118
k.u.k. Infantry Regiment 91, 74, 164
k.u.k. Infantry Regiment 98, 42, 82, 150, 159, 183
Landsturm (militia), 1, 51, 63, 83, 92, 123, 145, 148, 151, 184, 196, 201
Landwehr (territorial army of Austria), 1, 39, 42, 65, 71, 135, 145, 161, 184, 187,
language policy, 51, 160, 189, 258
military oath, 42, 47, 59n64
minority policies, 2, 37, 51, 159–172, 253–254, 258–259
mobilization, 4, 30–31, 37–49, 52–54, 62, 80, 127, 145, 160, 207, 251
morale, 51, 64–65, 69–70, 75, 84, 103n8, 131–136, 144, 146, 187–189, 191, 207, 209, 254–257
replacement practices, 51–52, 134–135
replacements, 103n8, 135, 160
reserve battalions moved out of Bohemia, 52, 61n119, 168, 200
supply crisis, 68–70, 78, 81–82, 100–101, 104n31, 123, 136, 145, 151–152, 170–173, 207, 252–254
universal conscription, 10, 34, 56n20, 79–80
awards, military, 118, 149, 156

Balkan Front (1916–1918), 3, 115–116, 123, 232
Banovo Polje, 118
battle. *See* combat
Belgrade, 30
Benko, Juraj, 132

Beroun (Bohemia), 38
Black, Jeremy, 10
Bochnia (Salzberg, Poland), 168
Bohemian Crown Lands, 1–4, 7, 14–19, 30–32, 37–39, 41, 50–53, 82, 123, 149, 160, 166–170, 200, 207, 240, 251. *See also* home front
Bohemian regiments, 162, 168, 200
economy, 64, 69, 87, 200–202, 207–209, 211, 215n90, 254, 257
educational levels, 18–19
levels of industrialization, 207
mobilization of 1914, 4, 30–31, 37–49, 52–54, 62, 251
mobilizations of 1909–1913, 39
politics, 2, 4, 10, 65, 160, 170, 183, 191–192, 201, 209, 259
rural population, 9, 19, 41–42
urban population, 9, 19, 37, 41, 189, 257
body, 10, 29, 72, 78, 83, 90, 93, 100, 116, 117, 129, 143, 163, 211, 219–221, 253–255
'body reflexive practices', 10
deformation, 80–82
destruction, 14, 234–240
disability, 235, 239, 243
and masculinity, 14, 78–81, 116, 124, 130–131, 157–158, 234–244, 249n121
as a symbolic space, 234–242
Bolshevik Revolution, 1, 64
Bosnian troops, 127, 166–167, 169
Bourke, Joanna, 7, 9, 128, 222, 228, 242
Bouška, František, 127, 224, 230, 237, 244
Braudy, Leo, 9
Brno (Brünn, Moravia), 29, 30, 79, 183
Brod, Max, 30–31
Brusilov Offensive, 67, 71, 118, 135, 162, 194, 195
Bukovina, 150, 152, 165, 167, 240

Caporetto (Kobarid), battle of, 64, 68, 74, 83, 209, 230, 248n81
Caré Alto, 189
Carinthia, 196
Carpahtians, 52, 64, 70, 73–74, 120, 145, 160, 167, 226–227, 244
Carso (Karst Plateau), 219

Čapek, František, 133, 135, 229
cavalry, 1, 77, 83
censorship. *See* post (military)
Central Powers, 64, 181
Cer, battle of, 50
Černý, František, 67, 71, 118, 135, 151, 185, 206, 224, 226, 230
Česká Skalice (Böhmisch Skalitz, Bohemia), 208
České Meziříčí (Böhmisch Meseritsch, Bohemia), 62
Charles I, Emperor of Austria-Hungary, 153, 164
Chauncey, George, 85
children, 31, 44, 47, 49, 52, 53, 92, 102, 126, 201–202, 205–208
 childhood, 35–36, 118, 132–133
 letters from, 206–207
 letters to, 192, 195, 206
 soldiers as, 132–133, 142, 153–154, 169
 soldiers remembering, 184–186, 227
 suffering, 208
 upbringing, 210
Chmela, František, 31, 158, 164, 244
Choceň (Chotzen, Bohemia), 127
Christmas, 39, 52, 124, 132, 151, 185–186, 191, 192, 252
cigarettes, 49, 68, 156, 185, 191–192, 194
class, 3, 4, 6, 9, 19, 47, 52, 78, 85, 86, 128, 133–134, 146, 149–151, 165, 170, 187, 253
 middle classes, 37, 44, 91, 148, 160, 172, 182, 187–192, 222
 officer class, 146–151, 257
 upper classes, 85, 187
 working classes, 7, 14, 31, 33, 44, 49, 52, 82, 123, 189, 240, 257
Clausewitz, Carl von, 220, 229
Cole, Laurence, 34, 37
combat, 15, 76, 219–242
 aesthetics, 222
 combat motivation (*see* motivation)
 discursive silence, 223–228, 231, 255
 as duel, 229–231, 242, 247n53
 dying, 102, 116, 184, 193, 205, 222, 227–228, 234–238
 firepower, 131, 144, 238

killing, 9, 196, 220, 222–231, 241
 levels of participation, 20, 231–233
 passivity, 20, 77–84, 119, 222, 228–231, 239–243, 252, 255
 practices, 72–77, 222–223, 229
 reality of, 70–78, 81–84, 240–242, 223
comradeship. *See* homosocial relationships
Connell, R.W., 6, 9, 10, 78
Conrad von Hötzendorf, Franz, k.u.k. Field Marshal, 159
Cornwall, Mark, 2, 69, 160
corporal punishment, 163–168
correspondence, 15, 18–19, 126, 129, 182, 186–197, 203, 207. *See also* post
 gender coding, 193–195, 209, 214n61
 importance, 126–127, 186–188
 self-censorship, 86, 195–196, 222–223
Croatia, 37, 68, 81, 92, 161, 169,
cross-dressing, 122–123, 129, 253
Crouthamel, Jason, 86
Čundrle, Jan, 138n51, 202, 206
Czech National Socialist Party, 4, 19
Czech Social-Democratic Party, 80
Czechs, 1–7, 10–15, 166, 254–259
 class identity, 61n118
 'cultural imperialism', 165–169, 254
 desertion (*see* desertion)
 historiography, 2–5
 national self-identification, 1–2, 19, 170–173
 nationalism (*see* nationalism)
 loyalty, 2–3, 4, 58n38, 59n67, 63–65, 160–165, 172–173, 230, 254–255, 256–9
 malingering, 3, 37, 43, 51, 63, 69, 231, 243–244, 256–257
 morale, 64–70, 133–136, 160–164, 170–173, 186, 206–210, 240, 254–258
 patriotism, 2, 37, 51, 256
 war enthusiasm, 4, 34, 37–38, 51, 251, 255
Czechoslovak Legion, 3, 15, 16, 33, 44, 202
Czernowitz (Černivci, Bukovina), 150, 240

Dalmatia, 38, 166, 199
Danube River, 30

Das, Santanu, 116
Deák, István, 80, 86, 232
Deist, Wilhelm, 12
desertion, 2–3, 14–15, 37, 69, 103n13, 105n39, 160–161, 164, 211, 230, 258
'green cadres', 105n45, 209, 259
diseases, 80, 97, 231,
venereal, 87–89, 242
Dolejší, Alois, 69, 76, 80, 95, 99, 122, 134, 151, 162, 166, 172, 208
Doležal, Václav, 92
Dolomites, 68, 73
Drina River, 50, 118, 124, 157, 184, 222, 225, 228, 236, 239
Duffett, Rachel, 78
Durazzo (Durrës), 181

Eastern Front, 3, 15, 33, 64, 98, 119, 122, 123, 142, 189, 223, 227, 232
specifics, 73–74
education, 18–19, 20, 85, 89, 128, 146–149, 154, 165, 172, 189, 202
Elias, Norbert, 82
emotions, 13–14, 16, 31, 34, 37, 78, 84, 116–122, 124–136, 166, 193–202, 206–209, 221, 237, 241, 253–254
aggression, 221
compassion, 94
display and expression, 13, 124–127, 194, 197
emotional support, 130–134, 182, 185–187, 196–198
emotional survival, 13, 102, 119, 124–126, 129, 133, 209
fear, 8, 14, 30, 38, 50, 53, 63, 70–75, 83–89, 92–97, 117, 125–129, 136, 172, 190, 195, 210, 226–228
fear of punishment, 12, 40, 53, 65, 69, 224, 251
gendering emotions, 31, 117, 119–122, 124–125, 136
love, 93, 102, 116–117, 127–128, 193
resignation, 41
stress, 20, 76, 102, 116–117, 121–123, 125–128, 224–227, 239, 254, 257
Engle, Jason, 135
Entente, 69, 181

Etappenschweine (rear-echelon troops), 233–234
exhaustion, 4, 13, 67–76
physical, 63, 70–72, 80–81, 84
psychological, 75–78, 81–83, 84
vegetative state, 71–77, 82

family, 14, 44–45, 63, 78, 132–133, 143, 182, 189, 192, 194, 197, 201–208
'military family', 152–154, 185
fatherhood. *See* masculinity
fatigue. *See* exhaustion
femininity. *See* women
First World War, 1–7, 9–15, 17–18, 39–41, 51–53, 83–85, 101, 116, 131, 142–144, 151, 164, 181, 205–207
in Bohemian Crown Lands (*see* Bohemian Crown Lands)
declaration of, 31–32
historiography, 1–5, 7, 9–11, 63, 75, 182, 222
reality of battle, 221–223, 237
food, 63, 82, 85, 104n21, 123, 136, 186, 189, 195–196, 233, 252
access to, 151–153
gendering of, 78
importance of, 66–72, 78
lack of, 64, 80–84, 151, 207–209
Forth, Christopher, 8, 20, 78, 82
France, 1, 3, 10, 15, 80, 90, 181,
French army, 5–6, 11, 12, 15, 72, 75, 181, 182, 204, 223, 224
Franz Joseph I, Emperor of Austria-Hungary, 2, 30–31, 37, 41, 153, 176n51,
Franz Ferdinand d'Este (assassination of), 30
Freud, Sigmund, 119, 153
furlough, 12, 65, 203–206, 217n105
dangers, 203, 216n105
frequency, 203, 209
importance, 203
Fussell, Paul, 182, 183

Galandauer, Jan, 37
Galicia, 3, 52, 62, 63, 68, 70, 73–74, 91, 93–94, 121, 123, 132–134, 151, 159,

165, 167, 169, 184, 226, 227, 228, 230, 231
gender, 8–9, 13, 31, 36, 44, 53, 66, 82, 84–85, 97, 101, 116–118, 122–124, 129–132, 143, 155–158, 162, 165, 191–193, 233, 238, 241, 244, 251–58
and First World War, 9–13
'double helix', 7
gender coding (communication), 191, 194, 209
gender and fear, 242
gender identity, 12–13, 18, 34–36, 53–54, 128–130, 136, 171, 193, 231, 241, 257
gender order, 11, 14, 31, 36–38, 45, 89, 92–95, 99, 100, 121–124, 144–148, 155, 171, 186, 193, 197–198, 201–210, 239, 255
gender performance, 14, 171, 209–210, 233–234
gender relations, 97–100, 144, 182
gender theory, 6–7, 13, 47, 78, 152
gendered social space, 13, 33–34, 47, 52, 126, 182–183, 192
and military history, 7–8, 31, 256
Germans (Austrian), 2–4, 14, 16, 29, 37, 133, 136, 154–173, 208, 223–224, 257
nationalism (*see* nationalism)
war enthusiasm, 34, 37, 55n10
Germany, 1, 10, 12, 37–38, 64, 101, 181, 234
German troops, 11, 12, 86, 97, 116, 131, 152, 155, 182, 222, 257
Gnila Lipa, battle of, 50
Göhre, Paul, 90
Goldstein, Kurt, 237
The Good Soldier Švejk (novel). *See* Hašek, Jaroslav
Gorizia (Görz, Austrian Littoral), 122
Gorlice (Görlitz), battle of, 64, 125, 126
Gray, J. Glenn, 11
Graz (Styria), 159

Habrman, Gustav, 80
Hála, Bohuslav, 186
Hämmerle, Christa, 9–10, 34
Haring, Sabine, 227
Hašek, Jaroslav, 3, 41, 63, 230, 243

Havlíček, Jaroslav, 77, 193
Healy, Maureen, 31, 43, 182, 210, 231
Hej Slované! (Hey Slavs!, song), 43
Hilfskräfte im Felde (Auxiliary Labour Force in the Field). *See* women
hinterland. *See* home front
Hirschfeld, Magnus, 130
historiography, 1–11, 63, 75, 182, 222
Czech, 3–5
First World War, 1–12
gender history, 6–9
military history, 11–13
new military history, 9, 131
Western historiography, 1–2
Holmes, Richard, 11, 71, 222
home front, 13, 31–32, 49, 51, 64, 77, 87, 89, 92, 93, 97, 126, 211, 212n9
soldiers' relationship with, 66, 181–209
See also Bohemian Crown Lands
homosocial relationships, 65, 120–4, 125, 127–129, 130–131, 133, 253
comradeship (concept), 115–117, 130, 139n72, 253
homoerotic undertones, 116–121, 129–131
hospitals, 62–63, 67, 83, 95, 98–99, 102, 115, 128, 133–134, 150, 155, 161, 184, 240, 243–244
Hradec Králové (Königgratz, Bohemia), 48, 50, 62, 244
humanity, 101, 120, 132, 252
dehumanization, 83–84, 144, 147
Hungarian troops, 114–115, 130, 160–162, 223, 243
hatred of, 167–168, 199–200
perceived qualities, 168
Hungary, 47, 52, 94, 149–150, 160,
hygiene, 72, 87, 120–121, 147, 167, 204
Hynes, Samuel, 182, 183

Isonzo front, 66, 73–74, 195, 209, 222
eleven battles of, 64, 186, 219, 237
Italian front, 64, 67, 118, 122–124, 127, 189, 191, 195, 196, 219, 237
specifics of, 72–75
Italian troops, 62, 65, 68, 70, 167, 225
perception of, 229–231

Italians (Austrian), 160, 166, 171, 259
Italy, 3, 68–69, 73–74, 83, 86, 104n31, 181, 209

Janošík, Jan, 33, 126, 151, 191, 195, 200
Janowitz, Morris, 11, 131. 144
Jarkovský, Josef, 134, 153
Jaroměř (Jermer, Bohemia), 39, 50, 150
Jaroš, Karel, 68, 93,
Jaroš, František, 98
Jaroslaw (Jaroslau, Galicia), 184
Jews, 16, 33, 51, 98, 224
Jílek-Oberfalcer, František, 183
Jindřichův Hradec (Neuhaus, Bohemia), 128
John, Jaromír, 121
Judson, Pieter, 170

Kaiser, Alois L., 81, 83, 100, 102
Kamarádství (veterans' magazine), 115, 169
Kápar, Josef, 121, 193–194,
Káposvár (Kopisch, Hungary), 94, 102
Kde domov můj? (Where Is My Home?, song), 37
Keegan, John, 11
Kerensky Offensive, 64, 105n39
Kienitz, Sabine, 79, 234
King, Jeremy, 16, 19, 33, 39, 40, 47
Kisch, Egon Erwin, 16, 19, 33, 66, 67, 70, 72, 75, 85, 87, 89, 92, 117–120, 127, 134, 135, 149–155, 185, 190, 192, 195, 204, 222–228, 233–241
Kitchener, 1st Earl, Horatio Henry, 39
Kolman, Jaroslav, 34, 47
Kolubara River, 226, 243
Kotrba, Jan, 127, 196
Kramář, Karel, 177n90
Kramer, Alan, 5
Krasnik, battle of, 50
Křenek, Jaroslav, 82, 115–116, 124, 129–130, 155, 234
Komarów, battle of, 50
Krakow, 50, 128, 133
Králova Lhota (Königshufen, Bohemia), 199
Krieghammer, Edmund von, Minister of War, 159
Křížek, František, 241
Kroměříž (Kremsier, Moravia), 210

Kučera, Rudolf, 4, 7, 14, 33, 49, 82, 87, 123, 170, 240
Kühne, Thomas, 13, 14, 116, 129–133, 148
Květoň, Vladislav, 95, 187
Kyšperský, Antonín, 195

Laška, Jan, 123, 147,
leave. *See* furlough
Leed, Eric J., 75, 76
Lein, Richard, 4, 64, 103n8, 160,
letters. *See* correspondence
Liebesgaben (gift packages), 191–192
liminality, 13, 75–77, 82, 229
Lirš, Ferdinand, 80, 147, 158, 161, 196, 229
Litoměřice (Leitmeritz, Bohemia), 30
Littoral (Austrian), 37, 122
Lipp, Anne, 12
Ljubljana (Laibach, Slovenia), 99
Loubal, František, 192–193, 197, 199
Lower Austria, 18
Lynn, John, 8–9, 257
  theory of combat effectiveness, 12–15, 38, 40, 52–54, 65–66, 131, 169, 221, 241

Macedonian front, 115–116, 181, 183
Magyars. *See* Hungary
Mail. *See* post
Malešević, Siniša, 9
manliness. *See* masculinity
Marshall, S.L.A., 11, 144, 153, 221, 224
Maršík, Ludvík, 123
Masaryk, Tomáš Garrigue, 3
masculinity (general), 6–14, 36, 85, 110n121, 196–197, 209, 227–229, 252–259
  and body, 78–83, 157, 234–240, 241–242
  and civilization, 66, 82–84, 165–167
  hegemonic, 6–10, 13–14, 33–36, 44–49, 53–54, 76–82, 89, 128–129, 145–155, 171, 197–205, 210, 228–233, 251–254
  hierarchy, 6, 10, 13, 45–47, 54, 124, 144–148, 152–154, 170–172, 175n30, 232–233, 251–254

fatherhood, 205–207
longue durée, 9, 36, 53, 76, 251
military, 8–10, 13, 35–36, 41–48, 53–54, 56n21, 76–77, 84, 102, 117–125, 129, 146–151, 161, 196–197, 227–233, 251–255
  patriarchal dividend, 6, 13, 44–49, 54, 84, 100, 146–159, 170, 173, 197, 206, 233, 251–252
  performance of, 93, 100, 125, 209–210, 233–234, 241
  and power, 6, 10–14, 44–45, 47, 76–77, 83, 100–101, 117, 144–162, 170–173, 197–205, 210, 238–243, 251–258
  public discourse, 34–36, 43, 45, 53, 80–84, 89–92, 101, 117–118, 124, 129–131, 149, 156, 183, 191, 197, 211, 231–233, 244, 251
  and social space, 10, 13, 31–34, 53, 97–98, 145, 182–183, 192, 210, 233–234, 251, 255
  and social status, 8–10, 13, 20–21, 41–46, 51–54, 146–155, 189, 233, 251–253
  subversion, 5, 77–78, 83–84, 86, 95, 116, 148–149, 165, 173, 208–210, 244, 252–259
  test of, 36, 227–232, 255
  theory of, 6–11, 13, 47, 78–79, 82, 118, 129, 152, 197
  venues of, 13, 181, 197–210
  victimization, 100
  and war (general), 8–11, 256
memoirs. *See also* personal accounts
Meyer, Jessica, 182
modernity, 8, 18, 76, 83, 86, 124, 162–163,
  and gender, 92, 117
  and masculinity, 5, 43, 78, 82, 85, 110n121, 162, 197, 205–206
  and medicine, 85
  modern consciousness, 182
  and warfare, 7, 13–14, 20, 39, 72, 75, 78, 84, 101, 106n60, 131, 144–145, 190, 209, 220–223, 242
Moltke, Helmuth von, the Younger, 160
Monfalcone, 68
Monte Meletta, 167

morale. *See* motivation
Moran, Lord (Charles McMoran Wilson), 11, 72
Morávek, Jan, 81, 187, 237, 239
Mosse, George L., 9, 182
motivation, 3, 5, 11–15, 19, 40–41, 64–65, 69–70, 84, 101, 125, 131–132, 136, 144–145, 159, 173, 203, 207, 211, 221, 240
  coercion, 5, 40–41, 54, 65, 84, 169, 172, 256
  combat, 12, 14, 131, 221–222, 241–242, 252, 253
  compliance, 40, 45, 47, 53, 63–65, 84, 146, 200
  consent, 5–6, 12–14, 38, 40, 50, 54, 169, 255–258
  initial, 12–13, 38–40, 44–47, 52–54, 101, 251, 256
  and masculinity, 47, 53, 131, 186, 197, 206, 241–242, 251–257
  normative, 40, 44, 53, 65, 170
  and primary groups, 12–13, 49, 54, 65–66, 116, 131–136, 221, 241–242, 253
  self-interest, 44, 135,
  sustaining, 12–13, 65–76, 82–87, 100–101, 131–136, 142–146, 164, 170, 173, 186, 201, 207–209, 221, 253–256
  social pressure, 7, 41–44, 49, 53–54, 189, 252
  theory of, 11–19, 40, 65, 221
Mudrák, Augustin, 45, 74, 84, 120, 162, 187, 203, 223, 224, 234, 235, 243
mutinies, 2, 11, 204, 259
  Bay of Kotor (Cattaro), 69
  Rumburk, 69, 105n40

nationalism, 2–3, 38, 43, 51–52, 69, 159–160, 166, 170–174, 209, 257–259
  Czech, 3, 17–19, 29, 166
  Austrian German, 4, 159, 160, 171
  in the officer corps, 160, 171
  pan-Slavism, 43, 223
  supranationalism, 160

Neumann, Stanislav Kostka, 16, 46, 102, 119, 130, 147–150, 183
Norton-Cru, Jean, 15
Nye, Robert, 92

Obilin (Croatia), 161
officer corps, 14, 18–20, 45–47, 63, 68–69, 72, 75, 85–93, 99–100, 142–173, 188–189, 191, 233, 241, 253, 257–258
   access to knowledge, 75
   casualties, 145–146, 160
   criticism, 69, 85, 99–100, 146, 151–152, 154–155, 158, 168–170
   language groups, 160
   leadership, 156–158
   masculinity, 20, 45, 145, 155–156
   patriarchal image, 153–154
   privileges, 68–69, 89, 91–92, 99, 150–152
   reserve officers, 145–146, 148, 160, 164, 171, 257
   social status, 47
   violence, 163–165, 168–169
Olomouc (Olmütz, Moravia), , 42, 168, 181,
Orwell, George, 66
Osijek (Croatia), 92
Osum River, 115–116

Palestine, 3, 68, 93
Pan-Slavism. *See* nationalism
parasites, 72, 98, 123, 147, 167
Pazdera, David, 4
physiology (contemporary), 237, 238
Piave River, 63, 68–69, 151, 156, 181, 209, 232
   battle of the Piave, 64, 75, 220, 227, 243, 256
Picq, Ardant du, 11, 131
Písek (Bohemia), 39, 66, 196
personal accounts (critical assessment), 15–20, 40, 63, 66, 153, 159
   diaries, 15–19, 50, 75, 86, 82, 126, 187, 203, 222–226, 234
   letters, 15–17, 117–118, 182, 192 (*see also* correspondence)
   memoirs, 15–19, 39, 40, 63, 72, 86, 153, 157, 159, 183, 222–224, 226, 234
Pluháček, František, 128
Plzeň (Pilsen, Bohemia), 47
Poláček, Karel, 46, 47, 142–146, 158, 165, 170
Poláček, Václav, 31, 184, 201
Poland, 73, 83
Poles (Austrian), 91–93, 166–173, 223
post, military, 181–182, 186–190
   censorship, 86, 189–191, 192
   War Surveillance Office (*Kriegsüberwachungsamt*, KÜA), 190–191
post-traumatic stress disorder (PTSD, shell shock), 239
Pottendorf (Lower Austria), 49
Prague (Bohemia), 19, 29–30, 37–39, 51, 139, 153, 160; 165–166; 194, 204, 239
primary groups. *See* motivation
prisoners of war (POWs), 3, 14, 15, 63, 80, 95, 105n40, 121–123, 145, 147, 157, 191, 202, 206, 232
propaganda, 3, 12, 16, 31–36, 69, 75, 97, 191, 231
   Austro-Hungarian, 31–32, 35–36, 53, 74–79, 84
   Czechoslovak, 3, 17–18, 51, 65, 105n39
   images of femininity, 92–99
   images of masculinity, 31–32, 74–79, 84, 204, 229, 236
   'letters from the front' (published propaganda collections), 77, 97,
Prudil, František, 153, 157, 172, 221, 227
Przemysl, 62, 232

Rachamimov, Alon, 14, 15, 122,
Radetzky von Radetz, Joseph, Field Marshal, 153
Rašín, Alois, 177n90
Rawa, battle of, 50
religion, 10, 20, 62–63, 93, 125, 166, 184, 194, 206, 257, 259
Rélink, Karel, 163, 198–199
Rezek, Josef, 229
Rezek, Ladislav, 197

Romania, 239
Romanian front, 67
Romanians (Austrian), 166–167
Roper, Michael, 182, 193, 237–238
Rose, Sonya, 198
Rothenberg, Gunther E., 159
Rovereto (Italy), 191
Russia, 1, 37–39, 50, 52, 54, 64, 69, 73, 74, 95, 123, 135, 181, 187, 202, 238
  captivity, 3, 14, 64, 95, 135, 138n51, 202
  'Slavic brethren', 2, 43, 223
  Russian troops, 33, 43, 118, 157–161, 194, 220, 223–226, 230, 235–236, 244
Ruthenians, 51, 166, 167

Sassoon, Siegfried, 181
Schmitz, Martin, 257
Schönberger, Bianca, 97
Scott, Joan W., 6
Šedivý, Ivan, 4
Šefl, Josef, 221
self-victimization (of soldiers), 7, 77, 81, 84, 100, 117, 228, 231, 239, 252
Serbia, 30, 50, 54, 92, 147, 155, 181, 205–206,
  Serbian Front, 16, 34, 47, 52, 66, 67, 74, 118, 125, 191, 195, 222–226, 233
Serbs, 2, 51, 72, 127, 155, 160, 224–226
sexuality, 13, 48, 66, 84–85, 100–102, 149–150, 246n42. See also women
  heterosexuality, 85–92, 215n87, 252
  homosexuality, 85–89, 117–118, 129–131, 252
  masturbation, 86–87
  prostitution, 87–90, 92, 99–100, 152
Shils, Edward, 131
Silverman, Kaja, 80
Šindelář, Jan, 124, 133, 153, 238–239, 241
Skála, František, 47, 82, 83, 94, 98, 102, 122, 125, 128, 132–133, 150, 154, 167, 172, 228, 230, 238, 239,
Slavonia, 37, 91, 94
Šlesingr, Jan, 33, 134, 243
Slezák, Josef, 62–69, 98, 118, 120, 125–128, 145, 156, 172, 184, 189, 193, 199–203, 211, 221, 236, 243–244

Slovaks, 3, 18, 166
Šmatlán, Jan, 47, 50, 120, 153, 187
Šmída, František, 46, 49, 68, 80, 86, 90–94, 125, 127, 134, 148, 152, 154, 161, 169, 172, 184, 187–189, 193, 205, 208, 229–230
Smith, Leonard, 5, 11, 222–224, 229, 237
socialism, 4, 19, 160, 209, 257–259
Sokol, 19, 80, 166, 172, 224, 230
  Slet of 1914, 29–30
Soušek, Vladimír, 223
Sperling, Bohumil, 64, 127, 185, 187, 225, 230, 235
Šrámek, Fráňa, 16, 67, 195, 201, 203
Šrámek, František, 187
Šrámek, Josef, 80, 89, 92, 95
Stouffer, Samuel A., 11, 131–132, 232
Suchý, Karel, 191
Sýkora, Jan, 135, 184, 231
symbolic spaces, 13, 97, 251
  body, 234–242
  comradeship, 117
  home, 182
  the military, 98
  war, 102
Szeged (Szegedin, Hungary), 150, 161

Theweleit, Klaus, 9, 101–102
Thirty Years' War, 1, 36, 39
Tirana (Albania), 124
Tolmin (Tolmein, Slovenia), 134, 222
Tosh, John, 9, 13, 118, 129, 197
trench warfare. *See* combat
Tříska, Jan, 67, 127, 201, 204, 214, 220, 229, 243
Tyrol, 37, 62, 121, 122, 127, 185
Tyrolians, 74, 167

Ulrych, Josef, 49, 80, 90, 92, 154, 193, 214n61, 228, 238, 243,

Váchal, Josef, 17, 50, 62, 66–70, 83–84, 120, 127, 136, 147, 167, 173
Václavek, Bedřich, 127–128, 193, 196
Vančura, Vladislav, 46, 85, 238
Vaněk, Karel, 41–44, 81, 161, 206–207, 211, 220–226, 234, 236, 241

Vařík, Ferdinand, 206
veterans, 133
   in Austria-Hungary, 34
   in Czechoslovakia, 139n72, 169, 224, 233–234
Verdun, battle of, 75
Vienna, 19, 38, 43, 47, 49, 113, 169, 201, 204–208, 231
Vítek, Jaroslav, 90–91, 133, 167, 169, 183, 199, 208, 219, 227–229, 238
Vittorio Veneto, battle of, 65, 156
Vlasák, Rudolf, 198, 206
Vraspír, Adolf, 206
Vysoké Mýto (Hohenmauth, Bohemia), 231

Wacht am Rhein (Watch on the Rhine, song), 37
Wagner, Karel, 28n83, 37, 43
Wagner, Rudolf, 83, 194
war, *passim*
   anthropology of, 8
   as a machine, 81–82
   and masculinity, 8–11, 251–259
Watson, Alexander, 12, 40, 131, 152, 257
Western Front, 1, 5, 11, 12, 65, 72, 131, 152, 181, 193, 204, 224
Westphalia (Germany), 38
women, 31, 33–34, 42, 48–49, 55n10, 92–102, 116–130, 148–155, 186, 200–210

breadwinners, 201–203, 210
disciplining, 197–199, 210
feminine tasks, 122–124
femininity, 6–7, 11, 34, 92–102, 116–119, 123–126, 129, 193–201, 210, 251–253
Hilfskräfte im Felde (Auxiliary Labour Force in the Field), 97–102, 252
mothers, 33, 39, 49, 101, 124, 184–186, 189–195, 199–201
nurses, 81, 95–100, 161, 239
objectification, 92–101, 253
partners, 33, 51, 101, 149–150, 180–211, 227
passivity (perceived), 92–94, 99–100
sexuality, 89, 91–101, 198–200, 215n87
wounded, 50, 97–98, 115, 127, 128, 133, 135, 145, 184, 196
wounds, 15, 62–63, 72, 74, 81, 98–100, 118, 239–243
   self-inflicted, 62–63, 243

Zahra, Tara, 19, 170
Zborov, battle of, 4, 105n39
the Zeman family, Pavel and Marie, 181–182, 189
Zeman, Josef, 200
Ziemann, Benjamin, 12, 182, 257
Žipek, Alois, 18, 157, 158, 242–243,
Zückert, Martin, 4

www.ingramcontent.com/pod-product-compliance
Lightning Source LLC
Chambersburg PA
CBHW072046110526
44590CB00018B/3060